# THE
# STRATEGIC METALS
# INVESTMENT
## HANDBOOK

# THE

# STRATEGIC METALS INVESTMENT

## HANDBOOK

MITCHELL J. POSNER
and
PHILIP GOLDBERG

**HOLT, RINEHART AND WINSTON**
New York

Copyright © 1983 by Mitchell J. Posner and Philip Goldberg

All rights reserved, including the right to reproduce this book or portions thereof in any form.

Published by Holt, Rinehart and Winston,
383 Madison Avenue, New York, New York 10017.

Published simultaneously in Canada by Holt, Rinehart and Winston of Canada, Limited.

Library of Congress Cataloging in Publication Data
Posner, Mitchell J.
The strategic metals investment handbook.
Includes index.
1. Metals as an investment.   2. Strategic materials.
I. Goldberg, Philip, 1944–     . II. Title.
HD9506.A2P64     332.63     82-1052     AACR2

ISBN: 0-03-059489-8

First Edition

Designer: Robert Bull

Printed in the United States of America

10 9 8 7 6 5 4 3 2 1

# CONTENTS

PREFACE                                          vii
ACKNOWLEDGMENTS                                   xi

## PART I   The Once and Future Resource War

ONE      THE GOLD OF THE EIGHTIES?                 3

TWO      TO HAVE AND HAVE NOT                      36

THREE    IS THIS REALLY WAR?                       53

FOUR     THE BATTLEGROUND                          73

FIVE     THE HOME FRONT                           113

## PART II   Investing in Minor Metals

SIX      INTRODUCTION TO INVESTING
         IN MINOR METALS                          161

SEVEN    INSIDE THE MARKET STRUCTURE              167

EIGHT    WHAT MOVES THE MARKETS                   180

NINE     BUYING AND SELLING                       208

TEN   INVESTMENT VEHICLES   **238**

ELEVEN   STRATEGIES AND TECHNIQUES   **261**

## PART III  Minor-Metals Investment Profiles

INTRODUCTION TO THE INDIVIDUAL PROFILES   **275**

ANTIMONY 281 · BERYLLIUM 283 · CADMIUM 284
CHROMIUM 286 · COBALT 290 · COLUMBIUM 293
GALLIUM 295 · GERMANIUM 297 · HAFNIUM 301
INDIUM 302 · LITHIUM 304 · MAGNESIUM 306
MANGANESE 308 · MOLYBDENUM 311
PLATINUM GROUP METALS 313 · RARE-EARTH METALS 320
RHENIUM 322 · SELENIUM 324 · SILICON 326
TANTALUM 329 · TELLURIUM 331 · TITANIUM 333
TUNGSTEN 336 · VANADIUM 339 · YTTRIUM 342
ZIRCONIUM 343

APPENDIX   **347**

INDEX   **357**

# PREFACE

**W**e became interested in strategic metals for two inter-related reasons: their potential as a sound investment in the coming years; and the intricate political and economic implications of the Western world's dependence on imported supplies, a situation somewhat reminiscent of that of oil. We have tried to do justice to these two areas of interest, keeping in mind both the importance of alerting our readers to a matter of national concern and the value that such information can have in the investment arena.

It is therefore fitting that the book is divided into three parts. The first provides the backdrop, describing the domestic and geopolitical scenarios that initially brought strategic metals into the news. This section tells why these functional metals are considered so critical. It examines the nature of the international "resource war" that many observers believe is being waged by the superpowers, as well as a number of domestic issues—social and political—associated with strategic metals. While Part I says little about investing per se, anyone contemplating such a plunge should first become familiar with the complex set of factors that can influence the market.

Part II is the primary investment section. It describes exactly how the market works, what affects supply/demand and prices, the role of the various participants in the market, and all the details of buying and selling, while explaining why these metals represent a good investment opportunity, and, equally important, why you might elect *not* to get involved. As with Part I, we try to provide an objective, sober analysis, presenting all relevant points of view, and shunning the hyperbole that too often has characterized writing on this subject.

Part III is a factual primer on specific metals, providing the salient information about the most important or closely watched minor metals. This section includes such facts as principal uses and geographical distribution of resources, and an investment outlook for each metal.

The metals under discussion were bought and sold long before anyone started referring to them as "strategic." Indeed, using the term can cause some confusion, because it signifies different metals to different people. Some firms identify only ten or twelve as strategic, although we have seen other lists as long as twenty.

The problem is really quite simple. *Strategic metals* is a political and, to some extent, economic term. The term used by industry professionals is the less precise *minor metals*. They are so named for several reasons: (1) they are primarily by-products of the more widely mined and used "base" metals, (2) many exist in small quantities (although some are quite plentiful), and (3) their applications and end uses in industry have been considered "minor" in importance (although today the uses of many of these metals cannot be considered minor).

"A minor metal used to be defined as a metal whose ore is present with that of a base metal and which is commercially worthwhile refining," says Howard Masters, Director of Lambert Metals Ltd., a London metals firm. "Hence cadmium, found with both zinc and lead, selenium, found with copper, and bismuth, found with lead. However, the 'minor' metals which we trade now also include metals which are mined in their own right and not as by-products, the obvious examples being mercury and antimony."

As for the term *strategic*, metals expert David Hargreaves writes, "A strategic metal can be considered one which, by virtue of its limited supply—geographically, geologically or both—and its critical end uses, industrially and militarily, has a high priority demand profile."

The U.S. government has determined certain metals to be of strategic importance. So has Germany, the Soviet Union, and just about every other industrial nation. Investment firms have added their own criteria, expanding the list of strategic metals to include not only those that are critical to the national defense and well-being, but also those that are likely to be in great demand in the years ahead and those without acceptable substitutes.

Reflecting those two terms, this book favors *strategic* when discussing geopolitics in Part I, and *minor* when investment is the main focus. For investors, it is almost always simpler and wiser to use *minor* metals, which is the broader term. Most, if not all strategic metals are minor metals as well, and the latter term is commonly used in the industry. One prominent Wall Street lawyer has been advising his clients to stay with the term *minor metals* because it is the traditional industry designation and therefore more objective. He is concerned that one of his clients might sell a customer a strategic metal that may later be judged not strategic at all. If that customer were to lose money, he or she could then claim to have been misled.

But terminology has nothing to do with the ability to make money investing in metals. The most sensible approach to minor-metals investment might best be summed up by a quote from a recent *Business Week* article: "As critical as a material may be, its price has less to do with flag waving and rhetoric than with the shifting forces of international supply and demand."

Of course, no single book can duplicate the expertise of investment analysts, political scientists, metallurgists, economists, industrialists, military leaders, and diplomats, all of whose disciplines deal to some degree with our subject. With the help of such experts, however, we have tried to provide a comprehensive, informative, practical book that the reader/investor can return to again and again.

Few readers will be expert enough to plunge into investing without the ongoing help of an adviser who can manage the practical details of buying and selling, and who can keep clients informed about day-to-day developments. But having read this book, the investor will be a well-informed client, capable of following the markets, capable of forming his or her own opinions, and perhaps most important, able to comprehend and interpret the advice and guidance of the experts.

# ACKNOWLEDGMENTS

In the course of researching this book we were aided by numerous people, whose assistance and expertise we deeply appreciate: Medard Gabel; Alfred Jenkins; Franz R. Dykstra; Dr. John D. Morgan and James Paone of the U.S. Bureau of Mines; J. Allen Overton, President of the American Mining Congress; Barbara Spillinger and Jack Carpenter of the AMC; Jane Troy and Tom Mansbach of the Overseas Private Investment Corporation; Debbie Cease and David Gardiner of the Sierra Club; Allison Horton of the Audubon Society; Paul N. Krueger of the Federal Emergency Management Agency; John Babby of the General Services Administration; Dr. Edgar F. Cruft of Nord Resources; Herbert E. Meyer of *Fortune* magazine; Representative Charles Bennett of Florida; Representative James D. Santini of Nevada; Tom Wolfe, Scott Higginson, and Sharon Cockayne of the House Subcommittee on Mines and Mining; officials at the Department of State who wished to remain anonymous; staff members of the Congressional Research Service and the Subcommittee on African Affairs.

Still more: Mr. Bryan Webb; Dr. Firoze Katrak and Bernard Reddy of Charles River Associates; J. Clarence Morrison of Dean Witter Reynolds; Ronald Shorr of Bear Stearns; Simon Strauss of ASARCO; Tony Leone of Afrimet; S. P. Prasadam of Strategic Metals Corporation; James Gourlay, Paul Gleason, and Brooks Newmark of James Sinclair and Company, London; Eliot Smith of Bache Metals; the South African and Australian consulates; Bud Kroll and James Sinclair of the Sinclair Group Companies; Montague Guild of Guild Investment Management; Roskill Information Services, the Commodity Research Unit; Francis Vassallo of the Chase Manhattan Bank; Dr. Brian F. Studd of Daniel C. Griffith and Company; Howard Masters of Lambert Metals Ltd.; The Minor Metals Traders Association; Dr. Frederick Collender of Doxford and Company, London; and especially Frederic B. Poneman, whose acute insights and moral support were a great contribution.

A special debt of gratitude to our wives, Renée and Jane, for their patience, understanding, and encouragement; and to Rosanne Malinowski, whose intelligent research and tireless typing made our task simpler and smoother than it might have been.

# PART I

## The Once And Future Resource War

# THE GOLD
# OF THE EIGHTIES?

## ONE

**A**T DAWN ON May 13, 1978, a gang of some 2,000 guerrillas attacked Kolwezi, a mining town in the central African nation of Zaire. Their goal was to seize Shaba province, formerly known as Katanga, and declare its independence. The same mission had failed just a year before, and still earlier, back in the sixties when Moise Tshombe had led the separatists for three bloody and futile years. Now they were trying again, having infiltrated mainly from Angola, where many exiled Katangese rebels have lived since the failed uprisings.

The invaders, joined by local supporters, captured Kolwezi airport and overran the town. Vandalism and propaganda occupied them for four tense days. Then things got vicious. White Europeans and blacks associated with the government of President Mobutu Sese Seko were slaughtered. Then, on May 19, 600 French Legionnaires parachuted into Kolwezi. Hundreds of insurgents were killed. The rest went into hiding or fled back to Angola. Shaba province was quiet. "Kolwezi almost overnight became a ghost town," declared *U.S. News & World Report*, "a rubble-filled wreck void of food, water, power or sanitation."

On the surface, the bloodbath appears to have been just

another in a long history of uprisings in postcolonial Africa, sound and fury, signifying nothing more than a defeat for a small band of stubborn radicals. But in fact, the Shaba invasions were important enough for nations as big as the U.S. and China, and as small as Morocco and the Sudan, to pledge aid of various kinds. And the region was important enough for the Soviet Union to have taken an interest, with the help of an estimated 20,000 Cubans in Angola. Said President Carter a week after the invasion was suppressed, "We believe that Cuba had known of the Katangan plans to invade and obviously did nothing to restrain them from crossing the border. We also know that the Cubans have played a key role in training and equipping the Katangans who attacked."

The charge, of course, was vehemently denied by Fidel Castro and the Kremlin, but few observers doubt that the Cuban presence in Angola was a major factor in the incident.

## A COVETED TREASURE TROVE

Why is everyone so concerned about a small province in a struggling undeveloped nation? For one thing, Zaire—formerly the Belgian Congo—is strategically located, right in the belly of Africa, bordering nine nations whose loyalties have been up for grabs since the demise of colonialism. Further, Zaire sits at the top of a region stretching down into South Africa that has come to be called "The Persian Gulf of Minerals," a treasure trove containing 95 percent of the world's known reserves of chromium, 52 percent of its cobalt, 53 percent of its manganese, 64 percent of its vanadium, and 86 percent of its platinum group metals (platinum, palladium, iridium, rhodium, and others). Anyone in need of those materials—or nickel, columbium, tungsten, and tantalum—will find Zaire attractive.

As for Shaba province, it is not just old tribal loyalties that make people covet it. Shaba is one of the richest mining districts in the world. Its resources are the envy of every nation whose cities light up at night thanks to copper wiring. Even more important, from one curved belt 30 kilometers wide and 300 long comes 60 percent of the world's current supply of cobalt—about 40 million pounds a year. By contrast, the second leading producer, neighboring Zambia, sends forth only 6.6 million pounds.

The United States currently produces exactly none of the slick, gray metal, which is crucial to the defense and aerospace industries. Without cobalt, experts say, we would be hard-pressed to build a functional jet engine, a missile, a decent machine tool, or a computer, the electric motors in which account for more than 10 percent of U.S. consumption. One reason we sent in $15 million worth of medical supplies, rations, and military equipment when Zaire was invaded in 1977 was that 75 percent of the cobalt we use originates in the nervous earth of Shaba province.

The Persian Gulf of Minerals is as resource-rich and as politically volatile as its oil-bearing namesake, and as such is a choice plum for industrial nations. Both power blocks would like secure access to the minerals of the region, and if history is any indication, they will go after them with craft and cunning—and, if necessary, commandos and cannons. That is why the echo of the Shaba invasion is still heard. It has become a prime anecdote and rallying cry for those sounding the alarm about a "resource war," one of the new buzz words in Washington.

## WHY WASHINGTON IS CONCERNED

"Resource war!" has been shouted by a large chorus of voices, including that of former Secretary of State Alexander Haig and high-ranking members of the defense establishment and private industry. Perhaps the most persistent voice belongs to Representative James Santini of Nevada, Chairman of the House Subcommittee on Mines and Mining, who has conducted a series of comprehensive hearings on the subject and has relentlessly pursued his position on Capitol Hill and in the press. According to the hawks, we are in a resource war whether we know it or not, and our chief adversary, the Soviet Union, knows it a lot better than we. When asked if we are in fact in a resource war, Henry Kissinger replied, "No. But the Soviet Union is."

The implication is, we'd better get cracking or else the war will be lost before we know it began. One Congressman has warned, "Our nation is facing a resource crisis potentially more devastating than any that could arise from a shortage of petroleum." In a nutshell, the justification for the alarm is based on the following assumptions:

1. Certain metals are crucial to the functioning of an industrial society, and vital for the national defense.
2. For many of these metals, the United States is entirely dependent on imports; for others we are nearly so.
3. Our primary sources in some cases are politically volatile areas such as southern Africa, or outright hostile ones such as the Soviet Union.
4. The U.S.S.R., which is abundantly endowed with many of the critical metals we lack, could potentially threaten our supplies.
5. Conditions in Third World nations, and certain domestic policies, have made us vulnerable to sudden supply cutoffs and price hikes.

As we shall see, not everyone agrees we are in a resource war, or that we are in imminent danger of a supply crisis in strategic metals. They feel the Soviet "menace" is nothing more than a new wrinkle in international economic competition, and that good sense and science will come to the rescue of our supplies like the Lone Ranger and Tonto.

## SHABA PROVINCE COMES TO WALL STREET

While national leaders were screaming "Resource war!" some people in the investment community were shouting "Opportunity!" Strong and growing demand and uncertain supplies—this situation often leads to large increases in prices in a short period of time, and in steady increases over the long run. That potential has stirred the interest of investors all over the world. At the turn of the decade, respected metals trader James E. Sinclair pronounced strategic metals the "gold of the eighties," and announced that his firm would create a division to specialize in this exciting new vehicle. Before long others followed suit, and strategic metals were being discussed everywhere investors congregated.

"Gold of the eighties" did not mean that molybdenum coins would become a means of exchange, or that the trendy would be sporting rings and baubles of vanadium. It simply meant that a category of metals, functional rather than ornamental, could become the big investment play of the decade. Like seventies gold, they could reap big dividends for those wise enough to invest in the right ones in the right way at the right time.

**Good Reasons to Invest**
The reasons for the bullishness were simple:

1. Technological advances have led to a rapidly growing need for metals with certain indispensable properties.
2. Economic recovery and a military buildup portend even greater demand in industrialized nations; anticipated growth will increase demand in populous developing nations.
3. The cost of mining is likely to increase more than the rate of inflation.
4. Political instability could lead to supply disruptions that can jack up prices overnight.
5. Many metals are relatively cheap now, during the recession.

If oil is the lifeblood of an industrial society, then metals are its flesh and bones. Not just iron and copper and lead and zinc, the old mainstays, but now the lesser-knowns—often called "minor metals"—whose names sound like the offspring of science-fiction writers. From antimony and beryllium to yttrium and zirconium, they sound strange and exotic, but they can be found in our cars, our airplanes, our televisions, our hospital equipment, our office supplies, our computers, our home appliances, and in the fighter planes, tanks, warships, and weapons upon which a nation's defense depends (the exact uses of each metal are described in Part III).

As with oil, demand is high and supply sources are often unreliable. As with oil, substitute materials are nonexistent in some cases, too expensive and not yet practical in others. As with oil, most of us have overlooked the importance of these metals, and will probably do so until we face the equivalent of gasoline lines. And, to carry the analogy one step further, people might be willing to pay high prices for strategic metals, and nations might be willing to fight for them, largely because they need them to fight with.

## Some Reasons to Be Bearish

Also like oil—and gold—the prices and market dynamics of strategic metals revolve around a set of overlapped and interwoven issues, touching on politics as well as economics, foreign affairs as well as geology or metallurgy. These issues—which affect all of us, even those with no intention of owning a thimbleful of titanium or columbium—are extremely complex. Not only do the implications vary from one metal to another, but many of the variables are simply too uncertain to predict with accuracy.

Largely because of that complexity, investing in strategic metals is not for everyone. While many investment experts believe that the alchemy of the market will inevitably turn chromium, germanium, and the others into pure gold, others point out the risks. People did get rich on gold in the seventies, but lots of people lost money too. Among the reasons to be cautious: this is a new, untested, unfamiliar form of investment, with few established precedents; any metal could plummet in demand due to technological breakthroughs or substitutions; events that influence prices are many and complex; there are a number of practical problems, such as relatively low liquidity and the need to begin with a sizable investment.

The pros and cons of investing in strategic metals will be discussed in detail in Part II.

## THE IMPLICATIONS OF THE SHABA SKIRMISH

The Shaba incident of 1978 stands as a good example of how complex the strategic metals situation can be. During the invasion, mining operations shut down for a while. Power for the mine pumps was cut off; ore hoisting in underground mines stopped for thirty days. No mining or metallurgical facilities were taken over or destroyed, but it took sixty days to resume operations fully. Lost production totaled $28 million.

The constant threat of sabotage, revolutions, strikes, and terror in the Third World makes mining there unsteady at best. Such incidents usually occur in a flash, but they can last a long time. Add to them the threat of cartels, embargoes, and sanctions in a world only now discovering the potency of economic warfare, and you can see why people in Washington are concerned.

On the other hand, despite the invasion, Zaire's 1978 production of cobalt was substantially higher than it was in 1977.

Raw material supply in multi polar world.

Wu, Kwan Li

D

CALL TO
SERVIC
Hawaii,
CANADA
and ask fo

8

*ate*_____

*ve questions regarding your order.*

| | Price for Paper Copy | |
|---|---|---|
| | **Soft cover** | **Hard cover** |
| | $20.00 ea. | $25.00 ea. |
| | $30.00 ea. | $35.00 ea. |
| e | $1.50 + $.75 per title | |
| | $2.00 + $2.00 per title | |

For a while, ore was airlifted out because of dangers to rail transport. Furthermore, the incident spurred cobalt consumers to look elsewhere for their supplies, and to step up the use of conservation, stockpiling, recycling, and substitution. In 1979, for example, Pratt & Whitney, the world's leading producer of jet engines, saved some 65,000 pounds of cobalt by replacing it with nickel in certain applications. Domestic cobalt reserves that had been off limits due to public lands policies were freed for development, largely because of the uproar created by Congressman Santini's hearings, in which Shaba became a kind of "Remember the Alamo."

Michael Calingaert, Deputy Assistant Secretary of State, told the National Materials Advisory Board that the diplomatic corps expanded its reporting requirements even before the Shaba invasion to keep Washington informed on cobalt production. Afterward, officials in all major producing and consuming countries stepped up information and intelligence reporting, a team of experts was sent to examine the Shaba mines, and, says Calingaert, "we were in direct contact with the government of Zaire to seek to assure a continuous flow of cobalt to American consumers and to rehabilitate facilities as quickly as possible."

In short, some people have countered the alarmists by showing how adaptable we are and how it is possible to prevent disasters even when supplies are disrupted.

But—comes the counterargument—to ensure stability those steps have to be taken before a crisis, and we are not always well prepared. The Shaba invasion failed, after all. What if it had succeeded? The cobalt on which we depend might have fallen into the hands of forces beholden to the Soviet Union. Besides, the disruption was short-lived and limited. What if the mine shafts had been destroyed? What if there had been a total cutoff that lasted a long time? What if the unrest had spread to other regions, where chromium, manganese, and other critical metals are produced? Under such circumstances, we would have been sadly unprepared. Our stockpiles are woefully short of their goals, and domestic sources of low-grade ores are years away from practical use. Substitutes for cobalt, chromium, and other metals are effective only in limited application; the lead time for new developments is long and the loss of quality would be high.

And what if a Shaba-like incident were to take place during a war? That is a contingency we don't like to contemplate but must be ready for nonetheless, particularly with tensions increasing throughout the world. Defense mobilization in the face of a major supply cutoff would be impotent.

While we might in the long run learn to adapt to the loss of a foreign supply, the short run could be disastrous, and the costs astronomical. We continued to get our cobalt in 1978, but we had to pay through the teeth to get it.

And that is where Shaba province and Wall Street really meet. Before the invasion, the price of cobalt was $6.85 a pound. Then it took off like the fleeing rebels, peaking at $53, $45 on the spot market. That is a handsome appreciation by anyone's standards.

But, it is prudent to note, the price soon fell precipitously, hovering at $25 for a long time before dropping to $20 early in 1981. Quite a drop, but still three times higher than the pre-Shaba price.

What does Shaba tell us? That metal supplies in the Third World are vulnerable to terrorism and other actions stemming from political instability. And that the "gold of the eighties" can be a lot like its precious namesake: lucrative and volatile.

## THE SHADOW OF THE BEAR

Making the Shaba incident all the more ominous, and the whole subject of strategic metals all the more complex, is the shadow of the Soviet Union. Not only was the invasion reportedly sanctioned by them, and abetted by Cuban and East German advisers in Angola, but it has also been alleged that Russian agents purchased every ounce of cobalt they could get their hands on just prior to the insurrection.

Was the Shaba invasion part of a Soviet strategy to disrupt Western supplies, or at least make us pay dearly for the metals that make up the weapons we might one day use against them? Some people have so concluded. Most observers will not go that far. But they will agree that Russia could not have been in a better position to know a guerrilla operation was imminent and that it might cripple mining operations. You don't have to be trained at a capitalist business school to know that prices might skyrocket under those conditions. Was their preemptive purchase, then, an economic move to stock up on cobalt while the price was right, either for their own use or for resale later?

As with most interpretations of Soviet motivation, there is considerable disagreement, lots of emotion, a great deal of speculation, and no unequivocal answers. There is considerable doubt that the preemptive purchase took place at all. Skeptics note that misinformation runs rampant at such times (several sources in the investment community, for example, incorrectly stated that the Katangese rebels had *taken over* the cobalt mines). A State Department spokesman claimed that the rumor of the Soviet purchase had been thoroughly checked out and that nothing out of line had been discovered. "All consumers were buying heavily at that stage," Gordon Brown, Deputy Director of the Office of International Commodities, told a House subcommittee. "There was a peaking demand for cobalt at that time so the Soviets were not the only people in the market." The State Department claims that Russian purchases at the time were consistent with their previous patterns.

But many people in the affected industries remain convinced that the Soviets did indirectly purchase close to 500 tons immediately prior to the invasion, and that they did it through surreptitious agents, making the ultimate destination of the ore undetectable. Hawks take that as a sign that the Russians are playing hardball in the resource war. Either they are using sinister means to deny the United States access to critical materials, or they are crafty, ambitious competitors who will resort to unsportsmanlike means to acquire the resources they need. They seem to be as omnivorous as any of our own corporate sharks, but with sharper teeth.

Further, contend the resource warriors, by Soviet standards Shaba was a victory, at least in part. Although the province remains in Zairian control and the West still gets its copper and cobalt, we are paying several times as much for it. The cost of jet engines soared as a result, industry sources claim. A number of similar events could damage Western economies as badly as oil prices have. In addition, the Kolwezi slaughter made it difficult to persuade white technicians, engineers, and managers to return to the mines of Shaba province, or for that matter to go anywhere in that troubled part of the world. Prior to the 1978 carnage, there werc 2,300 Europeans in Kolwezi, mostly Belgians. When the airlift arrived, about a dozen stayed. Now, despite vigorous recruiting, there are still under 1,000.

According to Eliahu Salpeter, writing in *The New Leader* (July 3, 1978), "There is evidence that the massacre in Kolwezi was not simply an outburst of spontaneous brutality; rather, it appears to have been a premeditated effort to frighten whites into leaving." With the danger of physical violence, and the financial uncertainties of Third World investments, Western presence in the rich mining areas has dwindled. For the host countries, who are dependent on mineral exports, the lack of competent engineering, administrative, and technical person-nel—not to mention capital—means slow growth and poten-tial turmoil. The result is a political and economic vacuum that many in Washington believe the Soviet Union is itching to fill. Unrest is in its best interests, and the Kremlin would no doubt welcome less Western involvement in Africa as much as we would welcome a Soviet departure from Cuba.

## BRONZE SPEARS TO TITANIUM TANKS

According to Isaac Asimov, the word *metal* derives from a Greek word meaning "to search for." It is an apt designation; humans have been searching for metals ever since a caveman discovered he could make a rock sharper by rubbing it against another rock. With the exception of gold, whose beauty and rarity have given it a worth far in excess of its practical value, the importance of a metal depends on its utility. For thousands of years, we have used metals in various combinations to make tools, weapons, consumer goods, and products that help manu-facture, store, and transport other goods. To a large degree, a society's level of technological achievement and physical com-fort derives from its access to metals and its ability to use them effectively.

Lustrous substances with a positive electrical charge, met-als are usually found in compounds with other elements, set into the earth's crust as rock. To use them, we first have to tear loose the metal atoms from the rock. This is the essence of metallurgy, and it probably began about 6,000 years ago with copper. A thousand years later, around 3000 B.C., some forgot-ten genius in the Fertile Crescent discovered that combining one metal with another can result in one with qualities unlike either of the originals.

We call this hybrid an *alloy*. The first was bronze, a combi-nation of copper and tin, which turned out to be so important that we named an entire era the Bronze Age. Warriors used bronze for armor and spear tips; bronze tools killed game, processed food, hewed stones into buildings, wood into ships, and marble into monuments. The metals brought sustenance and power to the user; no wonder men were willing to fight for them.

When the bronze-based societies began to run out of tin, they faced a choice. They could revert to the way their pre-bronze ancestors lived, or they could set out to find new sources of the metals they needed, while also searching for substitutes that might do the same job. In all likelihood, they gave no more thought to regressing than we would of going back to the agrarian ways of our forefathers, doing without our cornucopia of tools, machines, and gadgets, all of which, like a bronze spear, come from a hole in the ground.

As societies have done ever since, and as we continue to do, they looked for fresh supplies. The Phoenicians fought for and colonized an area that came to be called the Tin Isles, so important was that metal in their lives.

Sometime later, another metal was unearthed, and it turned out to be even tougher than bronze. Around 800 or 900 B.C., Hittite metallurgists discovered that by adding charcoal to iron, they could give it an extraordinarily hard surface that would hold up under demanding conditions. This was early steel.

Now it didn't matter quite so much if the tin supply ran low. Civilization had entered the Iron Age.

### The Eternal Search for Metals

Societies have repeated this process ever since: find a new material; discover new uses for it; imagine other uses beyond its range, or run low of supplies; find new sources and alternative materials. The search for metals and other minerals has set fleets to sail and armies to march. It has helped shrink the globe and spread people, goods, and ideas around the earth. It has contributed to technological breakthroughs and ingenious ways to make life longer, safer, and more comfortable. It has also led to great shifts of power and territory, to bloodshed, conquest, and oppression. It still does.

In short, along with fertile land, water, and fuel, the need for metals has been a driving force behind much of human endeavor, both noble and vile. To a large extent, metals have also been the *means* of the endeavor, for without them no strong tools can be made, no books printed, or weapons, or vessels, or implements forged. In the pithy phrase of a mining executive, "To make things, you need stuff."

The story is still the same, only now it is more complex. The discovery of new metals and new applications for old ones grew slowly over the centuries, but then, with the Industrial Revolution, that growth took off like one of the rockets built with lightweight, superstrong metals. Until the mid-eighteenth century, when cobalt was discovered, only twelve other elements had been recognized by civilization. Now we know of more than one hundred, about two-thirds of which are metals.

**New Metals for a New Age**
While we no longer call it the Iron Age, iron and steel still account for most of the world's metal production. Copper and tin, those old partners in the bronze business, now work separately for the most part, and new uses for them have been added over time (copper constitutes the veins and arteries of electrical systems). But other abundant metals, such as aluminum and silicon—discovered back-to-back about 150 years ago—have grown rapidly in use, replacing old standbys in many applications.

As extraction methods improve and new applications emerge, new metals are discovered, and that in turn helps create new products. Improvements on the products may require metals with special properties. Today a new set of metals has gained prominence. We have come a long way from those Hittite steelmakers; some of the metals that make high technology possible were not even known in their day. Indeed, some were not known fifty years ago. They are considered *strategic* and *critical*, terms that once might have been applied to copper or tin. The federal government defines strategic and critical metals as those that are necessary to supply our military, industrial, and essential civilian needs during a national emergency, and that are not found or produced in the United States in sufficient quantities to meet such needs.

That is why people in the Kremlin, the White House, and Wall Street are learning the difference between manganese and magnesium, tantalum and titanium, and why they are paying attention not only to who has access to what sources of raw materials, but also to the complex institutions required to harvest, concentrate, smelt, refine, alloy, fabricate, and transport the "stuff" we need to make our "things." They care because the demand for these metals as a group is expected to grow considerably. That is why this book devotes a great deal of attention to the unfolding geopolitical scenario, and to the equally complex domestic issues, that will affect the metals market. All of which would be irrelevant if not for the anticipated demand for certain metals in important applications.

## THE DEMAND FOR STUFF

Because we have come to take material abundance for granted, and because the goods with which we surround ourselves are so far removed in appearance, texture, and distance from the raw materials they are made of, we tend to forget that crucial first step—the hole in the ground. We have what J. Allen Overton, President of the American Mining Congress, calls "a hardware-store-shelf mentality." If we need something, we pick it off a shelf. But even the shelf comes from the ground (if it comes from a tree, then the tree was chopped, hewn, and transported by devices made of metal). Mr. Overton would have us remember the "stuff" while we enjoy our "things," even though "things have more sex appeal."

Perhaps we ought to remember, since Americans have more things than anyone else. Since 1940, humankind has consumed more minerals than it had from the point the first bronze shield was forged until then. Americans, most of whom have never seen a mine or a rock quarry, consume about one-quarter of the world's nonenergy minerals, despite having only 5 percent of the population and 6 percent of the land mass. If you include each person's share of public buildings and roads, every man, woman, and child in the United States requires 40,000 pounds of minerals a year. Over 4 billion tons of *new* minerals are needed every year, just to sustain our economy at present levels.

The next time you are driving down a highway, ask yourself which gifts of the earth make your automobile possible. No doubt you will think first of oil. But the oil is fueling a couple of tons of hard stuff, including: antimony, cadmium, chromium, cobalt, columbium, fluorspar, magnesium, manganese, molybdenum, nickel, platinum, tungsten, and zirconium, not to mention the obvious metals such as iron, zinc, and lead. In addition, metals were needed to extract those metals and turn them into a car. And high-strength metals were needed to drill holes, pump oil, and turn it into gasoline.

How about your telephone, another miracle we take for

granted? Forty-two elements are used in the handset alone (the ones with asterisks are described in detail in Part III):

| Element | How Used |
| --- | --- |
| Aluminum | Metal alloy in dial mechanism, transmitter, and receiver |
| Antimony* | Alloy in dial mechanism |
| Arsenic | Alloy in dial mechanism |
| Beryllium* | Alloy in dial mechanism |
| Bismuth | Alloy in dial mechanism |
| Boron | Touch-Tone dial mechanism |
| Cadmium* | Color in yellow plastic housing |
| Calcium | In lubricant for moving parts |
| Carbon | Plastic housing, transmitter steel parts |
| Chlorine | Wire insulation |
| Chromium* | Color in green plastic housing, metal plating, stainless steel parts |
| Cobalt* | Magnetic material in receiver |
| Copper | Wires, plating, brass piece parts |
| Fluorine | Plastic piece parts |
| Germanium* | Transistors in Touch-Tone dial mechanism |
| Gold | Electrical contacts |
| Hydrogen | Plastic housing, wire insulation |
| Indium* | Touch-Tone dial mechanism |
| Iron | Steel, magnetic materials |
| Krypton | Ringer in Touch-Tone set |
| Lead | Solder in connections |
| Lithium* | In lubricant for moving parts |
| Magnesium* | Die castings in transmitter, ringer |
| Manganese* | Steel in piece parts |
| Mercury | Color in red plastic housing |
| Molybdenum* | Magnet in receiver |
| Nickel | Magnet in receiver, stainless steel parts |
| Nitrogen | Hardened heat-treated piece parts |
| Oxygen | Plastic housing, wire insulation |
| Palladium* | Electrical contacts |
| Phosphorus | Steel in piece parts |
| Platinum* | Electrical contacts |
| Silicon* | Touch-Tone dial mechanism |
| Silver | Plating |
| Sodium | In lubricant for moving parts |
| Sulfur | Steel in piece parts |
| Tantalum* | Integrated circuit in Trimline set |
| Tin | Solder in connections, plating |
| Titanium* | Color in white plastic housing |
| Tungsten* | Lights in Princess and key sets |
| Vanadium* | Receiver |
| Zinc | Brass, die casting in transmitter, ringer |

Source: A. G. Cynoweth, "Electronic Materials: Functional Substitutes," *Science* 191 (February 20, 1976): 725–28, Table 20: Copyright 1976 by the American Association for the Advancement of Science.

Food and shelter? Since few of us live on farms now, we need metals for the machines that produce, transport, and store our food. And it would be back to log cabins without steel to build our buildings. For that we need manganese. "We don't know how to make steel without manganese," states E. F. Andrews, Vice President of Allegheny Ludlum. Twelve pounds of the metal are needed to make a ton of steel, a process one writer compared to the use of yeast in baking bread. No manganese, no steel; no steel, no cars, planes, factories, and so on.

Chrome, one of the metals foremost in the minds of resource warriors, is not only used to decorate cars and refrigerators. Without chromium there can be no stainless steel, that ubiquitous material so vital for its ability to resist abrasion and corrosion. Stainless steel—which is 14 to 20 percent chromium—is found just about everywhere in an industrial society, in construction, in transportation, in machinery and equipment, in defense materials.

In fact, you would be hard pressed to find anything around you that did not owe its presence to a hole in the ground. In most cases, a bunch of holes, in pieces of ground as far apart as Michigan, Brazil, South Africa, Russia, and Australia.

## WORLDWIDE CONSUMPTION WILL INCREASE

Will the demand remain high? For the most part, yes. Supply and demand for any given metal are influenced by business cycles, consumer tastes, government policies, geographic and geological factors, new technologies of extraction and production, the availability of substitutes and recycling methods, and a host of complex, unpredictable, and often shocking geopolitical events. Prediction is tricky business. As the International Economic Studies Institute put it, "We cannot predict the supply and demand for any raw material with precision, accuracy, or reliability. At best we can hope to establish orders of magnitude, directions of change, and a broad range within which actual results will fall."

It is safe to assume, however, that worldwide mineral consumption as a whole will increase, and that demand for strategic metals, as a group, will continue to rise. Any individual metal, of course, may run counter to the trend, at least for short periods. A growing world population, an evolving technological base, and the desire for rapid industrialization in developing countries all point to increased consumption.

Exactly how much consumption will grow depends on factors that are difficult to predict, such as worldwide economic conditions, and industrialization rates in developing nations. In the early 1970s, economist Wilfred Malenbaum of the University of Pennsylvania predicted that global demand for metals would double by the year 2000. Nobel laureate Wassily Leontief saw the world using three to four times as many minerals over the next three decades as it had until then over the course of human history. Many such dire predictions have since been lowered, as the worldwide Gross Domestic Product is not expected to increase as rapidly as once anticipated. Nevertheless, with world population expected to reach 6.4 billion by the end of the century, global production might increase at more than 3 percent per year—a lot of things, requiring a lot of stuff.

## CONSUMPTION PATTERNS WILL CHANGE

A 1973 study by the Wharton School of Finance and Commerce points out that increases in gross production and increases in raw materials needs do not move in perfect synchrony. In the boom years of 1957–66, for example, industrial production went up less than 20 percent. "As a rule," the study concluded, "less input is needed as precision of production improves, as end-use products are standardized, as materials strength is improved."

When a nation begins to industrialize, it needs increasing amounts of minerals for each unit of goods it produces. Later, more efficient manufacturing methods are discovered, new materials can be used, and the need for certain raw materials might decline in proportion to the continued increase in production. Recycling also comes into the picture, since old goods create scrap for new goods. In other words, a mature industrial society might produce more with fewer raw materials.

The rate of use over time varies with the material in question. During the decade from Sputnik to the first heart transplant, the use of zinc went up only 4.2 percent and copper 18.6 percent. But aluminum rose by 77 percent, and plastics rocketed by 240 percent, making the advice given to Dustin Hoffman in the 1967 film *The Graduate* excellent hindsight. Aluminum and plastic permitted cheaper, lighter, more efficient substitutes for many materials and opened the door for products that could not have been manufactured before.

The postwar era saw similar changes with regard to the minor or strategic metals under discussion here. The use of steel went up only 16.4 percent between 1957 and 1966, but the use of *alloy* steels—for which many of the strategic metals are essential—increased at nearly three times that rate. The ferroalloys—for example, vanadium, molybdenum, manganese, tungsten, chromium, cobalt—can combine with iron to produce steels with extraordinary strength and heat resistance. Both qualities are vital characteristics of the machinery that drives advanced technology. As always, new needs led to the discovery and application of new metals, and that in turn led to new products and new needs. Some of the strategic metals had been virtually ignored before World War II.

In the years to come, emerging nations will be erecting the basic structures of modern society—buildings, railroads, factories, airports, and so on—and they will use proportionately more of the basic metals such as iron, copper, lead, and zinc. The United States, Japan, Western Europe, and the Soviet Union, on the other hand, will use proportionately less of those materials (though total consumption will still increase), but will increase their use of strategic or minor metals, which is one big reason that investors are hopping aboard.

**Electronics Requires Special Metals**
The much-heralded transition of the U.S. economy from an industrial to a service orientation should not be taken as a sign of decreased demand for materials. For one thing, "reindustrialization" and the projected increase in defense spending could portend a resurgence of manufacturing. Moreover, you need raw materials in order to perform services. Transportation, medicine, utilities, and communications are quite materials-intensive, as we pointed out earlier when listing the minerals in an automobile and telephone. Even recreation and entertainment require large amounts of hard metals. Hans H. Landsberg of Resources for the Future pointed out in *Science* magazine (February 20, 1976) that more than two-thirds of our recreation expenditures are for durable goods, and portions of the remainder also require materials. Consider, for example, the equipment needed to produce the Super Bowl and to project it onto millions of color television screens. In fact, the TVs themselves are composed of thirty-five minerals, including

cobalt, which is used in the magnetic wave guide that creates the picture on the screen; strontium, which is used in picture tubes to eliminate harmful X-ray emissions; and yttrium, used in the phosphors that emit light.

Whether used for recreational, educational, industrial, or military purposes, electronic products are heralding a new era, and will surely be one of the boom industries in the coming years. These intelligent machines rely on exotic metals such as tantalum, which one expert notes "permits small volume, high capacitance devices [that are] used virtually in every electronic product produced by our country from hi-fis to computers to the most sophisticated space systems." While they are used in small quantities in each product, and while there are substitutes for most of them, the demand for the metals used in electronic gear should increase steadily. The substitutes in most cases are just other metals in the same group, and there is no doubt that vast quantities of electronic equipment will be produced in the next few decades. Electronics accounts for 62 percent of the beryllium used; 80 percent of the gallium; 60 percent of the germanium; 85 percent of the indium; 55 percent of the tantalum; and 85 percent of the yttrium. Selenium is widely used in photocopiers.

### Minor Metals Will Solve Major Problems

We need certain metals not merely to supply superfluous consumer goods for an ostentatious society. They will help solve critical problems. Already, lightweight, strong metals and electronics equipment have contributed significantly to improved medical and dental care. They will also play key roles in solving problems related to energy and the environment. Chromium and platinum, for example, are essential ingredients of pollution-control equipment.

According to Dr. John D. Morgan, Chief Staff Officer of the U.S. Bureau of Mines, "Accelerating defense and energy programs can be expected to generate increased demands for such materials as chromium, cobalt, columbium, molybdenum, nickel, platinum, tantalum, and titanium. Such programs require resistance to high temperature and corrosion and erosion." (Figure 1 shows the relative melting points of strategic and other metals.)

New sources of energy—coal gasification and liquefaction, oil shale and tar sand, magnetohydrodynamics, solar and ocean thermal, fission and fusion—will reduce our dependence on

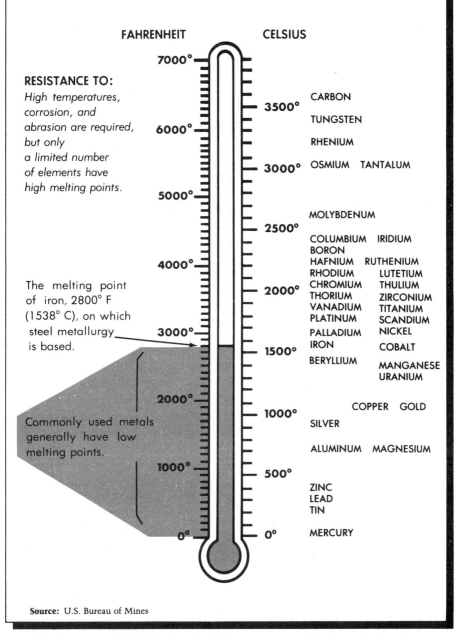

New and improved mineral-based materials are needed for a wide variety of defense, aerospace, and energy programs such as: jet engines, turbines, coal gasification and liquefaction, magnetohydrodynamics, fission, fusion, and pollution control.

**FAHRENHEIT**    **CELSIUS**

RESISTANCE TO:
High temperatures, corrosion, and abrasion are required, but only a limited number of elements have high melting points.

The melting point of iron, 2800° F (1538° C), on which steel metallurgy is based.

Commonly used metals generally have low melting points.

7000°

3500°    CARBON
         TUNGSTEN
6000°
         RHENIUM

3000°    OSMIUM  TANTALUM

5000°

         MOLYBDENUM
2500°
         COLUMBIUM  IRIDIUM
         BORON
4000°    HAFNIUM    RUTHENIUM
         RHODIUM    LUTETIUM
2000°    CHROMIUM   THULIUM
         THORIUM    ZIRCONIUM
         VANADIUM   TITANIUM
         PLATINUM   SCANDIUM
3000°    PALLADIUM  NICKEL
1500°    IRON       COBALT
         BERYLLIUM  MANGANESE
                    URANIUM

2000°              COPPER  GOLD
1000°
         SILVER

         ALUMINUM  MAGNESIUM
1000°    500°
         ZINC
         LEAD
         TIN

0°       0°       MERCURY

Source: U.S. Bureau of Mines

**Figure 1.** *This figure shows all known elements with melting points above iron and major metals melting at lower temperatures.*

imported oil in the future. But, they will require metals—many of which are mostly imported—for making the valves, pipes, and reaction chambers to harness alternative energy sources. Vanadium, columbium, and molybdenum, for example, are expected to be used increasingly in oil and gas pipelines. Beryllium, hafnium, and zirconium are used in nuclear reactors. Photovoltaic cells for solar energy will use metals with special properties; research is now centered on silicon, gallium, indium, selenium, tellurium, and others. To save energy, transportation will use lighter-weight metals such as molybdenum and titanium to replace heavier steels.

## AS THE COLD WAR GETS HOT, SO DO STRATEGIC METALS

Calling his country's attention to what he considers a critical shortfall in defense-related minerals, Congressman Santini summarized the relationship of mines and might: "A strong defense posture—power capability—is both a cause and

### STEEL INDUSTRY USES FOR STRATEGIC METALS

| Critical Metal Catalyst | Process | Use |
| --- | --- | --- |
| | Reduce iron ore (remove air bubbles) | Iron |
| Add manganese | To iron (coagulate grains) | Hardens steel |
| Add chrome | To steel | Stainless steel—autos, chrome plate |
| Add nickel | To stainless steel | Hardened stainless steel for autos and stainless plate |
| Add cobalt | To magnetic steel | Telecommunications, forklift trucks, etc. |
| Add cobalt | To steel | Resistance to heat, use in turboprop blades |
| Add vanadium | To steel | Toughens steel for drill rods, oil pipes |
| Add tantalum | To steel | Superalloy for high-precision aircraft joints and connectors |
| Add titanium | To steel | Noncorrosive |
| Add tungsten | To steel | Armor-plated steel |

**Source:** James Sinclair & Co.

effect of national resource security. Without materials for replacement and for other 'generations' of weapons technology, defense performance declines; without such a defense posture offshore mineral access and production become a high risk and dangerously vulnerable . . . the parallel to oil is unmistakable."

For that reason, much of the concern about defense has focused on minerals access—to strategic metals as well as oil—and much of the interest in strategic metals, by investors and others, revolves around defense needs. According to military and industry representatives, the United States is woefully deficient in the metals on which national security depend. According to Dr. William Schneider, an economist at the Hudson Institute and a longtime student of national security matters, "If we had a national emergency that required mobilization, the existing inventories of these raw materials would be utterly inadequate to the mobilization."

Each time the United States has gone to war in this century, it entered the fray with inadequate supplies and had to scurry about frenetically for materials once the crisis loomed large. Defense experts see the same pattern occurring and fear that this time, given the minerals self-sufficiency and the power of our likely adversary, the risk is too large to take.

Our "surge capability" has come into question; experts doubt that the kind of effort which enabled us to go from an ill-prepared start to a four-year production of 300,000 aircraft, 71,000 ships, and 86,000 tanks during World War II would be possible today. "Our systems are infinitely more complex, our defense industrial base does not have standby capacity, and we would be caught flat-footed for even the basic materials from which defense articles are made," says General Alton D. Slay, former Commander of the Air Force Systems Command.

Washington knows that adequate supplies of strategic materials are a key ingredient in a war effort, or perhaps even a sense of security in peacetime. "Adequate supplies of virtually every known material are a strategic necessity," says Dr. Morgan of the U.S. Bureau of Mines. Are we prepared? No, say many experts. The Defense Industrial Base Panel of the House Armed Services Committee published a report in 1980, the title of which expressed its dire conclusion: "The Ailing Defense Industrial Base: Unready For Crisis." One reason: "A shortage of critical materials, combined with resulting dependence on uncertain foreign sources for these materials, is eroding the foundation of U.S. defense capabilities."

The message is one the Reagan Administration has heard, and is taking seriously.

### Increased Defense Spending Ahead

The new Administration has called for huge increases in the defense budget. Although it might get slightly trimmed, the five-year plan requested by Reagan called for a 1984 defense budget of $250 billion and 1986 expenditures of $374.3 billion, more than double the 1981 level. In all, Reagan hoped to devote $1.5 trillion to the military between 1981 and 1986, enough to pay off the entire national debt with billions left over.

There are, of course, opponents who believe that current spending levels could handle any emergency, if the money were spent wisely and efficiently; there are those who accuse the military-industrial complex of using scare tactics to regain the power and influence it had before Vietnam. As of this writing, opposition to the proposed defense expenditures is loud, and it is likely to win some cutbacks. But military spending will soar way above present levels in any case. The Administration is determined to have a military capability "second to none."

Given the no-nonsense mood toward Moscow, we are likely to see fast action on defense procurement, although there is a raging debate over exactly what to spend the money on. Fast action is especially important due to the exceptionally long lead times required to gear up for new production and the long delivery periods typical of some defense items. The titanium shell that protects the pilot of an A-10 attack plane, for example, now must be ordered ninety-two weeks in advance.

In such an atmosphere we might see government action designed to ensure access to strategic materials. New initiatives in Africa, source of many critical metals, are already evident, as are changes in domestic policies that relate to mineral production. These will be discussed later.

We might look for increased use of Title III of the Defense Production Act of 1950. Entitled "Expansion of Productivity Capacity and Supply," the bill provides broad authority to the government to ensure that defense needs receive top priority. Guaranteed loans, direct government loans, purchase commitments, and supply subsidies are among the methods that can be used. The act has been employed infrequently in the last two decades, but during the Korean War it was responsible for $8.4 billion worth of transactions.

It all boils down to this: we will be producing a lot of hardware, for which manufacturers will need a lot of raw materials.

**An Arms Buildup Requires Metals**
The exact amounts of metals needed for defense are difficult to compute precisely, since direct defense consumption may not account for security needs such as communications and transportation. Also, a given product—a missile, for example—may require hardware from dozens, if not hundreds, of individual vendors and subcontractors. And, of course, some information is classified. But it is safe to say that an arms buildup will add up to a lot of cobalt, chromium, columbium, molybdenum, manganese, platinum, titanium—all the strong metals and ferroalloys needed to manufacture heavy-duty defense equipment. And a lot of antimony, beryllium, germanium, gallium, indium, and other exotic materials will be used in electronics, communications, and nuclear applications.

Take a look at what is needed to build one jet engine, in this case an F-100 Turbofan, which is used in a number of important fighter planes: 3 pounds of tantalum, 171 pounds of columbium, 720 pounds of aluminum, 910 pounds of cobalt, 1,656 pounds of chromium, 5,204 pounds of nickel, and 5,366 pounds of titanium. Very little of the unused residue can be recycled for the same application, since quality would be sacrificed.

A smaller engine, the LM-2500 Naval Gas Turbine, uses 14 pounds of tungsten, 16 pounds of silicon, 30 pounds of vanadium, 86 pounds of cobalt, 145 pounds of molybdenum, 749 pounds of titanium, 1,060 pounds of chromium, and 2,139 pounds of nickel.

That is a lot of "stuff" for one engine, and it costs a lot of money. At the current producer price of $20 a pound, the cobalt for the F-100 would cost more than $18,000, and you can't make a decent engine without it.

Nearly all primary structural metals and alloys used in the frames and engines of jet aircraft are derived from one or more strategic raw materials. The need for aircraft to withstand extremely high temperatures, and to be both strong and light, mandates increased use of the metals that are attracting investors.

Ground and sea forces also need the same materials. Chrome, for example, is used to line the barrels of the main guns on American tanks. According to Dr. Schneider of the Hudson Institute, this assures long barrel life—"a practical necessity in modern combat"—and since there are no known substitutes for chrome in this capacity, a shortage would lead to poor performance in a war. As the prime ingredient in stainless steel, chrome is, of course, also found in a wide range of machines and equipment used in defense.

The same goes for manganese, which Dr. Schneider says is "spread throughout the defense spectrum." As for cobalt, the importance of beleaguered Shaba province becomes clear when you consider that, according to some estimates, 70 to 80 percent of our consumption is tied up in defense. Dr. Schneider explains, "This is because it is used in high temperature applications and metal cutting applications, which are essential components of either inputs to the manufacture of defense products or are actually included in the defense products themselves." Many would argue with the figures, but not with the importance of these metals.

Quite possibly, the U.S. fleet will have to undergo modernization—in addition to the expected increase in size—since the Soviet Navy has grown enormously in numbers and strength. The U.S.S.R. recently unveiled a supersubmarine, which can dive three times deeper and move much faster than any of ours. It can do those things because its hull is made of titanium, which gives it the strength of steel with much less weight. Titanium, in fact, should figure increasingly in a wide range of defense areas. Indeed, each new instrument of destruction stimulates the invention of defenses to protect against it. The search is now on for alloys that can withstand attacks by laser weapons; the chrome and titanium now used for armor plating might not do the job.

Still other metals will be used in defense—in smaller amounts than those used in major hardware, but in quantities in excess of their current consumption. Because it is used increasingly in infrared night sights on sophisticated weapons, germanium has been booming since 1979. Beryllium is crucial in optical systems on missiles. Antimony is used in bullets, smoke bombs, camouflage, shrapnel, and incendiaries. And, of course, the special metals that are needed in long-life batteries, in computers, and for communications and all electronic and nuclear applications are vital to a modern war effort.

In some cases, substitutes can be used, but that usually means replacing one strategic metal with another. And substitution often lowers the quality of the product, something that is acceptable for, say, blenders, but not for fighter planes or missiles. If there isn't a resource war already, a worldwide arms buildup could easily cause one.

## U.S. PER CAPITA PRIMARY MINERAL DEMAND IN 1950, 1960, 1970, AND 1976 WITH FORECAST DEMAND IN 1985 AND 2000

Metals and Mineral-Forming Elements

| Commodity | Units | Per Capita Primary Demand | | | | | |
|---|---|---|---|---|---|---|---|
| | | 1950 | 1960 | 1970 | 1976 | 1985 | 2000 |
| Aluminum | Pounds | 12.3 | 19.0 | 39.7 | 49.7 | 84.2 | 137.4 |
| Antimony | Pounds | 0.2 | 0.2 | 0.1 | 0.2 | 0.3 | 0.4 |
| Cadmium | Pounds | 0.1 | 0.1 | 0.1 | 0.1 | 0.1 | 0.1 |
| Chromium | Pounds | 3.7 | 3.9 | 4.8 | 4.3 | 5.7 | 8.4 |
| Cobalt | Pounds | <0.1 | 0.1 | 0.1 | 0.1 | 0.1 | 0.2 |
| Copper | Pounds | 16.7 | 12.2 | 15.3 | 16.4 | 19.7 | 26.7 |
| Gallium | Grams | <0.1 | <0.1 | <0.1 | <0.1 | 0.1 | 0.1 |
| Iron in Ore | Pounds | 817.0 | 720.0 | 823.0 | 743.0 | 880.0 | 977.0 |
| Lead | Pounds | 9.2 | 6.0 | 8.1 | 8.7 | 9.4 | 11.2 |
| Lithium | Pounds | <0.1 | <0.1 | <0.1 | <0.1 | <0.1 | 0.1 |
| Magnesium—metallic | Pounds | 0.2 | 0.6 | 0.9 | 1.0 | 1.5 | 2.8 |
| Magnesium—nonmetallic | Pounds | 9.7 | 10.8 | 10.3 | 8.6 | 11.5 | 19.5 |
| Manganese | Pounds | 13.9 | 11.9 | 12.9 | 12.7 | 14.1 | 16.3 |
| Molybdenum | Pounds | 0.2 | 0.2 | 0.2 | 0.3 | 0.4 | 0.7 |
| Nickel | Pounds | 1.2 | 1.4 | 1.7 | 1.6 | 2.3 | 3.2 |
| Rare earth and yttrium | Pounds | <0.1 | <0.1 | 0.1 | 0.1 | 0.2 | 0.3 |
| Silicon | Pounds | 3.7 | 2.8 | 4.9 | 5.6 | 6.5 | 9.2 |
| Tin | Kilograms | 0.5 | 0.3 | 0.3 | 0.2 | 0.2 | 0.2 |
| Titanium—metallic | Pounds | <0.1 | 0.1 | 0.1 | 0.1 | 0.2 | 0.3 |
| Titanium—nonmetallic | Pounds | 2.7 | 3.8 | 4.7 | 4.7 | 6.3 | 10.5 |
| Tungsten | Pounds | <0.1 | 0.1 | 0.1 | 0.1 | 0.1 | 0.2 |
| Vanadium | Pounds | <0.1 | <0.1 | 0.1 | 0.1 | 0.1 | 0.3 |
| Zinc | Pounds | 15.1 | 10.6 | 12.6 | 11.9 | 12.7 | 15.3 |
| Zirconium—metallic | Pounds | <0.1 | <0.1 | <0.1 | <0.1 | 0.1 | 0.1 |
| Zirconium—nonmetallic | Pounds | 0.2 | 0.5 | 0.7 | 0.7 | 0.9 | 1.6 |

**Source:** U.S. Bureau of Mines

# WORLD PRIMARY MINERAL DEMAND IN 1976, WITH PROJECTED DEMAND IN 1985, AND CUMULATIVE DEMAND 1976–1985

Metals and Mineral-Forming Elements

| Commodity | Units* | 1976 | | | 1985 | | | Cumulative 1976–1985 | | |
|---|---|---|---|---|---|---|---|---|---|---|
| | | United States | Rest of World | Total World | United States | Rest of World | Total World | United States | Rest of World | Total World |
| Aluminum | Million ST | 5 | 12 | 17 | 10 | 24 | 34 | 69 | 163 | 232 |
| Antimony | Thousand ST | 27 | 49 | 76 | 31 | 67 | 98 | 262 | 526 | 788 |
| Beryllium | ST | 51 | 121 | 172 | 165 | 250 | 415 | 930 | 1,665 | 2,595 |
| Cadmium | Thousand ST | 6 | 13 | 19 | 8 | 18 | 26 | 63 | 141 | 204 |
| Chromium | Thousand ST | 461 | 1,756 | 2,217 | 670 | 2,400 | 3,070 | 5,300 | 18,800 | 24,100 |
| Cobalt | Million Lb | 19 | 55 | 74 | 26 | 74 | 100 | 208 | 584 | 792 |
| Columbium | Million Lb | 6 | 22 | 28 | 10 | 33 | 43 | 74 | 250 | 324 |
| Copper | Thousand ST | 1,766 | 6,273 | 8,039 | 2,300 | 9,000 | 11,300 | 18,400 | 69,100 | 87,500 |
| Gallium | Thousand Kg | 9 | 5 | 14 | 14 | 9 | 23 | 105 | 64 | 169 |
| Germanium | Thousand Lb | 47 | 128 | 175 | 60 | 150 | 210 | 484 | 1,261 | 1,745 |
| Hafnium | ST | 28 | 25 | 53 | 42 | 37 | 79 | 320 | 280 | 600 |
| Indium | Thousand T Oz | 546 | 954 | 1,500 | 804 | 1,486 | 2,290 | 6,132 | 11,045 | 17,177 |
| Iron in ore | Million ST | 80 | 494 | 574 | 103 | 650 | 753 | 870 | 5,200 | 6,070 |
| Lead | Thousand ST | 930 | 2,780 | 3,710 | 1,100 | 3,630 | 4,730 | 9,210 | 29,100 | 38,310 |
| Lithium | Thousand ST | 3 | 2 | 5 | 5 | 3 | 8 | 35 | 23 | 58 |
| Magnesium—metallic | Thousand ST | 112 | 148 | 260 | 170 | 300 | 470 | 1,280 | 2,020 | 3,300 |
| Magnesium—nonmetallic | Thousand ST | 923 | 4,654 | 5,577 | 1,350 | 5,650 | 7,000 | 10,300 | 46,800 | 57,100 |
| Manganese | Thousand ST | 1,364 | 9,674 | 11,038 | 1,650 | 12,700 | 14,350 | 14,000 | 102,000 | 116,000 |
| Molybdenum | Million Lb | 60 | 150 | 210 | 93 | 243 | 336 | 700 | 1,780 | 2,480 |

## WORLD PRIMARY MINERAL DEMAND IN 1976, WITH PROJECTED DEMAND IN 1985, AND CUMULATIVE DEMAND 1976—1985 (continued)

Metals and Mineral-Forming Elements

| Commodity | Units* | 1976 | | | 1985 | | | Cumulative 1976–1985 | | |
|---|---|---|---|---|---|---|---|---|---|---|
| | | United States | Rest of World | Total World | United States | Rest of World | Total World | United States | Rest of World | Total World |
| Nickel | Thousand ST | 167 | 493 | 660 | 260 | 750 | 1,010 | 2,100 | 5,900 | 8,000 |
| Palladium | Thousand T Oz | 522 | 2,043 | 2,565 | 795 | 2,270 | 3,065 | 6,200 | 19,500 | 25,700 |
| Platinum | Thousand T Oz | 786 | 1,954 | 2,740 | 920 | 2,370 | 3,290 | 7,700 | 19,600 | 27,300 |
| Rare earths and yttrium | Thousand ST | 14 | 5 | 19 | 19 | 11 | 30 | 148 | 72 | 220 |
| Rhenium | Thousand Lb | 8 | 4 | 12 | 7 | 4 | 11 | 60 | 34 | 94 |
| Rhodium | Thousand T Oz | 33 | 100 | 133 | 110 | 105 | 215 | 600 | 900 | 1,500 |
| Selenium | Thousand Lb | 987 | 1,786 | 2,773 | 1,390 | 2,410 | 3,800 | 10,800 | 19,100 | 29,900 |
| Silicon | Thousand ST | 604 | 1,828 | 2,432 | 755 | 2,600 | 3,355 | 6,200 | 20,100 | 26,300 |
| Tantalum | Thousand Lb | 1,278 | 851 | 2,129 | 2,300 | 1,700 | 4,000 | 16,100 | 11,500 | 27,600 |
| Tellurium | Thousand Lb | (withheld) | 200 | (withheld) | 370 | 220 | 590 | 3,080 | 1,900 | 4,980 |
| Thallium | Thousand Lb | 2 | 5 | 7 | 2 | 4 | 6 | 16 | 41 | 57 |
| Tin | Thousand MT | 46 | 195 | 241 | 48 | 216 | 264 | 420 | 1,860 | 2,280 |
| Titanium—metallic | Thousand ST | 8 | 46 | 54 | 22 | 72 | 94 | 170 | 530 | 700 |
| Titanium—nonmetallic | Thousand ST | 504 | 1,189 | 1,693 | 735 | 1,880 | 2,615 | 5,600 | 13,900 | 19,500 |
| Tungsten | Million Lb | 16 | 65 | 81 | 31 | 60 | 91 | 185 | 668 | 853 |
| Vanadium | ST | 9,779 | 21,462 | 31,241 | 15,400 | 31,300 | 46,700 | 114,000 | 240,000 | 354,000 |
| Zinc | Thousand ST | 1,276 | 5,150 | 6,426 | 1,500 | 6,190 | 7,690 | 12,600 | 51,500 | 64,100 |
| Zirconium—metallic | Thousand ST | 4 | 5 | 9 | 8 | 10 | 18 | 46 | 67 | 113 |
| Zirconium—nonmetallic | Thousand ST | 72 | 243 | 315 | 108 | 275 | 383 | 820 | 2,350 | 3,170 |

*ST = short tons; T Oz = troy ounces; MT = metric tons.

**Source:** U.S. Bureau of Mines

# WORLD PRIMARY MINERAL DEMAND IN 1976, WITH PROJECTED DEMAND IN 2000, AND CUMULATIVE DEMAND 1976–2000

Metals and Mineral-Forming Elements

| Commodity | Units* | 1976 | | | 2000 | | | Cumulative 1976–2000 | | |
|---|---|---|---|---|---|---|---|---|---|---|
| | | United States | Rest of World | Total World | United States | Rest of World | Total World | United States | Rest of World | Total World |
| Aluminum | Million ST | 5 | 12 | 17 | 18 | 46 | 64 | 275 | 682 | 957 |
| Antimony | Thousand ST | 27 | 49 | 76 | 50 | 92 | 142 | 907 | 1,669 | 2,576 |
| Beryllium | ST | 51 | 121 | 172 | 1,150 | 475 | 1,625 | 9,100 | 6,400 | 15,500 |
| Cadmium | Thousand ST | 6 | 13 | 19 | 13 | 28 | 41 | 216 | 477 | 693 |
| Chromium | Thousand ST | 461 | 1,756 | 2,217 | 1,100 | 4,200 | 5,300 | 18,400 | 68,500 | 86,900 |
| Cobalt | Million Lb | 19 | 55 | 74 | 39 | 120 | 159 | 698 | 2,030 | 2,728 |
| Columbium | Million Lb | 6 | 22 | 28 | 24 | 65 | 89 | 322 | 972 | 1,294 |
| Copper | Thousand ST | 1,766 | 6,273 | 8,039 | 3,500 | 16,000 | 19,500 | 61,800 | 255,700 | 317,500 |
| Gallium | Thousand Kg | 9 | 5 | 14 | 32 | 15 | 47 | 450 | 230 | 680 |
| Germanium | Thousand Lb | 47 | 128 | 175 | 81 | 200 | 281 | 1,517 | 3,920 | 5,437 |
| Hafnium | ST | 28 | 25 | 53 | 80 | 72 | 152 | 1,220 | 1,090 | 2,310 |
| Indium | Thousand T Oz | 546 | 954 | 1,500 | 1,520 | 1,780 | 3,300 | 23,458 | 32,057 | 55,515 |
| Iron in ore | Million ST | 80 | 494 | 574 | 129 | 1,020 | 1,149 | 2,600 | 17,700 | 20,300 |
| Lead | Thousand ST | 930 | 2,780 | 3,710 | 1,470 | 5,650 | 7,120 | 28,500 | 96,600 | 125,100 |
| Lithium | Thousand ST | 3 | 2 | 5 | 11 | 8 | 19 | 153 | 107 | 260 |
| Magnesium—metallic | Thousand ST | 112 | 148 | 260 | 365 | 585 | 950 | 5,230 | 7,860 | 13,090 |
| Magnesium—nonmetallic | Thousand ST | 923 | 4,654 | 5,577 | 2,550 | 7,920 | 10,470 | 39,100 | 150,000 | 189,100 |
| Manganese | Thousand ST | 1,364 | 9,674 | 11,038 | 2,130 | 20,000 | 22,130 | 42,000 | 348,000 | 390,000 |
| Molybdenum | Million Lb | 60 | 150 | 210 | 172 | 462 | 634 | 2,610 | 6,820 | 9,430 |

# WORLD PRIMARY MINERAL DEMAND IN 1976, WITH PROJECTED DEMAND IN 2000, AND CUMULATIVE DEMAND 1976–2000 (continued)

Metals and Mineral-Forming Elements

| Commodity | Units* | 1976 | | | 2000 | | | Cumulative 1976–2000 | | |
|---|---|---|---|---|---|---|---|---|---|---|
| | | United States | Rest of World | Total World | United States | Rest of World | Total World | United States | Rest of World | Total World |
| Nickel | Thousand ST | 167 | 493 | 660 | 405 | 1,255 | 1,660 | 7,100 | 20,900 | 28,000 |
| Palladium | Thousand T Oz | 522 | 2,043 | 2,565 | 1,125 | 3,730 | 4,855 | 20,500 | 64,500 | 85,000 |
| Platinum | Thousand T Oz | 786 | 1,954 | 2,740 | 1,070 | 3,625 | 4,695 | 22,300 | 65,200 | 87,500 |
| Rare earths and yttrium | Thousand ST | 14 | 5 | 19 | 34 | 40 | 74 | 541 | 425 | 966 |
| Rhenium | Thousand Lb | 8 | 4 | 12 | 10 | 6 | 16 | 193 | 113 | 306 |
| Rhodium | Thousand T Oz | 33 | 100 | 133 | 120 | 160 | 280 | 2,300 | 2,900 | 5,200 |
| Selenium | Thousand Lb | 987 | 1,786 | 2,773 | 2,450 | 3,980 | 6,430 | 39,600 | 66,900 | 106,500 |
| Silicon | Thousand ST | 604 | 1,828 | 2,432 | 1,200 | 4,900 | 6,100 | 21,000 | 76,000 | 97,000 |
| Tantalum | Thousand Lb | 1,278 | 851 | 2,129 | 4,600 | 3,400 | 8,000 | 64,000 | 45,000 | 109,000 |
| Tellurium | Thousand Lb | (withheld) | 200 | (withheld) | 510 | 260 | 770 | 9,680 | 5,520 | 15,200 |
| Thallium | Thousand Lb | 2 | 5 | 7 | 14 | 18 | 32 | 39 | 73 | 112 |
| Tin | Thousand MT | 46 | 195 | 241 | 50 | 256 | 306 | 1,160 | 5,440 | 6,600 |
| Titanium—metallic | Thousand ST | 8 | 46 | 54 | 40 | 150 | 190 | 630 | 2,150 | 2,780 |
| Titanium—nonmetallic | Thousand ST | 504 | 1,189 | 1,693 | 1,380 | 4,020 | 5,400 | 21,400 | 57,100 | 78,500 |
| Tungsten | Million Lb | 16 | 65 | 81 | 48 | 122 | 170 | 721 | 2,210 | 2,931 |
| Vanadium | Thousand ST | 10 | 21 | 31 | 33 | 57 | 90 | 470 | 890 | 1,360 |
| Zinc | Thousand ST | 1,276 | 5,150 | 6,426 | 2,000 | 8,400 | 10,400 | 39,100 | 161,900 | 201,000 |
| Zirconium—metallic | Thousand ST | 4 | 5 | 9 | 12 | 32 | 44 | 179 | 361 | 540 |
| Zirconium—nonmetallic | Thousand ST | 72 | 243 | 315 | 212 | 339 | 551 | 3,180 | 6,970 | 10,150 |

*ST = short tons; T Oz = troy ounces; MT = metric tons.
**Source:** U.S. Bureau of Mines

## WILL THERE BE ENOUGH?

One school of thought, Malthusian by inclination, sees the world running out of nonfuel minerals, just as it sees us running out of oil. "Most of the key metals will be exhausted within one hundred years," claims one analyst, "and some will be depleted within a decade or two."

The logic of such doomsday arguments seems on the surface to be plausible. With population and demand growing rapidly, exhaustion of consumable resources appears to be inevitable. Indeed, the known reserves of many minerals seem precariously low. But it is not that simple. It is wise to take any projection of future supplies with several grains of salt, salt being one raw material in plentiful supply. In the past, Cassandra-like predictions—about oil, for example—have been notoriously incorrect. In 1939, the Interior Department announced that U.S. oil supplies would last only thirteen years; yet, we subsequently discovered more new oil than the total of 1939's supply. Another dire prediction was made in 1947, this time by the State Department; then the following year we found twice what we had up to then consumed.

Predictions of metals depletion have fared no better. Less than half a century ago, for example, a noted geologist named C. K. Leith sounded the alarm over what he perceived as the imminent exhaustion of zinc, lead, and copper. At the time, our known reserves of zinc and lead were predicted to last only fifteen to twenty more years. Copper would last less than forty years. By those estimates, we should have run out by now.

What happened? Somehow, despite learned analysts like Dr. Leith, the United States produced more zinc in the next few decades than it had in the two previous centuries. In 1974, about twenty years after we should have run out, it was determined that our then-known reserves would last another sixty-one years. And the rate of consumption then was higher than it was when Leith made his projections. As for lead and copper, the rate of production in 1974 was pronounced feasible for another eighty-seven and fifty-seven years respectively, even without new discoveries.

Thus, we have more than we did half a century ago, even though we consumed more than anticipated and exhausted the reserves known to Leith and his colleagues. The doomsayers were wrong, partly because they underestimated the impact of new technology—an unpredictable factor in the minerals scenario, but one so important that one geologist called it the "inexhaustible resource."

We managed to invent better ways of finding and extracting ores and of using raw materials that were previously useless. Mining always begins by using the best and most accessible deposits. As these are used up, more sophisticated methods of harvesting, concentrating, smelting, refining, and fabricating are needed to make use of lesser-quality deposits. In 1900, for example, we were able to mine copper only from rocks with at least a 3 percent concentration of copper. By the 1970s, the cutoff level was down to 0.2 percent. In addition, as time goes by, we learn to dig deeper into the earth to reach remaining deposits, a costly process (there are problems of water removal, ventilation, temperature control, safety, mine hoists, and so on) but one that pays off—*if* the price of the metal is high enough.

## Be Reserved About Reserves

Catastrophic predictions are suspect for another reason, too. The term *reserve*, on which estimates are usually based, refers to that part of an identified resource that meets certain requirements, such as the quality of ore and its accessibility. To count as a reserve, a deposit has to be "economic"—that is, it has to be amenable to cost-effective development under current con-

### KNOWN RESERVES CAN CHANGE

| Ore | Known Reserves in 1950 (1,000 Metric Tons) | Known Reserves in 1970 (1,000 Metric Tons) | Percentage Increase |
|---|---|---|---|
| Iron | 19,000,000 | 251,000,000 | 1,321 |
| Manganese | 500,000 | 635,000 | 27 |
| Chromite | 100,000 | 775,000 | 675 |
| Tungsten | 1,903 | 1,328 | −30 |
| Copper | 100,000 | 279,000 | 179 |
| Lead | 40,000 | 86,000 | 115 |
| Zinc | 70,000 | 113,000 | 61 |
| Tin | 6,000 | 6,600 | 10 |
| Bauxite | 1,400,000 | 5,300,000 | 279 |
| Potash | 5,000,000 | 118,000,000 | 2,360 |
| Phosphates | 26,000,000 | 1,178,000,000 | 4,430 |
| Oil | 75,000,000 | 455,000,000 | 507 |

**Source:** Council on International Economic Policy, Executive Office of the President, *Special Report, Critical Imported Materials* (Washington, D.C.: U.S. Government Printing Office, December 1974).

ditions, or at least conditions that can reasonably be anticipated.

Reserves do not include resources as yet undiscovered, of which there may be plenty indeed, since a huge portion of the earth has yet to be explored. Nor do they include resources that geologists believe exist but have not yet verified. Further, there are deposits that are known to exist but are too costly to exploit or impossible to get at with current techniques. These also are not included in reserves. (See Figure 2.)

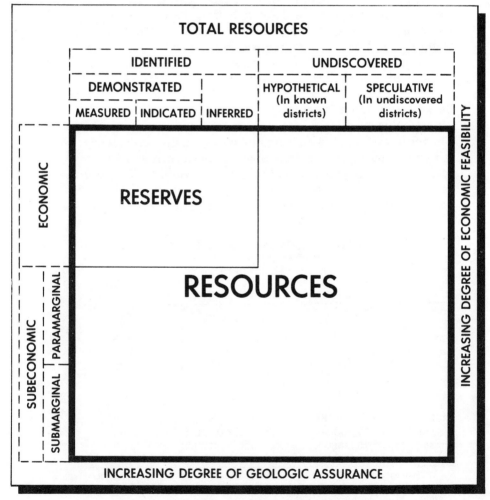

**Figure 2.** *Classification of Mineral Resources*

**Source:** *Mineral Trends and Forecasts*, Bureau of Mines, U.S. Department of the Interior, 1979, p. 6.

But at any time, any of those resources may suddenly become an official reserve. If consumers are willing to pay higher prices, miners will incur the cost of digging out the materials; suddenly, the resource becomes economic. The same could happen with a breakthrough in technology, enabling producers to dig a little deeper or turn a lesser-grade ore into a usable concentrate. Consider, for example, that our deepest mines reach no more than 5 miles into the earth—some people feel we've literally scratched only the surface.

## But Don't Be Complacent

On the other hand, blind faith in technology is not always justified. Human ingenuity can reach an impasse on any given problem, or it can simply react a few years, or decades, too late to avert troublesome and price-boosting shortages. Further, cost factors can create shortages that creativity cannot overcome. One of those costs is energy. Materials production accounts for nearly 16 percent of U.S. energy consumption. The deeper we have to dig, and the lower the grade of ore, the more rocks have to be moved, crushed, and ground in order to make a concentrate for smelting. Between 1972 and 1981, the cost of energy needed to produce a pound of copper increased by 832 percent.

At some point, energy or other costs may simply become too high to justify continued development of a particular metal. Or consumers will be forced to pay the higher price and look for substitutes, as we are doing with oil. Which decision is made depends on the importance of the end products for which the metal is used and the availability of alternatives. For most strategics, the uses are critical and substitutions are few or nonexistent.

The bottom line, then, on the depletion question is that we will not run out soon. But we may have to pay more. "For the coming decade," states the International Economics Studies Institute, "known reserves are generally adequate to cover anticipated demand, and the threat of widespread physical scarcities should not loom for at least thirty years. By that time economic adaptation may well overcome the threat of depletion. . . ."

For miners, industrialists, and guardians of the national security, depletion is irrelevant except in the very long run. What is worrisome is not how much is in the earth, but where it is located.

# TO HAVE AND
# HAVE NOT

## TWO

**N**ATURE HAS been generous with her metals, but not egalitarian. Deposits are distributed seemingly at random, encrusted like dried-up paint flicked onto the spinning globe by some cosmic abstract artist—a streak of cadmium here, a smattering of titanium there; here a spot of lithium, there a glob of tungsten. As with other natural resources, some countries happen to be "haves" and some are "have-nots." Some are well endowed with one or another strategic metal, but abject paupers with respect to others.

### THE UNITED STATES WAS ALWAYS A HAVE

For most of its history, the United States has been virtually self-sufficient in minerals. Indeed, it was exactly that prodigious endowment that seduced imperial Europe in the first place, causing ships to sail west to the New World as well as east and south. Combined with the pugnacity and resourcefulness of the settlers, our mineral abundance made possible the most advanced technology and most universal affluence the world has ever seen. Furthermore, we contributed to the economic growth of other parts of the world, because for most of our history we have been the world's chief supplier of raw materials.

To a large extent, we still supply the world. During the seventies, U.S. exports increased from 4.3 to 8.0 percent of the Gross National Product. A third of the earnings of U.S. corporations is from exports. We have trade surpluses from construction services and design, from agriculture, and from products demanding intensive research and development. We are so well endowed with foodstuffs that we spend proportionately less of our incomes on eating than any people in the world. In fact, we ship out fully a third of our harvest.

Among our chief dependents are the countries of the Third World, whose food imports have quadrupled in the last twenty years and are expected to increase by at least 50 percent in the next ten. Another customer is the Soviet Bloc.

Despite the fact that overall we are still more depended on than dependent, times have changed for the United States. We are no longer self-sufficient in raw materials. During the glory years that contributed to our feeling of omnipotence—and no small degree of complacency—we were the unscarred victors of World War II, and our resources were sorely needed by other industrialized countries who were cleaning up the rubble of war and rebuilding their economies from ground zero. Those days are over. We have competitors, and the world economy has become increasingly interdependent. No amount of protectionism can change that. "Americans," notes Leonard Silk of *The New York Times*, "are being forced to recognize that their economic well-being is greatly affected by a pervasive interdependence with other nations, whether highly industrialized or developing, Communist or capitalist, oil-rich or oil-poor."

The big shock, of course, came a few years ago when we found ourselves transformed from a self-sufficient exporter of energy to a helpless dependent of OPEC. Before World War II, the nations of Europe worried about being too dependent on the United States for oil; now we import half of our own.

## We Are Import-Dependent for Metals

The situation with nonfuel minerals is even worse. We rely on imports for some or all of more than twenty strategic minerals. Of the thirteen basic industrial raw materials, we import more than 50 percent of our needs in nine. Thirty years ago the figure was four of the thirteen. Thirty years from now it is expected to be all thirteen. In 1973, our trade deficit for nonfuel minerals was $2 billion. In 1978 it was $8 billion. Some estimate that by the year 2000, the deficit could reach $65 billion.

In short, we are now a net importer of minerals. Whereas in 1900 we produced 15 percent more raw materials than we consumed, we now produce 15 percent *less* than we consume, not counting petroleum.

The situation is most alarming with that group of special metals and ferroalloys whose uses and prices have multiplied over the past few decades. Many of them were not even discovered in the halcyon days of U.S. mineral independence. But as we began to find important uses for them, we realized that their global distribution was about as equitable as that of oil or wheat. In most cases, the United States had very little; in some cases none.

We are more than 90 percent import-dependent on several of the most critical metals: chromium (91 percent), manganese (97 percent), columbium (100 percent), tantalum (97 percent), cobalt (93 percent). We also import 87 percent of our platinum group metals (down from 91 percent in 1979), 73 percent of our nickel, 84 percent of our fluorspar, 62 percent of our cadmium, 53 percent of our antimony, and high proportions of a number of metals we will not be discussing in detail here. And some of those percentages are misleading, since the nonimported segment includes recycled metal originally obtained from foreign sources.

**Why Do We Import So Much?**
In many cases, we import these minerals for the same reason we import half our oil: it is simply more economical to do so than to mine our own deposits. Some of our best reserves have been used up, leaving us with less accessible deposits and lower grades of ore. Plus, mismanagement and questionable policies—taxation, depletion allowances, environmental regulations, and others we will discuss later—have weakened domestic production. We have reserves of certain metals sitting in the ground untouched because they are off limits due to federal land policies, or because they are too expensive to exploit given high interest rates and the costs of pollution control and production. The market has determined that the cost of reaching for self-sufficiency under present conditions is too high, financially and environmentally.

But that is not the whole story. With some metals we simply are a "have-not." Whatever deposits we have are either

# U.S. NET IMPORT RELIANCE[1] OF SELECTED MINERALS AS A PERCENT OF CONSUMPTION IN 1980

| Mineral | Percent | Major Sources, 1976–79[2] |
|---|---|---|
| Columbium | 100 | Brazil, Canada, Thailand |
| Mica (sheet) | 100[3] | India, Brazil, Madagascar |
| Strontium | 100 | Mexico, West Germany, Canada |
| Titanium (rutile) | 100 | Australia, Japan, India |
| Manganese | 97 | South Africa, Gabon, France, Brazil |
| Tantalum | 97 | Thailand, Canada, Malaysia, Brazil |
| Bauxite and Alumina | 94 | Jamaica, Australia, Guinea, Surinam |
| Cobalt | 93 | Zaire, Belgium-Luxembourg, Zambia, Finland |
| Chromium | 91 | South Africa, U.S.S.R., Philippines, Turkey, Zimbabwe |
| Platinum Group Metals | 87 | South Africa, U.S.S.R., U.K. |
| Tin | 84 | Malaysia, Thailand, Indonesia, Bolivia |
| Asbestos | 76 | Canada, South Africa |
| Nickel | 73 | Canada, Norway, New Caledonia |
| Gallium | 70 | Switzerland, Germany, Canada, Italy |
| Cadmium | 62 | Canada, Australia, Mexico, Belgium-Luxembourg |
| Zinc | 58 | Canada, Mexico, West Germany |
| Tungsten | 54 | Canada, Bolivia, Korea |
| Antimony | 53 | South Africa, Canada, U.K., Mexico, China |
| Mercury | 49 | Algeria, Spain, Italy, Canada, Yugoslavia |
| Titanium (ilmenite) | 47 | Australia, Canada |
| Selenium | 40 | Canada, Japan, Yugoslavia, France |
| Barium | 38 | Peru, Ireland, Mexico, Morocco |
| Gypsum | 38 | Canada, Mexico, Jamaica, Dominican Republic |
| Gold | 28 | Canada, U.S.S.R., Switzerland |
| Iron Ore | 22 | Canada, Venezuela, Brazil, Liberia |
| Vanadium | 15 | South Africa, Chile, U.S.S.R. |
| Aluminum | net exports | Canada, Ghana |
| Lead | net exports | Canada, Peru, Mexico, Honduras, Australia |
| Molybdenum | net exports | Canada, Chile |
| Lithium | net exports | Brazil, Canada, France, Japan |
| Silver | net exports | Canada, Mexico, Peru, U.K. |
| Magnesium | net exports | Norway, Netherlands, Canada, Italy |
| Beryllium | withheld | Brazil, India, Argentina, South Africa |
| Hafnium | withheld | Singapore, Mexico |
| Rhenium | withheld | West Germany, Chile |
| Tellurium | withheld | Canada, Peru, Fiji |
| Thallium | withheld | West Germany, Belgium-Luxembourg, Japan |
| Titanium (metallic) | withheld | Japan, U.S.S.R., U.K., China |
| Zirconium | withheld | Australia, South Africa |
| Germanium | n.a. | West Germany, Switzerland, Belgium-Luxembourg, U.S.S.R. |
| Indium | n.a. | Peru, Canada, Belgium-Luxembourg, U.K. |
| Thorium | n.a. | France, Canada, Netherlands |
| Yttrium | n.a. | Australia, Malaysia, Thailand, Canada |

1. Net import reliance = imports − exports
2. Sources shown are points of shipment to the United States, not necessarily the initial sources of the material. For example, the United Kingdom is listed as a source of platinum, whereas it actually processes ore from South Africa.
3. Figure for 1979; 1980 figure withheld.
**Source:** U.S. Bureau of Mines

so skimpy or of such poor quality that we can expect to remain import-reliant. That means a good chance of escalating prices. And if import prices go high enough to spur a move to substitution or domestic production, then the price of the substituting metal, or the shares of whichever mining company owns the claim to existing ores, could increase accordingly.

Unfortunately, some of the most critical metals, and the ores for which there are few acceptable substitutes, are the same ones with which we are least endowed: chromium, cobalt, manganese, the platinum group.

## Our Allies Have Even Less

It turns out that the spontaneous flicks of nature's brush have splattered strategic metals about the globe as if intended more for drama than function. John le Carré or Ian Fleming could not have done a better job. Not only do we have a pauper's share of some metals needed for industry and defense, but our allies in Europe and Japan have even less. Overall, we import only about 17 percent of our raw materials, while Europeans import 80 percent of theirs and Japan a stunning 95 percent. A West German study found that if that nation were to lose as much as 25 percent of its chromium imports, the ripple effect throughout the economy would produce a 20 percent decline in the Gross National Product, perhaps creating a recession as bad as that which preceded Hitler's rise to power in 1933.

## What Are the Implications of Dependency?

These numbers do not worry some observers. To them, interdependency is a fact of life, and it is not all bad. The United States has benefited from the use of imported raw materials. The International Economic Studies Institute notes, "They reduced U.S. costs for materials and facilitated U.S. exports of metals and of manufactured goods containing metal. Thus, they made possible larger real incomes in the U.S. than would have been possible if more expensive domestic resources had been developed."

The optimists are confident that new methods, discoveries, and technologies will reduce our vulnerability. "Given ten years or more to anticipate a particular problem," states one expert, "it is hard to imagine a mineral that would cause a severe industrial crisis because of a constricting supply from present sources."

Further, most of the minerals we and our allies import

come from widely dispersed and friendly nations, such as Canada and Australia, as well as from usually reliable sources such as Brazil. Indeed, 78 percent of our imports come from developed market economies.

All well and good, goes the counterargument, but such sanguine conclusions fail to take into account the fact that

## EUROPEAN ECONOMIC COMMUNITY (EEC)[1] NET IMPORT RELIANCE OF SELECTED MINERALS AND METALS AS A PERCENT OF CONSUMPTION IN 1978

| Minerals and Metals | Net Imports as a Percent of Apparent Consumption[2] | Major Foreign Sources, 1978[3] |
|---|---|---|
| Columbium[4] | 100 | Canada, Austria, Brazil |
| Manganese | 100 | South Africa, Gabon, Brazil, Australia |
| Cobalt | 100 | Zaire, Zambia, U.S., Finland |
| Bauxite and alumina | 83 | Australia, Guinea, Jamaica, Surinam |
| Chromium | 100 | South Africa, Turkey |
| Platinum group metals | 100 | South Africa, U.S.S.R., U.S. |
| Nickel | 100 | Canada, South Africa, Australia |
| Zinc | 71 | Canada, Peru, Australia, Sweden |
| Mercury | 79 | Spain, Algeria, China |
| Cadmium | 70 | Japan, Canada, Finland, Mexico |
| Tungsten | 93 | China, Thailand, Portugal |
| Gold | 99 | South Africa, Switzerland, U.S.S.R., U.S. |
| Silver | 85 | U.S., India |
| Selenium | 83 | Canada, Japan, Sweden |
| Titanium (ilmenite and rutile) | 100 | Australia, Norway, Canada |
| Vanadium oxide[5] | 100 | South Africa, Finland, Austria |
| Iron ore | 70 | Brazil, Sweden, Liberia, Australia |
| Antimony | 95 | Bolivia, Thailand, Australia, China |
| Copper | 100 | Chile, Zaire, Zambia, Papua New Guinea |
| Lead | 39 | Australia, Canada, Sweden, Morocco |

1. European Economic Community in 1978 included Belgium, Denmark, France, West Germany, Ireland, Italy, Luxembourg, the Netherlands, and the U.K.
2. Net Imports = Imports − Exports. Apparent Consumption = Domestic Mine Output + Net Imports.
3. Sources shown are points of shipment to the EEC and are not necessarily the initial sources of the material.
4. Trade of columbium, tantalum, and vanadium are reported together.
5. Vanadium ore is reported with columbium.
**Source:** U.S. Bureau of Mines

supply dislocations do not announce themselves ten years in advance; they can happen overnight, whereas the lead time needed to develop substitutes and new mines is typically several years. In addition, not only mining but also, increasingly, smelting and refining are done abroad due to the decline of the domestic industry. In fact, some of the ores extracted from American mines are shipped as far as Japan for processing.

Resource warriors also believe that optimists do not recog-

## JAPAN NET IMPORT RELIANCE OF SELECTED MINERALS AND METALS AS A PERCENT OF CONSUMPTION IN 1978

| Minerals and Metals[1] | Net Imports as a Percent of Apparent Consumption[2] ("E" Denotes Exports) | Major Foreign Sources, 1978[3] |
|---|---|---|
| Columbium | 100 | Canada |
| Manganese | 95 | South Africa, India, Australia |
| Tantalum | 100 | U.S., Malaysia, Australia |
| Cobalt | 100 | Belgium, Luxembourg, Zaire, Canada |
| Bauxite | 100 | Australia, Indonesia, Malaysia |
| Alumina | 27 | Australia |
| Chromium | 99 | U.S., West Germany, South Africa |
| Platinum group metals | 98 | U.S.S.R., South Africa, U.K. |
| Nickel | 100 | New Caledonia, Indonesia, Philippines |
| Zinc | 61 | Canada, Peru, Australia |
| Mercury | 0 | |
| Cadmium | E5 | |
| Tungsten | 51 | South Korea, Canada, Peru |
| Gold | 95 | Switzerland, U.K. |
| Silver | 60 | Peru, Mexico |
| Selenium | E123 | |
| Titanium (ilmenite) | 100 | Australia, Malaysia |
| Vanadium | 100 | South Africa |
| Iron Ore | 99 | Australia, Brazil, India |
| Antimony | 100 | Bolivia, China, Thailand |
| Copper | 91 | Canada, Philippines, Zambia |
| Lead | 76 | North Korea, Mexico, Australia |

1. Data not available for potassium, pumice, and volcanic cinder and strontium.
2. Net Imports = Imports − Exports. Apparent Consumption = Domestic Primary Production + Secondary Production + Net Imports.
3. Sources shown are points of shipment to Japan and are not necessarily the initial sources of the material.
**Source:** U.S. Bureau of Mines

nize the degree to which politics, ideology, and emotion can overrule the logic of the marketplace. Furthermore, it is felt that a close examination of global distribution figures reveals our gaping vulnerability in a few specific metals if not overall; this vulnerability is particularly critical in light of possible wartime needs. Perhaps most important, the Soviet Union seems as well endowed with the nonfuel minerals we lack as we are in the wheat they lack. And to add the final dramatic touch, the one area of the world besides the U.S.S.R. with a copious endowment of those strategic metals is also one of the most potentially volatile: southern Africa.

## THE WELL-ENDOWED SOVIETS

In contrast to the United States and its allies, the Soviet Union is 50 percent import-dependent for only three important minerals: bauxite (used to make aluminum), barium, and fluoride. In fact, the Soviets are self-sufficient in twenty-six of the thirty-six minerals considered essential for an industrial society. They have traditionally been net exporters of twenty minerals, including some of the very metals we need most: chromium, platinum, manganese, and vanadium. In terms of known reserves, production, and percentage of world exports, the Soviet Union has traditionally ranked first or second in those metals. The other leader is the Republic of South Africa—except for chromium, where Zimbabwe has more reserves than the U.S.S.R., but the latter produces more.

Even the eternal hope that new discoveries will balance things out has proved dim in recent years. Between 1975 and 1980, known world reserves of chromium nearly doubled, and new resource discoveries multiplied the world's total by an astounding ten times. Good news in one sense. But 93 percent of these new resources were in two areas—South Africa and the Soviet Union.

In a nutshell, that is why Washington is nervous. Together, two nations control between 90 and 99 percent of the world's known platinum (the variation is due to conflicting sources of information), 94 to 98 percent of the world's manganese, 84 to 96 percent of the chrome, and 95 to 97 percent of the vanadium. The implications of a collaboration between those two mineral giants or of Soviet control of southern Africa are enormous. (Details on the African factor in the equation are covered in Chapter Four.)

### The Bear Is Changing

For many years official assessments of Russia's self-sufficiency treated it almost as a blessing. Of course, we knew that their metals gave them a resource base for building advanced weapons. Sure, it might permit them to wage a subtle resource war with impunity. But those things we could live with. By and large, we saw the Soviets as suppliers. They were the world's largest producer of minerals, we the largest consumer. We needed their raw materials, they needed our currency, our wheat, our high-technology products.

Thus, despite decades of threats, fear, and animosity, we felt reasonably secure with our economic detente. In fact, our fear of being too dependent on volatile South Africa was partly assuaged by the belief that the Soviet Union could be counted on in a pinch. As recently as 1979, a government task force reported that although "the U.S.S.R. is an avaricious consumer of its own considerable production, it is also becoming an important supplier to the U.S. and to other market economies."

No longer. Not only can the Soviets apparently not be counted on, but their position may have undergone a complete reversal. Representative Santini told his Congressional colleagues, "It is more likely that the Soviet Union and the COMECON [Council for Mutual Economic Assistance, the Soviet Bloc "common market"] countries are headed toward confrontation with the United States and its allies over available resources."

Now, there is a wrinkle we had not counted on—self-sufficient Russia vying directly with the West for the same foreign sources of raw materials. It's as if we stopped selling grain to the Soviets and instead *bought* grain on the international market.

In July 1980, *Fortune* magazine reported that the Soviet Union "has now begun to import strategic minerals for itself and its allies from countries whose output traditionally has gone mainly to the U.S. and its allies." Writer Herbert E. Meyer went on to say that the new pattern "could well mean that our supplies of strategic minerals will tighten up in coming years, sending prices upward and perhaps creating spot shortages."

In 1979, exports of Soviet chromium dropped to half their previous quantity. Shipments of manganese and the platinum group metals also declined sharply. In addition, metal traders report, the Soviet Union virtually stopped signing new contracts for future delivery of titanium, vanadium, lead, and nickel. Interestingly, even Soviet exports to fellow COMECON members have been substantially reduced. Thus, the populous and increasingly industrialized nations of the Soviet Bloc might be looking away from Mother Russia for supply sources.

Even more ominous than the decline in exports is the other half of what some observers call a "historic shift" by the U.S.S.R. They have begun to purchase items that they have traditionally sold: for example, titanium, vanadium, beryllium, tantalum, lithium. Daniel I. Fine of MIT's Mining and Mineral Research Institute told *Fortune* that the pattern cannot be explained by temporary shortages or short-term speculation. He believes it is more than a passing phenomenon. "The mineral-resource balance of the U.S.S.R. is following oil into a new era of less-than-self-sufficiency." If that is so, then we have not only lost a supplier, we've gained a competitor, and a formidable one at that.

**Speculating on Soviet Motivation**
Since 1956, the Soviet Union has considered all data on production capacity and production plans for its metals a state secret, one indication of how important resources are in its international strategy. As a result, it has been next to impossible for Western nations to obtain reliable data on the Soviet mineral situation. This makes it difficult to determine the reasons for the Soviet shift from supplier to purchaser. By contrast, the West is virtually an open book when it comes to production data. This puts us at something of a disadvantage.

To some, the Soviet shift is evidence of a conscious, deliberate campaign to deny the United States and its allies the resources they need to maintain industrial and military strength. In this view, the Kremlin's strategy is one thrust in a long-range war of attrition. Others believe it is just a shrewd economic move by a major supplier, designed to improve its leverage in strategic metals. Perhaps it is an effort to raise world prices so that Russia's own stocks go up in value. Or part of a long-range plan to conserve in-ground resources for the future—to sell them when the West is scraping desperately for metals and willing to buy at any price, or to use themselves when technological advances make them easier and cheaper to exploit.

All of those factors may play a part in Soviet thinking. But most experts feel that the recent shift signifies something more: the Soviet Union is a lot less self-sufficient than we, and perhaps even they, believed. Moscow's primary motive may be to ensure that its own substantial industrial and military requirements are met. If the other results ensue as side effects, so much the better.

The major portion of Soviet minerals is located under the frozen earth of Siberia. Much of that region is covered with ice and snow several months of the year. To exploit those reserves requires huge capital investments and a tremendous amount of energy and manpower. On a purely cost-effective basis, therefore, acquiring minerals from abroad may be preferable to the long-standing Soviet goal of complete self-sufficiency.

James Sinclair summed up the possible reasoning behind the new Soviet strategy in his quarterly *Strategics Review:* "The Soviet Union recognizes that the value of its nonrenewable Siberian resources will increase in the long term as world energy and mineral supplies become short, and thus higher priced. Second, in the long term the world will need Siberian resources at any price, thus providing the Soviet Union with decisive political power in the affairs of the West. Third, outward access allows the Soviet Union to consume and deplete foreign energy and minerals while preserving a Siberian stockpile in the ground."

In this respect, Soviet strategy may be no more sinister than that of our own corporations. In the case of the Soviet Union's Siberian reserves, the benefits would go beyond short-range savings. Given the lead time afforded by the use of imported minerals, they could develop the technology needed to exploit Siberia economically. That technology, incidentally, could come from the United States. According to Dr. John F. Elliott, Professor of Metallurgy at MIT, the ability of the Soviets to develop their raw materials and produce high-performance metals and alloys depends on the acquisition of computers, automation techniques, and heavy excavation machinery—areas in which America leads the world.

### The Soviets Have Problems Too

The Soviet Union is reportedly besieged by management, labor, and technical problems; central planning is apparently not doing the best job of fulfilling Soviet mineral potential. According to MIT's Daniel Fine, "Mine design and planning in the Soviet Union appear less than adequate. Mineral processing capacity is deficient because of planning oversight. Labor incentives in the mining sector are not effectively achieving labor migration and higher productivity rates. Mineral recovery rates appear to be lower than in developing countries. A technological lag in the metals industry is evident."

Dr. Elliott agrees. Despite the Soviet Union's impressive achievements in space and military technology, he told a Congressional hearing, "There appear to be serious deficiencies in the system for producing metals and supplying metals and alloys for the civilian sector of their economy."

Because of inadequate production methods and equipment, the Soviet Union apparently has to accept higher costs, greater materials losses, or lower-quality metals. The alternative, Dr. Elliott notes, is "to use more highly alloyed steel to be able to meet the quality requirements. This action leads to an increased use of alloying metals, such as nickel, chromium, and molybdenum."

All of these pressures, it is believed, are compounded by basic supply/demand problems. The Soviet Bloc wants to step up its industrial development; this mandates increased consumption of metals. So does the continued buildup of Soviet military power. No doubt the Kremlin, evidently bent on achieving military superiority, is as concerned about future supplies of critical materials as is Washington. Indeed, if certain domestic critics are correct, they are a lot *more* concerned. Quite possibly, they are stockpiling for a future that might entail war.

Along with increased demand and a variety of technical and procedural problems, the Soviet Union may be experiencing a fundamental supply crisis. Their vaunted resources may not be as plentiful as previously assumed. "Mineral ore grades in existing deposits are declining without major new discoveries of new and richer supplies," states Dr. Fine. Like us, they may have used up their best ores. But they may be even less capable of developing substitutes quickly, and the amount of energy and manpower needed to exploit low-quality ores might strain their economic system even more severely than ours.

Manganese provides a good example. Historically, the Soviet Union has been the world's principal source of that vital ingredient in steel production. They are still the world's leading producer, as befits a nation with the world's biggest steel industry. But their exports have been cut back severely. Why? Perhaps, as minerals economist Franz Dykstra contends, Soviet estimates of their manganese reserves—essentially enough for 200 years at current consumption—are "hogwash." Dykstra believes that known ore bodies have been largely depleted, and that Soviet attempts to find new sources have either failed or faltered due to equipment and labor problems.

Robert L'Esperance of U.S. Steel agrees: "The evidence is that their costs are increasing and the productivity per man engaged in manganese mining is going down. I can cite for you their own statistics in one manganese operation from the period 1970 to 1975; the productivity dropped 23 percent."

Until recently COMECON obtained its manganese exclusively from Mother Russia, and the West accounted for a third of Soviet exports. But in the last five years, Soviet shipments to COMECON have dropped by 16 percent, and exports to the West have virtually disappeared. COMECON now imports about 1.5 million tons per year of high-grade ore, mainly from Gabon in West Africa—our chief source, too—and from Brazil, India, and Morocco. Mr. L'Esperance told Congress that he expects the Soviet Bloc to occupy a growing segment of the buying market in coming years.

This means that the United States, which imports almost every ounce of manganese it uses, might encounter increased competition for supplies. We can no longer count on getting it from Russia. "If somebody from the West came along and said, 'We would like a million tons of manganese ore,' " says Mr. L'Esperance, "there is no physical way they [the U.S.S.R.] can do it. Not in the near term . . . and in the far term they would have to sacrifice their own needs to do it."

A similar situation exists for chromium and platinum, both of which the Soviet Union has more of than any nation on earth outside southern Africa. Its ability to produce has deteriorated due to serious mining difficulties, according to U.S. experts.

Between 1975 and 1978, Soviet exports of chromium dropped from 1.2 million tons to 643,000 tons. Reportedly, a decline in ore grade led to unanticipated technical problems, forcing Moscow to turn to outside sources. Despite U.N. sanctions against Rhodesia, Russia purchased large quantities of choice Rhodesian ore, industry observers contend. Later they obtained ore from Albania, negotiated a mineral development accord with Turkey, which has moderate-sized chromium reserves, and began exploration in Syria. Reportedly, they recently purchased some chromite from Khomeini's Iran. What does all this portend? "Ultimately," Dr. Fine concludes, "the Soviet shift toward outward access and strategic dependency leads to greater conflict over southern African chromite," far and away the world's best reserves.

Platinum? In the last half of the seventies, Soviet exports dropped by about half, despite a favorable market for sellers (prices went up by 59 percent in 1978–1979) and the apparent Soviet need for hard currency. Shipments have increased, but are still one-third lower than the peak period of 1973. Experts believe that this, too, is a result of mining and processing difficulties. Eighty-five percent of Soviet platinum is mined in Norilsk, whose icy weather and remote location make it wretched for humans and exacting for current technology. Further, there have been reports of a natural disaster that closed underground operations.

Similar patterns have been observed for tantalum, vanadium, and titanium, all three of which have important military applications. Presumed to be self-sufficient, Russia has been importing. Allegedly, it has been importing about 80,000 pounds a year of tantalum from a mine in Mozambique formerly owned by Portuguese interests. Another example of the practical value of winning friends and influencing people in the Third World.

## Some Sinister Implications

What worries the resource warriors at home is not just the possible emergence of a voracious competitor, but one whose methods may overreach the boundaries of open competition and the rules of fair play. Dr. Robert Kilmarx, of the Center for Strategic and International Studies at Georgetown University, believes that "the Soviet Union is or will be evolving a minerals strategy that is adverse to the interests of the U.S. and its allies." Because of its alleged difficulties, Dr. Kilmarx contends, the only way the Soviet Union can achieve its mineral goals is to extend its sphere of influence, economically and politically.

One way to reach out is to provide technical expertise and financial support for exploration and development projects in poor but resource-rich countries. Reportedly, by the late 1970s the Soviet Union had formal assistance pacts with twenty-seven developing nations, including the African nations of Angola, Mozambique, Ethiopia, and the Sudan. This, of course, requires favorable political conditions.

As we shall see later on, the postcolonial period has created conditions in the Third World that make private investments there risky propositions. That has left a vacuum for the Soviet Union to step in to. By so doing, they could improve their political and military strength as well as their access to materials. The CMEA (Council for Mutual Economic Aid—essentially the Soviet Bloc) has brought on line projects that our own mining companies would not undertake because of volatile conditions or poor financial arrangements. The host countries were not necessarily pro-Soviet; they needed economic help, and they took it wherever they could get it, just as they do with arms. But they were often surprised to discover that dealing with Moscow was more ticklish than dealing with Wall Street or Washington.

The Soviet Union lacks the financial resources—the "buyer capability"—to engage in conventional market-style competition with the West. To Dr. Fine and others, this points to an inevitable conclusion: if they remain importers, they will have to play by different rules. With state-run economies for example, the Soviets may be in a good position to obtain what they need through barter, as in the oil-for-rice deal with India (their oil, India's rice) or the alleged cobalt-for-weapons exchange with Zambia. A state-controlled economy would be easier for the Soviet Union to work with, since it might provide terms less favorable to private investment, and since it is, in Dr. Fine's words, "easily mobilized for cartel formation, price gouging, supply restrictions, and Soviet/CMEA access. . . ."

But what about other tactics? What about sabotage, invasion, KGB subversion, or encouraging revolution to bring down a regime friendly to the West and replacing it with an accommodating ruler? Some of these methods are familiar to us, since we have used them ourselves on occasion. We call it "defending our vital interests." They come under the rubric "economic cannibalism" when your adversary uses them.

Conceivably, any of several incentives—disrupting Western economies, guaranteeing its own mineral needs, improving its political and military position—could be enough to make Moscow heat up the resource war. Some observers feel this is unlikely, that recent shifts in Soviet import/export patterns do not portend a coordinated, long-range turnabout, and that self-sufficiency will be pursued by the Kremlin despite recent production problems. Certainly, with respect to reserves, the Soviets have more than enough of most critical metals to meet

# PRODUCTION AND RESERVES
## BY MAIN GEO-POLITICAL GROUPING

PERCENTAGE SHARES IN WORLD TOTAL

| | Reserves | | | Primary Production, 1977–1978 | | |
|---|---|---|---|---|---|---|
| | Developed | Less Developed | Centrally Planned | Developed | Less Developed | Centrally Planned |
| Aluminum | — | — | — | 72 | 8 | 20 |
| Antimony | 24 | 19 | 57 | 35 | 37 | 28 |
| Asbestos | 56 | 11 | 33 | 42 | 7 | 51 |
| Barytes | 47 | 35 | 18 | 54 | 30 | 16 |
| Bauxite | 28 | 68 | 4 | 41 | 45 | 14 |
| Cadmium | 63 | 24 | 13 | 69 | 9 | 22 |
| Chromium | 68 | 31 | 1 | 45 | 23 | 32 |
| Cobalt | 7 | 72 | 21 | 19 | 60 | 11 |
| Columbium | 7 | 87 | 6 | 17 | 77 | 6 |
| Copper | 30 | 58 | 12 | 37 | 41 | 22 |
| Fluorspar | 52 | 38 | 10 | 37 | 31 | 32 |
| Germanium | n.a. | n.a. | n.a. | 56 | 34 | 10 |
| Gold | 64 | 14 | 22 | 68 | 12 | 20 |
| Industrial diamonds | 7 | 89 | 4 | 14 | 58 | 28 |
| Iron ore | 35 | 31 | 34 | 40 | 24 | 36 |
| Lead | 60 | 19 | 21 | 50 | 20 | 30 |
| Lithium | 24 | 68 | 7 | 79 | 4 | 17 |
| Manganese | 52 | 9 | 39 | 32 | 29 | 39 |
| Mercury | 58 | 13 | 29 | 36 | 19 | 45 |
| Molybdenum | 51 | 37 | 12 | 77 | 13 | 10 |
| Nickel | 32 | 53 | 15 | 48 | 27 | 25 |
| Phosphate | 19 | 75 | 6 | 43 | 31 | 26 |
| Platinum Group: | | | | | | |
|   Palladium | 86 | — | 14 | 33 | — | 67 |
|   Platinum | 55 | — | 45 | 72 | 1 | 27 |
|   Rhodium | 86 | — | 16 | 53 | — | 47 |
| Potash | 80 | 3 | 17 | 50 | 3 | 47 |
| Selenium | 29 | 52 | 19 | n.a. | n.a. | n.a. |
| Silicon | n.a. | n.a. | n.a. | 68 | 6 | 26 |
| Silver | 40 | 27 | 33 | 41 | 37 | 22 |
| Sulfur | 33 | 37 | 30 | 55 | 8 | 37 |
| Tantalum | 6 | 87 | 7 | 23 | 63 | 14 |
| Tin | 8 | 70 | 22 | 8 | 76 | 16 |
| Titanium: | | | | | | |
|   Ilmenite | 78 | 20 | 2 | 82 | 9 | 9 |
|   Rutile | 11 | 86 | 3 | 90 | 2 | 8 |
| Tungsten | 27 | 10 | 63 | 29 | 25 | 46 |
| Vanadium | 22 | 5 | 73 | 66 | 3 | 31 |
| Zinc | 68 | 21 | 11 | 54 | 19 | 27 |
| Zirconium | 70 | 16 | 14 | 83 | 2 | 15 |

**Note:** Developed countries are all OECD (Organization for Economic Cooperation and Development) countries and South Africa; Centrally Planned are COMECON countries, China, Albania, Vietnam, and North Korea; Less Developed covers the remainder.

**Source:** *James Sinclair Letter*, March 27, 1980.

their own needs for a long time, and probably enough to generate sufficient surplus to trade for badly needed foreign exchange. But they may decide to spend their rubles on other pressing problems instead of metals production. A policy of outreach could be more economic, at least for a while, and reap political benefits as well.

Whatever the Soviets decide will have a major impact on strategic metals supplies and prices. Either way, however, one unalterable fact remains: they have and we have not. If the U.S.S.R. chooses to remain a major supplier, it is problematic because it makes us dependent on our major adversary; if the Soviets stop exportng, and compete for Third World resources, that is even more problematic. Hot or cold, real or imagined, a resource war has implications that reach well beyond the metals markets. Both superpowers know that might and minerals are like chickens and eggs—powerful nations have always used one to obtain the other.

# IS THIS REALLY WAR?

## THREE

**B**ACK IN THE 1960s, few people, military analysts included, paid much attention to the Persian Gulf or the Strait of Hormuz. Now every schoolchild knows that the ships that deliver our oil must pass through those waters. After we sat through the indignity of gasoline lines, the suggestion of using force to defend our access to Persian Gulf oil elicited no more consternation than the idea of defending Lake Michigan. In the national consciousness, a small inlet halfway around the world became inexorably linked to our wallets, our prized mobility, and our standard of living.

The Persian Gulf was brought still closer to home when Iran, once the protector of Western interests in the region, became our enemy overnight. Concern became alarm when the Soviet Union invaded Afghanistan, whose southern border is about as far from the Strait of Hormuz as San Francisco is from Los Angeles. Also close by are pro-Soviet Syria and Iraq, as well as Cuban and East German military personnel in South Yemen and Ethiopia. Even if all this is not part of a Soviet plan to seize Mideast oil, it could conceivably be the result, as Washington is well aware.

The Mideast oil situation has alerted strategic planners to parallels elsewhere. Some of the resources of Southeast Asia—

coveted by Imperial Japan, and used extensively by the United States and Europe—have been lost to us, and others have been placed in jeopardy, by an adventurous Vietnam, now under the Soviet wing. Closer to home, the Cuban revolution meant more to Americans than the loss of cigars and a swinging vacationland. During World War II, the island was a vital source of cobalt, nickel, chromite, and manganese. Now the Soviet Union gets 40 percent of its cobalt from Cuban mines that we developed. It also has a vital link to the sea lanes of the Caribbean and an aggressive spear carrier to other parts of the world, such as Latin America, where political loyalties and formidable resource bases are up for grabs.

And then there is the "Persian Gulf of Minerals," perhaps the most critical of the former colonial regions. Both super-powers would love to have uncontested access to the area, just as they covet Mideast oil. The Soviet Union has taken major steps to counteract long-standing Western dominance in Africa, encircling the metaphoric "Persian Gulf" in much the same way it has the actual one.

## SOVIET INROADS IN MINERAL-RICH AFRICA

The Soviet presence in southern Africa has sounded the alarms in the Pentagon. Angola, Mozambique, Tanzania, the Congo, Zambia, and Ethiopia all have a significant Cuban/Soviet presence. Recently, Libya, an important Soviet client state, thrust successfully into its southern neighbor, Chad.

Add to that alleged covert activities in Namibia, South Africa, and Zimbabwe—stimulated, it is said, from Angola—and the Soviet Union seems to be sitting pretty, or at least a lot prettier than they have been since the sun began to set on the European empires. They are well placed to seize access to critical metals, or to disrupt the supplies of materials on which the West depends. Through Cuban and East German advisers, or KGB moles, they could foster sabotage, a form of disruption that could occur any time some disgruntled terrorist or political fanatic decided his or her life was worth risking to deal a decisive blow to the perceived enemy. Alert to unrest and instability, the U.S.S.R. could act as a catalyst to Shaba-like incidents; or to strikes such as the one in Chile where 10,000 workers walked out, closing the world's largest underground copper mine; or to outright revolution.

Washington has to think about what would happen if any

other nations in southern Africa were to align themselves with the Soviet Union. The possibility is enough to cause night tremors in the sturdiest soul in the Pentagon. To most political analysts, the chances of that happening to South Africa are not much better than it happening to Canada. On the other hand, not too long ago Ethiopia seemed securely in the Western camp, and so did Iran. South Africa is ripe for change. And what about Zaire, or Zambia, or Zimbabwe? They are not as powerful as South Africa, nor are their leaders as staunchly pro-West. And throughout the area poverty, frustration, anger, and desperation—the seeds of violence—are so rampant that explosions could occur without much help from the Kremlin.

## A Worst-Case Scenario

The Council on Economics and National Security (CENS), a Washington-based nonprofit group headed by former Rear Admiral William C. Mott, issued a white paper in 1980, in which the following worst-case scenario was concocted: "The possibility exists that the Soviets and their allies in Africa could create a cartel in certain critical minerals, particularly if the mineral resources of the U.S.S.R. and southern Africa were ever combined. Cuban infantry and East German security police could be used to sustain a cartel."

For a variety of reasons, scores of academicians and foreign policy experts have discounted the likelihood of such cartels having any significant clout, or even forming in the first place. The same authorities consider the other hawkish projections equally farfetched. But for now, let's consider only the worst case.

The CENS report goes on:

> . . . a Marxist "Commonwealth" in Africa would be inte-grated into the Communist economic system, COMECON, and exploited by the Warsaw Pact, somewhat in the manner that the U.S.S.R. has in the past exploited Eastern Europe. The arrangement perhaps would not be "efficient" in Western terms, but it might operate long enough to disrupt world trade and *cripple the West.* The state trading ministries of COMECON, after all, would have the bureaucratic know-how to organize commodity cartels and economic warfare, while the KGB and the revived East German "Gestapo" could answer to any complaints from African citizens. . . . Soviet-inspired economic "warfare"—waged through cartels in commodities like chromium and cobalt—would not have to be "profit-oriented" in order to

achieve Moscow's goals of creating financial chaos and wide-spread unemployment in the West and Japan.

Even if quite such a gloomy picture fails to unfold, the Soviet Union stands to gain from continued turmoil in southern Africa, and might therefore be motivated economically as well as politically to keep it going. As the only other well-stocked "have" in the world, Russia can only benefit from temporary disruptions in supplies, or from price jumps, if it has the capacity to turn seller again.

We have already seen one instance of this. When the United Nations imposed sanctions on the Ian Smith regime in Rhodesia to punish that country for its reprehensible racial policies, the United States went along, curtailing its imports of chromium. Yet we still needed the metal, and so we turned to an alternative supplier—the Soviet Union. In this seller's market, the Soviets were only too happy to accommodate us—at a price considerably higher than what we formerly paid Rhodesia. Thus, our economy suffered, Rhodesia suffered—the blacks, no doubt, more than anyone else—and only our official antagonist gained. To make the matter even more absurd, it is reported that the Soviets sold us chromium, not from their own mines, but from Rhodesia, which was so desperate for trade that they sold at a bargain-basement price to the only country that disobeyed the sanctions.

You don't have to be a capitalist to know a good deal when you see one.

A similar situation is likely to unfold if the United States ever went ahead with sanctions on South Africa. In fact, it could even be worse. The Soviet Union would gain by becoming chief supplier of certain minerals. But Western nations would not be the only losers. The black African nations that are sworn to do away with white rule in South Africa, and who would initiate efforts to impose sanctions, are themselves dependent on trade with South Africa. And some of them also depend on South African rails and ports to export their own goods and resources.

## JOCKEYING FOR POSITION

Turmoil, with or without outside assistance, can hit rails and ports as well as capital cities and mines. Without reliable transportation ore can't be moved to its destination. Nor can food and equipment be brought to mining sites. Thus, curtailment of transportation could be as damaging as curtailment of production.

Until 1975, manganese ore extracted from the rich deposits of Kisenge in western Shaba province was transported by rail over the Benguela line to the port of Lobito in Angola. From there it sailed west to Europe and the United States. The cost of moving ores to Lobito was 40 percent less than transportation to other ports. Then came the Angolan Civil War. The Benguelan line was disrupted. Even now, half a million tons of choice manganese sits in Kisenge. Alternative transport is too expensive and will be used only if consumers are willing to pay the price.

Because they are virtually landlocked, countries like Zaire, Zambia, and Zimbabwe are vulnerable to transportation problems in neighboring countries as well as in their own. Rail and inland water routes frequently traverse more than one country en route to and from the sea. Out of Zaire, for example, various routes go through Zambia, Zimbabwe, Tanzania, South Africa, and Angola. Not only its products, but also Zaire's critical imports depend on those routes. In 1979, 40,000 tons of coal, 90,000 tons of coke (a coal residue used for fuel), 30,000 tons of sulfur, and 180,000 tons of maize, along with other essential supplies, entered Zaire by rail from Zimbabwe and South Africa. We have already seen what it takes to make air shipments of Zairian cobalt economic: astronomical price hikes.

Gabon is another good example. This small nation supplies 30 percent of our manganese ore. Its known reserves are paltry compared to those of South Africa or the Soviet Union, but of the remaining producers only Australia has more. Gabon's ore gets to the sea over a rail route that runs through the Congo, perilously close to the Angolan border. Reconstruction of that line was stopped for a year, due to civil unrest in Angola. Experts fear that Gabon manganese shipments could at any time be interrupted by turbulence in neighboring countries.

Making the transportation situation that much more ominous is the general condition of disrepair. In Zaire and other nations, the systems can self-destruct without the assistance of a terrorist or a saboteur. According to Congressman Santini's Subcommittee staff, which visited southern Africa in 1980, "The Zairian national railroad . . . is slowly and surely grinding to a halt because of lack of foreign exchange to purchase vitally needed cars and locomotives, spare parts, and new track." Apparently, faulty tracks and equipment on one key line out of Kolwezi cause delays every day, adding an estimated $68 million to the annual cost of the metals produced there.

### The Vital Sea Lanes

The fragile railroad system is a chilling example of how sudden disruptions in supplies can occur. Even more chilling, however, is the stiff sea breeze blowing off the Cape of Good Hope.

From ports in Angola, Namibia, South Africa, Mozambique, and Tanzania, cargo ships sail eastward to Japan and westward to Europe and the United States. Many of them circle the Cape, which ranks with the Strait of Hormuz as a vital "choke point" in the flow of raw materials across the globe. Some 25,000 resource-bearing trade ships round the Cape each year. In their cargoes are 70 percent of Western Europe's mineral imports and 90 percent of its oil. A large portion of our own imports sails with them.

Military historians know that the nation that controls certain vital sea lanes enjoys a strategic edge over its opponents. "Any country aspiring to global power and influence must necessarily acquire the requisite means to exploit the seas," Rear Admiral Robert J. Hanks (U.S. Navy, retired) said at a Congressional hearing. "Exploitation in this context means, first, the ability to freely use discrete portions of the oceans when and where they must be used, and, secondly, to be able to deny such use to any and all potential adversaries."

At the height of its powers, the British Empire controlled almost all the vital choke points, thus securing both military and commercial leverage. The nation that rules the waves can often waive the rules.

In the past decade, the Soviet Union has expanded its navy considerably, while the United States has reduced its fleet to nearly half its former size. The U.S.S.R. now outnumbers the United States in every category of combat and support ships with the exception of aircraft carriers. Further, it is expected that the Kremlin, a careful student of history, will strengthen and expand its naval power over the next few years.

But what scares U.S. military strategists as much as the sheer size of the Soviet navy is its expansion geographically. In recent years, Russia has added to its Caribbean outposts in Cuba access to ports in Ethiopia, South Yemen, Mozambique, and Angola. While they are not all full-fledged military bases, the new ports represent important strategic gains. The Soviets also control the former U.S. naval base in Cam Ranh Bay, Vietnam. Needless to say, these developments have been greeted with alarm in the Pentagon; in wartime, Soviet ships would be poised to threaten shipments of vital materials.

Virtually all imported strategic metals, and 100 percent of all imported fuels, travel on the surface of the sea, through delicate passages like the Strait of Hormuz and the Cape of Good Hope. The ores mined in southern Africa sail a full six to eight weeks over the high and open seas before they are hauled ashore to make our airplanes and weapons.

Rear Admiral Hanks notes, "From bases at the North Cape, Soviet naval units—surface, subsurface, and air—transit the broad reaches of the North Atlantic to bases in Cuba. From there, where they can menace all of the shipping lanes lacing the Caribbean and the Central Atlantic, they can head southward to the West African coast and bases established in the Congo and Angola . . . it is obvious that Moscow currently has the capability to sever all of the main shipping lines in both the North and South Atlantic Oceans."

Hanks later qualified his statement by saying that traffic in wartime would probably continue to flow, but it would be reduced to the point where the United States could not support a "meaningful war effort."

During World War II the Allies encountered resource warfare in the form of German submarine attacks on merchant ships hauling strategic metals from Africa. Chromium shipments were constantly harassed. Tantalum and columbium were so critical, and the Nazi attacks so relentless, that we were forced to fly the ore in from Brazil. Russia is better positioned than Germany was.

Strategists point out with apprehension that there are more than 8,000 nautical miles of ocean stretching around the Cape of Good Hope from Liberia on the west to Mombasa on the east. On that vital loop there are no U.S. or European naval bases or airfields. While the defense capability of South Africa far exceeds that of its neighbors, military officials are loathe to place responsibility for the defense of the entire region in its hands. The political volatility of southern Africa, and the Soviet presence there make those sea lanes a high priority at any time, and especially during a conventional war.

Appearing before Congressional hearings a few months before his nomination as Secretary of State, Alexander Haig surveyed recent Soviet behavior and summed up the position of a large number of powerful people in these apocalyptic terms: ". . . these Soviet policies have the practical consequence of leading toward Soviet control of these vital areas. This control could, at any given point in time, interdict the vital lifelines of commerce of the Western world and its access to essential raw materials. The consequences of that would be the inevitable strangulation of our entire industrial complex."

## OR IS IT JUST COMPETITION?

The Soviet shadow hangs over critical pressure points on the globe. Some say the shadow holds a gun; others believe it holds only a calculator. Some say the Russian goal is ultimately to choke off the United States and its allies from their sources of vital minerals, thus bringing about an economic and military crisis in the West. Others say their goal is simply to obtain the currency and minerals they need to achieve their own industrial and defense objectives. To the hard-liners, we are in a resource war; to the others, we are engaged in economic competition. The distinction may be only semantic. Said Frank Shakespeare, former director of the U.S. Information Agency, and now president of RKO General, "When we jostle with Western Europe and Japan for strategic minerals— that's competition. When the Russians get into the act— that's war."

Henry Kissinger believes it is war; Alexander Haig believes it is war; Congressman Santini believes it is war; and a host of important figures in the defense establishment and private industry believe it is war. In June 1980, the World Affairs Council of Pittsburgh held a conference that was attended by an impressive array of ranking executives, academicians, and government officials. The speakers were unequivocal: this is war, and we must revise domestic and foreign policy so as to deflect our resource vulnerability. The conference's official summary, written by *Fortune* editor Herbert E. Meyer, concluded, among other things, that "the Soviet Union must be regarded as a hostile state, whose leaders may be attempting to injure the U.S. and its allies by impeding their access to strategic minerals."

### The Soviet Grand Design?
Those prepared to assign sinister motives to the Soviet Union believe the resource war is the latest chapter in Moscow's

historic grand design: to achieve global dominance and fulfill the destiny of world communism. Dismantling capitalism would be far superior to and far less costly than military victory. In this view, conquest, not conflict, is the objective, and the strategy is "economic cannibalism." Congressman Santini wrote to the *Washington Post*, "Every top Soviet leader from Lenin to Brezhnev has openly acknowledged that Soviet domination over the world's mineral resources, namely in the Persian Gulf and southern Africa, would bring the capitalist system to its knees."

In support of this contention, a hit parade of Soviet sources has been marshaled. Said Stalin in 1921: "If Europe and America may be called the front, the nonsovereign nations and colonies—with their raw materials, fuel, food and vast stores of human material, should be regarded as the rear . . . in order to win a war, one must not only triumph at the front, but also revolutionize the enemy's rear."

Brezhnev in 1973: "Our aim is to gain control of the two great treasure houses on which the West depends—the energy treasure house of the Persian Gulf and the mineral treasure house of central and southern Africa."

The sources of those quotations are somewhat uncertain and could be considered dubious. The latter is taken from Richard Nixon's memoirs and is attributed to a remark allegedly made by Brezhnev to Mohamed Siad Barre, President of Somalia, in Prague. Nevertheless, Soviet defectors have recently attested to the spirit of those quotes. In a paid editorial in *Newsweek*, Rear Admiral William C. Mott (U.S. Navy, retired) quoted one Galina Orionova, formerly with Russia's Institute of U.S. Studies. "The Soviet government behaves like any ordinary Soviet consumer," said Orionova. "He grabs anything which happens to be on the counter, even if he doesn't need it, knowing that tomorrow it may no longer be available."

That grabbing, resource warriors fear, can involve tactics that would make the "Ugly American" image look philanthropic by comparison.

Another defector, Igor Glagolev, who worked at the Soviet Academy of Science, claimed that the Soviet strategy of controlling the world's supply of key minerals was well under way. According to the *New Republic* (December 20, 1980), Glagolev alleged that plans were being made to invade South Africa and Namibia. "This is not a theoretical discussion anymore," the defector reportedly said. "It is a very practical instruction for immediate aggressive action. . . . I heard these instructions many times from representatives of the Soviet government."

### Or Cold War Bombast?

To many observers, these extreme views smack of Cold War paranoia and hawkish posturing. They are not yet prepared to characterize the U.S.S.R. as an adversary in an undeclared resource war and feel that there is as yet no concrete evidence of a concerted Russian attempt to deprive the West of its customary supply sources. These dissenters include representatives of the National Security Council and the State Department. According to *New Republic* writers Mark Hosenball and Peter Pringle, "When we posed Glagolev's plot to the CIA's minerals expert he giggled into the phone."

Indeed, the idea of an imminent invasion of South Africa strikes many analysts as ludicrous. That country is a lot stronger and a lot farther from Russia than is Afghanistan. It would be a huge risk militarily, and would no doubt inflame the world—even the anti-Western nations—to a degree that Russia is not prepared for at this time. Even barring such an invasion plan, the alleged Soviet plot to deny us our minerals is seen by many as pure inference and speculation. A minerals expert at the State Department, quoted in the same *New Republic* article, summed up the more cautious attitude we found elsewhere: "All one can say is that the Russians have proved they can play the game in the international market."

Other critics point out that Soviet gains in Africa have been minimal and have been balanced by an equal number of frustrations and defeats. While they have been backing revolutionary organizations since the late 1950s, they have been unable to transplant their political and economic ideologies. African nationalism, the dominant motivating force on the continent, is usually as anti-Soviet as it is anti-West. African leaders have cooperated with the Soviets on many occasions, but the loyalty does not always last once immediate objectives—obtaining military aid, for example—have been achieved. Indeed, Egypt, the Sudan, and other nations have reversed pro-Soviet stances. The strings attached to Soviet contributions and the West's clear economic superiority have kept Moscow's influence down. By all indications, despite definite Soviet inroads in the area, Western interests have not been seriously hampered, say the doves in the resource war.

Despite the turmoil in the region, traditionally Western or nonaligned states, such as Zaire, Botswana, and Zambia, have remained ensconced in the Western economy. Even the Soviet gains in Angola and Mozambique, while substantial, have not achieved quite what Moscow would have liked. Both nations cooperate with South Africa in trade, transportation, labor, and electrical power. Neither country has allowed Soviet military bases on its soil, and neither permits shore leave to Russian sailors. And placing pragmatism above ideology, both nations—as well as avowedly Marxist Zimbabwe—are stepping up trade with the West. Mozambique's largest commercial partner, the Congressional Research Service reports, is the United States.

But, counter the hawks, that does not mean the U.S.S.R. won't keep trying. Indeed, with its international reputation sullied, its global designs well behind schedule, and monumental problems at home, the Soviets may feel pressured into aggressive conduct, like a cornered bear. There can be no doubt that Moscow covets the mineral and strategic advantages of southern Africa. The big question is, What will it do to obtain them, if anything?

## THE NEED FOR OBJECTIVITY

In a sense, the debate over Russian motivation and ultimate objectives is irrelevant. Whether we call it war or Darwinian competition, the end result might be the same, particularly if the Soviets do play by different rules. If they have nothing more sinister in mind than we do—that is, securing reliable, low-cost access to the minerals they need—their achievement of that goal could have almost the same impact as if they deliberately cut off our sources. Japan did not set out to destroy the American automobile industry, but its automakers were such formidable competitors that they had almost that effect. Perhaps the distinction between *war* and *competition* is meaningful on the level of government policy, but to those who invest in and use strategic metals, it may not matter. Whatever the Soviet role, or goal, in the Shaba invasions, the price of cobalt went up to $45 a pound.

It is beyond the scope of this book, of course, to judge the opposing points of view. Quite possibly the hawks are macho toughs itching for a fight; perhaps they have resurrected Cold War rhetoric to further their own vested interests—home district votes in mining areas, favorable legislation for the mining industry, or a dynamic strategic metals market with big commissions for brokers. Quite possibly the doves are naïve, and fail to perceive the strategic implications of the scramble for metals.

Somewhere between the two extremes is a realistic vision. To be well informed, one must take an objective, impersonal view of the geopolitical and domestic issues that affect the metals markets, and pay attention to a variety of sources. Your personal political views should not influence investment decisions, nor should impulsive decisions be made on the basis of a single news item.

Two things must be said, however, regarding the hawkish point of view. First, many people in power adhere to it and, whether their views are accurate or not, they are influential. For years, James Santini was a lone voice in the Washington wilderness. Now he has a lot of company, and the Pentagon, defense contractors, and mining executives have sympathetic ears in the Reagan Administration. Key figures, especially Secretary of the Interior James Watt, are determined resource warriors. In a telephone conversation two months after Reagan's inauguration, Congressman Santini said he anticipated "an important shift in direction and emphasis, toward positive and responsible executive action." He wondered what he would do with all the acerbic speeches he'd accumulated over the years.

The other thing that must be considered is history. It is easy to underestimate the strategic implications of worldwide mineral distribution during a time of relative peace. But in the past when things got hot, raw materials access played a key role in determining the origins and outcomes of wars, and in the important decisions of world leaders.

## RESOURCE WARS PAST

"Too often," historian Alfred E. Eckes writes in *The United States and the Global Struggle for Minerals*, "orthodox diplomatic histories ignore substantive economic issues, like access to raw materials, perhaps because these themes frequently do not interest professional diplomats with a traditional bias toward political affairs. Such a correction is overdue. From World War I, when industrial nations awoke abruptly to the realization they lacked sufficient domestic minerals to satisfy the industrial requirements of modern warfare, the quest for secure foreign supplies has been a major consideration of great-power diplomacy."

Indeed, the relationship between resources and might goes back a lot further. The Phoenicians fought wars to gain control of the Tin Isles. The "tributes" paid to the Roman empire were a major consideration in expansion. Many even believe that Helen was just an excuse to plunder Troy, whose gold, ivory, and slaves appealed to the city-states of Greece. The Age of Exploration was undertaken by European nations for more than a sense of adventure; they needed certain resources and coveted others, and they were willing to fight each other and subdue native populations to acquire them: gold, silver, tobacco, and hides from the New World; cotton, silk, rubber, and spices from the East; diamonds, copper, and slaves from Africa.

Ever since two tribes fought over a water hole or a hunting ground, groups of people have used their resources to fight for other resources. In fact, access to critical materials has always been a major determinant of power. The guns of European colonists depended on chrome and manganese from Africa. Britain's coal deposits fueled the navy that ruled the waves and brought back nickel and tungsten and other metals that gave impetus to the Industrial Revolution, which further strengthened British might.

Richard Barnett, Senior Fellow at the Institute for Policy Studies and author of *The Lean Years*, writes, "Whoever controls world resources, controls the world in a way that mere occupation of territory cannot match. When vital materials are in heavy demand and short supply, that fact alone gives power to some people over others. Even the illusion of scarcity creates power. . . . As a variety of materials become scarcer and more expensive, estimating their future availability becomes a political act."

The Kremlin knows that, and so does Washington.

### Resources and the Great War
German historian Fritz Fischer believed that his country's instigation of World War I was, at least in part, a desperate attempt to catch up with France and Britain, whose colonial

outposts were providing them with the minerals that had become vital to industrial nations. Pathetically poor in vital resources, the proud, ambitious Germans set out to obtain manganese from Belgium, chrome from Turkey, iron and manganese from the Ukraine, and a host of minerals from Africa.

Minerals played a key role in the outcome of that war. The latest technologies of death—planes, tanks, submarines, mines—depended on metals that were in short supply in the belligerents' homelands. In the end, British naval superiority, which itself required access to minerals, was able to interrupt Germany's overseas supplies, and its convoy system out-maneuvered German torpedoes, keeping the supplies coming to British factories: manganese from India, chromite from Rhodesia and Turkey, nickel from Canada. Embargoes, blockades, and sabotage were used in addition to raw power.

World War I made it perfectly clear to industrial nations that depending on imports for strategic metals and ferroalloys was dangerous. The new scramble for raw materials now involved governments as well as private enterprise.

**Resource Prelude to World War II**
France and Britain took steps to develop and control the resources of their colonies, and to keep them out of anyone else's hands. In a wonderful bit of irony, the British tightened their grip on the Middle East because they were too dependent on their main source of petroleum, which they saw as unreliable and unpredictable. That source was the United States.

The shift in resource needs created by new technology made the United States less self-sufficient than it had been in the first three decades of this century, when we produced 96 percent of the minerals we used. Some people saw ominous portents. But to the Germans, Italians, and Japanese, true have-nots, the world's supply of minerals spoke English only. A full three-quarters of the world's production was in British and American hands. The sun had not yet set on the British Empire, and American investments abroad doubled in the 1920s, adding substantially to our overall abundance.

Postwar Germany was in particularly bad shape. It went from being the dominant producer of steel in Europe to a virtual have-not. The French now controlled all of Alsace-Lorraine and also the industrial region of Ruhr, acquisitions adding up to 80 percent of Germany's previous iron ore production, 30 percent of its steel facilities, and 30 percent of its coal.

Despite an energetic attempt to reindustrialize, to strike deals with foreign suppliers, and to develop substitutes and synthetics, Germany remained dependent on trade. But its trade position was embarrassingly weak, thanks to the Treaty of Versailles. By 1929, the exasperated Nazis had linked resource needs to national pride and German destiny. Deutschland must have land and minerals!

The unequal distribution of resources was apparently an important factor in the decision-making process. Axis powers were covetous; they complained bitterly about their second-rate economic status, which they attributed largely to the Allied control of resource-rich colonies. "From their perspective," Alfred E. Eckes wrote, "materials were both the vital precondition for successfully waging war and the goal of conquest—sufficient materials to assure long-term self-reliance." That assessment may, of course, go too far, degrading all the nonresource factors that led to war. Nevertheless, in Rome, Berlin, and Tokyo, the decision was made: they would expand their turf and obtain the raw materials they needed.

Hitler looked mainly eastward to the Soviet Union. "Where is there a region capable of supplying iron of the quality of Ukrainian iron?" he asked his people. "Where can one find more nickel, more coal, more manganese, more molybdenum?"

The Führer's dream was vivid and lyrical: "We shall be the most self-supporting State in every respect. . . . Timber we shall have in abundance, iron in limitless quantity, the greatest manganese ore mines in the world, oil—we shall swim in it."

He moved into Austria and Czechoslovakia, acquiring land rich in timber and minerals, and came within arm's reach of Hungary and Yugoslavia, with 23 percent of the world's bauxite, and Turkey, with 20 percent of the world's chrome. The Reich marched into Norway, securing the safe passage of half its iron ore, which came from Sweden. The nonaggression pact with the Soviet Union—soon to be broken—brought shipments of iron, chrome, platinum, and manganese. This made up for the loss of supplies from North and South America, which British economic controls had cut off.

While this was going on, Japan also decided it could not reach its economic goals by trading with stronger competitors. Its first objective was the area now called Indonesia, then in Dutch control.

Washington got the message. Southeast Asia was a major

supplier of certain materials. One geographer argued, "The United States would be compelled, for its existence as a major industrial state, to wage war against any power or powers that might threaten to sever our trade lines with this part of the world."

According to some experts, one reason for the attack on Pearl Harbor was to secure the seas for Japanese ships, so they could sail into the territories then controlled by the British and the Dutch.

By 1942, the have-nots had. According to Eckes, the Axis powers, whose homelands constituted only 3 percent of the world's land surface and contained about 5 percent of the world's minerals, now controlled 13 percent of the land and a full third of the minerals. In 1939 those nations had controlled only 6 percent of the world's iron production, 2 percent of its manganese, 3 percent of its chrome, and 6 percent of its tungsten. Now the respective figures were 46 percent, 30 percent, 30 percent, and 60 percent. Those acquisitions no doubt enhanced their ability to conduct a prolonged war, particularly since some of the gains entailed a loss of supplies for the Allies.

## Resources as a World War II Strategy

The belligerents waged a fierce resource war right from the start, wheeling and dealing for supplies, boosting domestic production, instituting embargoes, building stockpiles, and trying to keep materials out of their adversaries' hands. Early in the conflict, U.S. efforts were perfunctory at best. We continued to sell materials to Japan and Germany until shortly before Pearl Harbor. We served as middleman for shipments of cobalt from the Belgian Congo (now Zaire) and rutile from Brazil, enabling the Axis powers to do an end run around British trade controls. We also grossly underestimated our own materials requirements for eventual involvement in the war. We moved rather late to create the "arsenal of democracy," and to use our clout to cut off Axis supplies.

Nazi submarines were sinking Allied shipments of tin, chrome, manganese, nickel, and bauxite from South America and Asia. To make up for the losses, the United States frantically exploited domestic deposits and invented substitutes. We established development agreements with nearby sources, such as Mexico. One important resource move was to introduce U.S. technology to a certain nickel deposit, elevating it from zero production to the second largest output in the world. That mine was in Cuba.

The Allies waged the resource war with stealth and cunning, keeping vital minerals such as chrome and tungsten out of Axis hands. For example, we persuaded Spain—a major supplier of Germany's tungsten—to stop shipments. Our ace in the hole: Spain needed our oil. When we cut off chrome shipments to Germany from Turkey, Hitler's Armaments Minister, Albert Speer, issued a warning that sounds much like a Pentagon statement in 1982. Without chromium, he said, "the manufacture of planes, tanks, motor vehicles, tank shells, U-boats, and almost the entire gamut of artillery would have to cease from one to three months after this deadline. . . ."

Hitler reportedly paid little attention, a misjudgment that some people think was instrumental in reversing the direction of the war.

But Hitler did not always ignore Germany's mineral needs. According to minerals economist Franz Dykstra, when the Nazis breached their nonaggression pact with Stalin, their first target was Nikopol, in southern Russia, which has enormous deposits of manganese. German occupation meant ample manganese for Nazi steel mills. When they were finally driven out of Russia, Nikopol was one of the last areas the Germans abandoned; without that manganese, they were forced to produce inferior steel.

It is, of course, arguable just how much resources determined the outcome of the war, but they seem to have played a significant role. Not only was the Allied resource base superior, but we were able to keep foreign supplies coming in while keeping them away from the enemy. During the war, the United States imported sixty different minerals from fifty-three countries; twenty-seven of the minerals came exclusively from abroad. Some analysts believe that if Hitler had had sufficient supplies, the war in Europe might have dragged on another few years. By then Germany might have had an atomic bomb.

## THE SIDES CHANGE, BUT THE GAME'S THE SAME

No sooner was the ink dry on the Yalta agreements than the West was fighting for resources with the Soviets. Russia moved into the resource-rich areas of Eastern Europe formerly coveted by Germany. They also began to support leftist revolutionary activity, a move many perceived as an attempt to acquire resources and territory through subversion. At the same time, the United States found itself heir by default to the mineral-rich colonies of the Allies, who were reeling from the war. We viewed the resources of the Third World as a partial solution to three key items on the postwar agenda: rebuilding Western Europe, securing the minerals we needed to meet new demands and make up for wartime depletion, and keeping the Russian bear at bay.

As they had been ever since explorers first set sail from the shores of Europe, the lands of nonindustrial Africa, Asia, and South America were resource battlegrounds. The Soviets saw these areas as the sources of power that enabled the West to dominate the world. They would liberate these regions from "imperialism" and alter history. Many American leaders felt that Russian strategy called for spreading economic chaos in the West and sowing unrest in the colonies. If the U.S.S.R. succeeded, the National Security Council warned in the forties, the world balance of power would be decisively altered.

We did not launch the gunboats or colonialize. We marched in with capital, equipment, and expertise instead. Colonialism was in its twilight, nationalism was bubbling up, long-suppressed hostility was creeping to the surface. The result was an unpredictable investment climate. But the pressure of the Cold War, and the fear it might soon heat up, inspired the government to provide incentives—loans, guarantees, insurance against politically inspired losses. This set the stage for the worldwide outreach of U.S. companies; soon multinationals were reaping enormous profits and keeping the flow of resources moving to our shores.

The United States was not above protecting those investments by flexing its muscles—and occasionally using them. The CIA was given a mandate to protect our strategic industrial facilities, keeping them under "continuous surveillance." Political goals (that is, thwarting the "communist conspiracy") were often used to justify resource warfare; and resource goals were cited to justify political action. We bolstered regimes that welcomed our engineers and managers and tried to bring down less friendly forces. It is said that the CIA sabotaged Cuban industry after the Castro takeover; and its influence in places such as Iran, Guatemala, Chile, and various parts of Asia and Africa has been well documented.

Just how much resource access figured in those efforts is uncertain, but clearly it was in the minds of some key decision makers. Truman's Secretary of Commerce, Averell Harriman, for example, justified U.S. involvement in the Third World by stating: "I do not believe this country can survive if the sources of raw materials are in the hands of unfriendly people who are determined to destroy us."

## THE LATEST CHAPTER IN AN OLD STORY

Thus, our present resource war, if we choose to call it that, is part of the age-old struggle for strategic superiority. But this chapter has a few new wrinkles. One is the threat of nuclear war; another is worldwide intolerance of overt imperialism. Those two factors mean that resource wars have to be waged with subtlety. Also, this confrontation is not a simple matter of "haves" versus "have-nots." One side lacks what the other has.

For thirty-five years the two great powers have supplied each other with some of the resources each needs to destroy the other. Back in 1947, we were shipping foodstuffs, machinery, and industrial hardware to Eastern Europe. When we realized that some of those items could be used against us in a war, we established export restrictions and snickered at the Soviet Union's threat of retaliation. Some experts warned us not to take the threats so lightly. It so happened that we were obtaining 31 percent of our imported manganese, 47 percent of our chromite, and 57 percent of our platinum from the Soviet Union. We reconsidered, and limited exports of only items used for direct military purposes. And we cultivated other sources, including Cuba and southern Africa.

On and on goes the resource war, heating up, cooling off, heating up again. Sanctions, embargoes, and other strategies have been used by each side. At one point, just prior to the Korean War, the U.S.S.R. cut off our manganese shipments, a fact that resource warriors still use as proof of Soviet economic cannibalism. What they do not point out is that we stopped sending tungsten to Russia. Both nations found what they needed elsewhere, but they paid more for it.

And so it continues, right up to today with our constant reevaluation of trade agreements with each other, and slaps on the wrist such as the grain embargo imposed by President Carter after the Soviet invasion of Afghanistan, and President

Reagan's sanctions when martial law descended on Poland. Because of their unequal distribution and their critical defense applications, metals are one of the pawns.

Perhaps one day the consciousness of the world will be raised to a level at which everyone will appreciate the inherent interdependence of nations. But until this economic ecology dawns on us, the near future is likely to witness confrontation and competition rather than cooperation and trust. With Soviet inroads in the Third World and the change in their import/ export patterns, coupled with the hard-line attitudes of the Reagan Administration, we can anticipate more of the same. Moscow and Washington know that the "haves" usually win.

# THE BATTLEGROUND

# FOUR

IN 1970, Salvador Allende was elected President of Chile, largely on the strength of a promise to nationalize the copper industry immediately. This reflected a nationwide antipathy toward U.S. companies, primarily Kennecott and Anaconda. Even Allende's opponent, a Christian Democrat named Eduardo Frei, was opposed to U.S. corporate influence; but he called for nationalization of only a controlling portion of the mines. When Allende won, and expropriated the mining properties, the United States responded by cutting aid and food supplies to Chile and mounting the now-infamous CIA campaign of "destabilization."

Certainly, the divestment of U.S. corporate interests was not the sole or even chief reason for the intervention. The United States was acting on the domino theory, fearing that an unchallenged takeover by a socialist like Allende would lead to similar actions elsewhere in Latin America, and perhaps to the eventual spread of Soviet power. Allende lasted three years. On the heels of a brutal coup, the newly installed junta made an acceptable deal with Kennecott and Anaconda and opened the copper industry once again to foreign investors. Aid and food shipments resumed.

In those undeveloped parts of the world where resources

have helped Europe and the United States to prosper, passions have been running high for decades. Independence and nationalism have changed the way those nations relate to the industrial powers, and because of the distribution of resources—both actual reserves and potential—that changing relationship is an important factor in the metals situation.

## THE LEGACY OF COLONIALISM

Along with political freedom, the upsurge of national pride called for economic justice. The emerging nations saw themselves as victims, having been ripped off, exploited, dominated by colonists and corporations. They wanted not only a larger return on the resources of their lands, but also control over them. Thus, between 1961 and 1975, 128 foreign investments were taken over by host governments, often without what the investors termed "adequate compensation." To the more radical leaders of the Third World, such as Allende, "adequate compensation" was a laughable concept—the way they saw it, the foreigners had already received more than a fair share of profits.

Private investment in undeveloped countries is, of course, not the same as outright colonization, which even in the West is now seen as an arrogant and repugnant system. Indeed, the real impact of multinational companies is difficult to assess. No one knows what life would have been like in the former colonies without them. Foreign investments have often brought measurable benefits to the host countries, at least in economic terms: technology transfer, improved productive capacity and balance of payments, greater efficiency, higher employment, new products and industries. These, plus a number of less tangible gains, are thought by many to outweigh the fact that multinational companies historically removed far more in profits than they reinvested in the host country.

Whatever the actual economic scorecard, however, it is clear that, emotionally, the Third World's grievances are real. The legacy of colonialism is bitter and enduring, and the multinational corporation is frequently viewed by the Third World as not much different from an imperial overlord—rapacious, condescending, and just a step up from slavemaster on the scale of exploitation.

Determined that business shall not go on as usual, the governments of less-developed countries often took over industries. Where outright divestment did not occur, other ways to shift the balance went into effect: higher taxes on foreign enterprises, higher royalty payments, or concessions of various kinds, such as forcing the company to reinvest profits in the host country or to use domestic suppliers and contractors. Sometimes divestment was partial, with the state taking over a majority interest.

Essentially, the developing nations awoke to their inherent bargaining power and learned to make demands. And they learned to play one superpower against the other. Overpopulated, and sometimes catastrophically poor, they had been at a distinct disadvantage because the multinationals had all the technology, information, and organizational and managerial skills, as well as the military and political clout of their homelands. A country whose entire economy rested on the income derived from one or two industries could be held hostage to "demand interruption," just as import-dependent countries are vulnerable to "supply interruption." It was only when they learned of that mutual vulnerability that the developing nations were able to press for a better deal.

Revenue was not the only issue. Most developing nations realized that they had to diversify their economies, raise the level of skills of their workers, increase employment, and build a solid industrial and technological base. To do this, they had to shift from enclave extraction ventures run by foreign companies to integrated national industries that would not only extract raw materials and ship them out, but refine, process, and manufacture as well.

## A NEW ECONOMIC ORDER

Third World nations with a shared sense of historical outrage are frequently able to get together on fundamental issues despite the often huge differences between them. Control over resources is one of those issues. In December 1974, the United Nations General Assembly passed a resolution entitled "The Charter of Economic Rights and Duties of States," which asserts this basic premise: "Every state has and shall freely exercise full permanent sovereignty, including possession, use and disposal, over all its wealth, natural resources and economic activities." This has been the rallying cry for a "new international economic order."

The resolution goes on to grant each state the right to

"regulate and exercise authority over foreign investment within its national jurisdiction in accordance with its laws and regulations and in conformity with its national objectives and priorities." The states shall "regulate and supervise" the activities of transnational corporations to ensure that they comply with national laws and "economic and social policies." The resolution also grants the host nation the right to expropriate foreign property or transfer its ownership. "Appropriate compensation" is called for; disputes over what is "appropriate" are to be settled by domestic law in the host nation.

In such an atmosphere, the long-running battle between the superpowers for the hearts and minds—and ports and mines—of the Third World took on a new flavor. Since it was in their best interest to see nationalized economies pop up around the globe, even if the leaders were not overly friendly, the Soviets could support the new international economic order. Backing revolutionary forces, the U.S.S.R. could portray itself as a champion of freedom and the enemy of Western imperialism and white domination. The United States, on the other hand, was usually identified with the status quo, and we found ourselves backing those factions who favored a market economy and foreign investment. Human rights being a relative thing, each side could claim a monopoly on righteousness.

**Less Investment in the Third World**
But the status quo could not be maintained, which meant the United States had to either give up access to the minerals of demanding nations or learn to play by new rules. The end result was less investment in the Third World. The multinational companies that had extended America's reach around the globe, and brought within our borders a huge portion of the earth's bounty, found it too risky and insufficiently profitable to start ventures as expensive as mining under the new, hostile conditions. Who would want to spend hundreds of millions of dollars and several years just to see it all swept away by the mere signature of a newly installed leader? Far easier indeed to invest in a place like Canada or Australia, or to buy real estate in the Sun Belt. In the Third World, even where terms are decent, you have to deal with weaker infrastructures, potential currency devaluations or price controls, and the ubiquitous presence of terrorists and revolutionaries.

The increased militancy and accelerated demands of Third World countries, therefore, have exacerbated the resource war and magnified the vulnerability of the import-dependent West. It is one thing to rely on imports, quite another to be getting a worse deal than you once had, under less-than-stable conditions. Secure access and steady prices are top concerns of consumers, and conditions in many undeveloped countries make it unlikely we will have them, at least in the short term.

The situation is made even more complex because one of the best ways to deal with future worldwide supply problems is to step up exploration and development in areas that have not yet been exploited. So far, production has concentrated on a relatively small number of places. To the International Economics Studies Institute, this suggests that "the minerals potential of most of the developing countries has yet to be explored and developed. They undoubtedly harbor important mineral resources in their less accessible regions that have never been surveyed in a preliminary fashion. . . . Questions remain as to whether future increases in demand can be met without expanding minerals production in the less developed world, and how such expansion can be achieved if private capital continues to be deterred by the political risks that appear to be on the rise."

Good questions, and they won't be fully answered for a long time.

## OPECS ON THE HORIZON?

The bitter aftertaste of the oil shock and the ongoing success of OPEC have caused those concerned with defense and raw materials to wonder whether similar cartels could develop for nonfuel minerals. The thought of a strategic metals cartel is, of course, loathsome to industry and government leaders, who can envision producers banding together and wielding blows that could be even more crippling than OPEC's.

Certainly, joining forces would seem attractive to many developing countries. To them it could be a way to obtain from rich consumers a higher cash return, faster development, and foreign exchange to purchase manufactured goods. A cartel would also be beneficial in the long run, since the control of exports would enable the developing nations to stretch out the useful life of their resources. It is only natural that producers should seek to change a situation in which they are diffuse and unorganized and consumers are relatively few and well organized.

The big question is, Can effective cartels develop? Resource warriors tend to believe they can; others, probably the majority, feel the likelihood is very small. To these optimists, OPEC was a one-time-only occurrence, made possible by oil's unique importance and the right combination of circumstances.

## What Makes for a Strong Cartel?

It is generally agreed that several factors have to come together in order for a strong cartel to develop:

1. Producer control of a major portion of the world's production of the commodity.
2. Relatively few exporters; numerous and widely dispersed buyers.
3. Enough financial stability to offset any loss of funds due to restricting exports.
4. Inability of consumers to develop alternative sources of supply or to substitute for the commodity.
5. Absence of substantial stockpiles among consumers and low potential for recycling.
6. Inelasticity of demand—that is, price hikes do not substantially reduce demand or bring noncartel members into the market as sellers.
7. Cohesive policies and export discipline among members.
8. Similar political and economic objectives among members.
9. The commodity should be highly valued, difficult to store and transport, and a high percentage of its production should be traded internationally.

OPEC has many of those factors going for it. It deals in a vital commodity, used by most of the world in large amounts, with few alternative suppliers and substitutes. About half of all export revenues for oil go to only five countries, and while the members do not always agree, they share similar political and economic goals. And they can probably afford to outlast consumers if trade is curtailed. Yet, with all that in its favor, OPEC has had its troubles, and is now beginning to feel the impact of consumer backlash as industrial nations try to become less dependent.

## Why Metal Cartels Are Unlikely

By contrast, metals are exported by about forty different developing countries and a number of industrialized nations as well. Many of the exporters are very poor; they could not afford to do without export revenues for long. For example, the three largest exporters of copper—Zambia, Zaire, and Chile—earn more than half their export incomes from that metal. For Zambia, the figure is more than 90 percent. And loss of cash flow is not the only undesirable consequence of cutbacks—unemployment, and therefore unrest, would inevitably ensue.

In actuality, the major portion of the world's mining is not done in the impoverished Third World, but in places like Australia, Canada, and South Africa, not to mention the United States. In fact, an estimated 60 percent of the undeveloped countries have little or no mineral production. It would take a highly unlikely combination of events to get all countries that produce a given metal to act together against consumers with any consistency.

The possibilities for substitution, recycling, conservation, stockpiling, and alternative sources of imports are far greater for metals than they are for petroleum. We are not dealing with a single commodity here but with a few dozen, some of which are interchangeable, many of which are spread out on the globe. Quite simply put, an industrial nation can do without most metals a lot longer than it can do without oil. Compared to oil, the real impact of a major price hike would be relatively small, unless it affected a large number of metals.

If a metals cartel were to develop among Third World nations, it would probably win short-term increases in power and revenue at best. In the long run, industrial nations would lower their demand by substituting, mining inferior grades, or diversifying their import sources. They could also retaliate by cutting foreign aid, reducing technology transfers, or raising the prices of goods sold to developing countries.

For all these reasons, nonfuel cartels have not been very effective in the past. The International Bauxite Association has been able to raise the taxes and royalty rates paid by foreign producers in member countries, but the association has been unable to fix prices or manipulate the market significantly. For one thing, there are ways to produce aluminum other than from bauxite, albeit more expensively, and there are alternatives for many end uses of aluminum. The tax and royalty increases alone have stimulated the use of those alternatives, at least in limited measure. Additional pressure would no doubt lead to reductions in the demand for bauxite. And some countries that are not members of the cartel—Brazil, for example—have stepped up exploration and development.

Even less success has been achieved by CIPEC (a French acronym for the International Council of Copper Exporting Countries), the Primary Tungsten Association, and the Iron Ore Exporting Countries.

## Why Collective Action by Producers Can Be Effective

Congressman Santini is fond of quoting Robert Albier, an economist at the University of Chicago, who told the *Wall Street Journal* in 1975: "The oil cartel is in its early stages of breakdown. Crude petroleum prices are being lowered directly and indirectly by individual producing countries seeking to increase their exports. In the next several months the demands of OPEC-produced petroleum will decline sharply. The cartel will fall apart when its members are not able to share the necessary costs."

Skeptics feel that facile statements about metals cartels could meet the same fate as Mr. Albier's remarks. Certain plausible events could come together to make collective action feasible for some producing countries. Further, action by a group of nations does not have to emulate OPEC precisely in order to influence prices and supplies. Even if the cartel were to fold after a while, its short-term impact could be quite disruptive under the right conditions. And in wartime its impact could be devastating. After lengthy research, the International Economic Studies Institute was "skeptical as to whether OPEC's success can be repeated in other materials." But it added, "Successful or not, the effort to create effective cartels may tend to disrupt raw materials markets and increase uncertainty on the part of both industrial consumers and potential investors in materials projects."

For example, a cutoff of manganese would, according to Dr. John Elliott of MIT, put the U.S. steel industry under great pressure in a matter of three months. We could institute stringent conservation, alter production methods, and use lower-grade steel. But each of those reactions would take a long time to institute, and in some cases would lower the quality of steel and raise costs.

We could conceivably see embargoes, price hikes, or other forms of collective action if global politics heat up, even if such actions damage the perpetrators. Emotions can overrule pragmatism; Iran is a case in point.

Another argument offered by those who believe cartel-like action is possible is that even friends and political allies might participate if it was in their interests. The fact that stable, friendly nations are major suppliers does not entirely eliminate the potential for actions that work against consumers. In its role as exporter, the United States has proved that on several occasions. In 1973, for example, we imposed a total embargo on soybean exports and limited fulfillment of existing contracts to no more than half each order. Most of our customers were political allies, but we chose to curb the cost of feeding livestock for our farmers over honoring our commitments to Europe and Japan.

Canada is our biggest supplier of raw materials and our biggest customer as well. Two nations could not have a higher degree of economic interdependence, shared cultural heritage, and similar world perspectives. Yet Canada has been raising the price of the oil it ships to us when OPEC raises theirs. In order to conserve its deposits for domestic use, Canada has cut back oil and natural gas exports to the United States. In general, our neighbor is trying to create a national image as something more than a northern suburb of the United States, and many Canadians view U.S. corporate ownership of mines as a sign of American dominance. Although wealthy by comparison, Canada is similar to some undeveloped nations in that its mineral industry is its leading source of foreign exchange. Consequently, there has been considerable pressure to nationalize. While this has been done slowly, and through equitable means, it is nonetheless happening. In addition, Canada has recognized the economic advantages of vertical integration: they want to export less raw material and do more processing and fabricating at home.

Similar developments are taking place in Australia, Brazil, Mexico, and other friendly nations that supply us with minerals. They all seek growth, diversification, and greater self-sufficiency. Each nation looks out for itself first, and its self-interest does not always work to the advantage of the United States. If a cartel-like arrangement suited its national interests, a friend might participate.

## Can We Count on Other Sources?

It has often been said that we needn't worry about being dependent on South Africa and the Soviet Union for manganese, since Brazil, Gabon, Australia, and India can pick up the slack in a pinch. But according to Congressman Santini's Subcommittee, such an assumption would be folly. For one thing, it would take substantial capital to increase production enough to fill a sudden sizable gap. The producers would probably not make those investments unless purchase could be guaranteed over a long period of time or prices could be increased enough to make the investment worthwhile. In addition, it would take several years to build the infrastructure needed to increase production significantly. In the short run, present facilities would be insufficient to meet emergency needs.

Then again, would the producers—no matter how friendly—want to increase production if national priorities dictated the opposite? Due to rising internal demand, Brazil has been gradually decreasing its manganese exports since 1980. So far, each reduction has been small, but by 1989, total annual exports are expected to be about one-quarter of their pre-1980 level. Like Brazil, India has long-range plans to step up its steel production to meet domestic needs, and that means conserving its manganese. India projects a doubling of its manganese requirements by 1990. Australia, supplier of 15 percent of our manganese ore, has also been questioning whether to allow exports to increase. One political party, in fact, has proposed severe restrictions.

In this context, the fact that a hostile U.S.S.R. and a volatile South Africa together contain 80 percent of the world's known manganese reserves cannot be blithely ignored simply because our friends have the other 20 percent.

## New Forms of Collective Action

Dr. Robert Kilmarx, of the Center for Strategic and International Studies at Georgetown University, told a Congressional hearing that the chances of collective action by resource-rich Third World countries in the next decade is greater than most people realize. While producer cartels might not be organized for individual metals, we might see joint action by the entire group of developing nations, banded together over broad economic and political objectives, not a particular commodity. Despite vast differences in culture and ideology, developing nations have managed to act in unison on several issues that have come before the United Nations. Negotiations on the Law of the Sea Treaty (see "The Law of the Sea," p. 153) are a case in point. And poor developing countries have stood behind OPEC, despite the fact that oil price hikes have hurt them more than anyone.

One contingency Kilmarx warns against is increased involvement by OPEC in the sphere of nonfuel minerals. Kilmarx believes that the cartel might try to apply its clout more broadly. "Oil producers may change their behavior pattern with regard to nonfuel minerals, and seek to be the financier and supporter of more effective action by some of these so-far inefficient associations like the bauxite association."

It has also been proposed that OPEC could embargo oil to South Africa to protest that nation's racial policies. Although South Africa is the only nation in the world effectively producing oil from coal, such an embargo would be crippling to its mineral industry, and therefore threaten Western supplies.

## The Worst-Case Cartel

There is one item that experts agree on unanimously: if collective action were to occur, the metals most likely to be affected would be chromium, manganese, platinum, and cobalt. And the most effective and most devastating cartel would be one composed of southern African nations and the Soviet Union. The Kremlin might well cherish the thought of an economic alliance with Zimbabwe, Zaire, Zambia, and the Republic of South Africa.

Some believe that such an alliance is preposterous and that anyone who suggests it is either hopelessly paranoid or pushing some vested interest. Others say not to discount anything in today's world—OPEC seemed preposterous a decade ago.

E. F. Andrews, Vice President of Materials and Services at Allegheny Ludlum, believes that the potential for such a collaboration is strong enough to warrant preventive measures. Pointing out that OPEC has wreaked havoc on a U.S. economy that is only partially dependent on imported oil, Andrews contends that a cartel of metals producers on whom we are closer to 100 percent dependent could devastate the Western world. "That cartel, in my opinion, could not only seriously jeopardize the national security of the industrial world, which is virtually devoid of these commodities . . . [it would] shut the world down economically, if not indeed militarily, within a very, very short period of time. . . . I would think in less than six months."

His detractors contend that Mr. Andrews's hyperbole could be rooted in the fact that his company is the largest user of chromium and cobalt in the country and would benefit from government actions designed to lessen our import dependence. Nevertheless, some people have to examine worst-case scenarios and be prepared for them. Collaboration between two antagonists like the Soviet Union and South Africa may seem ridiculous at this time, but there are many "what-ifs"— revolution, for example—that could come together in the next few years to make such collusion no more ridiculous than American-Japanese-German economic cooperation after the smoke cleared from World War II.

But all the talk of possible and impossible cartels obscures one important point: cartels are only one way to hurt import-dependent nations. Given the strategic and economic positioning of the Soviet Union, the continued turmoil and poverty in most of the Third World, South Africa's alienation from the rest of humanity, and the delicacy of U.S. policy choices, it is far more likely that mineral disruptions will occur due to chaos, not collaboration. Remember, it does not take a cartel to produce price and supply shocks.

## THE FUTURE IN THE THIRD WORLD

In 1975, the CIA was given a $31.7 million budget to keep the leftist Popular Movement for the Liberation of Angola (MPLA) from taking over that country during its civil war. The MPLA—which was aided by the Soviet Union—was victorious despite the CIA, but we continued to spend money trying to bump them out of power. At the same time, Gulf Oil was paying the new leaders some $500 million a year in royalties for offshore drilling rights, just as it had been doing with previous regimes since 1968. The MPLA allowed Gulf to pump oil, pledged not to expropriate its property, and kept on cashing the handsome royalty checks, some of which were no doubt used to fend off the CIA. Thus, American dollars were supporting both sides of a civil war. The U.S. government stopped both the Gulf transactions and a contracted sale of Boeing airplanes to the MPLA, but not for long. Both nations opted for economic benefits over principle.

Angola is still a resolutely Marxist country. It harbors guerrillas determined to liberate Namibia from South African rule, and is host to 15,000 to 20,000 Cuban soldiers. At the same time, Gulf Oil is expanding its pumping capacity to 200,000 barrels a day. Recently, the Angolan government put out a welcome mat for more Western capital, techniques, and products. They have suggested that once the Namibian crisis is resolved, they would send the Cubans home and establish relations with South Africa, on whom they have tried to clamp sanctions in the United Nations.

### Pragmatism over Ideology
How to account for these contradictions? John Sassi, Gulf's Manager of International Studies, told the *Wall Street Journal*, "The surface indications aren't always as real as they seem. The Angolans adopted a pragmatic approach toward us. They're interested in seeing their resources developed and want the best technology and services."

Mozambique's President Samora Moïsés Machel, who owes his current status largely to Soviet support, has recently outlined conditions favorable to private traders, farmers, and industrialists, and stated publicly that "there is a place for foreign private enterprise" in his country. While he sides with Moscow on various foreign policy issues, such as the Soviet invasion of Afghanistan, he remains resolutely pragmatic at home, even allowing South Africa to trade in the port of Maputo. Reportedly, South African transit fees alone provide Mozambique's needy treasury with $12 million a year. Despite his official Marxist philosophy, Machel knows the difference between rubles and Western currencies and has sought far more foreign aid in the latter. "We are faced with a dilemma," Machel stated. "We don't have foreign exchange to finance development, and without development we cannot generate foreign exchange."

Such events lend credence to moderates who talk down the resource war and America's import vulnerability, for they suggest that economic pragmatism will overrule politics and emotions in the end. State-run economies may be more appropriate for some developing nations, and they are not necessarily beholden to the Soviet Union. (France's newly elected President, the Socialist François Mitterand, is more staunchly anti-Soviet than his predecessor, Valéry Giscard d'Estaing, a center-rightist. *Pravda* was pulling for Giscard.) The real difficulties in dealing with so-called Marxist regimes may lie in working out the logistics of doing business and in overcoming ideological biases at home.

## A Time of Transition

The colonial era is ending; a new economic order is taking shape. New forms of economic interraction are emerging. Perhaps the interests of poor producing nations and rich consumers can both be accommodated, and the benefits of development can flow both ways. Already there are positive signs.

Western nations and corporations have displayed a new willingness to pay attention to past grievances and present needs of the Third World. Developing nations—who realize that they need Western participation as much as, if not more than, the industrialized nations need their resources—are willing to listen to the demands of foreign companies for profits and security.

No supplier has a monopoly on any mineral. Producers know that substitutions, stockpiling, recycling, and new technology can put them out of business if their policies force those innovations on consumers. Further, many have decided that doing business with the West is preferable to linking up too closely with the Soviet Bloc. The West is seen to be more advanced, more competent, more wealthy, and more trustworthy. Said Secretary of State Haig, "An increasing number of black African states that have become the recipients of Soviet military equipment and increased levels of Soviet influence are having second thoughts about the desirability of that kind of relationship. . . . It is built almost exclusively on the provision of lethal weapons. It does not include the kind of developmental assistance that turns developing states into modern states."

Without the capital, technology, research, marketing, and administrative ability that the West can provide—not to mention the markets and products—the minerals of developing nations might just as well be mud. Further, nationalization can often backfire, as Zaire discovered when it tried to replace Belgian specialists with lesser-qualified Zairians. Like several other countries, Zaire was forced to recall Western talent after their attempts fell short of success. Indeed, the widespread unemployment and loss of revenues that followed nationalization of Iran's oil industry in the early fifties was one of the key factors that enabled the Shah, backed by the United States, to return to power.

"The fact remains that extreme nationalism militates against a nation's participating in and profiting from international trade," states Stanford geologist Charles F. Park in *Affluence in Jeopardy.* "It is also a fact that a nation suffers from private enterprise controlled by foreign investors intent only on exploitation. Perhaps in the future both extremes will be avoided."

That seems more possible now than at any time since World War II. Western powers are realizing that exploitation—both real and imagined—can be self-defeating in the long run, particularly now that undeveloped nations have raised their expectations. And Third World nations are realizing that true modernization requires more than just control over resources—it means learning to use technology, raising the labor skills of the people, diversifying economies, obtaining capital and reliable markets. Anti-Western and anticapitalist rhetoric will probably continue to be strident (it wins popular support if nothing else, and provides a convenient scapegoat), but words alone are not a threat to trade relations or a barrier to future ones.

Even staunchly Marxist leaders have been able to cooperate with U.S. corporations when it suits their needs. "Many are very free about labeling these recipient states as Marxist," said Secretary Haig. "Some have suggested they will be Marxists or democrats depending on their assessment of which label will bring them the progress for their people that they seek."

Even Lenin sought to revive the Soviet economy by granting concessions to foreign capital, social scientist Daniel S. Papp points out. Apparently contradicting his own ideology, Lenin allowed some mining operations to remain under private control, and permitted foreign-owned production, including a manganese mine in the Caucasus. Only Stalin's First Five Year Plan put an end to foreign investment in the Soviet Union.

### Adapting to the New Economic Order

Out of necessity, Western companies have demonstrated a greater willingness to contribute to the host nation's social and economic objectives. This might entail hiring and training local talent, or locating plants in areas the government wants to develop. It might mean refining and smelting minerals in the country of origin rather than shipping them out as raw ore. Joint ventures are becoming more popular, combining either government funds or private money with U.S. corporate capital. Often mandatory, such ventures spread the risk around and remove the onus of U.S. domination.

Problems can arise in joint ventures, of course. The big question is, Who owns the majority share? U.S. companies fear the host will make decisions that may help the ruling party politically or achieve certain social objectives, but at the expense of profits. Host governments in turn fear the opposite—that the foreign investor will be excessively profit-oriented and disregard the needs of the country. Perhaps for these reasons, many companies have taken to selling or leasing their equipment and expertise to the host country instead of making big capital investments.

Of course, in some countries the poverty level is such that no domestic capital can be utilized; joint ventures or consultant-type arrangements are not always possible. The result can be stagnation, if the producing nation can't share the risks but demands a higher share of the rewards. To solve the stalemate, a variety of loan and insurance programs have developed. The Overseas Private Investment Corporation, for example, is a government organization that insures U.S. companies against certain political risks in less developed countries. In addition, it provides financial assistance and investment counseling and finances the investigation and development of projects. The ninety "friendly less-developed countries" with whom it has agreements include Zaire, Zambia, and some of the smaller nations of southern Africa. International financial institutions such as the World Bank, the United Nations Development Program, and regional development banks, along with the U.S. Export-Import Bank, are helping developing countries meet their investment needs.

These changes are taking place in the context of an awareness that both consumers and producers stand to benefit from development and price stabilization. For that reason, there has been an increase in multilateral negotiations. The State Department, under the auspices of the U.N. Conference on Trade and Development (UNCTAD), has been engaged in discussions with developing countries since 1976, attempting to alleviate problems of price instability and lack of supplies. Along with the U.S. Geological Survey, the State Department is planning bilateral programs to assist developing countries in exploration efforts.

Despite the positive signs, however, investing in Third World countries can be risky. Indeed, even investing in France or Canada can be an "invitation to agony," as *Time* magazine put it. For that reason, executives are turning to specialists for political risk assessments before committing themselves to major capital outlays. Frost & Sullivan Inc., a New York firm, publishes monthly surveys of sixty-one countries for its clients, which include AT&T, Xerox, General Electric, General Motors, and about 200 other large corporations. The service costs $1,900 a year. Other services are more extensive and more expensive, often tailor-made for a particular project.

### Ambiguous Signals from Washington

But the risks often involve uncertainties in Washington as much as in the host nations. Despite its probusiness stance, the Reagan Administration has been making life difficult for firms investing in certain countries, such as Libya and Angola. The Administration is ideologically opposed to the Angolan regime and is pressuring it to remove the Cuban troops now there. According to *The New York Times*, Gulf and other companies with interests in Angola have been quietly lobbying, because they fear that hard-line policies could ignite a civil war or otherwise jeopardize their investments. The business leaders describe the Angolan government as "businesslike and nonideological," but the Administration sees it otherwise.

Liberals have been criticized by resource warriors for being so eager to please developing nations that they overlook the economic and strategic realities of our import dependency. There may be some validity in that argument. But it must also be said that conservatives often fail to appreciate that times have changed, and that cooperation and compromise may serve our long-range interests better than tough posturing and an inflexible adherence to the rules of the American market system. The resource battlegrounds of the Third World are no longer passive chunks of real estate on which the big powers maneuver for advantage. The developing nations are participants, and their leverage is improving. Viewing the call for a "new international economic order" as something just short of the *Communist Manifesto* could become a self-fulfilling prophecy.

Maintaining steady supplies of minerals requires shrewdness and strength. It also requires creativity, and cooperation with producing nations. In the long run, many experts believe, the United States stands to gain by helping developing nations meet their economic goals. Doing so could speed up mineral development, assure access to supplies, and minimize Soviet influence. A country with a strong and growing economy is less vulnerable to political turmoil, and less in need of give-away foreign aid. It also becomes a market for U.S. products.

Further, a nation that is treated respectfully—as a partner, not just a cheap source of labor and resources—will act more responsibly. Supply disruptions triggered by political or emotional pressures are more likely to come from nations whose attempts to fulfill their own social and economic objectives are frustrated.

Before we arrive at international economic enlightenment, however, all parties will have to come to terms with the past and work out mutually agreeable patterns of interaction. Given the East-West struggle, and the ongoing turmoil in developing nations, that day may be a while in arriving. In the meantime, uncertainty, political instability, and price volatility are likely to continue. Anyone interested in strategic metals must keep an eye on the three-way interaction between Third World nations and the two superpower blocs.

## THE PERSIAN GULF OF MINERALS

When you talk about oil, you talk about the Persian Gulf. When you talk about strategic minerals, you talk mainly about sub-Saharan Africa, and especially about the four countries that form a sickle-shaped curve from the navel of the continent to the Cape: Zaire, Zambia, Zimbabwe, South Africa (see Figure 3). Enormous reserves of platinum, manganese, vanadium, cobalt, and chromium are there, and heaven knows what else that hasn't yet been discovered or declared to be economic. Academics, diplomats, and Congressional researchers have examined the pressures, conflicts, politics, and economics of the area because it is so vital to our mineral needs and strategic priorities. Their findings are summed up in this chapter

## THE COBALT COUPLE

### Zaire
In 1960, Belgium got fed up with its troublesome colony and decided to turn the Congo over to its natives. With independence came years of power struggles between rival factions, with the CIA and KGB right in the middle. To the relief—and perhaps the dubious credit—of the United States and Europe,

Joseph Mobutu, former head of the army, took over the reins and has remained at the top ever since. Adept at political longevity, he has permitted no rivals.

By the early seventies, Mobutu's campaign for "African authenticity" in his nation had succeeded, at least in name. He dropped his Christian first name and became Mobutu Sese Seko. The city of Leopoldville became Kinshasa; the province of Katanga became Shaba; the country became Zaire. The copper and cobalt industry, owned by Belgium's Union Minière,

SOVIET INFLUENCED

AFRICA

ETHIOPIA

BENIN

GABON
MANGANESE

CONGO

ZAMBIA
COBALT
GOLD
MANGANESE

ZAIRE
COBALT
COPPER
DIAMONDS
TIN
COLUMBIUM
TANTALUM
GOLD
TUNGSTEN

ANGOLA

NAMIBIA

MOZAMBIQUE

ZIMBABWE
CHROMIUM
NICKEL
COPPER
GOLD
ASBESTOS

BOTSWANA
CHROMIUM
DIAMONDS

SOUTH AFRICA
CHROMIUM
MANGANESE
VANADIUM
PLATINUM

THE AREA OF SOUTHERN AFRICA HAS:
**95%** OF THE WORLD'S CHROME
**86%** OF THE WORLD'S PLATINUM
**64%** OF THE WORLD'S VANADIUM
**53%** OF THE WORLD'S MANGANESE
**52%** OF THE WORLD'S COBALT

Adapted from "The Air Force Command Statement on Defense Industrial Base Issues," Statement of General Alton D. Slay before the Industrial Preparedness Panel of the House Armed Services Committee, 96th Congress, Second Session, November 13, 1980.

**Figure 3.** *The Persian Gulf of Minerals*

was nationalized and renamed Gecamines. By any name, it supplies 60 percent of the world's cobalt.

**Unrealized Wealth.** The third largest nation in Africa, Zaire is potentially one of the richest. Its mineral wealth is enormous, even though large regions of the country remain unexplored. According to the State Department, 90 percent of Zaire's export earnings in 1979 came from minerals, and virtually all of that (95 percent) was divided in roughly equal shares between copper and cobalt. Small amounts of manganese, chromium, and nickel are also mined in Shaba, making that province the focal point of Zaire's economy, and one of the most important pieces of real estate on the globe.

Despite its inherent wealth, Zaire has serious problems. Like other former colonies, the country is depressingly poor, its services and infrastructure are falling apart, and it seems unable to get itself on a steady development track. Plagued by an inflation rate that reached 100 percent in 1978, several billion dollars of debt, and a growth rate of minus 4 percent a year, Mobutu's people have fallen into a state described by various observers as pervasive despair, cynicism, and inertia. The political scene is dominated by widespread corruption, which President Mobutu himself labeled the "Zairian Sickness."

Before independence, the Belgian Congo was a net exporter of food and was considered self-sufficient in crops. Two decades later, three-quarters of the Zairians are subsistence farmers earning an annual income approximately equal to the price of dinner for two at a good New York restaurant. Only one percent of the land is farmed. Food shortages torment city dwellers. The bottom line: Zaire has to import food, at the staggering cost of $300 million a year. Its main sources of food—Zimbabwe and South Africa—are also critical to Zaire because their transportation networks link the nation to the world outside Africa. Which makes the country's already delicate position that much more tenuous, and our dependence on it for cobalt that much more ticklish.

**Problems with the Infrastructure.** Shortages of fuel, spare parts, communications equipment, and managerial and technical skills have led to the deterioration of a once-strong transportation system. Only about 40 percent of the country's railroad cars are operational. Usable roads have shrunk from 140,000 kilometers to 20,000 since independence, according to one estimate.

Although Zaire has managed to produce and export an amazing amount of copper and cobalt during the last five years of turmoil, the mining industry is beset with problems. Without a large infusion of capital and expertise, the future is uncertain. Obsolete and worn-out equipment must be replaced, spare parts and other supplies must be made available, and foreign personnel must be attracted if the country is even to come close to realizing its production potential, not just for cobalt and copper, but also for columbium, tantalum, and other metals for which there are significant deposits.

In 1980, Congressman Santini and members of his Subcommittee staff visited Zaire, Zimbabwe, and South Africa. Their report, "Sub-Sahara Africa: Its Role in Critical Mineral Needs of the Western World," describes conditions in those vital nations. Zaire, the report concluded, "is on the brink of economic collapse . . . mining in Zaire is seriously burdened by government mismanagement and capital deficiencies. There's a real possibility that development of Zairian mineral resources could be brought to a halt by internal deterioration or external invasion."

**Instability Keeps Skilled Personnel Away.** Military security is reportedly better than it has been. As relations between Zaire and Angola have improved with the signing of a nonaggression pact, U.S. officials do not see any imminent threat of another invasion of Shaba. Apparently, many of the Katangan rebels have gone peacefully back to Zaire. However, the general political climate is somewhat tense, and the nation remains vulnerable to unrest. Sabotage in the mines is a potentially disruptive factor. The Santini report states, "It was acknowledged by mining and American representatives that a few explosive charges placed by terrorists at key installations could be disastrous." Recalling the 1978 disruption, the report cautions against undue optimism and points out that any threat of violence could set the foreign experts packing, perhaps for good this time.

Indeed, lack of homegrown expertise is at the heart of Zaire's problems, as it is in most former colonies. Mobutu's attempts to "Zairianize" his country in the early seventies were ill-fated on the practical level, no matter how meaningful they may have been psychologically. Native managers and technicians simply lacked the training and expertise to step in overnight and make the nation's industries work. Realizing this, the government has stepped up recruiting efforts, but the difficult living conditions, career uncertainties, and ever-present physical danger as dramatized by the Shaba invasions have proved unappealing to foreigners, particularly those who can command choice positions elsewhere. At the same time, Zaire's nationalization attempts closed off any substantial foreign investment, which left the country's industries disastrously underfinanced and dependent on foreign aid and international lending institutions.

**Uncertain Future.** In the meantime, Mobutu remains in power, largely due to the absence of alternatives. Any opposition, the Santini report contends, is either underground or ineffective thanks to a combination of Zairian apathy and Mobutu's elimination of opposition parties. But under conditions like that, recent history tells us, power is tenuous and surprises are almost predictable.

Santini's report concludes that the future of Zaire's mineral industry "hinges on the resolution of a number of severe operational, financial, and security problems . . . [ including] military security, major improvements in transportation, availability of sufficient foreign exchange for replacement equipment and spare parts, and the stabilization of managerial and technical expatriate personnel."

Experts in the State Department tend to agree with this general assessment, although they are usually more sanguine than Congressman Santini with respect to the future of Zaire's minerals.

### Similar Conditions in Zambia

Zaire's neighbor and fellow cobalt producer, Zambia, is in similar economic straits, facing the familiar amalgam of postcolonial problems. Blessed with fertile lands, Zambia was self-sufficient in food when it gained independence from Great Britain in 1964. Now its 5 million people depend on Zimbabwe and South Africa for their meals.

Zambia is not as critical to the United States as Zaire; its cobalt production is considerably lower, and the extent of foreign participation in mining is greater. However, with the opening of a new cobalt facility, the percentage of export earnings derived from that metal went up in 1981 from 5 to 12 percent. In a nation where minerals account for 99 percent of all exports, and just one product, copper, accounts for 83 percent, that increase is significant, and perhaps propitious. Zambia now supplies a larger percentage of U.S. cobalt imports than it did a few years ago, and if the plans to double production by 1985 are fulfilled, its role could increase still more, perhaps taking some of the pressure to supply off Shaba province.

According to Michael Calingaert, Deputy Assistant Secretary of State for International Resources and Food Policy, Zambia has potential for rapid growth and development. In recent times, however, that potential has been thwarted by depressed copper prices, internal economic difficulties, and political and transportation problems resulting from Zambia's support of the Zimbabwe liberation movement. Now things are looking up. Says Calingaert, "The independence of Zimbabwe and the opening of frontiers with that country have greatly improved morale among the expatriates in the mining sector and facilitated the import of essential goods." While Zambia is officially nonaligned, President Kenneth Kaunda has purchased Soviet weapons, but has resolutely resisted Kremlin influence.

## A Minicartel

Significantly, Zaire and Zambia have formed a minicartel for cobalt, despite their moderate political positions, their poverty, and their extreme reliance on mineral exports. Based on the accepted criteria for success, the cartel seems to have little or no chance of exerting a major impact on prices. They were able to stabilize the cost of cobalt at about $25 a pound after the sky-high escalation following the 1978 Shaba invasion, but that fourfold increase over pre-Shaba prices spurred efforts by consumers to develop substitutes and exploit sources that had not been economic when prices were low.

The most recent decision by the Zaire-Zambia cobalt cartel was to *lower* the price to $20 a pound and most experts expect it to drop still further. While that is still a lot higher than the $6 price of 1978, the trend indicates that there are limits to price fixing in the metals market. Perhaps the higher prices will prove advantageous in the long run by providing Zaire and Zambia with badly needed cash that could help modernize the mining industry, and by alerting Western consumers to the need for alternatives. But perhaps the most revealing aspect of the new cartel is the fact that it was formed at all. It illustrates the way Third World producers are thinking and their desire to milk their resources for all they are worth while the industrial nations still need them. Those resources represent their one strong suit.

Supplies and prices of metals from the cobalt couple will be as stable as their politics. An atmosphere that encourages the confidence of Western governments and corporations will keep the cobalt coming and permit those countries to expand and solidify their industries. But turbulent politics and tenuous economics have been around a long time in that part of the world and are not likely to disappear overnight. Zaire and Zambia, important pieces on the resource chessboard, are worth a close watch.

## PLEASANT SURPRISES IN ZIMBABWE

To the astonishment of most of the world, seven years of bloody civil war ended rather calmly in April 1980, and white-ruled Rhodesia became black-ruled Zimbabwe. The new ruler is an avowed Marxist, Robert Mugabe, whose years as a guerrilla leader were marked by heinous brutality not limited to whites. Mugabe's victory left Western analysts and Rhodesia's privileged whites trembling in anticipation of the worst. But the worst has so far failed to materialize.

Mugabe surprised everyone by promising to uphold the new constitution, which ensures the safety of whites and their property. So far, the new government has kept its word, and has not undertaken the wholesale nationalization of industries that had been anticipated. Mugabe is a socialist still, but he has actively sought private foreign investment, issuing a statement in February 1981 that read: "Government will encourage and welcome the participation of private enterprise in productive activities which create employment opportunities for Zimbabweans and which make a net contribution to the economy."

Apparently, the conciliatory attitude extends even to South Africa, whose white rulers and official racism are disdained by Mugabe. In the face of growing antipathy between South Africa and the rest of the continent, Mugabe recently stated, "Our own position is that we shall continue to maintain trade relations with South Africa, to the extent that South Africa makes it possible for us to do so."

Perhaps Mugabe is more pragmatic than idealistic. He has so far displayed a remarkable awareness of the forces that created chaos and destitution in other newly independent countries, and has taken pains to avoid them. He has also proved remarkably adroit at domestic politics, solidifying his position and winning the trust of whites and blacks alike. In a country with numerous and bitter rival factions within each race, that is no small feat.

Mugabe apparently felt that the abrupt departure of skilled whites and the sudden removal of incentives for capital investment could in the end make conditions worse for his people than when they were under the thumb of the white minority. Thus, during his first year anyway, he managed to push black advancement enough to prevent massive resentment from those who have waited a lifetime for their rightful place in their own country. At the same time he satisfied whites that their safety and their property were in no immediate danger. During the first year, only a few thousand of Zimbabwe's 200,000 whites left the country, and those who remained were as comfortable as they ever were—more so, perhaps, now that the violent civil war was over.

According to *New York Times* reporter John F. Burns, Mugabe's government seems to be "committed to a multiracial, democratic state that will encourage whites to remain, preferring lingering white wealth and advantage to the chaos attendant on a policy of retribution." Recent reports, however, indicate that large numbers of whites are leaving, apparently in fear that the open-arms policy won't last.

The U.S. government is apparently pleased with developments in postwar Zimbabwe. At a meeting of thirty-six nations in Salisbury, Zimbabwe's capital, in May 1981, the United States pledged $225 million in aid over the next three years. Why such a generous handout at a time of fiscal austerity and cutbacks in foreign aid? For one thing, if we did not come forward, we would have looked awfully foolish when other nations were contributing $1.4 billion. Reluctance to help out might have caused Zimbabwe to snuggle up to the Soviet Union instead. Also, the Reagan Administration was eager to demonstrate its support of black majority rule in Africa in the light of criticism of the President's conciliatory remarks toward South Africa.

But the gesture was also a way of expressing tacit approval for Mugabe's impressive beginning and what it stands for. The U.S. delegate to the Salisbury gathering, M. Peter McPherson, said, "The creation of Zimbabwe is one of the most remarkable political and diplomatic achievements of this generation. In committing our support we are also providing support for peaceful settlements to international conflicts."

## A Healthy Prognosis

The massive aid, and the vote of confidence, should help Zimbabwe recover from the ravages of war and keep its economy rolling. The health of that economy is of major concern throughout the world. The nation is blessed with rich mineral deposits and fertile land. Aside from South Africa, it has the healthiest and most diversified economy on the continent, with a solid infrastructure and the highest percentage of blacks with education, skills, and literacy. Along with its southern neighbor, Zimbabwe has taken on the role of food provider to Africa's hungry millions, and is expected to assume an even greater share of that burden as black leaders try to cut their dependence on South Africa. According to *The New York Times*, Zimbabwe already produces more than 2.5 million tons of food a year, about 5 percent of Africa's total consumption.

For a country whose recent past has been tumultuous, Zimbabwe's economy is in remarkably good shape. It has so far enjoyed real economic growth, and its inflation rate is low by African standards. Scientific and technical personnel are insufficient, but the stable, peaceful conditions that have generally prevailed under Mugabe might encourage both foreign personnel and domestic training programs. Its transportation system is far superior to most of its neighbors, but there could be problems if mineral development increases to the degree expected. According to the Santini report, there is a scarcity of railroad lines, and the ports in neighboring countries are insufficient to handle even present traffic. But overall, the prognosis is positive, particularly in light of the aid commitments and Mugabe's overtures to Western capital.

## Mineral Bounty

Although its economy is diverse, mining is as important to Zimbabwe as agriculture. Over forty minerals are produced, with 90 percent of the country's output coming from six: gold, copper, nickel, asbestos, coal, and chromium. Its lithium deposits may also prove important, since demand for that metal is expected to increase substantially.

It is, of course, Zimbabwe's chrome that most concerns the United States. Known reserves are estimated at three billion tons, of which a third is the high-grade metallurgical ore from which ferrochrome is produced. Running north-south through the central part of the nation is a geologic phenomenon called the Great Dyke, which is believed to contain chromium resources of up to 10 billion tons. These reserves are second only to South Africa's. Together, the two countries contain about 95 percent of the globe's chromium reserves, enough to supply the world far into the twenty-first century, and probably a lot longer.

According to the State Department, Zimbabwe is poised for a major mining boom, with gold and ferrochrome expected to show the biggest increases. Prospecting is underway, and is likely to snowball if foreign investors remain confident in the Mugabe government.

**Proceeding with Caution**
Despite the pervasive glow around Zimbabwe at the moment, there is circumspection. As the recent exodus indicates, white citizens, while relieved, are not entirely relaxed. They remember the firebrand that was Mugabe, and wonder how long the honeymoon will last. Might he be holding back to attract foreign capital and white know-how only to let loose the forces of retaliation later on? When the economy is strong and the black population better trained, might he then nationalize the mining industry? Will blacks who oppose Mugabe's moderate approach become embittered and impatient, and might they mount a new reign of terror? These questions remain, despite the present optimism. As one white in Zimbabwe told *The New York Times*, "He [Mugabe] says all the right things . . . but somewhere along the way there's always that little phrase, 'for the time being,' 'at least for now,' 'as far ahead as we can see.' What does it mean?"

To Congressman Santini it means proceed with caution. "The threads by which civilization and modern industrial society are suspended are much thinner, much more fragile than most Westerners ever imagine," his report states. "The thinning, not to mention the breaking, of those threads which allow an economy or an industry to function—such as financial incentives, tax policy, transportation network, communications systems, worker safety and freedom—can destroy ever so slowly, but effectively, the ability of a mining industry to fulfill its nation's own needs, not to mention those of another country." U.S. companies are watching closely.

### Leaning to the West

At the moment, the United States could hardly ask for a better Zimbabwe. We are, for a change, on friendly terms with a revolutionary government; we have publicly supported it and we participated in the orderly transition from white domination. Mugabe, leaning to the West despite his Marxist convictions, is demonstrating that practical concerns can, and should, override differences in ideology. The chances of Zimbabwe collaborating with the Soviet Union on resource war strategies—by forming cartels, withholding minerals from the West, price fixing, or supporting regional terrorism—are remote. Mugabe is vehemently anti-Soviet.

Realistically, the cartel possibilities are limited under present conditions. Chromium is the only commodity that Zimbabwe could possibly join forces to market, but that would require collusion with South Africa. Right now, the two countries are as diametrically opposed as, well, black and white. Cooperation between them is about as likely as a Kennedy-Nixon campaign ticket. But conditions in South Africa could change that.

A friendly, cooperative Zimbabwe is of inestimable value to the United States, not only for the minerals it can supply, but for its influence on the rest of the continent. A stable Mugabe regime would help stabilize the entire "Persian Gulf of Minerals," and act as a vital buffer to Soviet influence.

Our relations with South Africa may have as great an impact on our relationship with Zimbabwe as our Zimbabwe policy itself. Just before the U.S. pledge of aid, Mr. Mugabe expressed regret that his good relations with the United States were jeopardized by our support of South Africa, which he called a "regional aggressor and delinquent."

## SOUTH AFRICA: THE SAUDI ARABIA OF MINERALS

Like a cork in a funnel, the Republic of South Africa sits at the nadir of the continent, with all the other countries exerting downward pressure on it. Looking at a map, you get the impression that if the cork were to crumble, everything else would go tumbling into the South Atlantic.

Geologically and politically, the Republic of South Africa may be just that critical, and the situation just that delicate.

## Mineral Abundance

Nature was extravagant when it stocked South Africa with minerals, and the country has been resourceful in taking advantage of its endowment. It has developed one of the most efficient, technologically advanced, and financially sound mining industries in the world. Some forty-three mineral commodities are exported to more than ninety countries. Gold represents the largest portion of those, with 69 percent of the country's export revenues.

In terms of total annual output, South Africa—which is about the size of the southwest corner of the United States (covering California, Nevada, Arizona, and Utah)—is the world's fourth largest mineral producer, behind the Soviet Union, the United States, and Canada. But because it uses a lower percentage of its production domestically, and because it has a virtual Western-world monopoly on certain metals, it is, arguably, the most important exporter in the world. For good reasons it has been labeled "the Saudi Arabia of minerals."

The troubled nation ranks number one in the world for producing ferromanganese, antimony, zirconium, titanium, and asbestos. In terms of total exports, South Africa is number one in platinum, vanadium, gold, diamonds, all forms of manganese, chromium ore, and ferrochrome. It is second in fluorspar and zirconium exports, and third in titanium exports.

Sitting in the coveted earth of South Africa is an estimated 86 percent of the world's known platinum, 83 percent of its chromium ore, 64 percent of its vanadium, and 48 percent of its manganese. It is those metals about which the United States is most concerned. In 1980, the United States produced no chromium of its own; 40 percent of our chromium ore, and 62 percent of our ferrochrome, came from South Africa. We did produce vanadium, but we relied on imports for 27 percent of our needs; more than half of that came from South Africa. Our allies imported 73 percent of their vanadium from South Africa. For manganese ore, we depended mainly on Gabon and Brazil; but for ferromanganese we looked to South Africa for almost 40 percent of our needs, and an additional 10 to 15 percent came from sources that process South African ore.

As for platinum, the United States imports essentially all of its needs. In 1980, South Africa supplied 53 percent; 22 percent came from the Soviet Union. But even that understates the situation. Of the remaining 25 percent, half came from

Great Britain, which in actuality has no platinum of its own—it processes concentrates that it gets mainly from South Africa.

Making the numbers even more interesting are two facts: the only significant alternative source of some of these metals is the U.S.S.R.; and some constitute only a small portion of South Africa's exports. Chromium ore and ferrochrome, for example, represent less than 3 percent of the nation's revenues. They can afford not to sell.

Like Canada and Australia, South Africa's management is compatible with the American way of doing business. It is motivated almost exclusively by market dynamics; it is sophisticated and technologically progressive; it has ample capital; it is philosophically committed to the West. Said the Santini Subcommittee about its visit, "It was most impressive to witness firsthand the mineral wealth and technological advances. South Africa is at the apex of both the free world mineral solutions and potential problems."

Those problems, stemming from the grave racial situation in South Africa, could imperil the future of the country, and therefore the Western world's supplies of critical metals. The peril is magnified by South Africa's strategic maritime position on the Cape of Good Hope, and by its military and economic clout, which has helped keep the Soviet Union from making greater inroads into the region. A friendly alliance with South Africa could ensure the minerals prosperity of either super-power and its allies for the foreseeable future. But no one wants to embrace a government considered immoral by much of the world.

### Are Supplies Threatened?
The potential for supply cutoffs from South Africa and the extent of U.S. vulnerability if one occurred have been hotly debated in Washington. The Santini report states that a disruption "would be so severe in the case of certain metals that the President of the United States would have almost no other choice but to assume economic mobilization powers, impose resource-use priorities, and provide for domestic production capacity if possible. Neither the stockpile nor substitution would compensate even in the near term for the loss of South African mineral exports to the West. . . ." The report also points out that Europe and Japan are even more vulnerable, since they import virtually everything. Certain disruption

## SOUTH AFRICAN AND SOVIET MINERAL STRENGTH

| Metal | World Reserves | | | | World Production | | | | World Exports | | | |
|---|---|---|---|---|---|---|---|---|---|---|---|---|
| | South Africa | | U.S.S.R. | | South Africa | | U.S.S.R. | | South Africa | | U.S.S.R. | |
| | Percent | Rank | Percent | Rank | Percent | Rank | Percent | Rank | Percent | Rank | Percent | Rank |
| Antimony | 5 | 3 | 5 | 4 | 12 | 3 | 11 | 4 | 5 | 8 | 0 | — |
| Chrome | 81 | 1 | 3 | 3 | 34 | 1 | 23 | 2 | 28 | 1 | 15 | 3 |
| Ferrochrome | n.a. | n.a. | n.a. | n.a. | 24 | 1 | 16 | 3 | 51 | 1 | 5 | 4 |
| Manganese | 78 | 1 | 16 | 2 | 20 | 2 | 39 | 1 | 52 | 1 | 22 | 2 |
| Manganese ore | n.a. | n.a. | n.a. | n.a. | n.a. | n.a. | n.a. | n.a. | 30 | 1 | 15 | 3 |
| Ferromanganese | n.a. | n.a. | n.a. | n.a. | 9 | 3 | 22 | 1 | 20 | 1 | 9 | 5 |
| Platinum | 75 | 1 | 15 | 2 | 49 | 1 | 46 | 2 | 58 | 1 | 36 | 2 |
| Titanium | 7 | 6 | 12 | 3 | 3 | 6 | 10 | 4 | n.a. | n.a. | n.a. | n.a. |
| Vanadium | 49 | 1 | 46 | 2 | 40 | 1 | 29 | 2 | 59 | 1 | 19 | 2 |

Compiled from data supplied by the South African Mineral Bureau and U.S. Bureau of Mines. All data for 1978.

scenarios could also compromise South Africa's delivery of foodstuffs within the continent.

E. F. Andrews of Allegheny Ludlum was even more apocalyptic: "We would have to revert forty to fifty years in our standard of living and technology if deprived of the minerals and metals of South and southern Africa. Without these strategic metals, all production of steel, aircraft, missiles, tanks, naval vessels, automobiles and weapons of all kinds would cease."

In response to such grave alarms, the Subcommittee on African Affairs of the Senate Foreign Relations Committee conducted a study, the results of which were published in September 1980: "The key conclusion of this report, contrary to conventional wisdom, is that South African minerals are of significant, but not critical, importance to the West." The report cites ways, albeit expensive ways, to deal with possible interruptions without having to become dependent on the U.S.S.R. These include stockpiling, conservation, substitution, design changes, recycling, and the use of untapped reserves such as the manganese deposits on the ocean floor. "In sum," states the report, "it does not appear that the West faces an imminent threat of interruption of South African mineral supplies. More importantly, such an interruption would not spell disaster; the entire Western world would not be shut down in six months, and we would not be forced to revert forty to fifty years in our standard of living, should we have to do without South African minerals."

Despite that optimistic conclusion, however, the report did caution against "equanimity." It called for a comprehensive nonfuel minerals policy, to be formulated with our allies. "Failure to take prompt action," said the Subcommittee, "will risk repeating in southern Africa the same mistakes we have made in the Middle East."

### Three Disruption Scenarios
The McGovern Report (we will call it that, since George McGovern was then Chairman of the Subcommittee) outlined three possible scenarios that could disrupt mineral shipments from South Africa: a trade embargo on South Africa, imposed by foreign nations opposed to apartheid; an embargo *by* South Africa, in which it stopped shipping metals to protest international pressure or sanctions; internal disruptions such as

strikes, demonstrations, and revolutionary violence (one assumes that sabotage and terrorism fall into the last category). The report more or less ruled out Soviet naval aggression in the critical shipping lanes, since such an act would constitute the sort of blatant provocation that Moscow would not dare make at this time.

**An Embargo on South Africa?** In the United Nations there have been repeated calls for economic sanctions against South Africa, the most recent stemming from that nation's continuing presence in Namibia (South-West Africa) long after its U.N. mandate to govern the area has expired. But, says the McGovern Report, a Security Council call for a mandatory embargo can be vetoed by the United States, Britain, or France, and a voluntary embargo would certainly be limited in scope and ineffective, since many nations and corporations would continue doing business with South Africa, just as they have during periods of sanctions on other nations, such as Rhodesia.

**An Embargo by South Africa?** The threat of an embargo is there, and has been voiced by South African authorities in moments of pique. They have been miffed at Western powers for the pressures placed on them to clean up their racial policies. South African leaders have accused the West of everything from naïveté to ingratitude to political blackmail for failing to appreciate their country's strategic importance as mineral supplier.

Said Prime Minister P. W. Botha in 1980, "Naturally we are disappointed that Western nations who are dependent on our mineral resources, who have an interest in our stability and are fully informed on our strategic importance, are apparently not prepared to stand up and be counted in defense of what is of decisive importance to the free world in southern Africa."

One official, quoted at a Congressional hearing by E. F. Andrews, reportedly said that South Africa is tired of being "the world's scapegoat," and might be forced into a policy of "economic counterattack."

The South African government has a strong diplomatic hand to play. Confronted with a restriction of U.S. investments, for example, or a cutoff of OPEC oil, they could conceivably retaliate by restricting exports of vital minerals. They could also use their minerals leverage to try forcing the United States into a more conciliatory position. Any such embargo would probably have a more powerful impact than sanctions imposed by an international body, since it would be enforced by the exporter itself. It could even extend to minerals from other parts of southern Africa, if the South African government denied access to its rails and ports.

However, any embargo initiated by South Africa is likely to be limited in scope and brief in duration, because minerals contribute a major portion of the country's foreign exchange. Minerals production makes up almost 20 percent of South Africa's Gross Domestic Product; its 900 mines employ 772,000 workers, more than 600,000 of whom are black. A study by the South African Foreign Affairs Association, quoted in the McGovern Report, states that "any attempts to place an embargo on the export of minerals and their processed products from South Africa would have a disastrous effect on South Africa's balance of payments, and indeed on the whole economy."

A limited embargo on, say, chromium might have a significant impact without damaging the South African economy, but it might inspire political retaliation. South Africa has a lot to lose by further alienating the United States and the Western allies. Staunchly anti-Soviet, and alarmed by Soviet inroads in their part of the world, they need close links with the West for security. South Africa is strong militarily, and can probably resist anything short of large-scale invasion à la Afghanistan— a highly unlikely prospect, but one that South African leaders cannot entirely ignore.

In a statement published in James Sinclair's quarterly *Strategics Review*, Dennis Etheredge, a mining executive and former president of the South African Chamber of Mines, said, "I think it would be very silly of us to use our strategic minerals as a weapon against the West, particularly the U.S. I am a business man, not a politician. We have acquired a reputation in South Africa, right around the world, despite the fact that we are a polecat in many other senses. The one reputation we have is that we deliver. We deliver regularly and reliably."

That businesslike attitude is supported by South Africa's Minister of Mines, F. W. de Klerk: "It is our firm policy to trade, and we fully support the principle of open trade. We do not favor the formation of cartels, such as OPEC."

South African leaders want us to ease off some of the pressure, let them move ahead socially at their own pace, give them credit for changes already made, and leave politics out of our mineral dealings. Those may be difficult requests to grant, given the nature of South African racism and the militancy and impatience of the Third World leaders with whom the United States wants to strengthen ties.

**Disruption by Unrest?** The third possible scenario for a disruption of South African exports—violence and unrest—is a less predictable matter. Depending on the exact nature of the outburst, a disruption may be inconsequential or devastating. As the McGovern Report concludes, "The impact of revolutionary violence on mineral exports cannot be assessed at the present time." The report states that a lengthy cutoff is highly unlikely, but it does admit that "revolutionary violence within South Africa is a continuing possibility and one which could at least temporarily endanger mineral supplies."

Which is precisely the point that minerals activists have been making, only they believe that the implications of even a temporary cutoff are grave. Economically, that would seem to be so. Mining in Shaba province was interrupted for only a short period of time, but prices quadrupled. Further, say the activists, we are not as well prepared as the McGovern Report suggests. In a letter to Senator McGovern dated October 22, 1980, Congressman Santini objected to the "pat and almost offhanded solution" offered by the report. "Careful inquiry into each of these 'solutions' reveals very real infirmities, not to mention national and international ramifications and side effects."

Santini's analysis attacked the report for failing to acknowledge the costs and logistics involved in some of the recommended prophylactic measures: long lead times for developing substitutes and "design changes"; high costs and lowered quality from the use of alternatives; insufficiencies of current stockpiles; political and economic hindrances to the development of "untapped reserves"; the implications of shifts in Soviet export/import patterns. Above all, Santini felt that the national security implications of even limited supply interruptions were dangerously underplayed by the McGovern Subcommittee.

The McGovern Report might well have been naïve and perhaps overly optimistic about the possible impact of supply cutoffs. What Santini's rebuttal did not adequately address, however, was the report's contention that a serious interruption of South African minerals was improbable. That remains the crucial question.

It seems somehow glib to dismiss the possibility of violent disruptions simply because, as the McGovern Report put it, "it cannot be foreseen with any precision." It is precisely because it cannot be foreseen that unrest is so worrisome. Further, such upheavals—whether a stick of dynamite in the hands of a single saboteur, or an outright civil war—are probably more plausible than an embargo by either side. The South African security system is second to none, yet even the sanguine McGovern Report concluded that violence was a "continuing possibility." After all, a few years ago, anyone who predicted that the Shah of Iran would be replaced by Islamic fundamentalists, and the U.S. Embassy there held for over a year by a gang of disorganized student militants, would have been classified an incurable paranoid.

If an embassy, why not a mine? Indeed, there have been two attacks on South African petroleum complexes. The Soviet-backed African National Congress (ANC) claimed responsibility. It would not take much to create at least a short-term disruption of key metal supplies, and probably soaring prices. Privately held stocks would then be the only source outside the U.S.S.R., unless the government released the strategic stockpile.

### Will South Africa Remain Stable?

That is a complex question, too complex for detailed discussion here. We will simply sum up the current situation.

Within South Africa, change is taking place—too slowly for black leaders, too quickly for some whites, just the right pace for others. There are reasons to be hopeful. Chester A. Crocker, now Undersecretary of State for African Affairs, wrote in the journal *Foreign Affairs* (Winter, 1980–1981): "Black politics are characterized by an increasingly confident experimentation with various strategies for challenging white control, while white politics are demonstrating a degree of fluidity and pragmatism that is without precedent in the past generation. The combination does not make meaningful evolutionary change certain, but it does make it possible for the first time in decades."

The writing is clearly on the wall; blacks will ultimately gain control of their country. Apartheid is doomed. The remaining questions are: How soon will the change occur? What form will the new South Africa take? Can it be done peacefully? How will the transition affect the mineral industry?

At the present time, total revolution is not very likely.

South African military strength is more than sufficient to put down any rebellion. The U.N. embargo on arms shipments to South Africa forced the country to arm itself, and it now has the tenth largest weapons industry in the world. But chaos and protracted guerrilla warfare are certainly within the bounds of possibility. The militant ANC is active, despite government attempts to suppress it. Everyone hopes that change can come about peacefully, but not everyone believes it can.

Within both the black and white communities, there are vast differences of viewpoint. Blacks in general are becoming increasingly political, and, after the Zimbabwe settlement, increasingly hopeful. Yet there is widespread disagreement on tactical issues and competition to fill the leadership vacuums. Within the white community, attitudes and feelings seem to be as diverse as they were in the United States during the civil rights campaign of the 1960s. Some diehards are prepared to resist change to the end. Others, perhaps more numerous than we realize, accept the future and are prepared to help usher it in gracefully.

Yet despite hopeful signs, change is creeping along at a pace that is, at best, frustrating for blacks. The atmosphere remains tense; cosmetic modifications of apartheid will not satisfy.

### The United States Is Walking a Diplomatic Tightrope

As for U.S. policy, that is one of the great diplomatic conundrums of all time. It requires the vision of a prophet and the balance of a tightrope walker. Essentially, the United States must support the aspirations of the black majority for full participation in their country and for equality before the law— goals that are consistent with our stand on human rights, our promises to black African leaders, and our long-range strategic interests. At the same time, we must recognize that the fate of South Africa is in the hands of its people; our power to influence events is limited.

While continuing to apply whatever pressure it can to promote equitable and rapid change, the United States has to avoid appearing self-righteous or imposing its own solutions on another country. Nor can we afford to completely alienate the present leadership in Pretoria, or provoke reactionary measures that could be destructive to black Africans as well as ourselves. If we are to ensure access to African minerals and apply counterpressure to Soviet expansion on the continent, we need the trust and support of both the black leaders of other countries and the white South African rulers.

All of this will require consummate diplomacy. Domestically it will require careful communication between Washington and citizens concerned about the moral issues. The situation is so complex and so hotly emotional that the full implications of any given action are seldom understood. As Mr. Crocker put it, "The problem is that the land of apartheid operates as a magnet for one-dimensional minds."

In the past, experts believe, U.S. policy has been subject to confusing oscillations, reflecting the ambiguities of the issues and differences between administrations. During the Carter years the emphasis was on human rights. Rather than strengthen the white government's hand by acknowledging our mineral dependence, Carter threatened an embargo on imports as a way of exerting pressure on Pretoria. At the same time, he tried to ingratiate the United States with emerging black nations by taking a strong stand against apartheid and siding with them on issues such as Rhodesian and Namibian independence. Many observers feel that while our position was morally impeccable, our actual influence on South Africa during those years was minimal. It may even have damaged communications with the white leadership, heightening the threat of a serious conflict between Washington and Pretoria. Such a rift might have jeopardized both our mineral situation and racial progress.

The Reagan Administration lost little time in shifting gears. Long aware of our mineral dependency, both the President and Secretary of State Haig expressed the desire to forge better communications with the Pretoria government. In a television interview with Walter Cronkite, Reagan described South Africa in the friendliest terms heard in Washington in decades. "Can we abandon a country that has stood by us in every war we've ever fought," he asked, rhetorically, "a country that, strategically, is essential to the free world?" He then made the gesture that white South Africans have been pleading for. He praised the government's "sincere and honest efforts" to achieve racial justice.

There are, of course, millions of people who would be reluctant to characterize South Africa's efforts as either sincere or honest. The hue and cry was predictably swift. Was Reagan laying the groundwork for a major shift in policy, toward appeasement of white South Africa? Or were his remarks intended to illustrate the hypocrisy of refusing to talk to one human rights violator, South Africa, while calling for talks with the Soviet Union? Liberals were understandably bracing for the next move.

And the next move did little to assuage fears. The new Administration urged Congress to repeal the Clark Amendment of 1976, which prohibits the use of covert aid to rebel forces fighting the leftist government in Angola. Angola, of course, is now playing host to 15,000 to 20,000 Cuban troops, and to the South-West Africa People's Organization (SWAPO) guerrillas who are seeking to oust South Africa from Namibia. As of this writing, the Senate Foreign Relations Committee voted for the repeal, but the House Foreign Affairs Committee voted to retain the amendment. Along with the U.S. refusal to back U.N. sanctions against South Africa, the proposal on the Clark Amendment raised further doubts about the Administration's commitment to human rights and black majority rule in Africa.

Predictably, those moves were greeted with a sigh of relief from the South African government. To America's embarrassment, Reagan's overtures were quickly followed by a South African bombing mission 200 miles into Angola, where the SWAPO forces are based.

Balancing those controversial actions, the Reagan Administration reaffirmed its commitment to "the path of negotiation" in Namibia, and has tried to revive the stalemated talks that had been attempting to work out a peaceful transition from South African rule to independence. Secretary Haig tried to assure the world that he wanted to repeal the Clark Amendment for general procedural reasons, not because of any planned mission in Angola. Reagan's show of support and generous aid offering to Zimbabwe also helped placate disgruntled African leaders. Perhaps most important, he has repeatedly reasserted the United States stand on apartheid, which he termed "repugnant."

To convey these positions and assuage the fears of black Africa, Reagan dispatched Chester Crocker to Nigeria, Kenya, and the so-called "front-line states" of Angola, Botswana, Mozambique, Tanzania, Zambia, and Zimbabwe. Crocker also went to South Africa, where he told white leaders that the United States would like to work with them in harmony, but that apartheid was unacceptable and we would not consider military cooperation. At the same time, Secretary Haig told the

Senate Appropriations Subcommittee on Foreign Operations that the Administration is "sensitive to a number of inherent contradictions" in African affairs, and said he was confident that we could "maintain effective dialogue" with South Africa while also solidifying relations with black nations, including those now labeled Marxist.

As the government walks the diplomatic tightrope, the minerals keep coming. Just how long we can stay balanced and whether the Administration will come up with a policy that can satisfy all parties in the long run remain to be seen. Clearly, even if the moral issues were not so unequivocally clear, self-interest would mandate an uncompromising commitment to racial justice in South Africa. To do otherwise would only increase the chances of violence, and that would foster Soviet inroads in the region, making minerals access even more tenuous. It would also alienate the rest of the Third World, whose friendship and resources we may ultimately need more than we need South Africa's.

Chester A. Crocker writes, "Clearly, the fundamental goal is the emergence in South Africa of a society with which the United States can pursue its varied interests in a full and friendly relationship, without constraint, embarrassment, or political damage. The nature of the South African political system prevents us from having such a relationship now."

South Africa is the most important piece on the resource chessboard. The future of prices and supplies depends in large part on what happens there in the next few years. And what will happen is anybody's guess.

# THE HOME FRONT

# FIVE

**F**OLLOWING WORLD WAR II, the United States began its transition from a propeller-driven Air Force to one carried aloft by jet engines. Judging columbium to be a critical metal in that transition, the Defense Department called on the appropriate government agencies to see what they could do about supplies. By the time the Korean War started, surveys had been taken all over the world, and it was determined that production could not exceed a million pounds a year. Three years later, the U.S. government had 15 million pounds in its stockpile.

How did that feat of legerdemain occur? In May 1952, officials in the Bureau of Mines shrewdly concluded that miners would somehow find previously undiscovered deposits if they were given the proper incentives. So the government announced that it would purchase up to 15 million pounds at *double the price*, which was then $1.60 a pound. The goal was considered unattainable, but it was announced anyway, to encourage exploration. At double the price, new companies jumped into the columbium business; old companies were willing to invest more capital on exploration and to use more costly procedures in the process. Not only was the government's 15 million pounds supplied in three years, but additional quantities were sold to private industry.

The story illustrates not just the tenuous nature of prognostications in the realm of metals. It was related by Dr. John Morgan, Chief Staff Officer of the U.S. Bureau of Mines, to dramatize his conviction, shared by many colleagues, that the United States is more import-dependent than need be. Given adequate incentive, the mining industry is often capable of small miracles. The real enemy in the resource war, Dr. Morgan believes, is ourselves. "The wicked Americans will probably get us before the wicked Russians do," he asserted. "We won't be brought to our knees, if we get off our butts."

To back up his point, he related two other incidents. In the late forties and early fifties, when the United States was importing its uranium from South Africa, the government offered a $10,000 bonus for the discovery of small quantities of the metal. The uranium rush was on, aided by government-guaranteed prices for production. Soon the United States was virtually self-sufficient in uranium. Similarly, the government in 1951 anounced it would buy tungsten at $63 per unit, a nearly fourfold increase over the going price. The reason: prior to the Korean War, we had been importing half our tungsten from China. Two years later, the domestic industry had increased its production by four times.

### THE DECLINE OF DOMESTIC MINING

Executives in the mining industry couldn't agree more with Dr. Morgan's assessment. Once virile and robust, the industry used to extract and process enough minerals for our own needs and much of the world's. In the last decade, however, it has become somewhat enfeebled and has lost its competitive edge. Part of the problem is geologic: declining ore grades, and the absence of certain newly important metals. Another factor is increased competition from abroad. Japanese, German, and other smelters and refiners have emerged as viable alternatives to the United States, which once dominated global production.

Part of the blame must also be placed on the shoulders of mining executives, who some observers feel have grown rigid and inflexible, unable to respond to changing social and economic conditions. The large companies that dominate the mining field, some argue, became overly obsessed with the P to

E ratio and other short-term or intermediate-range objectives, and made decisions that might have been counterproductive in the long run. Further, according to Business Week (July 2, 1979), some metals experts feel that producers made fundamental misjudgments a decade or so ago, and as a result have become overly burdened with debt.

### Misguided Government Policies?

Then there is the influence of government policy. By virtue of its importance to the national defense and its impact on the environment, the mining and processing industry is deeply affected in a number of ways by governmental actions. Industry leaders feel that the decline of domestic mining, and our consequent dependence on foreign sources, can be traced to a series of questionable policies, shifts in national priorities, excessive regulation, ambiguous and erroneous assumptions, and a failure to recognize the importance of minerals in the overall economic and strategic scheme of things.

Indeed, some of the most vocal resource warriors feel that domestic policies are the true villain. They are using the Soviet menace the way others use OPEC—as an emotional trigger to force changes such as: more favorable tax incentives; upgrading the strategic stockpile; reducing environmental regulations; opening public lands to exploration; establishing a more coherent and consistent official posture toward minerals; and better cooperation between the mining industry and government.

### We Can Produce If the Price Is Right

The interplay of a variety of domestic events—and the effectiveness of corresponding lobbying organizations—might have a stronger impact on the strategic metals picture than will geopolitical factors. Technological innovations can suddenly make one metal almost obsolete—or at least far less critical— and another a prized possession. Policy changes might create a domestic mining boom, or the opposite.

Some of the metals on which we are most import-dependent can conceivably be developed domestically, given the right set of conditions. We have, for example, considerable deposits of chromium in Montana, California, and Oregon, which could produce several hundred thousand tons per year. In fact one of them did so during the Korean War. But the deposits are considered submarginal. At current prices, it is far cheaper to import from South Africa, Zimbabwe, or the Soviet Union. The price of chromium would have to go up several times to make it worthwhile for miners. In addition, certain environmental restrictions might have to be waived, and tax and other financial incentives thrown in.

Similarly, we now produce some 25,000 tons of titanium a year. But we import virtually all of our rutile, the raw material from which titanium sponge, and eventually metal, is derived. A different ore, ilmenite, could be used, and there are vast supplies of it in the United States and Canada. Indeed, we already use it to make pigment, and the technology for turning it into metal is known. Why don't we do it? Because it is cheaper to import rutile. Without a firm market at an adequate price, Dr. Morgan contends, companies are not willing to make the huge investments needed to mine ilmenite and turn it into titanium metal. There have been occasions when it looked as if they might, but the B-1 bomber and the SST were canned, and with them the incentive to produce large amounts of titanium. Even now, with defense spending about to soar, potential producers will not budge without firm, long-term contracts.

Dr. Morgan contends that, "We can pretty much produce anything we want, *if* we're willing to pay the price." That price is not only financial. It could mean compromising the clean air and water, occupational health and safety, and other social legislation of the seventies. The supply and prices of strategic metals, therefore, will be strongly affected by the attitudes of the government and the public in the years to come.

So far, the Reagan Administration seems favorably disposed to the kind of changes the mining industry has been espousing. The climate in Washington has never been better— or worse, depending on your point of view—for reordering priorities. One can anticipate that forthcoming decisions will lean in the direction of alleviating import dependency by rejuvenating domestic industry. Further, we might end up with a less ambiguous and more consistent government stand on the issue, which could help stabilize the metals market.

Mining executives are chomping at the bit, anxious to be let loose after years of what they have perceived as strangulation. Before the picks and shovels penetrate the earth, however, and even after they do, the opposition will be heard, and it will be loud and tough. Most Americans apparently do not want development at any price, despite economic woes. Yet surprises may occur at any time due to foreign events or technological breakthroughs in laboratories.

The situation is complex and unpredictable, and it should not be supposed that a simple change in one area, no matter how important, will necessarily induce a logical shift in the supply/demand picture. All factors have to be weighed.

## THE STATE OF THE INDUSTRY

When a mineral deposit is discovered—itself an expensive process, involving sophisticated instruments and highly skilled professionals—geologists must then assess whether it can yield ore economically enough to warrant development. Detailed examinations are made. Some sites will then warrant further investigation, and of those a small percentage are inviting enough for geologists to gather still more detailed information. Some will then be judged inadequate, some will be declared resources presently uneconomic, and a few will be termed reserves. The percentage of the last is small. Of every 10,000 "conceptual deposits" identified by geologists, an estimated *one* is immediately productive.

If a deposit is good enough to warrant production, the land must be prepared for mining, and that requires a permit procedure that industry leaders view as interminable and fickle. Assuming the company is given permission to go ahead, preparation may require sinking mine shafts or constructing tunnels. Once the ore is extracted—by an increasingly expensive labor force, using increasingly expensive energy—it is sent to a mill, where the useful components are separated from waste, and the waste is then discarded. That step involves compliance with strict environmental standards.

The concentrated ores are then sent to a smelter or a refinery where they are further reduced to a useful metal. This is the most polluting step. Then the metal is sent to other plants where it is fabricated into the shapes used by industry: bars, rods, sheets, tubes, wire, and so on. To the degree that doing so is cost-effective, residual values of the metal are then reclaimed and put back to use.

### Mining Is Expensive

From discovery to production, the process takes an average of six or seven years, sometimes longer, with an enormous amount of regulatory paperwork and red tape at every stage. It is extraordinarily expensive, not to mention risky. "These capital expenditures dwarf those normally associated with manufacturing," James Boyd wrote in *Science* (February 20, 1976). "The gross capital investment and the capital investment per worker are on a scale not contemplated by manufacturers of plastics, textiles, or other products in the manufacturing sector." Boyd quotes the cost of a new magnesium plant at $75 million, and that of an integrated steel complex capable of producing 4 million tons a year at $2.4 billion. Those were 1976 dollars.

Nord Resources, a growing mining firm, owns a site in Papua New Guinea believed to contain reserves of 400 million pounds of cobalt and 3 billion pounds of chromium. Dr. Edgar Cruft, President and Chairman of Nord, is understandably excited about the property, which he believes contains the largest amount of those strategic metals outside southern Africa and the Soviet Union. Anticipating that consumers will welcome a reliable alternative to those suppliers, Cruft is eager to begin exploiting the deposit. A lengthy and costly series of studies was completed in early 1982, which revealed that it would cost $750 to $800 million to go ahead with operations. Assuming the capital can be acquired, Nord can expect its first salable metal to leave the ground sometime around 1988. Dr. Cruft will attempt to raise the funds through loans and by putting together a consortium of mining companies and financial institutions.

That provides an example of the time and cost involved in new mining ventures. It may not be easy for Dr. Cruft to raise the money, even though the site is less expensive to work on than American sites and New Guinea is considered one of the safest Third World countries to invest in.

Mining is the most capital intensive of all industries; some projects can cost upwards of a billion dollars, and the profit margins are relatively low.

## Some Reasons for Increased Costs

Inflation and high interest rates have kept investment down in all industries, but mining has been particularly hard hit. In 1958, it cost Phelps Dodge 18.2 cents to produce a pound of copper. In 1964, it cost 19.4 cents, and in 1970 it cost 27.8 cents. It then doubled within the next five years, and has been climbing ever since.

One of the factors involved is the rising cost of equipment. According to Commerce Department figures, the price index of capital goods used in manufacturing rose 116 percent between 1970 and 1978; the same data for mining indicate a 170 percent increase. The problem is magnified by what some mining executives believe are inadequate depreciation allowances for replacing equipment. U.S. producers are working with outdated plants compared to those in Japan and Germany, and in some cases companies have chosen to close down because the cost of replacement, added to other burgeoning costs, was simply too high.

Energy prices also have shaken the mining industry. According to George B. Munroe, Chairman and President of Phelps Dodge, the cost of energy required to produce a pound of copper increased by 832 percent between 1972 and 1981, and energy now constitutes one-quarter of the cost of production, compared to 7 percent in 1972.

But the costs that rankle mining executives most are those associated with environmental regulations, which they consider excessive and wasteful. Mining and processing minerals is a dirty, smelly business that rips up pristine land, belches huge clouds of toxic smoke into the air, and dumps large amounts of waste into rivers and streams. No one knows of a truly clean way to get the minerals society requires, but we have determined that it shall be done cleaner than it has been. The cost of cleaning up has skyrocketed since the nation first made it a priority. *Business Week* reported that environmental regulations, along with those for occupational safety and health, have raised the cost of mining 25 percent without increasing output. According to McGraw-Hill studies, pollution control in the last eight years of the seventies averaged 8 percent of the total cost of mining. The production of nonferrous metals required an even greater percentage: 19 cents of every dollar spent was allotted for pollution control. The average for all other industries was less than 6 percent.

Mr. Munroe of Phelps Dodge contends that the "torrent of regulation" added 15 cents to the cost of producing a pound of copper (copper costs are relevant to this discussion, since many strategics are produced as by-products of copper mining). Government figures project the cost of full compliance with Environmental Protection Agency regulations at $552.7 million in 1985, using 1975 dollar values, and the total investment required at $2.7 billion. That is for the copper industry only.

Iron and steel makers will spend between $6 and $8 billion on environmental regulations between 1979 and 1983.

## A Crunch on Capital

The upshot of all these accelerating costs has been to magnify the risks already inherent in the nature of mining. Once strong enough to finance new ventures from internal cash flow, mining companies are now forced to seek investment capital through outside private sources. From 1967 to 1977, the debt structure of ten major mining companies rose from 11 percent to 42 percent of capital. Nonferrous producers carried an average of 34 percent debt in 1979, compared with 24 percent for manufacturing companies in general. One reason for this is the decline of government support. The federal assistance, stockpile purchases, subsidized loans, and favorable taxation policies of the 1950s have virtually disappeared, and with it much of the mining industry.

Ten years ago, the United States produced more than a million tons of zinc metal a year. It now produces half that amount. Ten zinc smelters have closed since 1969, and only one was replaced. This is a sharp contrast to overseas, where zinc production has increased by 25 percent in the same time period, and new smelters have been built in Japan and Europe. We import twice as much zinc as we did a decade ago, and much of it is in the form of metal, which makes our costs much higher than if we import ore. Indeed, virtually all zinc smelting is done overseas.

The zinc example is used by industry sources to illustrate the decline of mining and producing in general. Not only is zinc an important metal, but it is one for which we apparently have ample reserves. Part of the problem is the fact that while other countries also shut down obsolete plants, they do a better job of replacing them. The U.S. economy, however, has worked against that level of capital investment.

The steel industry also is in trouble. Much of the world's steel production has transferred from the United States to other countries. In 1950, the United States accounted for 40 percent of world production; in 1978, that figure was less than 10 percent. We imported 10 percent of our consumption in 1950; 35 percent in 1978. During the same period, worldwide production tripled. Troubled steel companies mean less capital for expansion, exploration, research, and development. And that affects a wide range of metals, notably the ferroalloys.

In 1978, the average increase in research and development expenditures was 7.3 percent in the metals and mining industry, compared with 16.4 percent in all others. It is further believed that a significant portion of research expenditures in mining has gone into environmental protection, not into finding better ways to extract and process minerals.

Naturally, investors are reluctant to hop aboard a long-range mining project with enormous start-up costs and a morass of red tape. Moody's Investor Service has given major mining companies a poor credit standing, and so has Standard and Poor's. For good reason, apparently: a 1978 Citibank survey of sixty-four industry groups ranked nonferrous metal manufacturing fifty-fifth, and metal mining dead last in the rate of return on net worth. All of which has increased the cost of borrowing and reduced the availability of funds.

The depressed capital picture has caused the demise of many independent mining companies and the merger or sale of others. In the latter part of the seventies, a number of nonferrous producers were acquired by giants such as Atlantic Richfield, General Electric, and Standard Oil of Indiana. Bendix and other companies acquired major portions of others. More recently, a new wave of mergers and acquisitions took place: Kennecott, the nation's largest copper company, was purchased by Standard Oil of Ohio; Standard Oil of California, already a 20 percent owner of AMAX—a major producer of molybdenum and nickel—moved to acquire the other 80 percent; Fluor Corporation acquired St. Joe Minerals. According to *Time* magazine, "Wall Street investors expect that other mining companies will soon become targets for takeover bids" because many stocks are depressed at the moment, whereas anticipated increases in defense spending may spell a revived future.

### Is the Government to Blame?
Critics of the mining industry are reluctant to accept the miners' analysis of the problem. The miners view is narrow, it is said, and they have been unable to adapt to a new set of national priorities, or to realize the value of gains that have been made in other areas of national and international concern. Industry spokesmen, however, see the government as the prime reason for its problems. Excessive regulation and fiscal

policies that discourage investment where foreign governments encourage—and even subsidize—it have made domestic mining less competitive, they feel.

While the situation is complex and no one party is exclusively to blame, the consensus is that government action, right
or wrong, has indeed hurt the industry. Even the General
Accounting Office (GAO) during the Carter Administraton
assigned some of the blame to the government. Its 1979 report
on the mining and mineral processing industry stated that one
cause of decline was "the cumulative effect of government
actions which have tended to discourage investment in domestic mineral projects." The report cited the same villains that
are so popular among mining executives: environmental and
health/safety regulations; land withdrawals; antitrust regulations that restrict joint ventures and other forms of economic
cooperation among companies; and the failure of government
to appreciate the implications of its policies on the nation's
supply of strategic materials. Said the GAO report, "The U.S.
government has not established a mechanism to identify and
resolve conflicts that arise between goals in the mineral area
and those associated with environmental and other national
concerns."

## CHANGES IN THE AIR

To whatever degree the government is responsible for the
decline of domestic mining, and to whatever degree it is capable of changing the situation, it looks as though it is now
determined to reverse the trends of the past decade.

Resolved to strengthen the nation's defense posture and
the business climate in general, the Reagan Administration
has already inspired optimism in the mining industry. The
Republican platform included a section on raw materials
access, calling for reduced dependence on foreign sources, the
elimination of land use and tax policies that inhibit mineral
development, and the serious consideration of mineral requirements in foreign policy and treaty negotiations. The opposition
fears that these goals may be achieved at the expense of ten
years of progress on environmental protection, and perhaps
some important relationships with developing nations.

## Reagan's Pro-Mining Team

If personalities are any indication of future policies, it would seem that changes are in store. Murray Weidenbaum, Chairman of the President's Council of Economic Advisers, was a member of the Strategic Minerals Task Force that Reagan appointed even before his inauguration. Weidenbaum is a strong opponent of overregulation. Indeed, within months of taking charge, the new Administration moved to cut down on regulations in general, and on environmental restrictions to mining and processing in particular. A formidable task force headed by Vice President Bush was charged with sniffing out red tape for cutting.

Then there is James Watt, the Secretary of the Interior, who has turned the Department abruptly away from its previous emphasis on protecting public lands toward opening them up to exploration and development. Said Democratic Congressman John F. Sieberling of Watt, "You've got to go back a long way in American history to find leadership so dedicated to exploiting the natural resources on our public lands."

When Watt was a lawyer in Colorado, he was President of the Mountain States Legal Foundation, which battled the Department he now heads in an attempt to open Western land to private development. Citing our import dependence on strategic metals, the new Secretary told the Senate he hoped to reverse the policy of limiting permits for exploration in wilderness areas. That and similar pronouncements by Watt have set off a cry of protests from the timber forests of Maine to the threatened coastline of California. In the first few months of Watt's reign, the Sierra Club had collected more than a million signatures on a petition calling for the dismissal of the man it claims "shows no concern for the protection and enhancement of our environment."

Watt has been joined by some old friends and comrades in the "Sagebrush Rebellion." Anne Gorsuch, head of the Environmental Protection Agency (EPA), vigorously opposed that agency's hazardous waste and pollution regulations when she was a Denver lawyer and State Legislator. She has pledged to reduce the EPA's regulatory "overburden." Also aboard is rancher Robert Burford, another Coloradan, who heads the Bureau of Land Management (BLM), which administers the Wilderness Act. Burford led a major assault on the bureau when, as a private citizen, he tried to get it to turn control of federal lands over to the states. Watt's choice to head the Office of Surface Mining (OSM) is former Indiana State Senator James R. Harris, who once challenged the constitutionality of parts of the Federal Surface Mining Act. In effect, he is now in charge of an agency that is bound by that law.

With the Cabinet stacked with officials of such strong conviction, the domestic mining industry is more optimistic than it has been in a long time. J. Allen Overton, President of the American Mining Congress, has already given Reagan and Watt "an 'A' for the course—a first-rate performance in terms of recognizing the problem and doing something about it." No doubt Overton and his colleagues are equally delighted with the turn of events in the Senate, where James McClure now chairs the Senate Energy and Natural Resources Committee and Strom Thurmond heads the Armed Services Subcommittee on Military Construction and Stockpiles. With liberals such as Frank Church and George McGovern gone, men like Thurmond and McClure can be expected to push for aggressive development and stockpiling policies. And in Congress, James Santini should have more sympathetic ears than he is accustomed to as he fights for passage of his National Mineral Security Act.

The issues are volatile, and both sides can be convincing. Let's examine the key questions and opposing points of view. The outcome could strongly affect the metals markets.

## THIS LAND IS YOUR LAND

A team of geologists found indications of a mineral deposit rich enough to justify further investigations. They staked a claim. Later, the claim was withdrawn when the geologists discovered that they had been exploring on public land declared off limits to mining. It was protected because of its historic importance. Curious, the geologists asked why it was such a valuable piece of American history. The answer: it was the site of a famous gold mine.

That story typifies the rather ambiguous attitude our nation has toward mining. On the one hand we venerate it as a major reason for our affluence. On the other we vilify it as an omnivorous destroyer of land, air, and water. We want the "stuff" with which to make the "things" we crave—including the vehicles that transport us to mountain trails and pristine lakes—but we don't want to blemish the earth to get it. For most of our history, the developers had their way. They produced, but they also destroyed, and society decided that too much damage had been done. It demanded a shift in priorities. Miners and smelters became villains; we clamped down on their activities in order to protect our natural heritage. Some people think we've gone from one extreme to another; but environmentalists say, in essence, we can't turn back the clock, so learn to do with less and find cleaner ways to do it.

Our schizoid attitude was illustrated by two Congressional acts in 1980. On the one hand, Congress refused to include a large area of Idaho under the Wilderness Act because it might contain major deposits of cobalt. It was the first time Congress acted against the inclusion of a piece of land since the act was passed in 1964. On the other hand, the same Congress placed off limits more than 100 million acres of land in Alaska, even though mining executives believe it contains nearly thirty important minerals and has not been adequately assessed for its potential.

Before 1968, the federal government withheld 17 percent of all federal lands from mining and exploration. Since then, vast tracts have been swept under Uncle Sam's coattails. Five hundred million acres, about two-thirds of all public property, is restricted. That represents an area the size of all land east of the Mississippi, excluding the state of Maine; almost all of it is located west of the Mississippi. "The areas locked out," claims American Mining Congress President J. Allen Overton, "are precisely those where geologists tell us we are most likely to have what we need."

## How Much Is Off Limits?
Federal policies on public land overlap so many departments and agencies that it is impossible to determine exactly how much land has been withdrawn and under what conditions. No accurate inventory exists. "We found that there is no single source of cumulative withdrawal statistics," reported the General Accounting Office in 1979. "Each land-managing federal agency keeps its own records and, to some extent, sets its own requirements for mineral exploration and development within the lands under its jurisdiction."

One study of land withdrawals, conducted by the Department of the Interior in 1977, indicated that 42 percent of federal land has been closed to hard rock mineral activity; 16 percent has been "highly restricted"; and 10 percent "moderately restricted." Congressman Santini believes that an additional 10 to 15 percent has since been restricted. Industry sources generally estimate that 70 percent of all public land is either closed or in some way impossible to explore. Recently, the Department of Interior concurred, stating that 70 percent of the land is "encumbered by some degree of restriction inhibiting mining." Those restrictions include such things as prohibitions on building roads.

In addition, the industry contends, no adequate surveys were taken before the land was withdrawn, so no one really knows what minerals might lie under the public land. That, plus improved technology, make it likely that much of the land can be profitably exploited, mining executives say.

Industry spokesmen feel that one obvious but vital point is missed by large segments of the public: minerals can be extracted only where they are found. Sometimes that happens to be on land we would like to leave untouched, for aesthetic, historical, recreational, or other reasons. Miners want the land open at least for exploration, so that its true potential can be adequately assessed before we decide whether to lock it up.

### Can We Explore Without Destroying?

Of all stages of mining, exploration is the least destructive, and only a small portion of surveyed land ever ends up being mined. Indeed, all the mining done in the course of U.S. history has involved a mere 0.3 percent of our total land area. Of the 2.3 billion acres in the fifty states, 6 million are used in mining—about the same amount used for airports and railroads—whereas 1.3 billion acres are used for farmland, and 24 million for highways.

Further, some miners contend that even the extraction phase can be done so as to protect, and even enhance, the land. "The operation of a mine," writes Stanford geologist Charles Park, "does not have to lead to the defacement or destruction of natural beauty or wildlife. Some of the most beautiful and best managed lands in the world are to be found around the mines of central Europe."

American miners point with pride to former mine sites in the Southwest that were turned into lovely parks, and to reclaimed land in Indiana that now has a more fruitful crop yield than it had before mining was done beneath its soil. Mineral economist Franz Dykstra contends that the old rapacious days are over, and that most mining executives are glad of it. "Most of us got into mining because we love the out-of-doors," he said. "We know more about environmental impact than most of the environmentalists, and we probably care more. Mining people are not a bunch of tyrannical thieves. Environmentalists have done a good job in making this a point of awareness; things are much better now, and it is possible to satisfy both sets of priorities."

### The Conservation Argument

Naturally, it will be quite difficult to convince the large and vocal environmental lobby that miners love the land they rip apart. Affectionate platitudes can easily be dismissed as so much public relations—the ecological equivalent of a segregationist claiming that some of his best friends are black. Give miners an inch, some fear, and they will dig up a mile.

For one thing, environmentalists disagree with the industry's estimates regarding the percentage of public land that cannot be mined or explored. Depending on how you read the figures, they contend, you can juggle them to show, not 70 percent withdrawn or restricted, but as little as 30 percent. The industry's figures, the Sierra Club claims, are out-of-date—gathered before the Alaska Lands Bill was finalized and another 50 to 100 million acres were released—and they also lump all restrictions, even trivial ones, together. Further, at least 23 million acres of public land that cannot be used to mine metals have not been set aside as wilderness. Rather, they are reserved for extracting oil shale or nonmetal minerals, such as phosphorus.

Environmentalists also claim that any time a significant mineral argument has been raised, the government released the land in question to permit development. The original Wilderness Act, passed in 1964, allowed for new mining claims up to 1984. Twenty years, conservationists feel, is ample time to explore, and any claim can be developed as long as it is done with "minimum degradation" to public land. If little mining has been done on public land, they believe, it is not because it has been off limits, but because very little of it has anything that can be mined economically. Of the land areas surveyed by the U.S. Geological Survey, 69 percent were declared as having no mineral potential. Much more remains to be surveyed.

Perhaps the inevitable confrontation might be resolved by

a comprehensive inventory of the mineral potential of restricted land. Until everyone agrees on just what lies beneath the surface, consensus is unlikely.

### If Public Land Is Opened Up

In the long run, any significant changes in public land policy could change the strategic metals picture, since new discoveries would lessen our import dependence, alter stockpiling practices, and perhaps cause changes in consumption patterns. Any immediate impact is likely to center on two key metals— cobalt and the platinum group.

The Blackbird Mine in Idaho, owned by Noranda Mines of Canada, is known to contain large deposits of cobalt; indeed, it was once a working mine. The land adjacent to the mining district might contain significant deposits also, and for that reason the boundaries of the River of No Return Wilderness Area were pushed back after the second Shaba incident and much hue and cry in Congress. There are still areas that cannot be explored, however, and some industry representatives would like to see the remaining restrictions removed. But environmentalists point out that the Blackbird Mine has not produced in years, not because of governmental restrictions, but because it is cheaper to import cobalt at present prices. If we do start producing cobalt domestically, the public land issue may become significant.

The Stillwater Complex in Montana, perhaps the largest single deposit of platinum group metals in the world, could conceivably provide 25 to 30 percent of our palladium needs and 9 percent of our platinum needs by 1986. Containing potential for chromite, nickel, and copper as well, Stillwater is currently being assessed by companies with claims in the geologic area. But parts of the area are on national forest land and cannot be explored because to do so would require drilling, which is forbidden. If that land is freed up, and if it is determined to contain economic deposits, it might have an impact on the platinum group market, and possibly on the chromium one as well. However, it should be remembered that economic factors might play a more important role in these matters than land policy.

Mining executives feel that even if the land is not used immediately, preliminary work will help prevent panic and unpreparedness if foreign supplies are threatened in the future.

Conservationists, on the other hand, feel that keeping the miners away will avert reckless development—which, they point out, cannot be reversed—and also preserve minerals in the ground for an uncertain future.

Given the complexion of the Reagan Administration, changes can be expected, although pressure from environmentalists and Democratic Congressmen may keep them minimal. If Secretary Watt has his way, miners will be able to stake claims on public land well past the current 1984 deadline; he wants to extend it by twenty years. Watt appears to be serious about his stated desire of making his chief legacy the bolstering of strategic minerals reserves.

## CLEAN AIR VS. MINERALS

In September 1980, Anaconda, one of the nation's oldest and largest mining firms, shut down its smelter and refinery in Montana. The reason, according to the company, was that it could not risk the expenditure of the $400 million needed to comply with pollution standards. The firm had already spent $60 million on compliance and could not be sure the additional modifications would be sufficient. As a result of Anaconda's decision, 1,500 workers lost their jobs, and this somewhat preposterous situation was created: Anaconda now loads its copper concentrates onto railroad cars bound for San Diego; from there the material is shipped all the way to Japan, where it is smelted and converted to wire tubing and sheet metal; then it is shipped back to the United States for sale.

The mining lobby has milked that story for all it is worth. To miners, it illustrates how destructive to business U.S. environmental regulations are. Unemployment, foreign dependency, and other economic costs, they feel, are too high to pay for pollution standards that many consider unrealistic in the first place. They believe the policies are dominated by procedural convolutions that are time-wasting and prohibitively complex. The executives have sympathetic ears in Washington now.

According to one estimate, there are currently eighty different laws administered by twenty different federal agencies that directly or indirectly affect mining. Of these, there are twenty major environmental statutes, administered by ten agencies. The industry maintains that compliance expenditures have eaten away at funds badly needed for replacing equipment, research and development, and other critical functions.

Smelting and refining are particularly unclean operations, and even the staunchest supporter of deregulation would not suggest a return to the reckless ways of the past. If nothing else, it would be bad politics to take any position other than one of concern for clean air and worker safety. The spirit of environmental regulation, therefore, is unchallenged. It is the letter of it that makes the issue volatile. "Environmental, health and safety goals conflict with the objectives of national minerals policy not by their nature, nor their desirable objectives," states a report issued by the Santini Subcommittee, "but through uncertainty, delay, excessive costs and the snuffing out of innovative approaches to problem solving."

Basically, the industry contends that existing procedures are too cumbersome, ambiguous, and inflexible; promulgated without sufficient knowledge of the industries affected; based on standards that are often unfeasible and of questionable validity. Further, because of U.S. tax law, companies have it more difficult than their counterparts in countries like Japan and Germany, where depreciation procedures for antipollution equipment ease the burden.

### The Impact of Regulation

H. Stanley Dempsey, Vice President of AMAX, Inc., presented Congress with an analysis of the impact of regulations on mineral goals. Those goals are: to secure an adequate supply; to obtain minerals at a reasonable price; to rely on the private sector for production. Against these objectives, the impact of various regulatory provisions were analyzed and presented as shown opposite.

These are, of course, industry assertions, and as such can be regarded with skepticism. But the Reagan Administration is clearly more sympathetic than its predecessors. Until now, regulatory agencies and affected industries acted as adversaries; cooperation and trust are likely to increase over the next four years, and the adversarial role will be played by environmental organizations and the Democratic opposition. In addition to eliminating some regulations and streamlining others, the Administration is likely to push for greater control by state and local governments and to make cost-effectiveness a major component of all decisions.

| Environmental Policy Elements | Mineral Policy Goals | | |
|---|---|---|---|
| | Adequate Supply | Reasonable Price | Private Sector |
| CZMA — Coastal Zone Management Act | No impact | No impact | Minimal impact |
| ESA — Endangered Species Act | Minimal impact | Minimal impact | Minimal impact |
| W&SR — Wild and Scenic Rivers Act | Minimal impact | No impact | No impact |
| HCRS — Heritage, Conservation, and Recreational Service | Minimal impact | Minimal impact | No impact |
| MSHA — Mine Safety and Health Act | Significant impact | Significant impact | Severe impact (major disruption) |
| OSHA — Occupational Safety and Health Act | Severe impact (major disruption) | Severe impact (major disruption) | Severe impact (major disruption) |
| SDWA — Safe Drinking Water Act | Minimal impact | Minimal impact | No impact |
| TSCA — Toxic Substances Control Act | Minimal impact | Minimal impact | Minimal impact |
| RCRA — Resource Conservation and Recovery Act | Significant impact | Severe impact (major disruption) | Severe impact (major disruption) |
| CWA — Clean Water Act | Severe impact (major disruption) | Severe impact (major disruption) | Severe impact (major disruption) |
| CAA — Clean Air Act | Severe impact (major disruption) | Severe impact (major disruption) | Severe impact (major disruption) |

Legend:
- ○ No impact
- ⊕ Minimal impact
- ◑ Significant impact, causing delays and additional costs
- ◕ Severe impact, causing major disruption, cost increases, and delays
- ● Severe impact, causing foreclosure, inability to operate

As submitted to the Nonfuel Minerals Policy Review, Part II, House Subcommittee on Mines and Mining, 96th Congress, First Session.

**Figure 4.** *Impact of Environmental Programs on Mineral Policy Goals*

Industry leaders are pushing for greater self-regulation. Standards would be set by the government, but the method of compliance would be left to industry, which feels it can do a better job, and more economically, if left to its own devices. With the government issuing strict engineering and design criteria, unfeasible or uneconomic practices abound and the ingenuity of private industry is stifled, critics feel. They will also push for lowering standards to what they consider a more realistic level, and for stricter verification procedures on studies that determine those standards. And they want to streamline the process of obtaining permits, which they feel has been characterized by long and costly delays, leading to the sort of uncertainty that stifles economic growth.

**But the Public Wants Clean Air**
Despite a sympathetic and determined Administration, and a public that seems eager for industrial revitalization, wholesale changes in environmental regulations may not be easy to achieve. The American people clearly want clean air and water, and workers will not backtrack readily on agreements that protect their health and safety. While we also want less inflation, more jobs, and continued abundance, few are convinced that we have to compromise the public health to get them. Business leaders, including those in the metals and mining industry, have yet to persuade the public that regulation is the main villain, or that there aren't ways to have both economic growth and strict compliance.

Indeed, there are indications that the public is not of a mind to let industry have its way; no one has forgotten that there were good reasons for instituting regulations in the first place, and there is no assurance that deregulation won't bring about a return to the careless past. An opinion poll of Arizona residents, for example, showed that 60.3 percent do not favor relaxing air and water standards, even if doing so means stimulating economic growth. (Arizona is one of the leading smelting and refining locations in the country.) Nor is it clear that "cost-effectiveness" means as much to the public as it does to business. How does one measure the "cost" of dirty air or unsafe working conditions? The U.S. Supreme Court, in a recent ruling confirming federal standards on cotton-dust exposure, decided that the benefit of worker health must be placed above "all other considerations," including cost. Justice William J. Brennan wrote, "The legislative history [of the

Occupational Safety and Health Administration's law] demonstrates conclusively that Congress was fully aware that the act would impose real and substantial costs of compliance on industry and believed that such costs were part of the cost of doing business."

The Supreme Court ruling might serve as a signal that it will not be easy to undo the regulatory apparatus, at least not without prolonged Congressional debate. The Sierra Club, the Wilderness Society, and others are gearing up for a battle, and they represent a formidable lobby with considerable public support.

### Will We Keep the Clean Air Act?
The first major test will be the Clean Air Act, which expired in September 1981. A cornerstone of environmental legislation, the act is, as we write, the focal point of a major brouhaha. Environmentalists will concede nothing except some streamlining measures—they agree that some of the apparatus is overly cumbersome, but feel that the law as it stands is fair, and in fact has not been enforced rigorously enough. Proposed changes, they feel, will weaken standards and jeopardize the health of those who most need protection: the very young, the very old, and those with existing health problems.

As for the industry's contention that the act has damaged their economic standing, environmentalists don't buy it. While they acknowledge that delays have been bothersome, they point out that no permits for new facilities have ever been denied since the Clean Air Act came into being in 1970. The infamous Anaconda closing, they contend, was not forced by environmental costs, but other factors. According to David Gardiner of the Sierra Club, a study by the EPA and the Montana State Legislature found that regulations were a "relatively minor" component in the closing. Gardiner contends that a major part of the excessive costs and delays the industry complains about come from their own attempts to sidestep the law.

At the moment, the Clean Air Act is being rewritten in both Senate and House committees. The Administration and industry lobbyists are expected to weaken the revisions made by the Senate Environment Committee and lean toward the House version, which is said to have taken much of the bite out of the original act. By the time this book is published, both bills will probably have come to the floor of House and Senate, but the debate is expected to be fierce before a compromise is achieved. The final outcome might have a significant impact on the domestic mining industry.

We may have underestimated the economic costs of regulation, just as we previously underestimated the social costs of unrestrained development. Or, quite possibly, environmentalists fail to realize how much the things we hold dear hinge on access to minerals. Indeed, one of the great ironies in the debate is that some of the metals that miners want to produce more of are needed to clean up the air; chromium and platinum are vital components of antipollution equipment.

On the other hand, the industry and the Administration may be forced to take a different approach to easing the pressure created by environmental standards. A well-informed public might just ask, "If other countries can do it, why can't we?" Japan, Germany, Canada, and other industrial nations spend proportionately as much on pollution control as we do. Indeed, the Japanese and Germans have even stricter environmental standards, and yet manage to outproduce us.

After all is said and done, we will probably see important changes in environmental regulations, and these will make life easier for domestic producers. But the changes may not be as sweeping as the industry would like.

## STOCKING UP, PILING ON

In the 1930s, while Japan, Germany, and Italy were stocking up on strategic minerals, the United States, wary of involvement in another foreign war, decided against doing so. We started a National Defense Stockpile in 1939, but it was a desultory effort, and when war came the United States was forced into emergency measures that, while ultimately successful, were costly and wasteful. The lesson was not lost. In 1946, Congress enacted the Strategic and Critical Materials Stock Piling Act, designed to decrease "dangerous and costly dependence" in times of crisis. During the Korean War, the act was used to increase production of materials and stockpile them in key locations around the country.

Since then, the stockpile has, in the words of the American Mining Congress, "suffered from constant tinkering with stockpile goals for reasons unrelated to national security." Various administrations have used stockpile acquisitions to stimulate foreign trade, to bolster domestic employment, to meet peacetime industrial needs, or to control prices and buffer inflation. According to some experts, this "tinkering" has disrupted the market at various times, resulting in dangerous shortages. The Santini Subcommittee report states, "The heavy liquidation of stockpiled commodities during the 1960s, for example, was a factor in inhibiting expansion of new mineral capacity, which helped to bring about the major shortages of 1973–74."

At one time, the report points out, the cobalt stockpile contained more than 102 million pounds. Then, a government faced with budget deficits reduced the stockpile goals, and much of what we had was declared surplus. Between 1964 and 1975, 60 million pounds were sold. This may have helped keep inflation down, but it also kept the price of cobalt down, discouraging producers from making investments. When the Ford Administration later raised the cobalt stockpile goal to 85.4 million pounds, only 40.8 million were left of the 102 we started with. We were faced with filling a huge stockpile deficit at drastically inflated prices.

**The Revised Stockpile Act**

To correct this situation, the Strategic and Critical Materials Stock Piling Revision Act of 1979 reaffirmed the need for stockpiles, and mandated that "the purpose of the stockpile is to serve the interest of national defense only, and is not to be used for economic or budgetary purposes." As it now stands, the stockpile goal for each of the ninety-three materials singled out by the government is based on the amount the nation would need during a three-year conventional war.

The separation of strategic and economic needs suits most experts just fine; they feel an economic stockpile would be susceptible to political manipulation and could cause unnecessary price volatility. Others have argued in favor of an economic stockpile as the only way industry can be sure of having what it needs. Theoretically, such a stockpile would exist as a separate entity from the defense stockpile and be used in the event of embargoes or other supply disruptions.

The National Commission of Supplies and Shortages studied the question and concluded that economic stockpiles would be too expensive, and that it would be too difficult to enforce price controls. The American Mining Congress concurs, adding that only with such critical and import-dependent minerals as cobalt, platinum, and manganese should an economic stockpile even be considered, and that if an economic stockpile were to be enacted it should be administered by a nonpolitical entity chartered in a manner similar to the Federal Reserve Board.

Current opinions make it highly unlikely that a government-run economic stockpile will come about. Experts seem

## SELECTED STOCKPILE GOALS (DESIRED INVENTORY MIX) AND INVENTORIES AS OF JANUARY 1, 1981

| | Units* | Goal | Inventory |
|---|---|---|---|
| Aluminum metal group | ST Al | 7,150,000 | 3,444,06 |
| Alumina | — | 0 | |
| Aluminum | ST | 700,000 | 1,73 |
| Bauxite, metal-grade, Jamaica-type | LDT | 21,000,000 | 8,858,88 |
| Bauxite, metal-grade, Surinam-type | LDT | 6,100,000 | 5,299,59 |
| Antimony | ST | 36,000 | 40,73 |
| Bauxite, refractory | LCT | 1,400,000 | 174,59 |
| Beryllium metal group | ST Be Metal | 1,220 | 1,06 |
| Beryl ore 11% BeO | ST | 18,000 | 17,98 |
| Beryllium copper master alloy | ST | 7,900 | 7,38 |
| Beryllium metal | ST | 400 | 22 |
| Bismuth | Lb | 2,200,000 | 2,081,29 |
| Cadmium | Lb | 11,700,000 | 6,328,80 |
| Chromite, refractory-grade ore | SDT | 850,000 | 391,41 |
| Chromium, chemical and metallurgical group | ST Cr Metal | 1,353,000 | 1,173,23 |
| Chromite, chemical-grade ore | SDT | 675,000 | 242,41 |
| Chromite, metallurgical-grade ore | SDT | 3,200,000 | 2,488,04 |
| Chromium, ferro, high-carbon | ST | 185,000 | 402,69 |
| Chromium, ferro, low-carbon | ST | 75,000 | 318,89 |
| Chromium, ferro, silicon | ST | 90,000 | 58,35 |
| Chromium, metal | ST | 20,000 | 3,76 |
| Cobalt† | Lb Co | 85,400,000 | 40,802,39 |
| Columbium group | Lb Cb Metal | 4,850,000 | 2,510,52 |
| Columbium carbide powder | Lb Cb | 100,000 | 21,37 |
| Columbium concentrates | Lb Cb | 5,600,000 | 1,780,46 |
| Columbium, ferro | Lb Cb | 0 | 930,91 |
| Columbium, metal | Lb Cb | 0 | 44,85 |
| Copper | ST | 1,000,000 | 29,04 |
| Fluorspar, acid-grade | SDT | 1,400,000 | 895,95 |
| Fluorspar, metallurgical-grade | SDT | 1,700,000 | 411,73 |
| Lead | ST | 1,100,000 | 601,03 |
| Manganese, chemical and metallurgical group | ST Mn Metal | 1,500,000 | 1,586,58 |
| Manganese ore, chemical-grade | SDT | 170,000 | 221,04 |
| Manganese ore, metallurgical-grade | SDT | 2,700,000 | 3,378,7 |
| Manganese, ferro, high-carbon | ST | 439,000 | 599,9 |
| Manganese, ferro, low-carbon | — | 0 | |
| Manganese, ferro, medium-carbon | ST | 0 | 28,9 |

to feel that there are better ways to help industry maintain large enough inventories to offset potential supply disruptions. Relief from the high operating costs that burden the mining industry would help considerably, as would lower interest rates. Further, adds Dr. John Morgan of the Bureau of Mines, tax laws could be amended to help industry stock up on its own. Currently, raw materials costs can be deducted only in the year they are used. In Sweden, by contrast, deductions can be made in the year of purchase.

| | Units* | Goal | Inventory |
|---|---|---|---|
| Manganese, ferro, silicon | ST | 0 | 23,574 |
| Manganese, metal, electrolytic | ST | 0 | 14,172 |
| Manganese dioxide, battery-grade group | SDT | 87,000 | 247,827 |
| Manganese, battery-grade, natural ore | SDT | 62,000 | 244,816 |
| Manganese, battery-grade, synthetic dioxide | SDT | 25,000 | 3,011 |
| Mercury | Flasks | 10,500 | 191,391 |
| Molybdenum group | — | 0 | 0 |
| Molybdenum disulfide | — | 0 | 0 |
| Molybdenum, ferro | — | 0 | 0 |
| Nickel | ST Ni + Co | 200,000 | 0 |
| Platinum group metals, iridium | Tr Oz | 98,000 | 16,991 |
| Platinum group metals, palladium | Tr Oz | 3,000,000 | 1,255,003 |
| Platinum group metals, platinum | Tr Oz | 1,310,000 | 452,640 |
| Rutile | SDT | 106,000 | 39,186 |
| Silicon carbide, crude | ST | 29,000 | 80,548 |
| Silver (fine) | Tr Oz | 0 | 139,500,000 |
| Tantalum group | Lb Ta Metal | 7,160,000 | 2,391,940 |
| Tantalum carbide powder | Lb Ta | 0 | 28,688 |
| Tantalum metal | Lb Ta | 0 | 201,133 |
| Tantalum minerals | Lb Ta | 8,400,000 | 2,551,302 |
| Thorium nitrate | Lb | 600,000 | 7,145,112 |
| Tin | LT | 42,000 | 200,452 |
| Titanium sponge | ST | 195,000 | 32,331 |
| Tungsten group | Lb W Metal | 50,666,000 | 81,216,792 |
| Tungsten carbide powder | Lb W | 2,000,000 | 2,032,942 |
| Tungsten, ferro | Lb W | 0 | 2,025,361 |
| Tungsten metal powder | Lb W | 1,600,000 | 1,898,911 |
| Tungsten ores and concentrates | Lb W | 55,450,000 | 88,436,637 |
| Vanadium group | ST V Metal | 8,700 | 541 |
| Vanadium, ferro | ST V | 1,000 | 0 |
| Vanadium pentoxide | ST V | 7,700 | 541 |
| Zinc | ST | 1,425,000 | 375,970 |

*ST = short tons; LDT = long dry tons; LCT = long calcinated tons; LT = long tons; SDT = short dry tons; T Oz = troy ounces.

†The purchase of 5.2 million pounds of cobalt in June 1981 brought the inventory up to 46,002,393 pounds.
**Source:** Federal Emergency Management Agency

### The Stockpile Is Deficient

As for the strategic stockpile, it is woefully short for about a third of the materials included. Cobalt, for example, is at only 53 percent of the desired level; titanium sponge is some 163,000 tons short of its 195,000-ton goal; platinum is about 65 percent short of its goal. Overall, it would take $12 billion at current prices to get the stocks up to desired levels; in some cases, supplies would run out in less than a year of conventional warfare.

Some of the materials currently in stock are of such low quality as to require replacement. They were purchased so long ago that they do not meet today's more stringent standards for advanced applications. Paul Krueger, head of the Resource Preparedness Office of the Federal Emergency Management Agency (FEMA), which sets stockpile goals and priorities, believes that "perhaps 10 percent might not meet today's quality standards." Others feel Krueger's estimate is overly optimistic.

### New Purchases for the Stockpile

During the Carter Administration, attempts to fund new acquisitions were denied. The lame-duck Congress of late 1980, after several compromises, agreed to allocate $100 million for fiscal 1981. President Reagan confirmed this early in his term, announcing that the funds would be used first to purchase cobalt, and that other commodities were being considered for future purchase. These include bauxite, columbium, fluorspar, nickel, platinum group, tantalum, titanium, and vanadium. In June 1981, the government purchased for $78 million 5.2 million pounds of cobalt, the first significant addition to the stockpile in more than twenty years.

Congressman Santini called the Reagan announcement a "substantive and symbolic beginning . . . long overdue." Mr. Krueger called it a "foot in the door," enabling FEMA to "get off the ground on a modest level." While $100 million sounds like a lot of money, it must be kept in mind that at that rate it would take 120 years to meet official goals. The cobalt alone would cost almost a billion dollars.

### How Are Stockpile Goals Determined?

Mr. Krueger explains how his office sets stockpile goals:

Basically, we use information which originates from many different departments and agencies, principally the Department of Defense, the Department of State, the Bureau of Mines at the Department of Interior, and the Department of Commerce. Given the scenario guidance that this should be a major three-year war, we find out what the Defense Department will use in the way of weapon systems and match this up with a very extensive civilian economic scenario. From this base, we estimate what the requirements for various metals and minerals are, and offset these requirements by what we perceive and estimate to be the available supply during wartime. Where the supply is insufficient to meet the needs of the Nation, in not only the military, but also the essential civilian and industrial needs, we would establish a stockpile goal for the material in question.

Each year, an interagency committee, chaired by Krueger, draws up a shopping list based on goals, deficits, excesses, and current market conditions. Senior level staff from various departments determine the plan, based exclusively on strategic considerations. Materials for which inventory and domestic production is low and defense needs are high are given top priority—hence the decision to begin acquisitions with cobalt.

## How Stockpile Transactions Are Made

Budget requests have to be approved by Congress. No money can be spent unless it has been earned through the sale of surplus items in the stockpile. The $100 million allocated in 1981 was earned from the sale of a variety of items, chiefly tungsten and industrial diamonds. The $120 million requested for fiscal 1982 had to be covered by selling some of the estimated $6 to $7 billion in surplus materials now in stock, much of which is tin and silver. Tin is now being sold; silver sales, however, have been postponed pending hearings.

Written into the stockpile policy is a provision that purchases and sales are to be made without disrupting markets. Whenever possible, purchases are made when the market is slack, and sales are made when the market is tight and materials are in short supply. It doesn't always work out that way, as we shall see later, but overall the American Mining Congress has given the government high marks for avoiding market disruptions. The administration of transactions—as well as storage, security, maintenance, and other managerial functions—is the charge of the General Services Administration (GSA).

For the most part, the GSA acts like any other consumer, trying to strike as good a deal as possible for each transaction. When purchasing, the GSA solicits bids and proposals from sellers. These might include registered representatives of foreign companies and sometimes foreign governments. Solicitations come in, and the best bids are followed up with negotiations. Sometimes, several sources are used and materials of varying grades and stages of processing are purchased. The cobalt purchase was made entirely from Zaire, at well below the official producer price.

### The Future of Stockpiling

Most authorities close to the mineral scene feel that the situation has improved considerably since FEMA and the GSA were created in 1978 and the Stockpile Act was passed in 1979. Materials set aside now can be used only under certain circumstances: on the order of the President; on the order of certain other officials; in time of war or national emergency. In some cases, FEMA might recommend release of materials to the President. For example, the Defense Department might ask FEMA to apply for Presidential approval to release a key material for defense acquisitions during peacetime.

The stockpile program may seem to be a simple matter of buying what is needed and selling surplus. In fact, it is awash with politics—different agencies and officials have conflicting interests—and arcane budgetary convolutions. Overall, everyone seems to be in favor of maintaining stocks, but just how to fund the purchases and what criteria should be applied are controversial matters. So far no one seems ready to allocate the big bucks needed to meet stockpile goals, and it is highly unlikely they will come from tax revenues. Said one spokesman, "The reality has not matched the rhetoric. If you don't see purchase levels of $400 to $500 million by 1985, the whole thing will have been a waste of time."

### Alternatives to Stockpile Purchases

Outright purchases, however, are not the only way to meet stockpile goals. Both Paul Krueger and John Morgan strongly feel that domestic production should be encouraged as part of the national minerals policy. "The creation or enlargement of domestic productive capacity," says Dr. Morgan, "if it can be done at reasonable prices, should in most cases provide greater flexibility than stockpiles. In fact, one ton of domestic productive capacity is equal to three tons of stockpiled material under current stockpile planning."

Essentially, if a good mine is in operation, stockpile goals for that metal can be lowered; production offers greater stability in the long run. Krueger believes that a careful blend of stockpile acquisitions and enhanced domestic production is the most cost-effective way of reaching national objectives, except for certain metals, such as chromium, that are too expensive to mine at this time.

### The Defense Production Act

A good mechanism for stimulating domestic production already exists, experts believe, in the Defense Production Act of 1950. Title I of the act provides specific authority for priorities and allocations as required by defense mobilization needs; Title III provides broad authority for expanding the supply of materials, through exploration, development, mining, research, and the allocation of loans and loan guarantees. During the Korean War, $8.4 billion worth of transactions were made under the act, with a probable real cost of less than one billion. Says Dr. Morgan, "In a few years these programs doubled U.S. aluminum production, increased U.S. copper mine capacity by a quarter, initiated U.S. nickel mining, created the titanium industry, quadrupled U.S. tungsten mining, and greatly expanded the world columbium-tantalum mining and processing industries, as well as expanding supplies of many other materials for production needs and stockpiles." The act has not been used since 1967.

Some form of guaranteed government purchase arrangement—for example, where the government agrees to purchase a specific quantity over a fixed period of time at a set price— would, experts feel, significantly stimulate domestic production and help meet stockpile goals. Experts feel that Noranda might forge ahead faster with its Idaho mine if such an agreement were announced for cobalt; with the stockpile goal 39.7 million pounds short, it would seem to be in the government's interest. Where to get the money to pay for guaranteed purchases is the major obstacle.

FEMA already has the authority to apply the Defense Production Act, but has no money with which to do it. Mr. Krueger is trying to find a way to work out the budget obstacles, which he characterizes as a "sticky mechanical problem" rather than a matter of policy. For the moment, stockpile acquisitions will move ahead, but slowly, and other FEMA programs will creep along without the budget needed for large-scale action. However, if the resource war heats up, and the Reagan Administration places the stockpile higher on the priority list, government influence on the market could increase. The market implications of stockpiling are discussed in Part II.

## INVENTION AND INNOVATION

In 1942, German railway locomotives were made with 2.3 metric tons of copper; a year and a half later, a tenth of that amount was used. Early in World War II, German submarines used 56 tons of copper; later they were made with only 26 tons. Pressed by shortages in critical materials, German ingenuity was charged with finding new ways to build things. Plentiful materials were used in place of scarce ones, equipment was redesigned, scrap was recycled—to save not just copper, but scarce ferroalloys as well. More vanadium and silicon were used, for these were abundant. As a result, the monstrous German war machine was able to press on longer than it might have otherwise.

The United States too was pressed to unleash its national imagination. When Nazi submarines disrupted shipments of bauxite from Dutch Guiana, we learned to use lesser-quality bauxite mined in Arkansas for the aluminum needed to build planes. When the Japanese conquered Malaya in 1942, our rubber supply was cut off. Since there are no rubber trees in the United States, we were forced to come up with a substitute. The result was synthetic rubber, which not only helped us win the war but had important civilian uses as well. Rubber technology continues to be critical to this day, in fact, as we still get the natural form from unstable Southeast Asia. Since synthetics are inadequate for certain applications, and since they are derived from exorbitantly priced petroleum, scientists are experimenting with other alternatives, such as a plant called guayule.

### Technology Can Affect Supplies
The foregoing are only a few examples of technical innovation changing the supply/demand picture. There are number of ways this can occur: new manufacturing processes can cut raw materials waste; new product design might require less of a

given mineral and more of another; better-quality products might mean less frequent replacement; recycling methods can be introduced; users might learn to substitute a cheaper and more abundant mineral for another.

In addition, scarcity can be overcome by new ways of detecting deposits; techniques to improve extraction methods; reaching previously inaccessible ores; reducing waste; and utilizing low-grade ores.

Research in all these areas is going on all the time, although everyone wishes it were better funded and better coordinated. At any moment, an important breakthrough can be announced that has profound implications for the market. Whether the effects will be accurately predicted, however, is another matter. Often, the obvious does not occur, since these events are more complex than they appear on the surface. For one thing, just because a new procedure is perfected does not mean it will be applied. It will have to be judged cost-effective.

### Technology Can Reduce Demand

In the decade ending in 1979, the consumption of copper increased by only 32 percent, more than a third less than the previous decade's increase. According to George B. Munroe, Chairman and President of Phelps Dodge, a major reason for the reduced growth rate was the "substitution of cheaper competing materials, such as aluminum and plastics, in some applications, and economization in the use of copper." The telecommunications industry, for example, invented processes that enabled it to transmit over existing facilities messages that previously would have required additional copper wiring. Manufacturers learned to use thinner-gauge wire and thinner tubing, and to substitute semiconductor circuits for mechanical switching devices and hand-wired circuits that use more copper. Now the demand for copper may be reduced still further with the development of fiber optics, a technique by which information is transmitted along hair-thin cables of glass. The chief components of this new technology are oxygen and silicon, the two most abundant elements on earth.

But many times a decrease in demand from one source will be accompanied by an increase elsewhere. Developing nations, for example, are stepping up their use of copper dramatically. And industrialized nations are finding new applications for the venerable metal, such as in solar energy devices and electric vehicles. Further, any substantial reindustrialization or

THE ONCE AND FUTURE RESOURCE WAR / **144**

increase in defense spending usually portends increased copper use. Finally, while plastic and aluminum have replaced copper in the past, the increased cost of petroleum, from which plastics are made, and the large amount of energy needed to use aluminum might reverse that trend.

The copper example provides a good illustration of the many variables that affect the relationship between technology and supply/demand. Cost is a big factor, for it not only serves as an incentive for research and development, but it also determines whether a new procedure will be applied. In any given instance, there is a point at which a new procedure becomes economically feasible. Sometimes the equation can get complicated. Once it was assumed that lightweight, abundant metals such as aluminum and magnesium would replace heavier metals such as steel. So they did, for a while. Then the high energy costs of producing the lighter metals slowed the substitution process. Yet in some instances, the lighter metals are still the cost-effective choice—in transportation, for example, where the energy savings in use outweigh the extra cost of production.

**Technology Can Affect Different Metals in Different Ways**
Making the situation even more complex is the fact that an innovation can decrease demand or increase supply of one metal and precipitate exactly the opposite for another. For example, a new mining procedure may make it possible to use lower-grade ores of a certain metal, thus increasing its supply; but the procedure itself might necessitate an increased use of, say, tungsten to make drills strong enough to get to the ore. Similarly, advanced electronic equipment may mandate the consumption of certain rare metals with special properties, such as gallium or beryllium. But the same technology might enable manufacturers to improve the design of their products and thereby cut down on consumption of other metals. Or the new technology might lead to social changes that affect supply and demand: advanced communications equipment might cut down the need for business travel, thus affecting materials use in the transportation industry; electronic sensing devices might reduce waste in manufacturing, thus cutting down demand for some metals; integrated circuits can lead to miniaturization, so that the same function can be performed by a product that requires less raw material to build. The work

of a pocket calculator, for example, once required a large, bulky computer.

After the Shaba shock of 1978, industries began to find ways of doing without cobalt. Television manufacturers devised new cobalt-free magnets. The electronics industry began to use barium and strontium alloys in loudspeakers. Engine makers used nickel in some parts and stepped up the recycling of cobalt. Most of the changes were based on techniques that had already been known, but were not worth instituting until the invasion shook up the cobalt users.

But you can't wait for a price change or a revolution to begin looking for alternatives. For that reason, basic research is proceeding at all times in private industry—and in government agencies as well, since mineral availability is crucial to national defense. Both are hurting for funds, but nevertheless experimentation is underway that could affect supply and demand down the road.

## DEVELOPMENTS IN EXTRACTION METHODS

Microwave, radar, infrared, and ultraviolet technologies have created new sensing devices. Some of the 2,500 communications satellites now orbiting the globe are capable of detecting an undiscovered mineral deposit that ground-level procedures might pass over. The Columbia space shuttle is expected to extend our capacity to survey the earth and sea. In addition, advances in the knowledge of how ores are formed are proving useful in discovering new deposits. At any moment, major deposits hitherto unknown might be announced—or kept quiet, if secrecy suits the discoverer.

Both the U.S. Bureau of Mines and private industry sponsor research on mining technology designed to maximize resource recovery and cut costs. Techniques for improving the way mine shafts are sunk and rocks are broken are always being investigated, as are ways to manage materials and people underground. For fifty years, the Bureau of Mines has been researching ways to produce aluminum from inferior sources found in the United States. It is also researching ways to use submarginal nickel deposits in California and Oregon and ways to make economic the use of ilmenite in producing titanium. One important project has to do with extracting chrome, nickel, and cobalt from laterite deposits. These are residual geologic deposits created in ancient times by the leaching away of other materials by acid rain. Laterite could one day be a major source of those metals.

We are also learning how to dig deeper into the earth. It is felt that below 5 kilometers large deposits of manganese, chromium, cobalt, nickel, and other metals can be found. Sophisticated engineering procedures are being used to create instruments that can get to those ores. Such equipment will have to withstand extreme heat and pressure, thus mandating the use of superstrength alloys—metals being used to get metals.

Will we ever get to those deep ores? Experts believe that technology will inevitably conquer the challenge. The real questions are: When will it happen? And will we use the technology once it is available? Those questions will be settled largely by cost factors. In any event, unless economics and politics intervene to change the timetable, the technology is thought to be two decades away.

## SUBSTITUTION

Users of metals are constantly trying to cut down on expensive or scarce metals by finding ways to use cheaper, more abundant metals to perform the same job. Advances made by private sources are seldom revealed prematurely, to avoid losing the finder's competitive edge. Surprises, therefore, are possible.

Fundamental research is seeking a better understanding of corrosion, which accounts for the replacement of more than $20 billion worth of materials a year. A substantial portion of the steel we produce is used to replace rusted and corroded steel. Research, therefore, could one day lead to a longer life for metals, and decreased demand for some alloys and increased use of more efficient substitutes.

### Looking for New Alloys
The search is on for cheap, abundant materials that can form alloys with great strength and durability. Interchangeable metals would spread out demand and provide some insurance against shortages. In fact, some substitutions might be non-metals for metals. Plastics, polymers, and other new com-

pounds might fulfill roles typically played by metals, particularly in appliances and automobiles. Ceramics also offers promising possibilities, with some metal parts already being replaced in engines and cutting tools. Composites of various materials are also being examined. The use of thermoplastics, for example—mixtures of glass fibers and polymer—has been growing rapidly.

In February 1981, *Fortune* reported that new methods for producing alloys might one day lower the need for chromium, cobalt, and other strategic materials. Called metallic glasses, the superalloys are produced by several methods, the most promising of which, according to *Fortune*, is rapid quenching, in which alloys of iron and inexpensive substances such as silicon are frozen in their liquid state. The substances emerge with various properties depending on the speed at which they are cooled. One, sold by Allied Chemical under the name Metglas, is "three to four times as strong as the toughest steel alloys and up to 100 times as corrosion-resistant as the best stainless."

However, metallic glass cannot be used in high-temperature applications because it becomes brittle. Microcrystalline alloys, produced with slower cooling, are less corrosion-resistant but are tougher and can withstand higher temperatures. According to *Fortune*, microcrystalline bars cost no more than alloys made with cobalt, tungsten, or molybdenum, and in some applications last as much as four times as long. The magazine reports that more than 100 manufacturers are testing these new materials, and producers are working on ways to use them to coat ordinary metals, thus increasing the resistance of those now in use.

Scientists in the defense and aerospace industries are attempting to create useful alloys with common metals (such as silicon, aluminum, boron, and carbon) for use in engine blades, aircraft skins, and other products that now use metals which are in short supply. Such new alloys may ultimately force down the demand for some of the critical metals on which we are import-dependent. Also, new weaponry will require new raw materials. For example, new alloys will have to be found to further strengthen armor plating on tanks and planes in order to resist laser weapons. When such an alloy is found, the demand for the materials involved could soar, depending on current defense policies.

**Substitutes for Platinum?**
One of the metals most vulnerable to geopolitical shenanigans is platinum, which is of crucial importance as a catalyst in oil refining and other industrial processes. Scientists are now looking for ways to use common iron in this capacity, and are hopeful of success before the year 2000. Platinum is also used in the conversion of hydrogen-rich fuel cells into electricity, an energy source that experts hope will decrease oil consumption. But in 1976 it was concluded that if the nation were to use that method to produce 10 percent of its electricity in 1990, we could consume one-third to one-half the world's platinum production each year in the process. In anticipation of that problem, scientists have been developing nickel-based electrodes to do the work of platinum catalysts.

Platinum's sister metal, palladium, is used as a contact material in the millions of electromagnetic relays used in telephone systems. Since palladium costs so much, scientists have been looking for substitutes for half a century, but with little success. The only functional alternative is an alloy of 60 percent palladium and 40 percent silver. However, new switching systems are expected gradually to replace the electromagnetic relays now in use, thereby eliminating the need for palladium. This is an example of what technicians call "functional substitution"; substituting for the metal itself is called "material substitution."

**Replacing Cobalt and Other Metals**
Among other research projects currently underway are experiments to replace cobalt in magnets with combinations of more common metals such as iron and copper. Since 20 percent of U.S. cobalt consumption is for permanent magnets, success in that research could have a major impact on the cobalt market. Chromium supply is a major concern, and current research is focused on replacing it in high-strength steel. The Bureau of Mines is experimenting with something called ion implantation, which would, if ultimately feasible, cut down on chrome usage considerably. Composite materials using aluminum and copper are being investigated by the Defense Department as substitutes for titanium. As much as half the titanium used in certain applications might be saved, experts feel, but the Defense Department says it would take five years and $100 million to explore and develop the process. Defense also uses

30 tons of beryllium a year, mainly in components of guidance systems. Composites are being explored tht could save as much as $185 million a year. Developing a feasible substitute, however, would take five years and $34 million.

### Don't Count on Substitutes

As these brief examples illustrate, substitution possibilities abound; given ample time, incentive, and money, researchers can be expected to have a strong influence on the metals market in the future. The trick is to know how a given innovation will affect each metal, and when. This is not always easy. The time factor is one uncertain element; it might take years from the time of discovery to actual application, and some inventions that receive a great deal of fanfare may never see the light of day. Indeed, many of the projects described in this chapter won't yield anything practical until the next century. The hot discoveries described by *Fortune*, for example, hardly raise an eyebrow among government officials, who see them at this point as romantic visions.

Further, the unexpected has a way of cropping up. For example, the price of cadmium doubled in 1980 when it was expected to be used widely in batteries. Then it was found to be carcinogenic and prices tumbled, leading to heavy losses for investors.

For all these reasons, resource warriors do not buy the argument that technology will protect us from supply shortages. "Large-scale substitutions," contends the Santini Subcommittee report, "often cited, sometimes glibly, as a solution to major interruptions of foreign mineral supplies, could result in major dislocations of the economy, and could only be accomplished through an allocation process under Government control. Moreover, seldom can the availability of substitutes in sufficient quantities be guaranteed, or can it be fully known how decreased performance through their use affects such things as productivity."

Experts believe that some of the most important functions of metals on which we are most import-dependent are simply irreplaceable. We come once again to the riches of southern Africa: chromium, manganese, cobalt, vanadium, and the platinum group. According to the National Research Council it would take fifteen years to substitute for chromium significantly, given today's technology. For stainless steel there are no alternatives. Nor can manganese be replaced in its steel-making function.

In some cases, the impediment to substitution is a big one: loss of quality. Fifty years of research on palladium alternatives in relay systems did not come up totally empty. Scientists did find other materials to do the job, but their performance and reliability were significantly inferior.

The same is apparently true with chromium, cobalt, and other strategics. Dr. Edgar Cruft of Nord Resources pointed out that the failure rate of a jet engine, based on material cracking or breaking, should be no more than one failure per 100,000 hours of flying. As a further safeguard, airlines are required to replace engines every 5,000 hours. To a passenger, those figures are comforting. But suppose an engine manufacturer replaced the cobalt or chrome in its product with titanium, the only feasible substitute. The failure rate, says Cruft, might then be one in every 2,000 to 3,000 hours, so great would be the loss of quality. Not so comforting. The substitution may be permissible for stainless steel silverware—who minds a broken fork?—but not in jet engines.

Can we reliably state that no feasible substitutions for those crucial functions exist? According to industry representatives, we can. The major strategics, they say, have been researched for years, as industry and government have not lacked for incentives. Some feel that chromium substitution has been investigated to 95 percent of its limit, enough to know that large-scale substitution is not feasible.

"You can't imagine the research that's been done," says mineral consultant Franz Dykstra. "By everybody—the steel industry, Bureau of Mines, universities. World War II drove us to an incredible effort." He adds that people in Washington who lack technical expertise too often make policy based on theoretical technological solutions that may have no practical utility.

We can probably expect to see moderate substitution in the next few years, but it would take a major research breakthrough or an explosive political/economic event for it to have a wide-ranging impact. But even small shifts in usage can affect prices, particularly over the long run.

The substitution possibilities for each metal are covered in Part III, and the various effects on the market are discussed in Part II.

## RECYCLING

According to metallurgists writing in *Science* magazine, an estimated 10 million pounds of chromium, 2.5 million pounds of nickel, and 250,000 pounds of molybdenum are lost each year in the waste products of stainless steel manufacturing. The *Washington Post* reported that "nearly three-quarters of the metals consumed in the U.S. are used just once and then thrown away." Such statistics are often cited as examples of American profligacy and to demonstrate that greater use of recycling can reduce our dependence on foreign materials.

In many respects the argument is a good one. Not only would we import less if we recycled more, but we would use less energy as well. It takes nearly twice as much energy to extract and process ores than it does to recycle the equivalent amount of waste. And there is definitely room for improvement: countries like West Germany and Japan make much greater use of scrap than we do. In fact, they make good use of *our* scrap.

### Recycling Depends on Cost

But once again science mixes with economics. Recycling can be expensive. If the price of a metal is high enough, companies will use whatever recycling methods are available. If the cost of purchasing raw materials is cheaper than recycling, they won't bother, even if it means depending on foreign suppliers. Also, if prices are high, recycling plants have the incentive to increase their reclamation activities. The social or strategic inadequacies of market motivation in this regard will have to be addressed by the government, perhaps through economic incentives to recycle.

### Obstacles to Recycling

The industry is upset by what it considers a form of public hypocrisy. The government wants it to recycle in order to conserve strategic metals. Yet it has mandated such stringent pollution standards that recycling—a dirty process by any standard—is less economic than ever. Since the advent of antipollution regulations, increased amounts of scrap have been exported, and companies have closed large recycling plants. Indeed, the United States is the only nation in the world to export stainless steel scrap, which contains large amounts of chrome and other metals. Not only do we lose valuable materials by exporting them, but the ones that find their way back here end up costing more.

Another potential problem with recycling is loss of quality. You can, for example, reuse waste elements created in the manufacture of jet engines, but you can't reuse them to make jet engines. Critical properties are lost in the process.

## The Future of Recycling

Because of rising costs, uncertain supplies, and national security, government and industry continue to do basic research on recycling technology. In the long run, it might prove an effective way to reduce import and consumption levels of major strategics, perhaps more effective than substitution, since it has the added advantage of leaving ores in the ground. Interest is picking up, and if regulatory changes alter the economics of recycling, it may pick up still more.

Two developments are worth keeping an eye on. The first is the conversion of flue dusts—waste products of steel manufacture—into usable nickel, chrome, and cobalt. Some companies are already using this process. According to the Bureau of Mines, flue dust conversion could be done on a large scale now, but the cost is too high.

There is a related technology that is finding increased use, and it could reduce total consumption significantly. Called "powder metallurgy," it is accomplished by reducing scrap metal to powder form, and then compacting the powder into the shape of the finished product—say, a part for an automobile transmission—under extreme pressure. One writer compared it to stamping cookies with a cookie cutter. The process reduces waste by about half: a pound of powdered metal will produce a product weighing almost a pound, whereas traditional methods would lose half a pound to waste. There has been concern over possible losses of quality, but industry officials claim that the strength and endurance of powdered products are virtually the same as with traditional processes. Further research will determine precisely how widespread the method is likely to become.

Recycling has the potential to cut down the consumption of raw strategic metals, but for that to happen the price of the metals or the uncertainty of supply will have to increase considerably.

## SEA AND SPACE

Someday, the present anxiety over some metals may be just a memory. Five-sixths of the earth is covered with water, and beneath much of it is a potential bonanza. Scattered about the ocean floor, at depths of 12,000 to 20,000 feet, are potato-shaped nodules containing copper, nickel, cobalt, and manganese. Some estimates project up to 100,000 tons of metal per square mile. Preliminary studies by a number of mining consortiums have led to the conclusion that deep-sea mining is technically feasible. Indeed, one of those consortiums, having spent $125 million during seventeen years of research, is willing to spend an additional $125 million on a pilot program and then to design and build one billion dollars' worth of equipment to mine the nodules. But no one will take the next step until the international politics of ocean mining are settled.

### The Law of the Sea
For the past decade, representatives of 158 nations have been locking horns in an attempt to hammer out an agreement on the use of the sea and its resources, which everyone seems to agree, however reluctantly, are "the common heritage of mankind." Achieving consensus on more concrete questions, however, has not been easy. Elliot Richardson, U.S. Ambassador to the conference during the Carter years, characterized the negotiations as "by far the toughest that I've ever had any part in" (and his career has included four cabinet posts with Nixon and Ford). Despite the obstacles, it seemed that most of the rough edges of the Law of Sea treaty were ironed out and a final draft had been expected in April 1981. But the Reagan Administration heeded the calls of treaty critics, and to the consternation of convention delegates announced that it would review the negotiations before signing.

The crux of the matter is the basic difference in interests between Third World nations, who have tried to instill the spirit of the "new international economic order" into the treaty, and the industrialized nations, who stand to be the ones making the initial investments of capital and technology and therefore want rewards commensurate with the risks involved. Critics of the agreement as it now stands feel the United States has "knuckled under" to the Third World in the area of seabed mining. Mr. Richardson, who no longer leads the delegation, feels that the deal was close to the best that could be expected, and in fact represented considerable compromise on the part of the Third World nations, particularly in aspects of the treaty unrelated to mining. In short, he feels it is a fair treaty; he fears that renegotiation could lead to the loss of important long-range gains—both practical and psychological—in international relations.

For the moment, however, the opposite view prevails, and the Administration's new delegates will be seeking major changes in the treaty before submitting it to the Senate for ratification. All of which means that the fruitful harvesting of seabed minerals—a long-range prospect to begin with—is even further away.

### Objections to the Treaty
The areas of the Law of Sea treaty as it now stands that are of concern to the Reagan Administration include the following, according to James L. Malone, the new chief negotiator for the U.S. delegation:

- It places under "burdensome international regulation the development of all of the resources of the seabed and subsoil beyond the limits of national jurisdiction."
- It would establish a supranational mining company called the Enterprise, to be funded initially by nations in proportion to their U.N. contributions, which could eventually monopolize production.
- It calls for the transfer of technology and the sale of proprietary information from privately owned sources to the Enterprise and to any developing country.
- It limits the annual production of seabed nodules and the amount any company can mine for the first twenty years. It would also protect land-based producers from competition with seabed miners.
- It calls for a one-nation one-vote organization, and an Executive Council, the makeup of which is felt to favor the Soviet Bloc over the United States.
- It imposes revenue-sharing obligations on mining companies, and some of the revenues would go to liberation movements such as the PLO.
- It lacks provision for protecting investments made prior to the treaty.

**Mining the Sea Is a Long Way Off**
The review process will be a lengthy one, and some officials predict that no final agreement will be reached before 1984 or 1985. While this has infuriated delegates of the developing countries (recently they announced that they might ratify the treaty without the United States), it has pleased U.S. mining interests who hope to get an early lead on developing seabed resources. The Reagan team is apparently acting in accord with the Republican Party platform, which stated that the Law of Sea negotiations had "served to inhibit United States exploitation of the seabed for its abundant mineral resources. Too much concern has been lavished on nations unable to carry out seabed mining with insufficient attention paid to gaining early American access to it."

Anticipating that companies would stop investing in seabed research because of Law of Sea developments, Congress, in June 1980, passed a law that empowers the Commerce Department to issue mining licenses. The law prohibits commercial mining until 1988, by which time the Law of Sea treaty should have been signed. However, if negotiations drag on beyond 1988, domestic companies could dive right in. Some observers feel that the main value of the law is to serve notice to the international community that the United States is determined to have what it considers its rightful share of sea resources, preferably under the auspices of an acceptable agreement, but failing that, on its own. This may hasten the adoption of an acceptable Law of Sea. It also served to inspire U.S. companies, who feel more confident about continuing their exploration and the development of expensive, sophisticated equipment needed to mine the ocean floor.

Once mining begins, it could conceivably change the complexion of the international minerals situation. Billions of tons of nodules are known to bear important minerals, and no one knows exactly what might lie beneath the surface. The most abundant area so far explored is in the Pacific Ocean between Mexico and Hawaii. Within twenty years from the start of development, the United States could conceivably be self-sufficient in nickel, cobalt, manganese, and copper. But for work to begin in earnest, the climate will have to be right for the consortiums to justify the financial risks—anywhere from $500 million to $750 million for a commercial facility, depending on its size.

We are not likely to see large-scale mining in the ocean before the year 2000, and some would say that is overly optimistic. The current review of the Law of Sea will be a big factor in determining the actual timetable.

### Resource Star Wars?

Although much closer at hand, the sea is actually more of a mystery to scientists than another possible source of minerals: outer space. From all indications, the moon and nearby planets could supply metals in the not-too-distant future. Furthermore, manned space stations are considered an excellent location for creating alloys and new materials that cannot be produced under the influence of gravity.

But such projects are dozens of years and billions of dollars away. Before companies will risk money developing equipment and conducting experimental manufacturing operations they will have to be assured of the future of the U.S. space program and be provided appropriate political safeguards. But given the exhilaration created by the successful Columbia shuttle, and space competition from the Soviet Union, the dream of Cecil Rhodes—the adventurous financier who opened Africa to mining—that man would one day mine the stars may not be that far off. If not the stars, then certainly the moon, which is no further from our technology than the Tin Isles were to the Phoenicians.

## TOWARD A NATIONAL MINERALS POLICY

Concern over foreign dependence on minerals is nothing new in the United States, nor are attempts to come up with a coordinated minerals policy. Over the years, at least twenty mineral or material policy studies have been prepared by various federal agencies and numerous others have been undertaken by private organizations. Despite all the research, and the official concern that stimulated each one, the government seems to have been unable to come up with a coherent, consistent apparatus for addressing mineral issues. It seems to be the kind of item that gets swept under the rug until a crisis comes along and everyone starts shouting that something ought to be done. Now is one of those times.

One major complaint of those associated with mining and related areas is the absence of a clear, explicit policy or set of guidelines that expresses the nation's attitude on minerals. So many government agencies and departments affect mineral supplies in one way or another, their jurisdictions so often overlap or are unclear, their priorities are so often contradictory, and their policies so often at odds with one another that it is difficult to avoid confusion and waste. For that reason, one recurring suggestion has been for a Cabinet-level department to oversee a coherent national minerals policy.

**A National Mineral Security Act**
That suggestion along with others frequently mentioned by the mining industry and concerned government officials was incorporated into a bill introduced to Congress in April 1981. Sponsored by Congressman Santini, the National Mineral Security Act is said to be the result of over a dozen hearings conducted by Mr. Santini's Subcommittee in the two previous years.

The Congressman summarized the principal provisions of the act this way:

- "Establish a 3-member Council on Minerals and Materials within the Office of the President to coordinate and review all government activities affecting minerals, and submit policy recommendations to the President for maintaining a minerals policy.
- "Provide a means whereby the Secretary of the Interior may increase the accessibility of public lands for mineral exploration. It does not automatically reverse previous legislation, it simply sets out a procedure for the secretary to, upon nomination, review areas of mineral potential for possible exploration.
- "Amend U.S. tax laws to assist the mining industry in making the capital investments that are necessary to locate, develop and produce the minerals on which our economy and security are vitally dependent. These amendments provide tax-exempt financing for pollution control facilities and allow accelerated amortization of pollution control and government mandated expenditure.
- "Amend the stockpiling act to allow the immediate expenditure of funds generated by the sale of stockpiled materials. These funds will be used for acquisition of other strategic and critical materials."

Of all the provisions in the bill, the most effective might be the one dealing with taxation. According to Dr. John Morgan of the Bureau of Mines, accelerated amortization of capital expenditures strongly encouraged investment during the Korean War, and is said to have increased steel-production capacity by 25 percent.

Also under consideration are current U.S. antitrust regulations, which prohibit joint ventures in foreign investments and other forms of economic collaboration between companies, and between companies and the government. This, the industry contends, puts them at a distinct disadvantage compared with Japan, Germany, and other nations, where cooperation is not only accepted but encouraged.

While the climate in Reagan's Washington certainly favors the kind of legislation and executive affirmation implied in the Santini bill and urged by private industry, the machinery lumbers slowly. The National Mineral Security Act is now being evaluated by five Congressional committees, and there is no telling how long that will take. In the meantime, each day brings something relevant to the strategic metals market, either on fiscal, environmental, technological, or international grounds. Investors are well advised to stay on top of the news.

# PART II

# Investing in Minor Metals

# INTRODUCTION TO INVESTING IN MINOR METALS

## SIX

### **S**EVERAL GOOD REASONS TO INVEST IN MINOR METALS

Essentially, price is a function of three factors: supply, demand, and costs. Taking a broad view, we expect the price of metals to rise steadily because there will be (a) steady but slow growth of supply, (b) steady but slow growth of demand, and (c) increasing production costs.

But many commodities are expected to increase in price over time. Why invest in minor metals? Because they can be a worthwhile addition to your portfolio in several ways.

**Minor Metals Can Be an Inflation Hedge.** Most mining experts agree that production costs are rising at a rate far in excess of the rate of inflation. Assuming that demand will remain steady and grow slowly, we can expect prices to outpace inflation over the next three to five years, although not necessarily on a year-by-year basis.

**Minor Metals Are a Business Cycle Investment.** Historically, minor metals purchased during a recession would appreciate substantially during the recovery. To take advantage of this pattern, you must buy a "basket" of metals; this is because a single metal may diverge from the general economic cycle at any time, if demand for it were to drop for reasons unrelated to the business cycle.

**Minor Metals Can Serve as a Hedge Against Political Unrest.** If you sincerely believe that the arms race will continue to heat up, or that revolution in central or southern Africa is inevitable, buying certain minor metals makes a great deal of sense. Even the most conservative analysts believe that in the next five to ten years at least a few of the countries producing minor metals will experience enough instability to cause a spurt in the price of the metals they export. The problem is determining which countries will be involved and when it will happen.

**Minor Metals Can Be a High Technology Investment.** At a time when investment advisers around the world have been touting genetic engineering companies, personal computer producers, and alternate energy firms, minor metals offer a unique but viable way to capitalize on the technology boom, since they will play a key role in the new technologies in areas such as electronics, chemicals, optics, defense, and energy.

## SEVERAL REASONS TO BE CAUTIOUS

Understanding how to buy and sell minor metals is simple enough. But determining when to buy and sell and comprehending market behavior are not easy. These aspects of trading confound experts ranging from local scrap dealers to Soviet senior traders.

If you are to be successful in minor-metals investing, you must learn to live with several basic difficulties.

**Many Variables.** The variables include: geopolitics, new deposits being discovered continuously, advances in technology, the world economic picture, labor actions, environmental regulations, above-ground stocks, interest rates, substitutions, and stockpiles. All these factors and several others affect the market.

**Accuracy.** The mining and metals industry is awash with words and numbers, many of them confusing. In addition, some of the most important statistics are not quite accurate. And while no expert would dare accuse any metals firm of intentionally distorting or fabricating their production, consumption, stock, or reserve data, no expert would stake his or her reputation on the validity of industry reports. This is a competitive industry, and producers and consumers are reluctant to tip their hands. If they had their way, most mining folks would rather not give out any statistics at all. However, they must provide some data, lest they appear to the government and to their stockholders to be uncooperative. But what they release is not much more than "smoke signals," useful in determining the general direction and little else.

Certain vital statistics with strategic importance, such as the level of above-ground stocks, are simply unavailable to the general public, even in the form of estimates. For this reason, most successful metals and mining analysts, and some traders, have a network of moles that they rely on to gain access to confidential data. Usually they will keep this information to themselves to discourage leaks. Many firms specializing in metals research rely on costly site visits and access to confidential internal industry documents, which they gain by providing something in return and guaranteeing anonymity. Very cloak-and-dagger, and clearly beyond the capacity of most of us.

**Information Overload.** Reliable or not, studies, reports, and statistics are never difficult to find. A tremendous amount of information is disseminated worldwide through the governmental mining bureaus of producing and consuming countries, industry watchers, think tanks, and trade publications. Monitoring all that data is virtually impossible, even for the trade. Professionals often develop preferences for one publication over another, but no single publication provides all the data.

**The Two Market System.** Buying and selling minor metals can be done in two arenas: *the producer market*, in which the price is set by the producers and adhered to on a contractual basis by consumers; and *the free market*, where there is a freely floating price determined by short-term supply and demand. In sizing up the markets, you must keep tabs on both the producer and free markets. The fine art of market watching will be discussed in Chapter Eight, "What Moves the Markets."

**Confusion over Who Has Jurisdiction over Minor-Metals Trade for Investment Purposes.** At the present time, there is no government agency charged with regulating minor-metals trading or settling disputes. The Commodity Futures Trading Commission (CFTC), which deals with base and precious metals traded on exchanges, has been quick to disqualify itself in most cases. In a *New York Times* article on May 11, 1981, CFTC spokesman Bruce Stoner pointed out, "As our name implies, we are only charged with supervising the futures markets. We have no power to intervene in cash markets. The business in strategic metals, as we understand it, is confined to cash deals."

There are some instances in which an investor might deal in forward contracts, which involve buying a contract on margin for future delivery. Says Stoner, "If so, a case could be made that such deals involve contracts and are not strictly cash deals." Theoretically, at least, the CFTC could attempt to curb abuses in such instances (see "Forward Contracts," p. 265).

In some cases, the state attorney general, charged with protecting the rights of consumers, can take action. In July 1981, for example, a scandal erupted in New York involving a strategic metals dealer. The operation was quickly and dramatically closed down by a raid authorized by the attorney general.

### ARE YOU INVESTING FOR THE RIGHT REASONS?

Assuming that you are willing to press on and invest in minor metals in spite of the difficulties, you must do some soul-searching to determine if your motivations, expectations, and suitability are reasonable.

**Political Beliefs and Moral Convictions.** An investor we know sincerely believes that the Soviets are hell-bent on destroying the United States and turning our nation into one of its satellites. He therefore finds the notion of an aggressively fought resource war quite feasible. He is firm in his belief that the Russians are holding back exports of critical materials and are attempting to control foreign sources in order to undermine our defense and economy.

This conviction has led him to invest in minor metals such as titanium and germanium, the stuff with which wars are fought.

South Africa? He thinks it's a great place. While it saddens him to do so, he is betting that the Russians will finance and arm a terrorist takeover of the South African government in order to control much of the world's minor metals. Every week he calls his broker for price quotes on manganese, platinum, and vanadium.

Another investor deplores the "racist" policies of South Africa, and would dearly love to see its government fall. When it does, she hopes that the new majority-rule government will form a minerals cartel with other black African states and proceed to jack up the price of several important metals, a la OPEC. As far as she is concerned, it would be just deserts for our support of a white supremacist regime. Therefore, she doesn't object to profiting from the "liberation of the oppressed."

To both of these investors we say: "Strong political beliefs, moral convictions, or intense dislike of a foreign power do nothing to alter the supply/demand situation, nor are they likely to increase the odds of a government being overthrown. *Invest with your head, not with your heart."*

**Get Rich Quick.** If you are looking for a quick killing— large profits in a short period of time—strategic metals is probably not the place. In some forms of investment, such as commodities futures, the potential for quick and dramatic profits is greater because it has been designed into the system through the use of leveraged contracts, where a small amount of cash controls a lot of product so that a very small price movement can produce very large profits (or losses). But there are no futures markets in minor metals. And *while quick, substantial profits, or the quadrupling of price in a short time, can and does happen with minor metals, it is seldom by design, and quite rare.*

In order to make a large profit in minor metals, you need a large change in price: to make 20 percent in three months, the price of the metal must move 20 percent in the same three months. It is appropriate to refer to minor metals as a new *alternative* investment, but there are far more *aggressive* investments available.

**High-Sounding Terms.** A few years ago, a stock named Goldfields became very popular. It seemed that whenever the price of gold moved up, it moved up, and vice versa. Many investors assumed that it was a gold-mining stock. Ironically, Goldfields was not a mining firm but a bakery.

Names and labels have a way of giving an investment luster. In applying the term *strategic* to several metals in its stockpile, the U.S. government has given metals dealers a sales concept that Madison Avenue would envy.

The term *strategic* refers to metals that are vital to industry and national defense. But *from an investment perspective, strategic has nothing whatever to do with potential profitability.* And in that sense, the distinction between strategic metals and all other metals, minor or base, is artificial.

Each and every metal can be analyzed in essentially the

same way to determine if there is an opportunity for profit. Whether it is used in tanks or toilets is of little importance to the investor if the overall supply/demand picture looks bullish.

As we shall see, there are many instances when investing in metals that happen to be strategic does make sense. But one should not rule out an opportunity in, say, copper or aluminum simply because they are not considered strategic.

Investing in base metals is old hat, while minor metals is a fresh area. That is the basic reason why promoters have been playing up strategics and playing down industrial metals. Everyone is tempted by that old "get in on the ground floor" investment line. But it is a mistake for investors to divide metals into industrial and strategic and then buy only those with strategic importance. Instead, buy with a simple view of where the market appears to be going, and buy whatever metal or metals appear to be increasing in price. Otherwise you will narrow your opportunities unnecessarily. "You can make a very good case for aluminum as an investment metal," says Bryan Webb, past president of the Minor Metals Traders Association, "even though it is plentiful and not generally regarded as strategic by politicians and defense experts." You should be looking for opportunities to make the right investment decisions, so do not get locked into words like *strategic, political instability*, and so on. Rather, look for the opportunity that best puts the odds in your favor.

**Financial Suitability.** Investments can be glamorous, too. Hard-sell salespeople gravitate toward "sexy" investments— those with a "come hither" rationale that is hard to resist. To some people, strategic metals have an exotic, esoteric image. But stay away from minor metals if your financial condition doesn't justify the purchase, even if owning them appeals to your sense of style.

# INSIDE THE MARKET STRUCTURE

## SEVEN

## THE PRODUCER MARKET

Economically speaking, metals markets in general are *oligopolies*. They are characterized by having just a few sellers of the same product or, in some cases, of slightly different products. For example, there are fewer than a dozen producers of columbium in the world, and although the grades may differ, most of them sell the same basic product, some form of ferrocolumbium.

Several prevailing factors are responsible for this situation:

**Scarce Raw Materials.** Most metals lie below the ground, and you've got to own or lease that ground in order to get your hands on them. Securing mining rights is often a matter of money, influence, geopolitics, and sheer bold-faced gambling. Competitive pressures tend to limit the number of mining firms that gain access to the ores.

**Financing.** The mining business requires huge capital expenditures for exploration, mining, and equipment. Very few firms have been able to afford these costs or to obtain the necessary funds from other institutions.

**Low Margins.** Because profit margins are low, a firm must capture a large segment of the market in order to increase revenue. Therefore, it is not worthwhile for firms with only a small market share to stay in business, and so large mining conglomerates have tended to swallow up the marginal firms. In fact, many smaller mining companies are started on the premise that if things go well, the owners will have the opportunity to sell out to a large firm at a sizable profit.

**Mergers and Takeovers.** Not only do large mining companies take over small ones, but they also buy, or merge with, refiners, smelters, and fabricators. The result is the creation of mining conglomerates.

The North American mining industry has tended toward vertical mergers and takeovers, resulting in several large conglomerates that control every phase of the process.

### How Are Prices Determined in This Situation?

Most economists agree that there is no single model that adequately explains how oligopolies behave. Prices tend to be rigid, remaining unchanged for fairly long periods of time.

Here is a case in point. From 1926 to 1938, the price of sulfur remained $18 per ton, in spite of major changes in demand and production. Some theorists offer this reason: if a producer were to lower its price, it is likely that other producers would lower their prices to match it. This would eliminate any advantage that might have been gained from underselling the market. If a producer were to raise its price, the company runs the risk that competitors might not raise theirs, and the producer could then lose some of its business to those who offer more favorable prices. In short, in an oligopoly, a producer usually cannot increase his share of the market by lowering prices, and he usually can't increase his profits by raising prices.

Faced with this no-win situation, the best strategy for a producer is to sit tight until something major happens to supply or demand, causing *all* producers to raise or lower their prices.

When the price of a commodity is set by the sellers, it is called a *managed* or *administered* price. In the metals markets it is referred to simply as the *producer price*. But it is not entirely under the producers' control. They can't just pick a price and ram it down the throats of the consumers. Even in a market where one or two producers supply almost all the metal, attention must be paid to supply and demand; so the producer price lies somewhere between a monopoly price, in which the seller can dictate terms, and a *free-market price*, which is determined by free trade between buyers and sellers.

The producer-price system is used extensively throughout the world. It is common in North America where vertically integrated conglomerates control not only the mining, smelting, and refining, but in many cases also the fabricator and the fabricator's main customer. With this kind of control, imposing a producer price is a *fait accompli*.

Most consumers are not unhappy with this arrangement. The system provides them with the security of a steady supply and the comfort of knowing that their competitors are paying the same price for metals as they are. There is less chance of being undercut. In addition, the producer-price system does not involve the day-to-day price fluctuations that can be hard on metals purchasers.

### How Is the Producer Price Fixed?

Producers revise prices up or down when they feel that market conditions dictate or justify a change. They like to adjust their prices gradually, based on costs and profit margins, and they are more interested in steady growth than in trying to capitalize on temporary shortages. Most would be quite satisfied if they could raise their prices enough to keep pace with inflation.

Very few metals markets permit the producer to get precisely what it wants. So the sellers must constantly try to gauge supply and demand. Is the market strong? Is it soft? Are competitors showing any signs that they might raise prices? Lower them? In addition, sellers must keep tabs on overall costs of production for their competitors as well as themselves. Taking all these factors into account, the producer must determine what price will yield the greatest possible profit—that is, the price at which it can sell the most metal with the largest profit margin.

It is very easy to lose your way in such a price-setting process. Increasingly, producers of minor metals are relying on a short cut: they let the free market tell them the score. The free market is the portion of the metals market (usually very small in comparison to the producer market) that trades strictly in accordance with supply and demand. Prices are negotiated daily between buyer and seller, and even though the amount of metal changing hands is a drop in the bucket of total world consumption, the free-market price tells the producers a great deal about what they should be charging. The free-market system is important enough to warrant separate treatment, and we'll explore it in depth later in the chapter.

### The Role of Price Leaders
Brazil is the world's leading producer of columbium; it is responsible for about 75 percent of the total output. When the primary Brazilian producer adjusts its price, it isn't long before the other producers follow suit. Indeed, in many metals markets, one or two firms are consistently the first to change a price, with the rest of the pack following close behind. Such firms are called *price leaders*. There are two basic types: *dominant firms*, which have captured the lion's share of the market, leaving the remains to be divvied up among a bunch of smaller firms who have no choice but to follow the lead of the larger ones; and *barometric price leaders*—producing firms that are especially good at monitoring market forces and anticipating changes in supply, production costs, or demand. They are often the first to change prices because they are first and best at judging the market. Such firms are not necessarily the largest producers.

Recently, smaller firms have grown bolder about breaking away from the rigid pricing structure of the larger producers, because the growth of the free market has allowed them to sell their output through merchants.

### Why Is All This Important to the Investor?
It is highly unlikely that you as an investor will ever purchase minor metals directly from a producer. But you must keep track of their production costs and all other factors that affect pricing. For example, suppose a dominant producer is having balance-of-payment problems. It might well wish to lower its price to encourage demand and increase foreign exchange input.

Getting even a vague idea of the producer situation is not all that easy. Following the trade publications might help, but your best bet is to find a merchant with good sources of information, and stay in close touch. If you have any friends or relatives in the mining business, or in any business involved with metals, don't be shy. Every little bit of information helps. Minor metals are still dominated by the trade, and are likely to remain that way in the foreseeable future.

## Contracts

Producers like to make money producing metals, not speculating on them. They are after a healthy profit over an extended period of time. Similarly, consumers buy metals to use as raw materials in their products, not to trade and gamble with. Their profit comes from the sale of the goods they make with these metals. Pratt & Whitney, for example, makes jet engines that use cobalt. Profits come from the sale of these engines, not from speculating in cobalt.

The cobalt producers in turn want Pratt to continue making and selling jet engines that use cobalt. Pratt & Whitney, meanwhile, is bidding against competitors for contracts to build jet engines. They would like to have a reasonable idea of what each metal is going to cost over the next year, or over several years if possible, so they can plan accordingly, and price their engines to reflect the cost of the metals in them.

In short, both producers and consumers use contracts because they dislike surprises. The bulk of world production is tied up in contracts, and the contract terms dictate the relationship between the free-market price and the producer price, since this information provides a clue to how much noncontract metal is available and how many consumers are able to buy on the free market.

Simple *fixed-price contracts* involve the purchase of a specific amount of metal at a set price, to be delivered and paid for at specific times. However, contracts for large metals purchases by major consumers are often more flexible. Some, for example, have clauses that tie the price to the inflation rate, production costs, the size of the ultimate purchase, and other variables.

*"Cost plus" contracts* involve a price set according to a specific formula based on a firm estimate of the production cost per unit of metal, plus a fixed amount. Another type is a "cost plus incentive fee" contract, in which the markup is based on the amount of metal eventually supplied. This is used when a consumer wants a certain amount of metal, but the producer is not sure that he can supply the full amount.

*Flexible contracts* are also quite common. They usually call for the purchase of some minimum amount of metal over a given period of time, with the understanding that the customer will probably buy much more. The cost is often the prevailing producer price at the time of each order. Such contracts are actually an acknowledgment of common interest and cooperation, an informal agreement to do business with each other.

Technically, users with more flexible contracts can turn to the free market to take advantage of a very low price, since they need purchase only a minimum amount to honor their contracts. Those bound by firm contracts have a bit more difficulty, but even they can find a way if they want to buy free-market metals badly enough.

However, major consumers rarely want to use the free market. They are loyal to the producers, because they know that violating an unwritten agreement or harming a relationship just to save a few bucks is not smart business. The consumer doing business through a contract always knows what it is getting, and it is secure. In times of shortage, the free-market price will probably be higher than the producer price, so the contract holder will, in effect, be buying at a discount. During severe scarcities just getting the metal, regardless of price, is a major achievement. Only regular loyal customers can expect to be supplied by the producers. And producers might be forced to allocate among users, in which case the size of the allocation is usually determined by the size of past purchases. Therefore, in order to get metal from producers when there is a shortage and the free-market price is high, the consumer must be willing to buy from producers when there is a surplus and the free-market price is lower.

In a competitive marketplace, however, even loyalty has limits. If the free-market price were to fall to a level a *great deal lower* than the producer price, consumers might consider risking a break with a producer.

The amount bought and sold under contract differs from metal to metal. Molybdenum, for example, is sold largely by contract. The major producers are American and Canadian, and they prefer to do business that way. With silicon, on the other hand, it is almost totally a pay-as-you-go, free-market situation, with very little contract business.

## THE FREE MARKET

The free market is simply the market for metals that are freely traded, rather than those sold by producers at their managed price. It is a negotiated market, usually made by specialized metals dealers operating out of London and, to a lesser degree, New York and Chicago. Business is conducted primarily over the telephone and Telex lines. In most cases, the metal sold on the free market is only a small amount of the total tonnage produced, and is often referred to as marginal tonnage.

Although the free market is relatively small, its influence is usually far greater than its size. In many cases, it drives the producer market, forcing producers to adjust their prices by establishing trends that are hard to ignore.

In almost every case, investors purchase and sell metals through the free-market system. So this is the market to watch.

### Where Does the "Excess" Tonnage Sold in the Free Market Come From?

There are several sources of excess tonnage. The first is a number of small, less well-organized producers with marginal tonnage and without the muscle to support a large international marketing division. They also need to convert metal to money more quickly. Such firms are less able to negotiate favorable contracts with major users. They rely on merchants (whose role is explained later in this chapter) to unload whatever they can produce.

Another source is the Soviet Union and the COMECON nations, controlled economies with unpredictable mining operations and sales policies. Market watchers are frequently surprised at how suddenly these nations will stop supplying a metal, often after a period of tremendous exporting.

The Soviets and their allies dislike acting in concert with Western producers and would rather keep everyone guessing. Besides, they are unable to sustain long-term contracts in many metals because their production is just too erratic. So they use the free market, which allows them to throw a smoke screen over their activities.

In addition, some consumers resell unneeded excess stocks, re-refined or secondary metals from manufacturing processes, or metals that were sold to merchants, perhaps at a discount, by the producers.

### Who Buys from the Free Market?

Primarily, those who buy from the free market are small independent users who don't have the clout, the finances, or the need for the large tonnages required to negotiate a favorable contract with producers.

There are other players, and the extent of their involvement varies greatly from metal to metal. The situation often depends on the market share controlled by the producers. If a very large segment of world output of a particular metal is sold through merchants, even major consumers who would prefer doing business by contract have no choice but to turn to the free market.

For example, tungsten ore trade is conducted primarily on the free market, because the Chinese, who produce about one-quarter of the world's total output, prefer selling through merchants. When the dominant producer of a metal chooses to sell on the free market, it makes the formation of a meaningful producer-price structure rather difficult.

There are other factors that could enhance the importance of the free market literally overnight. Almost every consumer has an occasional need for the free market. A sudden strike or mine closing could result in a producer being unable to live up to its commitment. That would send its customers to the phones looking for supplies. Suddenly, the free market is very active. In the case of the Shaba incident in 1978, it was not the fact but simply the *fear* of mine closings that sent major cobalt users scrambling to cover themselves. If production were to cease, they wanted to have sufficient cobalt stocks to weather the storm.

Smart consumers plan ahead. They like to keep their options open, knowing full well that a politically inspired supply dislocation is always a possibility. Many make it a practice to buy marginal tonnage from the free market regularly, even when they can meet all their metal needs through producers. Thus, when and if a crisis arises, the merchants might regard them as regular and therefore preferred customers.

This arrangement can be beneficial to the investor, because it means that there are many dealers who trade regularly with major users. Thus, a dealer with good contacts should be able to give a serious investor a general idea of how several major consumers feel about a metal's price. Don't expect specific or detailed information, though. Dealers value the major consumer's business (which is steady) a great deal more than they value your relatively small purchases.

When comparing the free-market price with the producer price, you will often notice that the former is slightly lower.

Do not be misled into thinking that a surplus is brewing; do some simple arithmetic. In the free market, cash-and-carry is quite common, and payment terms rarely extend beyond thirty days. On the other hand, producer terms might be as long as six months. Also, in some instances the consumer doesn't want the metal delivered immediately, but would like the producer to hold it for several months. It is therefore only fair that a producer might want the price to reflect interest charges that would accrue while waiting for the money, as well as storage charges while the metal shipment awaits the delivery day. In many cases, then, the difference between the producer and free-market price is only a function of interest and storage charges, while the basic price is just about equal.

## THE TWO-PRICE MARKETPLACE

No economist has ever adequately explained how a two-price market can exist for long in a free economy. This merely dramatizes the shortcomings of economic theory, because in reality there are two prices in most metals markets.

Under normal circumstances, the producers hold sway over the market. They can guarantee steady supplies and discourage price cutting. Usually the larger mining concerns buy out small companies before they get successful enough to pose any real threat.

Major suppliers can discourage smaller, weaker firms from expanding capacity by lowering their prices to a level that makes such expansion unprofitable. A break in the producer price signals consumers that the softness in the free-market price is not a short-term aberration. Producers are in effect saying that they don't expect prices to firm for some time, and they hope that consumers will increase their consumption of the metal at the more favorable price.

This would appear to be all in a day's work in an oligopoly. The producers are simply adjusting their price in accordance with changes in the supply and demand situation and protecting their position as the dominant suppliers. But not all breaks in the producer price are carried out in an orderly and controlled manner.

Dissension among major producers prevents them from presenting a uniform pricing policy to consumers. Many analysts believe that cobalt pricing is undermined in part by the fact that Zaire and Zambia don't get along very well and don't trust each other. Thus, major consumers can play one against the other to get a lower cobalt price.

**Consumer Loyalty and Producer Price Breaks**
The relationship between large producer and large consumer is akin to a marriage. But it is a marriage of convenience, and there might be times when a consumer finds the free-market prices too sexy to resist. Indeed, as this book is being written, the temptation is especially strong, because the current economic slump has resulted in the worst metals markets in forty years, with large surpluses causing free-market prices to dip well below those of the producers.

Sooner or later consumers start asking whether it is wise to continue paying the higher producer price when the company is fighting for economic survival. This happens in a different way at a different time for each industry, each metal, and each type of end user. But it does happen.

Some consumers keep the faith with their main supplier, but purchase a little less from them while quietly buying some metal at the lower free-market price. The mixture of lower free-market prices and higher producer prices serves to lower the "average price" per unit that the company is paying, thus reducing its overall costs. Some boldly buy large amounts on the free market—even if it means building up excess stocks—thus reducing their average costs. And they can juggle their books so that they are in essence using the lower-priced metal now, and saving the higher-priced metal for a time when prices rebound. Still others abandon ship and plunge deeply into the free market, while a significant number of consumers, confronted with slow growth, will simply buy a lot less metal or none at all.

The first major consumers to turn to the free market are usually firms with the most flexible product requirements. If a consumer has qualified as acceptable for use several different grades and origins of a metal, it has more of a choice and a bigger potential supply. It can be faster on its feet, quick to adjust to a changing situation, and more able to buy at lower prices on the free market. But a firm that requires a very specific grade of metal, mined and refined in perhaps one or two places, has less flexibility and less chance of finding exactly what it wants in the free market. Therefore, it is much more likely to hesitate before moving away from its major suppliers. For example, chemical companies that use titanium as a pigment are more flexible than those that require high-grade metal for aircraft.

How the producers react to a falling free-market price depends on the condition of the principals. If, as in the case of many metals, the main producers are developing nations with heavy debt and balance-of-payments problems, they must continue to dig metal out of the ground and convert it to cash, since it is likely to be one of their few sources of foreign exchange. They will lower the price to keep the demand and market share up, regardless of the long-term consequences.

### How Low Can the Producers Go?

It is difficult to generalize about how much producers can lower prices. However, down-side price potential is often based on estimates of the cost of production for the major producers. Many experts have pointed out, for example, that before the Shaba incident the African suppliers did quite well selling cobalt at $6.00 per pound. Taking inflation and other price factors into account, it is now estimated that they could make a profit selling cobalt at $8.00 to $10.00 per pound. So, even though the producer price for cobalt has dropped to $17.00 per pound at the end of 1981, there appears to be plenty of room below. The free-market price sunk as low as $9.50 per pound by November. Copper, the other major metal export of these nations, is depressed as well, which tightens the screws still further.

## THE BLACK MARKET

In lesser-developed nations, when the principal sources of revenue are foreign aid packages and the sale of raw materials, patronage and theft are simpler and more direct than in industrialized nations. Often, payoffs take the form of secret (and not-so-secret) allocations of valuable minerals to a favored minister or his relatives by the state-controlled mining concern. In some cases, the beneficiary simply sells the allotment of minerals on the free market or to a multinational firm willing to look the other way in the name of goodwill. He then pockets all the money. In other cases, the receiver of the allocation must pay a price for the minerals. This price is low enough to assure a profit when he turns around and sells the stuff.

This "black market" supply of metal usually doesn't show up in the books of producers or purchasers. Other black market supplies are the result of outright theft at the mine site, hijacking in transit, or pilferage from consumer stocks. Most experts feel that black-market trade does not have significant impact on the market as a whole, but it does help to explain in part how metals have a way of showing up for sale when there is supposedly none available at any price. And while the market might not feel its impact, the black market has made several individuals quite wealthy.

## THE DEALER

According to S. P. Prasadam of Strategic Metals Corporation, merchant trading in minor metals began about thirty years ago when Leonard Hillyard (now a Director of Strategic Metals Corporation) created a company to solve a sticky problem: how to transfer exotic materials from lesser-developed nations to the technologically advanced nations in the United States and Europe.

The *dealer* is the middleman who puts buyer and seller together or buys from producers and sells to consumers. He neither takes ore out of the ground, nor refines it, nor manufactures products that utilize metal. For this reason, many market economists have long held that the role of the dealers is unnecessary in the metals markets, and that they will go out of business as the markets become more orderly and efficient.

That is unlikely, as the metals markets show little sign of becoming more orderly and efficient. Dealers exist because both producers and consumers require their services. The market participants are a hodgepodge of parties with differing philosophies, political and economic ambitions, suspicions, perspectives, and short- and long-term goals. The dealer is the great equalizer, the referee. The only philosophy he or she adheres to is that of the free market: supply, demand, profit. Bryan Webb, former Chairman of the Minor Metals Traders Association, says of this possible demise of merchants: "If it hasn't happened by now, it's not going to happen."

Trading minor metals is a quiet business, unlike businesses such as futures, government securities, and currencies. Market monitors and news services do not flash up-to-the-minute prices, because there is no formal structure for determining price. Rather, it is a friendly business in which traders call around in search of buyers and sellers. Most of the people know each other, and the trading is quite civil. Many of the firms involved started in base metals and other raw materials, and several of the London firms have been in operation more than 200 years, although they have traded in minors for only a short time. Curiously, the public is largely unaware of their existence.

As a potential investor, you will not be able to buy tungsten directly from the Chinese or sell germanium directly to General Dynamics. Therefore, you must establish a relationship with dealers either directly or indirectly through an investment adviser or minor-metals investment program.

Dealers have the information. They speak to scores of buyers and sellers each day to get a sense of what is happening in the markets. Even the respected trade journals such as *Metals Week* and the *Metal Bulletin* must resort to polling selected merchants to arrive at free-market price quotations for minor metals and to assess general market sentiment. There is simply no other way to tell, because there are no exchanges that trade minor metals and no form of official price. So if you are unwilling or unable to get to know several dealers before investing, link up with someone who is.

Some dealers discourage speculators because they have legitimate fears. First, they are afraid that inexperienced investors will get hurt and that the dealers will ultimately be blamed. Second, they do not want to call attention to themselves. Discretion is an important part—indeed, *an unwritten code*—of the trading industry.

In the near future, dealers and investors will probably form some kind of uneasy alliance. The investor represents another potential customer, and the dealer is the only real source of supply for small investment. At the same time, the novice buyer can cause problems for the dealer, and the dealer can take advantage of the investor.

# WHAT MOVES THE MARKETS

# EIGHT

**S**INCE MARKET behavior is a function of many variables, the best an investor can do is arrive at some sort of "snapshot," freezing the situation at some point in time. Professional market watchers do this at regular intervals, hoping to identify trends by comparing snapshots.

The information provided in this section will help the reader understand how the market works, and identify metals that are worthy of investment consideration.

### SUPPLY

Most of the world's major mining companies were created to exploit the base metals that helped spur the growth and development of the industrialized world in the nineteenth and twentieth centuries. Minor metals were either a by-product of base metal mining or, when mined by themselves, a side business, generating a minute portion of overall revenues.

With respect to economics, the situation has not changed a great deal. However, producers recognize that the outlook appears bright for minor metals and that they may account for a greater percentage of revenues in the future. They can be expected to be far more responsive to market demand. Let's look at the major factors that influence supply.

**Expansion of Economic Reserves.** There is every reason to believe that there are enough resources of most minor metals to last well into the next century. But *only that which can be exploited easily and profitably plays a role in the market supply.*

Reserves are by definition that portion of a proven resource base, including developed mines, that can be economically exploited. Seabed mining, for example, has the potential to impact the manganese market quite severely. But at the current time, seabed mining appears to be at least a decade away, and costs may render it uneconomical even then. So the market simply pays no attention.

However, supplies can increase rapidly if (a) in the normal everyday course of geological exploration, new reserves are discovered; (b) unusually large demand, high prices, or government incentives cause an intensive search for a particular metal; or (c) known resources suddenly become economic.

The U.S. Bureau of Mines keeps tabs on resources and reserves in several classifications, both domestic and worldwide. The trade press reports new discoveries and all announcements of attempts to exploit reserves. In addition, the press keeps the trade abreast of the progress firms are making in expanding capacity or getting new mines operational.

**Industry Output.** Available economic reserves are one thing. Getting the metals out of the ground is quite another. Suppose, for example, a mining company is sitting on a huge economic reserve, and the directors know they can sell twice as much ore as they are currently mining. If the mine is already operating at full capacity, nothing can be done about it over the short term. Expanding capacity takes time, as well as money for new construction and equipment.

If demand is steady and projected to remain so, the industry will take the steps necessary to expand supply. This happened when a shortage of molybdenum in the late seventies spurred producers to increase production capacity. Now most experts expect to see ample molybdenum supplies by 1983 and for some time thereafter, despite the strong demand due to the use of molybdenum in oil pipelines.

Industry capacity bears watching very closely because it has been shown to be a vital factor in determining price. A metal in short supply may rise in price in the face of steady demand. But sooner or later, if they can, the producers will seek to increase their capacity. If they were to produce even a little more than anticipated demand, they could create a surplus that would soften prices significantly. Thus, if you were to purchase a metal in the hope of higher prices, you might be disappointed if the operation of some new production capacity were only months away.

Announcements of new capacity must be watched for and interpreted. What is the likely overall impact of this new capacity? Will it increase total world output by 0.5 percent or 5.0 percent? Is annual world consumption roughly equal to production, or is there a shortage? A surplus?

**The Cost of Production.** In mining, the principal costs are labor, capital, land, energy, and machinery. All of these have been rising in excess of the inflation rate, with labor and energy leading the way. The lower grades of ore now being exploited also increase the costs. And well-meaning environmental standards force the purchase of pumps, fans, ventilators, and other devices, along with the energy to drive them. If costs rise at a greater pace than the price of the metal, they could render a previously economic reserve marginal or subeconomic, thereby restricting the supply, at least until the metal price catches up a bit.

**Technology.** Advances in mining engineering and minerals processing techniques usually result in increased production and more economical or efficient extraction of by-products. Occasionally, a major breakthrough will permit the economic mining or refining of a grade once considered too expensive or unfeasible to exploit. As a result, such an advance may require a revision of reserve estimates.

Our understanding of mineral formation is rapidly increasing. Satellites carrying elaborate sensing equipment have greatly improved mineral detection, especially the location of "blind ore bodies" not readily apparent from the earth's surface. It is almost certain that by the end of the century we will be mining mineral reserves that have not yet been discovered.

Considerable progress has been made in the development of new mining and processing methods that require less energy. This, along with the utilization of alternate energy sources, could result in substantially lower costs. Another potential cost-cutting innovation is new, labor-saving mining machinery. But whether or not these advances will mean lower or even more stable prices remains to be seen.

**Ecological Considerations.** Strict regulations concerning air and water quality and land conservation can restrict supply. In the first place, conservation laws can curtail the exploration and exploitation of deposits that lie on protected lands. Laws aimed at fighting environmental pollution and waste disposal also restrict mining and refining activities.

**The Amount of Base Metal Production.** Often, several minor metals are found in the same rock as a base metal and are separated out in the smelting process. Others may lie in close proximity to base metal ores and are mined along with the base metal. In both cases, the supply of minor-metals by-products is directly related to the amount of base metal being mined.

If production is down for the base metal, it will be down for the by-product, regardless of demand for the latter, since it doesn't pay to mine a lot of unwanted base metal just to get a small amount of by-product. Simon Strauss of ASARCO, a major mining firm, quips: "Do you run a lumber mill to produce sawdust?" The base metal by-product relationship, and exceptions to the rule, will be explored later on.

## DEMAND

As we have noted, there has been a distinct trend toward increased use of minor metals, due to the industrialization of less-developed nations, advances in electronics and other high-technology industries, the use of superalloys, and other factors. Let's look at the basic components of demand.

**The Number and Size of Customers in the Market.** In the case of many minor metals, the number of consuming firms has been growing steadily. In many other cases, the number of firms remains small, but they have been growing larger, increasing their consumption of specific minor metals.

**Level of Related Metals.** The demand for one metal is often affected by the supply and demand pattern of another when the two are often used together.

**Need for Finished Products.** Minor metals are required in finished products representing virtually every area of advanced design and manufacture, from life-saving bioelectronic devices to life-threatening advanced weaponry. In general, such products are on the rise, but it is the anticipated acceleration of the arms race that has caused many analysts to predict a bull market for minor metals. For example, if there is a large demand for advanced aircraft, the demand for titanium can be expected to increase because it is often an important raw material used in their construction (and is expected to become more so in the future).

An increase in a demand for a particular finished product might not cause an increase in overall demand for the metal if other uses are declining, or if the amount of metal actually involved is not significant, compared to total world production.

**Consumer Preferences.** In certain situations, two or three metals are similar enough to provide a choice of which metal to use for a specific application.

But suppose a purchasing agent prefers one metal because he or she finds it easier to obtain, or because of a good relationship with a dealer who supplies it; or an engineer or plant manager, for reasons that few are able to explain, likes working with a particular metal and not another; or perhaps a designer is simply too busy—or too lazy—to make a change, and would rather stick with an old favorite. Even in the world of heavy industry, the choice of materials sometimes boils down to subjective preference.

Subjective or not, the preferences of purchasers, engineers, and designers can have a profound effect on demand. This is a closely knit group, and certain metals have a way of becoming fashionable, which means the industry as a whole might tend to think as one in its preference for one metal over another, even if the reasons aren't quite logical or clear.

## PRICE

The price of a metal is not simply a symptom or reflection of supply and demand. Price *interacts* with the supply/demand balance, and in many cases actually alters the picture. In fact, some economists view the relationship between supply/demand and price as a version of the old chicken-and-egg question.

If there is a dramatic change in the price of a metal, you can expect the market to react to it, and usually the supply/demand situation will shift accordingly. Often, the obvious occurs: consumers buy less when the price is high.

Higher metals prices reduce the income of the user if he or she can't readily pass the increase along to customers. So, the user has less money to spend, which in turn can mean fewer dollars available to spend on the metal.

For example, a manufacturer of a titanium component for the aircraft industry has a contract to supply those components at a set price. But if titanium prices go up, and the manufacturer can't raise the price of the components, the firm will have less money available for expansion and continued manufacturing.

Shortages and price rises can ultimately be very damaging to a metals market, because they encourage substitution and conservation, thereby reducing demand and softening prices in the long term.

Engineers and scientists have been enthusiastic about tantalum in recent years, and the projections were for steady growth through the year 2000. But when the price ran from $28 per pound to almost $100 per pound in just a few short months, it discouraged new and widespread use of tantalum, ultimately resulting in a slackening of demand. Prices have declined sharply as a result, with free-market prices falling below $40 per pound in 1981.

Investors must regard a sudden dramatic rise in the price of a metal as a red flag; they must examine the situation carefully to see how prices will affect the overall health and profitability of the consumers and the use and development of substitutes. If consumers are relatively unaffected by the price and substitution remains a difficult or unwarranted option, the dangers of a slackening demand are lessened, and investing in metal may be a wise decision.

The concept of *elasticity* is helpful in understanding how metals prices are reached. Basically, elasticity is a measure of the relationship between price and supply and demand. There are several types of price elasticity: elasticity of supply, elasticity of demand, and cross elasticity.

### How Prices Affect the Supply of Minor Metals

The sensitivity of supply to a change in price is measured by *price elasticity of supply*. It is said to be high when the supply is very sensitive to a change in price, that is, the supply changes when the price changes. Supply is said to be inelastic when a price change has little effect on the supply. Several factors directly affect this sensitivity, and they are evaluated by experts in an attempt to determine whether a price change will affect supply:

**Time Frame.** Time frame is generally viewed in terms of two broad categories. The *short run* refers to the time period during which plants and equipment cannot generally be changed. The *long run* refers to the time in which major changes can be implemented. Because companies have more time to adjust, supply is generally more sensitive to price over the long term.

Always evaluate price elasticity of supply in terms of a time frame. For example, suppose a mining firm announces plans to increase its output of titanium sponge. Find out how they are going to do it. Are they building a brand-new mine in a new area? That will take some time. Or are they converting a processing plant once used for aluminum to one that can handle titanium? That will probably take a lot less time than exploiting a new mine. If they are reopening a mine that was closed only six months ago, it could start running again in a matter of months.

Knowing when new supply will hit the market can make the difference between a profitable trade and one made too early or too late.

If a supply squeeze is but a few months old, producers are running at capacity, and the outlook points to continued strong demand, it is likely that higher prices will continue, all other factors being equal. Supply probably won't be very elastic. On the other hand, if supplies have been tight for a year or two, there is a pretty good chance that at least some of the producers have done something about it, and it may be only a short time before new capacity comes on stream. This new supply might stabilize or even depress the price.

Generally, a minimum time frame for the introduction of new mining capacity is about two years. This can be accomplished when it is simply a matter of expanding an existing operation and ordering equipment that can be supplied off the shelf. To exploit new properties, it may take three to four years if the properties are in mining districts that already have housing, power, and transportation. But it may take eight to ten years if there is no infrastructure.

Refineries and smelters can usually be expanded in one to one and a half years, and scrap refineries can be converted to accept primary material if the need is there.

**Significant Changes in Industry Output Capability.** A war or natural disaster that restricts the ability of the mining industry as a whole to meet demand will, of course, make supply less price-elastic. If an earthquake closes a major silver mine, one can't extract silver no matter what the price. How severe an effect this has on the market depends on how important the mine is to total world output and the condition of above-ground supplies, as well as the ability of the rest of the industry to absorb the loss. Therefore, don't rush to buy a metal simply because you hear that one of the mines is in some sort of trouble.

**The Cost Structure of the Metals Producers.** How the producers will react to a rise in price is largely a function of their cost structure. There are three basic types of cost structures in mining:

1. *Constant cost,* in which an increase in output brings no significant change in the production cost per unit, and the profit per ton does not increase no matter how much more is mined. This kind of situation is very rare in the mining industry.

2. *Increasing cost,* in which the cost of production increases with the amount of metal produced. In such a situation, a price increase must be high enough to justify the added costs of expanding production. This cost structure is very common in the mining industry, because mines tend to extract the easiest reserves first, that is, the minerals that are cheapest to mine. There may well be ample deposits of metal farther below the surface, or contained in a different kind of rock, but these deposits might require more costly mining and smelting procedures. If the price is high enough to allow a producer to turn a profit, the deposit will be exploited. If not, the market might not get additional supplies despite a rise in price.

3. *Decreasing cost,* in which an increase in output decreases the cost of production; the more tonnage the producer mines, the cheaper the cost per ton. Such producers might be predisposed toward encouraging consumption rather than trying to get the absolute highest possible price for their metal, favoring stable, slowly rising prices instead. The producers fear that too high a price might reduce demand, thereby cutting into their profits. They will also do what they can to ensure a

steady and adequate supply, reassuring consumers that they need not fear a shortage. This would discourage consumers from looking for substitutes.

The best way to find out about the cost structure of a particular metals industry is through a mining industry analyst attached to a major stock brokerage firm.

### How Prices Affect Demand

The sensitivity of demand to price is measured by the *price elasticity of demand*. It is said to be high when demand changes as the price goes up. Demand is considered inelastic when price changes have little effect on it.

Consider cobalt. The producer price has fallen at least $7 over the past year, but this drop has failed to stimulate demand. An economist might say that cobalt demand is currently price-inelastic. However, every situation is different, and metals should not be classified as elastic or inelastic based on only a few situations. Cobalt would have been considered price-elastic when demand dropped about 8 percent from 1978 to 1979, the period of its meteoric price rise. This wasn't due to a shortage. Production for that period actually increased.

Several factors affect elasticity of demand:

**Time Frame.** Generally, the demand for a metal is more sensitive to price over a long period of time than it is over a short one. The longer the period, the more time consumers have to find substitutes, redesign products, and otherwise reduce their need for that metal. But during that time frame, many other things can happen to counteract such reductions in demand. New uses and new discoveries may keep the need for a metal strong, even after years of high prices. Thus, the timetable for new applications of a metal must be an important consideration as well.

**Substitutes.** Demand for a metal may prove very sensitive to price if consumers can find a less expensive substitute. The extent to which substitution will render the demand for a metal price-elastic depends on how widespread the substitution is expected to be. If substitution takes place only in "fringe" areas, demand will not be greatly affected.

**The Importance in the Overall Budget.** Suppose the price of black pepper were to double. Would you stop using it as a seasoning? Probably not, because pepper represents a very small portion of your grocery budget. On the other hand, were beef prices to double, you might buy less meat, as that change could have quite an impact on your total budget.

The scenario is not much different in minor metals. While it is true that almost every builder of automobiles uses cobalt, only a small amount per car is required. Strategic Metals Corporation estimates that between $1 and $2 worth of cobalt is used in a $10,000 automobile. As in the black pepper example, the manufacturer probably would not bother to replace the cobalt it is using even if it were to double in price. If the cobalt in that car were to sell for $4 instead of $2, it would not affect the overall cost of the auto. (If a minor ingredient were to increase in cost sufficiently—say 600 percent—it might warrant substitution.)

Thus, if a price change in a metal has only a minimal impact on the user's total costs, it is unlikely that demand will be greatly affected.

### How a Price Change in One Metal Can Affect Demand for Another

Change in demand for one commodity is often the result of a change in the price of another. This relationship is measured by *cross elasticity of demand*, and is useful in determining the extent to which two commodities are substitutes or complements. It is very likely that if the price of butter drops, the demand for margarine will drop with it, because most people will prefer the higher-quality product if the price is within their budget. (One exception: to the extent that margarine is used instead of butter for health reasons, demand would probably remain unaffected by the butter price.) In such cases we say that the cross elasticity is positive, that is, the price of one commodity and the demand for the other move in the same direction, and the two commodities are regarded as *substitutes* for one another.

Consider another example. If the price of gin were to drop, the demand for tonic would probably rise, because people would buy more gin and require more tonic to mix with it. In this case, the cross elasticity is negative, that is, the price of one commodity moves in the opposite direction of the demand for the other, and the products are referred to as *complements*.

Cross elasticity can be applied to the supply component as well—a change in price of one metal will often result in a change in the supply of another. This is useful in understanding how price can affect the base metal/by-product relationship. For example, if the zinc price declines, the supply of germanium decreases, because lower prices usually mean less zinc production, and less zinc output means less germanium coming out of the ground with it. Since both zinc price and germanium supply move in the same direction, the cross elasticity of supply between zinc and germanium is said to be positive. Even a basic understanding of this concept allows an investor to see how a drop in the price of one metal may trigger a buying opportunity in another.

## SUBSTITUTION

The press has oversimplified the concept of substitution of minor metals. It isn't simply a matter of finding a suitable replacement for a metal in short supply or one that is overpriced. Rather, it is a complex process involving many variables. One must ask: At what price do consumers start looking for substitutes, and for which applications? How much time does it take to effect a substitution program once the decision has been made by the consumer? When it is claimed that there is no known substitute for a particular metal, does that mean that the product or products cannot be made without it, or that there will be some loss of quality, or slightly different characteristics? Can the end users live with lower quality if it means a cost savings, or must they have the very best?

Government agencies, mining conglomerates, and major consumers pay thousands of dollars to think tanks for answers to these questions. At best, they are correct only some of the time. The U.S. Bureau of Mines publishes up-to-date information on new use patterns and substitution possibilities, and the last section of this book includes that information as of 1982, along with the major end uses of each metal. This will help you answer questions such as: Is substitution viable in several major applications, or only a specific case? How much will the annual consumption be affected by a substitution? A substitute for chromium in metal plating, for example, would have far less impact than a substitute for stainless steel.

Let's look at the factors that influence substitution.

### High Prices
Somewhere in the price behavior of the market, there exists a price high enough to send consumers all over the world

searching for suitable substitutes. It is not a price you get by calling Merrill Lynch, however. It exists in principle, but no one seems to have located it with a great degree of accuracy. Such a price, if known, could be quite helpful in projecting the "top" of a market, because one would know that once a certain price level was reached, serious attempts would be made to reduce consumption of that metal.

In 1979, skyrocketing cobalt prices triggered a major decision by Pratt & Whitney to eliminate the need for 65,000 pounds of the metal in its J-5 engine. Said Executive Vice President Richard J. Coar in *Business Week* (July 2, 1979), "There was no reason to change as long as cobalt was $6 a pound. But at $45 per pound, you make the change."

In the long run, high prices can actually have a negative impact on substitution programs. At a high enough price, producers will increase their output. If that price is reached, considerable amounts of new supply could enter the market before any meaningful substitution program gets off the ground. Then, if the added supplies lower the price of the metal, plans for further substitution might be discouraged.

## Time
Substitutes must be located, ordered, and delivered. The plant must be adapted to accept new materials, a complicated procedure in many cases. The lead time involved is usually a minimum of two years. In more extreme cases, new technology may be needed to find or formulate a substitute or to redesign the product to accept one. It is difficult to predict exactly how long that will take.

## Time/Price Combination
While there are many technical and mechanical limitations on how fast substitution can take place, the price pattern can accelerate or slow down the process. A high price might motivate a producer to embark on a substitution program that takes about five years. But if the price moves still higher, the producer might speed things up, implementing it in only three.

Producers who misjudge the time/price combination can inadvertently encourage substitution and a decrease in demand by raising prices excessively or withholding supply. For example, the world's oil producers appear to have raised the price of oil too high in too short a period of time. OPEC was well aware that the industrialized nations would act to reduce consumption, but it did not anticipate the speed and effectiveness of energy programs.

### Progress
Substitution is not always the result of shortages or high prices. Sometimes, it is simply the result of the forward march of innovation. The nature of science and technology is to advance, and businesses must remain competitive. Designers are therefore always searching for better ways to make things. In this context a certain amount of substitution is inevitable for virtually every metal, no matter how unique or indispensable it may appear. Once, beryllium was the darling of aerospace designers. A short time later, metallurgists developed a beryllium-copper alloy that was superior to the pure metal in many applications, while requiring far less beryllium. Recently, titanium has come into widespread use in aerospace only to be threatened by the advent of new ceramics and composites.

Since no one can predict exactly when and in what form a breakthrough will occur, it seems wise for the serious investor to purchase an assortment of metals. If a few of the minor metals in the portfolio fall out of favor, perhaps several others will be just coming into their own. (For more on the "basket approach" to investment, see page 270.)

### Relative Price of the Substitute
Before becoming aggressive about replacing a metal, consumers must first consider whether the substitution will prove economical.

While many metallurgical engineers believe that new ceramic and composite materials will greatly reduce metal consumption, the price of these miracle substitutes could one day be dearer than the metals they replace. The pattern might then reverse itself, with the demand flowing back toward the metals.

This kind of cyclical behavior of a metal and its substitute, as explained by mining expert Dr. Frederick Collender, is depicted in Figure 5.

### Suitability
Elements may be similar in atomic structure and properties, but no two are exactly alike. So whenever you make a substitution, you make a change in the end product.

Sometimes, achieving the same quality and performance with a substitute is simple. One need only do some minor redesigning, or alter the method of manufacture, or juggle around the other ingredients, like a chef substituting honey for refined sugar.

But there are many instances when the use of a substitute means downgrading the performance of the product. In some applications, a manufacturer might be able to live with the change. For example, tantalum is used in the manufacture of high-quality electronic capacitors. Aluminum and ceramic capacitors can serve as substitutes, but they are used mainly in home entertainment equipment, where the requirements are less demanding than in certain ultrahigh technology applications.

In many instances, there are no suitable substitutes.

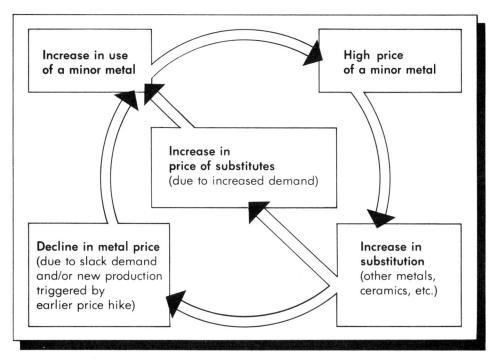

**Figure 5.** *Substitution resulting from high prices may occur in a cyclical manner.*

Replacement of the vital metal would change the product significantly or make it prohibitively expensive. In 1978, the National Materials Advisory Board concluded that, "An estimated 90 percent of the aircraft industry consumption [of chromium] is considered essential. Elimination or even reduction of the chromium content in the alloys would severely downgrade aircraft performance unless a technological breakthrough is achieved in materials development programs."

It would seem that profit opportunities exist in metals that appear to have no substitutes at anything short of an astronomical price. While this alone is not sufficient reason for investing, it does eliminate one of the consumer's primary methods of responding to a shortage or high price. Keep in mind, however, that the development of a viable substitute could be just around the corner.

### Shifts in the Projected Use Pattern

A metal may be slated for use in several major applications that are only in the development stages. But further down the road, designers may have second thoughts about using that metal—because of its price, the discovery of a superior material, or a change in technology. Copper, for example, is expected to be a major component of solar thermal energy systems. Forecasters take this into account when arriving at demand forecasts for the next two decades. But it is entirely feasible that solar electric energy, not thermal, will become the dominant method of harnessing energy from the sun. It would use far less copper, and far more silicon, which is needed for the manufacture of photovoltaic cells.

So a bright demand picture can be tarnished before a metal has a chance to show what it can do. This kind of shift in the use pattern is not really a form of substitution, because the metal was never really put to use in the first place, but it could mean that your expectations of great profits have to be revised downward. And it may mean that you should think about selling your holdings altogether.

### Subjective Variables

Designers, engineers, production and financial executives may for months, or even years, grumble about the high price of a metal or the difficulty in obtaining it. Then suddenly, a decision is made to go ahead with a substitution program. A designer or metallurgist who has been too busy or too lazy to search for a suitable substitute may suddenly decide the time has come. He may be responding to pressure: when times get tough, the cost accountant's voice often gets louder.

Or perhaps a purchasing agent has some harsh words with a producer, and attempts to get the company to substitute away from that producer's product; or a new production manager comes in who wants to work with a metal she is more familiar with.

While the pressures to substitute may be economic and somewhat measurable, the actual go-ahead decision sometimes boils down to decidedly human factors, such as personality, preference, and serendipitous discovery.

### The Substitution Ladder

The following table is an attempt by R. U. Ayres to demonstrate the different circumstances and mechanisms that bring about technological substitution. At the bottom of the ladder, mechanisms used by supply forces dominate. As we go up the ladder, methods used by demand forces are represented.

| Level (Rung) | Brief Description | Example |
|---|---|---|
| VII | Shift in social or personal values or goals resulting in shift in demand | More consumer goods versus quality of life |
| VI | Shift in strategy to achieve goals | Telecommunication versus personal travel |
| V | Shift in technical means (i.e., systems) to implement strategy | Individual personal transport versus mass transport |
| IV | Shift of subsystems, within a system (design change) | Internal combustion engine versus battery powered vehicle |
| III | Shift in components (design change) | Piston engine versus turbine engine |
| II | Shift in materials for specified component | Aluminum versus cast iron for engine blocks |
| I | Shift in materials processing technology | Ingot casting versus continuous strip casting of metals |

Source: *Materials in World Perspective* by D. G. Altenpohl, Berlin, Germany: Springer-Verlag, 1980, p. 161.

## STOCKS

Let's consider another side of the base metal/by-product relationship. What happens if demand is great for the base metal, but weak for the by-product?

For example, during an economic boom, when base metal production is near or at full capacity, the amount of by-product being mined will naturally be quite substantial. Producers will sell as much base metal as they can mine profitably. But if demand for the minors is not sufficient to utilize the additional supplies, producers will be faced with an oversupply and the market will become soft. Producers then create stocks, literally piling up the by-products in the form of residues from base metal processing, slag, or pure metal. The producers are banking on the notion that demand for the by-products will eventually pick up, and they will be able to sell the metal out of stock.

During the recent recession, with base metal production down, the output of the minor metals was down as well. But in certain cases, producers have simply supplied the market with by-product stocks built up during the boom years of the mid-seventies. For some by-products though, the stocks built up during the last boom aren't sufficient to keep pace with current demand, and tight supplies are expected to continue until the picture brightens for the base metals. With the relative growth of minor-metals consumption far outstripping that of the base metals, it appears likely that producers will have difficulty maintaining and building stocks of their by-products.

A graphic example of the above-ground stock situation is provided by germanium, a by-product derived largely from residues and wastes associated with the smelting and refining of zinc. There are enough reserves of recoverable germanium to meet demand for quite some time, but because of depressed zinc production and inadequate methods of germanium recovery, stocks have held the key to the market supply.

To be considered even a potential source of germanium, the zinc ore must contain at least 10 parts per million (ppm) of germanium. Most ores do not contain even this minute amount, but there are some that contain up to 50 ppm. It is from these ores that zinc concentrates containing 100 ppm are produced.

Because it is very expensive to recover, *germanium is extracted only to meet existing demand*. The number of zinc producers providing germanium is very small, and many simply sell off their germanium residues to smelters or other producers, rather than extract it themselves. Most of the flow of recoverable germanium is being wasted, and at this time it could make a real difference since supplies are tight.

For many years, demand for germanium has been met from inexpensive stockpiled residues accumulated years ago by the two largest free-economy producers, Eagle Picher and MHO. Lately the situation has been changing, however. Zinc production has been way down in the wake of the recession, and demand for germanium is much greater than had been anticipated even in the late 1970s thanks to the widespread use of germanium in electronics and infrared optics.

As a result, the traditional stocks of residues have been dwindling, and the producers have had to turn to "leaner" residues from which it is more costly to extract germanium. The high price of the metal reflects this apparent shortage.

At current prices, it is considered worthwhile to replenish stocks of the residues, and to use residues with lower ppm of germanium. Many experts feel that there will be sufficient germanium around to meet demand within three to five years. Since the recovery costs could be higher, however, germanium could well remain at a high selling price.

The stock situation for a metal is one of the most important determinants of price behavior, and some say the most important. Unfortunately it is among the most difficult to assess, because the producers and consumers are not in the habit of telling the world how much they have on hand. They will give the various research groups and government agencies some ball-park figures, but experts all agree that those figures can range from slight exaggerations to complete fabrication. The industry tells the public just what they want it to know or believe.

In assessing minor-metals stocks, one must make the distinction between demand and consumption. Demand is the tonnage that is required by consumers; consumption is the amount actually used. *When users fear a shortage, demand will exceed consumption*, because users will often buy more than they consume, building up stocks to assure an adequate supply. *In times of surplus, consumption will often exceed demand*; the users will buy less than they use because they are drawing on their inventories. Users then feel comfortable drawing down these stocks because they know there is plenty of metal out there in the market should they need more on short notice.

The simplest way to assess the stock situation is to ask, "Is the amount being produced approximately equal to the amount demanded?" And, "Is the amount of metal actually demanded approximately equal to the amount being consumed?" The answer to the first question should tell you something about the situation with respect to stocks held by producers: if they are taking more out of the ground than they can sell, they will stockpile it. The answer to the second question hints at what the *users* might be doing: if they are buying a lot more than they are using, they are not throwing the metal away—they are building an inventory.

The current trend has producers holding much of the excess stock during slow periods. Consumers have been saying to producers: "You hold the stocks, and we'll draw them down as needed at an agreed-upon price."

Ideally, you or your adviser should spend some time looking at metals statistics for past years in yearbooks and Bureau of Mines publications. Stocks are created or depleted over time, so you can't deduce much from the examination of a single year. If it is clear that a shortage existed five years ago, starting then would make good sense, because it is likely that there wasn't much above-ground stock around at that time.

Remember that minor-metals stocks tend to accumulate during booms and are depleted in downturns. However, there are exceptions. Demand for a metal may surge and stay strong for several years, through boom, recession, or a full business cycle. The industry may be caught off guard, and never get a period in which to build adequate stocks.

## SUPPLY OVERHANG

In some cases, when the trade is aware of a large stock, who owns it, and its approximate size, its very existence can actually put pressure on the price—even if the stock remains unsold. Such a supply "overhang" is especially apparent if it becomes known that the holders of the stock have no intention or means of using the metal. They may be hoarding the stock for some unknown reason; or they may simply be private speculators who are seeking to make a sizable profit by trading in a metal they have no use for, and waiting for the price to climb high enough to merit cashing in. When they do liquidate, the flood of additional supply is likely to bring the price down again. Thus, even the producers know that a sudden price rise will result only in a sudden increase in supply, so they would rather the price stay low to protect market stability. In this manner, a supply overhang can put downward pressure on the price, undermining the very purpose of the speculators' investment.

It is for this reason that many experts believe large private purchases of minor metals will not pay off, and disagree with proposals to give tax incentives to those who purchase them. Private purchasers may be helping the nation, they contend, but it is unlikely that they will make money, because they will create an overhang.

In the spring of 1980, a buyer or group of buyers (several experts implicate a group of Beverly Hills movie and television millionaires) apparently tried to "corner" the cadmium market. They reportedly bought about $3 million worth, driving the price from $2.00 to $3.50 per pound. Their $3 million was then worth about $5 million on paper. Apparently, the group thought they would slowly take out some of their profits, so they sold a mere $200,000 worth, about 4 percent of their holdings. But even such a small sale was enough to signal the markets that the speculators were unloading. The result: a price reversal that sent the cadmium price back to where it came from.

There were probably other factors to help account for the pullback. But even today, the entire industry believes that this group is still sitting on almost $3 million worth of cadmium that they can't use. That stock has hung like the Sword of Damocles over the price.

## HOW FAR DOWN THE LINE?

The extraction of metals from ore is a complex process involving several steps. By-products are usually extracted in a sequence, which is determined by the technology in use and the relative importance of the by-products involved.

Consider germanium. There are several methods of processing zinc ore, and which one is used depends on the kind and grade of ore as well as the end products desired. But with all the methods there are by-products such as cadmium and arsenic that are recovered first because they are considered to be of greater economic importance than germanium. Because of this "extraction line," a slackening in demand of one by-product may affect the production of another.

There is one important benefit to being at the bottom of the extraction line. After the residues have gone through several extraction steps, each one removing still another by-product, what is left is usually a very high concentration of the "final" by-product or products. This makes recovery more feasible. Indeed, it is fairly easy to recover germanium from the residue and the precipitate left over at the end of zinc processing.

## CONSERVATION

While recycling superalloys was virtually unheard of before 1978, the possibilities are now being explored with some encouraging results. Certain high-technology procedures require two to four times as much raw material as actually goes into the final product. Only about 15 percent of all titanium metal used ends up as finished parts. Sixty-eight percent is recoverable scrap, and the rest is not recoverable. If this excess metal could be recovered and used, we could reduce our overall requirements significantly.

Some experts, including ASARCO's Simon Strauss, believe that recycling improvements will not be a substantial factor in meeting our overall consumption needs. Strauss also points out that some metals are totally consumed in the alloying or processing stage. Hence, there is nothing left to recycle, and little in the way of discarded scrap.

However, experts such as Charles River Associates' Dr. Firoze Katrak believe that we can continue to improve on the *kind* of recycling being done. He points out that there is free-market competition for scrap as well as virgin metal, and the forces of supply and demand will have their effect on conservation, recycling, and scrap supplies. A few years ago, much of the waste was sold off as all-purpose junk metal, which usually got mixed in with other metals in steel production, rather like the "meat by-products" used for filler in lower-quality hot dogs. Recently though, fabricators have begun to segregate their scrap for remelting so that the waste material is converted into usable metal of specific types and grades. For example, high-quality titanium scrap is very valuable, and its most efficient use is in titanium alloys. But the scrap market has traditionally sent much of that titanium to the steel industry, which doesn't really require such high grades in its manufacture. As titanium prices go up and demand for ingots increases, the scrap distribution pattern is certain to change.

When considering the impact of a conservation or recycling program, first consider where the conserved metal is going. Will it be used wisely, helping to meet a primary demand, or will it wind up in a product where several less costly or lower-grade metals would do just as well?

## ENERGY

Energy is a major cost component of the mining and refining of minor metals. But the impact of rising energy bills on the cost of production and, ultimately, the selling price of the metal vary with each individual situation.

For certain metals, the selling price is so close to the cost of production that if energy costs go up so must the price of the metals. This can be likened to a building that rents for little more than the mortgage payments, taxes, repairs, and utilities. If the heating oil and electric costs rise substantially, the landlord must raise the rent to survive.

Other metals have a much larger profit margin to work with. In 1979, when cobalt was selling for $40 per pound, its selling price obviously bore no relationship to the cost of production, because a short time earlier the producers were making money selling it at $6 per pound. A doubling or tripling of energy costs could be absorbed with little difficulty. Of course, producers could try to use energy costs as an excuse to raise the price even higher, but the point is that an increase in energy costs does not always *necessitate* a rise in the selling price.

Generally, the energy cost is a larger component of the production costs of metals that are abundant or easy to recover. Most of the money is spent on smelting and refining, where a lot of energy gets used, and far less on exploration and mining. Abundant metals usually involve less costly mining techniques as well.

For example, the raw materials cost of silicon and ferrosilicon is minor. There is plenty of silicon around, and it is easy to mine. Most of the production cost is for the power required to drive the electric arc furnace used for smelting. Silicon prices are therefore intimately connected to energy costs. This caused some speculators to buy up silicon during the 1974 oil embargo on the hunch that if energy prices skyrocketed, so would silicon. Indeed, the price almost doubled that year, but that wasn't due to energy costs alone, and subsequently the price did level off quite a bit from its high.

The energy cost of metals processing can also vary according to the heat required to remove the metal from the ore. Titanium, for example, requires a tremendous amount of heat to refine, while copper generally requires much less.

In the seventies, it was estimated that the metals industry consumed about 9 percent of the nation's energy. But the rapid rise in oil prices has already spurred metals producers to look for ways to reduce energy costs, including more efficient methods of refining and alternate forms of energy.

As the world uses more of its easily recoverable resources, it will have to turn to reserves that are more difficult and costly to extract. This may result in additional costs for advanced technologies and mining equipment, and make energy less dominant in the overall cost of production. On the other hand, as producers are forced to mine "leaner ores" with a much lower content of metal, they will have to use more energy to extract the same amount of metal.

## SPECULATION

Metals industry representatives are in the habit of referring to speculation in minor metals as something new. However, it is clear that some speculation has been taking place for a while.

For years, minor metals was a "fringe" business for traders. The amounts traded were small, and so was the dollar volume. The market could turn on a single innovation or a very modest change in the supply/demand picture. Many traders felt that the way to make minor-metals dealing worthwhile was to take a position—that is, to speculate on the price.

In recent years, minor-metals dealers have tended to speculate a bit less, as the recession and continued high interest rates have made that practice even more risky than usual. Also, many traders have been "burned" by unscrupulous or reckless brokers.

Minor-metals traders nevertheless continue to maintain positions. They might take possession of a metal at a price they consider favorable, and hold it for a while on the belief that it will go higher. The traders are confident that they will be able to get rid of the metal somewhere, even if a great profit doesn't materialize.

Less common is the process of "shorting" the market: a dealer, believing the price is going lower, will agree to sell a specified amount of metal at a fixed price, for delivery at a future date, because he or she believes that by the time the delivery date rolls around, the price will be much lower. The dealer will then buy the metal at the lower price and sell it to the buyer at the higher fixed price, pocketing the difference. This is a very risky business because the dealer often has no metal in stock. If there is a shortage, he or she may have to pay an outrageous price to meet the obligation to deliver.

Technically, producers, consumers, and dealers are all speculators to a degree, because they form opinions on which way the prices will move and take action accordingly, which may involve some risk. Large consumers may at times purchase more metal than they can use and stockpile it because they believe that the metal is underpriced and going higher.

"Users always have a view of the market," says Eliot Smith of Bache Metals. "If they think it's going up, they might be more aggressive buyers. Is that speculation? I call it smart buying. They know that they will eventually use what they buy."

This is the primary difference between trade speculators and private speculators, or investors. The trade can use the metal in a product or service; the investor's only choice is to sell it back at some future time or to hold it indefinitely.

Sometimes a savvy metals purchaser may find his hands tied by the firm's financial officers. When interest rates are high, they tend to discourage the maintenance of large inventories. Purchasers, on the other hand, may sense a bargain during such periods, especially if the high rates have softened the economy, and metals prices with it. Ironically, several industry officials have told us that when metals rise in price, the financial officers are the first to ask why stocks are so low.

Admittedly, the financial officers' actions may have been necessary to protect the company during hard times. And of course, the purchasers are often wrong about the future price. As an investor, you must learn to play both roles, that of the risk taker and the conservative manager. Later on, we'll take a look at the kind of questions you must ask before deciding to invest and at some of the strategies you can use.

Many experts are quite concerned about the effect of private speculators on the minor-metals markets. They are quick to point out that such participants do not understand the markets or how to trade them, and that speculation might bring about excessive and magnified swings in prices, causing the markets to become disorderly and dangerous. They maintain that, by contrast, professional trade speculation is done on a reasonable scale by players who have a vested interest in a stable market.

Others see it differently. "There is no doubt that private client interest has always been present and that it is better to have it organized and fairly visible than hidden," says Howard Masters, director of Lambert Metals Ltd., a prominent London metals dealer. In this manner, Masters feels, any price movements caused by speculators can be detected and, if the market wishes, discounted. The end result could be minor-metals prices that more accurately reflect market conditions. On the other hand, Masters does not expect many quick or easy fortunes to be made through buying and selling minor metals.

In general, the overall effect of speculation on price has been limited. The amounts involved are small, and the players are not in the habit of "dumping" their holdings under pressure, a practice that could cause the price to collapse. Merchants tend to liquidate slowly, finding buyers for their inventory. Consumers simply use the metal in their products, looking a bit foolish for having paid too much for the stuff. On occasion, one or several large investors have set out to make a bundle by taking a large position in the metal, and have lost a bundle instead.

Things could be different in the future. The volume of minor metals produced and consumed is very small when compared to the potential capital that investors could inject into the market. In some cases, it appears plausible that a group of investors could "corner" the market for a time. The entire annual world production and above-ground supply of germanium could probably be purchased for under $200 million, a relatively small amount in the investment industry. Even a small portion of that, perhaps $20 million invested in germanium, would undoubtedly impact the market.

But for how long? The production of germanium is a continuous process, and new supplies are constantly entering the market. If there were a steady stream of investors to meet that supply, buying up every kilo in sight, the situation could conceivably become unruly, with investors bidding against users.

If investment interest were to abate, the market would eventually readjust as more and more germanium production increasingly diminished the overall impact of that $20 million cache.

If the group of speculators holding the germanium were capable of acting together, they might continue to buy up a portion of germanium production in an attempt to maintain their grip on the market. But individuals are no match for the combined buying power of two dozen multinational industrial firms. Therefore, it is highly unlikely that a small group of investors could keep the market out of kilter for very long.

Another factor in the overall effect of private speculation is the staying power of investors. How long will the average investor hold minor metals? The most current advice ranges from as little as six months to as long as three to five years. Compare this to the prevailing wisdom on gold and silver bullion or coins: precious metals have been promoted as a form of insurance or "hard money," and investors are encouraged to hold a portion as part of their estate, retirement plan, or long-term investment portfolio.

There is no sense of history attached to minor metals, no feeling of inherent worth. Therefore, don't expect to see many people passing them on to their grandchildren, or giving them as gifts at confirmations and weddings. Minor metals must still be regarded as a "shot" at some potentially good profits over a period of several years. After such time, people will probably seek to take profits, or else grow impatient if there are none. Some Wall Street executives have mentioned the idea of limited partnerships that could take positions in minor metals and hold them for a set period. When that period had elapsed, the remaining metals would be sold off. Several funds with expiration dates could put all sorts of pressure on the market. In essence, these funds coming on line in a certain period would be functioning with the buying power of major producers for the period during which they are accumulating metals holdings. (Of course, they wouldn't be treated like consumers, because they would be one- or two-time buyers). Years later, they would be acting in a manner similar to producers, releasing large amounts of metals into the market.

In order to meet investment demand, producers can increase their production and possibly sell "extra" output not required by the trade to the investing public. If this can be accomplished in some markets, the investors' long-range effect on that market would prove negligible. Another possible scenario: a surge in investor interest could catch the market off balance, and cause a spurt in the price. But the producers might react quickly, possibly flooding the market with enough metal so that consumers who use the metals would not find themselves competing with the investors.

As of this writing, there does not appear to be enough interest in the majority of minor-metals markets to pose any threat to their price stability. And since we are in a serious and protracted economic downturn, investors can quietly accumulate certain metals without seriously affecting the market. In many cases, there are large supplies available. James Gourlay of James Sinclair and Company believes that, in the long run, investors will probably stabilize the markets by creating a "buffer stock," which will be drawn on by consumers when there is a shortage. This investment buffer stock will tend to build up when prices are low, because investors will consider the metals relatively low risks with good profit potential. The investors therefore might be willing to take excess supply off the hands of producers. In this manner, the investing public might actually assume the role that industry has asked various governments and international trade organizations to take—that of a stabilizing influence, propping up low prices and supplying the market during a shortage. Whether or not investors could profit from such a role is a topic of debate, as discussed earlier in this chapter (see "Supply Overhang," p. 198).

## GOVERNMENT INTERVENTION

Whether the intention is to help the metals industry or restrict it, the action of the government has an impact on the market.

Several years ago, the United States government began pouring money into a program to develop a method for producing better-quality silicon at lower costs. In anticipation of the project's success, producers tabled their expansion plans. Why enlarge or build new plants equipped with older technology only to be rendered obsolete? The government was out to reduce costs, so the older plants could never hope to compete with the new generation. The result was a short-term supply squeeze in silicon, because the growth of demand was steady while the supply remained flat.

Another example: In June 1981, the General Services

Administration entered into an agreement with SOZICOM (the world's largest cobalt producer, in Zaire) to purchase 5.2 million pounds of cobalt for $78 million, as part of the U.S. stockpile program. One might expect that the price of cobalt would rise in the wake of such a large purchase. Instead, the free-market price dropped about $3. A little simple arithmetic tells why: the GSA purchase works out to precisely $15 per pound, agreed to at a time when the producer price was $20. Zaire's willingness to sell at that price sent several messages to the market: first, that Zaire had a lot of stock they needed to get rid of, and there weren't enough buyers at $20; second, they were short of foreign exchange, and $78 million provided some help; third, the producers were in a weakened position, and the consumers could reasonably expect the producer price to come down from $20. One London dealer specializing in cobalt commented, "The consumers will be saying to the producers at the next meetings, 'Why should we pay $20 when you sell to the U.S. government for $15?' They will be expecting a break, and they'll probably get it."

A great many investors had previously bought cobalt in the hope that the government would eventually increase its stockpile, forcing the price up. They got their wish, but not their profits. For the moment at least.

As we discussed in Part I, the government's methods of affecting the market are manifold: environmental restrictions that drive up the cost of production; outright mine closings and smelter shutdowns due to violations; changes in the tax laws affecting the industry; import and export quotas and tariffs; and the general resource policy followed by the executive and legislative branches.

# BUYING
# AND SELLING

## NINE

### HOW FEASIBLE IS MINOR-METALS INVESTMENT?

Several market characteristics affect the feasibility of investment. In many cases, those metals with the brightest supply/demand pictures, presenting the best outlook for price appreciation, possess market characteristics that make them unsuitable for investors. Therefore, it is vital that every potential investor assess the overall investment feasibility before making a purchase.

**Liquidity**
Liquidity simply refers to the ease of buying and selling in this market, that is, how readily you can convert your metals to cash and your cash to metals. Liquidity is usually a function of several factors.

**The Size of the Market.** How many tons of the metal are produced and consumed each year? Some minor metals are produced and consumed in large volumes, and the larger, the better. For example, the annual world production of chromium and manganese exceeds that of copper.

**The Dollar Value.** At current prices what is the total dollar value of the metal changing hands? Again, the larger, the better.

**The Number of Buyers and Sellers.** This is as important as the amounts involved. For example, a large dollar-volume of tantalum is freely traded, but there are only a few buyers. As a result, the market is a lot less liquid than the volume would indicate.

**The Marginal Tonnage.** How much metal is in the hands of merchants and what is that amount worth? There are no figures on free-market trade, so it is difficult to determine these amounts. You must rely on the merchant—who will have a feel for how much marginal tonnage is in circulation by how easy it is to buy and sell varying amounts. S. P. Prasadam of Strategic Metals Corporation (SMC) considers $200 million the minimum value a metal traded on the free market must have before his company will invest for a client. Another criteria SMC follows is never to buy more than one percent of the annual world consumption, and to buy only in cases where SMC is confident it can liquidate that amount within twenty-four hours without seriously affecting the price.

**The Tightness of the Supply/Demand Situation.** In most cases suppliers try to produce just enough to satisfy demand, and consumers try to buy only what they will need now and in the future. Some markets allow very little margin of error. For example, total world production of aluminum is around 14 million tons annually, but under certain conditions, the aluminum market could swing on a shortage or surplus of as little as 100,000 tons.

### Volatility

The prices of some metals have a tendency to fluctuate more often and to a greater degree than others. Price fluctuations are important to the investor because they create the opportunity for profit. If the price just sits there, you can't make money. It has to move.

Volatility is more than simple price fluctuation, which is a normal healthy component of any commodity investment. Rather, volatility often connotes very rapid, exaggerated movements, sometimes triggered by news, actions taken by producers or consumers, or even unsubstantiated rumors or fears. Trading in an extremely volatile metal can therefore be dangerous, because you can suffer large losses before you have a chance to close out your position.

As with liquidity, price stability is greatly affected by the amount of metal being traded on the free market. Dealers may buy and sell where and to whom they please at whatever price. Therefore, if they are holding a large amount, the producers, who operate under certain self-imposed restrictions, will be less able to keep the price from moving up and down as the free-market players see fit.

When making an investment decision you must evaluate volatility from three points of view:

**The Historic Volatility.** How volatile has the metal been in the past?

**Future Volatility.** This must be a personal estimate, based upon your and your broker's or trader's view of just how rapid the supply/demand factors are shifting, the state of market flux, and how much metal is in the free market.

**What the Market Believes.** Does the market consider the metal's price to be volatile or relatively stable? If volatile, have the participants taken steps to protect themselves? Are speculators standing aside?

Most professional traders try to come up with a risk/ reward ratio. For a given trading period, they will estimate how much they can reasonably expect the market to drop before they would sell—the risk. And, if they are right, what will be the approximate upside potential price movement—the reward. For a speculative trade to be worthwhile, the potential reward should always be greater than the potential risk, and in most cases, several times greater.

In general, minor-metals prices are not very volatile when compared with precious and base metals. Says Bud Kroll, a minor-metals specialist formerly with Sinclair and Company, "Minor metals prices don't usually move. They ooze."

### Size of Trading Quantities

Minor metals are industrial metals, and the lots traded are sized to conform with the kind of quantities that consuming firms might tend to use readily. By most investor standards, these quantities are quite large. Purchasing a standard amount might require a great deal of money. A 5-metric-ton lot of antimony selling at $2,500 per ton would cost $12,500, a large sum to invest in a single metal.

Smaller lots are not readily tradable. As an investor, you

usually have to deal as the industry does, at least for now. So when looking at prices, consider not only the price per pound or kilo, but also the minimum size of purchase. Recently, some investment firms have been selling smaller lots to clients by simply buying commercial lots and breaking them up for investment clients. There are, however, a few problems associated with this method that we will discuss shortly.

### Storage Feasibility

In many cases, storage is quite a simple matter. Some metals, though, are highly toxic or tend to deteriorate with time, requiring special handling that can substantially increase the cost of your investment. Generally it is wise to stick to metals that have long shelf lives and a high value per unit of weight.

Another storage consideration is the bulk of the metal. For example, the most liquid form of chromium is not the pure metal itself but ferrochrome, which is only part chromium and contains a lot of iron. Storing any worthwhile quantity, therefore, means assuming the warehousing costs of large bulk. Holding metal ore is generally not recommended, since the actual amount of the metal contained is such a small percentage of the overall weight.

The form of the metal also may present problems. Suppose at the time of your purchase, dioxide is the most widely used form, and several years later it is phased out in favor of the sulfide form. Or suppose you purchase a drum of ball metal only to see it replaced by powder. An astute trader will advise his client of a coming change in sufficient time to exchange the metal for a more up-to-date form.

### Grade

Minor metals are sold in varying grades. Grades or purity of the metals are the result of different origin (which often means different types of ore), the method of refining, and the intended end use. Any knowledgeable merchant will be able to advise you as to which of the grades are most liquid at the time. The problem arises when that grade is not immediately available. In some cases, it is better to stand aside than invest in a metal with a less-liquid grade. In other cases, having some metal is better than having none, especially if the market for the less-liquid grade is sufficient to make you feel safe. Just be certain that you are not paying high-grade prices for a lower-grade metal.

### Tax Advantages
In most cases, profits made from the purchase and subsequent sale of minor metals will be treated as capital gains. If you are investing through a corporation, there may be added tax benefits. It is wise to inform your accountant of your intended actions.

### Optimum Holding Period
When purchasing a metal, you must form a concrete idea of how long you are willing—and able—to hold the metal. If this time varies greatly from the holding period judged optimal for investment potential, you might want to pass. For example, if it looks as if we will see a big move in titanium in two or three years, but you can tie up your money for only six months to one year, you would be foolish to invest.

### Foreign Exchange
When you deal in minor metals, the price may not always be denominated in U.S. dollars. Therefore, if the purchase and the sale of that metal must be made in a foreign currency, you are also speculating on the rate of exchange between that currency and the U.S. dollar.

For example, if you were to purchase germanium at £400 per kilo when one British pound was worth $2.50, it would cost you $1,000.00. Suppose that six months later you wish to sell, and germanium is then worth £410 per kilo. On the surface, it looks as if you will make a profit of £10, or $25.00 per kilo. But what if, in the interim, the pound dropped in value and was then worth only $2.25? The value of your germanium is £410 times $2.25, which equals $922.50. So you have actually lost money.

If you cannot deal in dollars, you have two choices: (1) gamble, in the hope that the currency you are trading in will get stronger against the dollar, or (2) use one of several methods to "hedge" against currency fluctuations. Your broker or merchant should be able to advise you on a hedging program that is best for you.

## DEALERS

Because by industry standards their purchases are small and irregular, most private investors are not suitable candidates for a contract with a producer, or even a dealer accustomed to doing business with the trade. The vast majority of investors do their buying in the free market, either directly through dealers or through investment firms that arrange free-market transactions.

Many dealers are unwilling to work with the public, whom they regard as uneducated, undisciplined, and, in the words of one metals trader, "a lawsuit waiting to happen." Recently, a small number of dealers have decided to experiment with a few private speculators to see if such investment business is worthwhile. None of these firms is yet willing to solicit private clients actively. Most have declined to advertise, and almost all reserve the right to refuse to do business with a customer they regard as unsuitable.

Yet it is possible to find a dealer. Start by calling a few to see if they are willing to deal with the public, and more specifically, to deal with you. The names and addresses of minor-metals dealers are readily available in several reference works, such as *Metals Statistics.*

Even if a dealer is unenthusiastic, it pays to ask if he or she would be willing to give you a price quote on one or more metals, as well as a feeling about the direction of those markets. This will enable you to get an idea of how professional metals traders speak to investors, the kind of questions they ask, and how they answer the questions you put to them. A trader who declines to sell to you might well refer you to someone who will or give you some insights into the direction of the market.

If possible, select a dealer who is a member of the Minor Metals Traders Association (MMTA), a London-based trade group that has been in existence since 1973. Since that time, standardized contract forms have been drawn up and adopted by the members. (See Figure 6, pp. 221–22.) Rules of arbitration have been established, and an arbitration board created to settle disputes that might arise from trading between members. In such disputes, the MMTA is able to gain access to the appropriate records of most Rotterdam warehouses, a task that is extremely difficult for an individual.

The MMTA is a selective, tightly knit group, most of whose members know each other. While newcomers tend to regard it as a closed club, using MMTA member firms can provide the investor with a kind of insurance. In addition to the arbitration clauses, transactions between MMTA members tend to be a bit smoother than those between nonmembers.

Says Howard Masters, director of London-based Lambert Metals Ltd., "Even though we are a cliquish world, the closeness that binds us gives us a special understanding of each other's trading problems. . . . This bond makes us unique in the metal world."

Perhaps the best reason to stay with MMTA members is the built-in screening. All candidates for membership must be recommended by a current member. With the growing interest in strategic metals, the professional traders are determined to keep their businesses and reputations from being undermined by investment hucksters who travel from one business to another, leaving a string of lawsuits and victims in their wake. Recently, the MMTA issued a memo to its members alerting them to a California firm that was dealing in minor metals in an unethical manner. It is hoped that such firms will change their ways rather than risk losing the cooperation and assistance of the MMTA members.

## INVESTMENT FIRMS

Most investors lack the time and discipline to do the homework necessary to trade minor metals on their own. Indeed, the language and procedures involved can be quite complicated. It is not surprising that a large number of investors rely on investment firms.

There is a wide range of investment firms offering minor metals to the public. Some are older, established firms that are providing the service to clients as a kind of side business, developed in response to client demand. Others are firms that were set up solely to deal in minor-metals investments. A third variety consists of firms that were previously involved in some other form of alternate investment that no longer attracts the public. Such firms may have pushed gold and silver coins, collectibles, or commodities during the "hard money" seventies, and have been looking for something new to sell.

In most cases, the investment house has struck a deal with one or several trade merchants; this allows the merchants to purchase metal on the free market on behalf of the investment firm's clients. In short, the firm makes the calls to the dealer that the client can't or won't make himself.

Several companies claim to be able to deal directly with producers through some kind of flexible contract. We have never seen proof of this. Theoretically at least, these firms offer competitive prices, and have a source of supply when the free market is tight.

For its role as middleman, an investment company may be compensated in a variety of ways, including commissions, a markup of the metals price, management or administration fee, or even a percentage of the profits. In most cases, the firm will have a resident expert or consultant to advise investors in minor metals.

Finding minor-metals investment firms should be easy. In fact, they will find you. "Retail" business from private investors is their bread and butter, so they advertise aggressively in the principal business and investment publications and in the major metropolitan daily newspapers. They conduct direct-mail and telephone-sales campaigns, and most have toll-free 800 numbers. Their staffs have envelopes stuffed with brochures and reprints to mail to you.

Whether to trade through a dealer or an investment firm is a highly individual choice. If you have the sophistication, wealth, and desire to follow the market carefully on a regular basis, the dealer route might be best. That is, if you can get a dealer to do business with you directly. If you use a dealer, you might also want to consult an expert regularly, paying him or her for advice on an hourly or retainer basis.

For most people, however, investment firms offer the most suitable route. They have made a point of tailoring their programs to the qualified investor, while the dealers have not.

## CHOOSING A FIRM

Once you have decided whether to go with an investment firm or a dealer, you must decide which company or companies to do business with. Here are the questions you should find answers to:

### Is the Firm Highly Regarded?
The best way to assess the reputation of a dealer firm is to phone several other dealers. In many instances, a dealer may be well respected as a trader of certain metals, but may not be considered expert in others. Be sure to specify not only the dealer you are interested in but also the metals you are thinking of trading.

If you are considering an investment firm, begin by asking other investment advisers you rely on if they have heard anything about the ethics and expertise of the firm you have in mind. It is surprising how many rumors that float around Wall Street turn out to be true. There is a chance that your stockbroker or financial planner may have heard or read something that you haven't.

The next step would be to ask the investment firm for the names of the dealers who execute their orders. Call those dealers and get an opinion of the investment firm's knowledge, trading expertise, efficiency, and integrity. Presumably, the investment house has convinced the dealers that it will generate enough business and has enough financial stability to deserve good treatment as a steady and reliable client. So don't expect to get a negative response from the dealer. However, don't be afraid to get specific. Ask the dealer about the investment firm's past trades, how they fared, and other pertinent questions.

Finally, contact the MMTA and ask if there have been any cases brought up before the arbitration board involving the firm, any reports of widespread abuses by them, or any claims against them.

### How Good Are Their Prices?

There will always be a variation in free-market price quotations—that is the nature of a negotiated market. The range is usually no more than 10 percent, however. A price quote that is 30 percent higher than the range of the rest of the quotes is a sure sign that the firm is trying to rip you off.

Don't choose a firm simply on the basis of the lowest quoted price. A slippery salesperson may deliberately feed you a low quote just to get your business. Then, when you open the account, he or she will claim to be unable to fill your order at that price. It may be worth paying a few cents or even a few dollars more per pound to get better, more reliable service and expertise.

### How Knowledgeable Is the Staff?

Does the firm have experienced and knowledgeable metals traders in house? Do you have access to their advice, either by phone, newsletter, or both?

There are many people in the "alternate investment" field who simply go where the action is, as one investment cools off and another gets hot. One year it was diamonds. The year before, gold, silver, coins, and stamps. In principle there is nothing wrong with an attempt to keep up-to-date, as long as the individual advising you knows what he or she is doing. Unfortunately, such alternate investment specialists are often too impatient to do adequate research, too selfish to concern themselves with their client's best interests, and very often just plain irresponsible. In short, they may know less about minor metals than you do (especially now that you've read this book).

Is the firm equipped to keep tabs on all the factors affecting supply and demand? Do they monitor the changes that may cause a metal's outlook to go from sweet to sour? Don't assume that every dealer is knowledgeable. Because of the small volumes involved, many of the larger metals firms have used minor metals as a training ground for new traders. Many of the traders are learning the ropes while they wait to graduate to trading the base metals.

Fortunately, this is not always the case. There are many traders who have spent many years in this field, and lately minor metals have become attractive enough to be regarded as a business worthy of seasoned traders. Make sure that there are several in the dealer firm you deal with.

### Watch Out for High-Pressure Sales Tactics
It is simply amazing what pushy salespeople can do when you are caught off guard. They will appeal to your greed—promising fantastic profits and telling you that "this is your last chance to get on board"—and to your fears—urging you to put some money in strategic metals "before it is too late."

Even if you agree with the salesperson, think clearly about the deal being offered to you, and remember that there are many firms to choose from.

Many firms will advocate the "buy-and-hold" approach to strategic metals as an insurance policy against world instability—the collapse of our economy, the devaluation of currency, or a world war. Keep in mind that minor metals, unlike gold and silver, are not a traditional form of money or stored value. Certainly, minor-metals prices might go up in unstable times, but so will rice, and rice will keep you alive. If there is a major economic collapse, much of the world's industry and technology will slow down or stop, reducing the demand for these metals. Thus, the ideal political situation for long-term investment is not total disaster but a world economy of sustained growth, with a steady arms buildup and, perhaps, a deteriorating situation in southern Africa thrown in for good measure.

## WHAT A GOOD METALS BROKER SHOULD DO FOR YOU

**Provide Information.** In the minor-metals markets, the trader is both the source and receiver of information concerning the "going rate" and liquidity of the metals. Trade journals rely on them for free-market prices. And you must rely on your dealer to provide you with the information necessary to make the proper investment decisions. Besides giving you price quotes, your dealer should be able to give you a sense of the market's direction, of any new developments, political, technical, or otherwise, that the market might be watching carefully.

**Help You Time Your Trades.** Unfortunately, some of the dealers in the minor-metals investment business are anxious to sell you metals as soon as you open your account. They would like to make the purchase, arrange the paperwork, be done with you, and then move on to the next customer. But just because today is the day you *decide* to commit some money to minor metals doesn't necessarily mean that today is the best day to buy all or any of them. A good dealer takes some pride in "buying smart" for a client. He or she will hunt for the right opportunity and will be patient.

A trader must also have the skill to know when to get you out of the market. At certain times, he or she might have to act quickly, and for that reason you might want to give a trustworthy dealer power of attorney (see "Managed Accounts," p. 240). "There is nothing worse than for a trader to let a bull market go stale on him," notes Bryan Webb.

**Keep You Abreast of Sudden Changes.** From time to time, certain intangible changes take place in the market. In many cases, by the time the trade press publishes the information, it is too late to act on the news. And some situations are so subtle they escape the journalists entirely.

Your dealer should inform you of any unexpected buying or selling, the actions of the Russians and other centralized economies, the impact of late-breaking economic figures on the market, and other short-term events. As one London trader told us, "Traders don't rely on analysts or newspapers to tell them how certain events are influencing the price of minor metals. We let the market tell us."

Consider, for example, what happened when news broke in the press about the large purchase of cobalt for the U.S. stockpile. For months prior to the purchase, analysts and salespeople had been telling clients that such a purchase would mean higher prices. But if you had called your broker after the transaction, he or she would have told you that the traders had detected no new buying and that the market had actually softened, with free-market prices dropping several dollars.

**Detect Irregularities.** Although considered rare by most market watchers, there are undoubtedly attempts made from time to time to manipulate or squeeze the markets. A good broker with your best interest in mind will advise you to get out or stand aside if he or she senses any kind of collusion— unless, of course, he or she is part of it. (In that case, just hope the broker will allow you to make a killing equal to his or her own.)

**Be Aware of All Trading Strategies.** An active trader will know all the tricks. He will use them and will recognize situations in which they are being used against him. Several traders have mentioned the common gambit of driving the price down by selling small amounts into the market, and then turning around and purchasing larger amounts at the lower prices.

**Handle the "Traffic" Efficiently.** Once the metals have been purchased, the process of securing them, having them stored, assayed, and insured, and handling the flow of funds should be swift, efficient, and free of errors. This is not as easy as it sounds, but a good broker will make the extra effort to be accurate and prompt.

## BUYING

### Get a Quote

Whether you are dealing with merchants or investment houses, always get several price quotes. Six or seven is not considered excessive, even by professionals.

Minor-metals dealers normally mark up the price of the metals they sell. The difference between their purchase price and selling price is often called the "spread." In some cases the

INVESTING IN MINOR METALS / **220**

dealer will be able to buy the metal at the bid price, and turn around and sell it to the client at the offer price. He or she makes the difference, or spread, between the two prices.

Investment buying usually involves smaller lots than consumer buying, so prices are usually not as low. In addition, the investor has to pay more for the firm to assume the administrative and financial risks of buying a commercial lot and breaking it up into smaller lots. Sometimes, simply finding the metal can be quite a chore, requiring as many as twenty phone calls.

Beware of excessive markups. It is difficult even for traders to arrive at what they consider an accurate price. Nobody is in this business as a public service, and it is not uncommon for firms to make a small markup. But when dealing with an inexperienced client, they just might be tempted to get greedy. Don't let this happen. If a brokerage firm is charging very low commissions, it could be a red flag—they may be making their money in another way. Recently, *The New York Times* discovered a Florida firm selling cobalt at $55.00 per pound at a time when the free-market price was $18.50.

Many investment firms prefer to give the clients a "ballpark" quote, reserving the right to some flexibility in actually closing the sale. This is understandable, since they would otherwise be required to make a phone call every time the quote was changed by even a penny. However, most reputable firms are willing to take a "limit" order in which they may fill the order only at a specified price or lower. Within the trade, a person's word is good enough to seal a deal, but the quotes can't be expected to hold steady for long. Once you agree to make the purchase, the dealer sends a Telex, specifying a price, quantity, delivery, material, packing, and payment terms. The confirmation that follows should contain the information specified in the MMTA Contract Form "B" (see Figure 6).

Make sure that there is a clear understanding concerning the size, grade, origin, and delivery terms that the quote applies to. The quotes may be for a certain grade and origin, but the seller has the option of delivering a slightly different grade or origin, as long as the price is adjusted accordingly. Most good brokers have given notice to the merchant with whom they do business that they will not accept delivery of a grade lower than the minimum specified; however, the seller may deliver a higher grade than the one on the confirmation if he or she so wishes.

In certain cases, even your dealer won't know the precise grade and origin he or she will be able to buy until attempting to execute an order. For example, the bulk of the zirconium output is handled by a few producers. Most free-market activity is confined to scrap alloys and ore. A private investor who wanted to own some would have to be very flexible in grade and form requirements.

When you accept a quote and authorize purchase, you will be required to put up a minimum margin of about 25 percent of the purchase value within twenty-four hours. In most cases, the balance will be expected in a few days, although some brokers require full payment in advance or funds placed in a trust account. Generally, payment is on a 100 percent cash-against-documents basis. Most dealers will require that payment in full be in-house before they will transfer title to you.

**Steer Clear of Small Amounts**

We noted earlier that the trade is accustomed to dealing in lots of metal that would be considered large by the standards of most private investors. Most investment firms will sell you the smallest amount they think is negotiable. If the quantity offered to you is packed in a container that is standard in the industry, in its original drum or bottle with all the proper seals and markings, you know that you have a unit that can at least be grouped with other containers to form a lot large enough for the trade to consider buying. This makes a purchase feasible, although somewhat risky since the investment firm must be relied upon to put a tradable lot together when it is time to liquidate.

Do *not* buy little cans, boxes, or bottles that are filled by opening a drum and parceling it out. First of all, the assay does not hold if the seal has been broken, so you would have to have your small amount assayed again, and that could cost a lot in relation to the amount of the metal. Second, if you tried to sell, say, 100 pounds of cobalt, a merchant would probably laugh, scream, hang up, or do all of those things—anything but do business with you.

**Commission**

Some firms charge a straight commission for each transaction. This can be a flat fee, or a percentage, such as the 4 percent of contract value currently charged by Strategic Metals & Critical Materials, Inc. When comparing, you must look at total costs,

## THE MINOR METAL TRADERS' ASSOCIATION
## CONTRACT FORM "B" (1980)

Contract No. _____ Date _____

_____ agrees to sell, and

_____ agrees to buy, subject to

the conditions overleaf:—

Quantity

Material and Purity

Price

Form and Packing

Origin

Place of Delivery    In Free or Bonded Warehouse _____

Time of Delivery

Terms of Payment    Prompt nett cash against presentation of the following documents either direct to buyer or through a Bank:

1. Warehouse Warrant or evidence of unconditional release by Warehouse to buyer
2. Signed Commercial Invoice, stating origin of material
3. Sellers' or Producers' detailed Weight Certificate showing individual gross and nett weights of each unit of packing
4. Sellers' or Producers' Quality Certificate showing analysis in conformity with description of material above

Unless otherwise stated in the contract, the "Uniform Rules for Collection" of the I.C.C., 1978 Edition will apply

Other Conditions

Signature of Buyer _____ Signature of Seller _____

Courtesy of MMTA, London.

**Figure 6.** *Sample Contract Form. A revision of this contract is currently underway.*

## CONTRACT CONDITIONS

1. This contract is governed by the Uniform Laws for International Sale of Goods, as laid down in the Uniform Laws on International Sales Act 1967 (U.L.I.S.) the whole of which is incorporated into this contract.
   In the interpretation of this Law, English Law shall apply, unless otherwise laid down in the contract by agreement between parties.
2. The formation of this contract shall be governed by the Uniform Law on the Formation of Contracts for the International Sale of Goods as laid down in Schedule 2 of the above Act, the whole of which is incorporated into this contract.
3. The governing contract is to be issued by the Seller. The duplicate is to be countersigned by the Buyer and returned promptly.
4. Delivery of the goods, handing over of documents, transfer of property, payment of the price and passing of the risk, shall be in accordance with the provisions of Chapters III, IV, V and VI of U.L.I.S.
5. With the exception of Mercury, the total net weight of material delivered can vary by plus or minus 2% from the contractual quantity.
6. Part deliveries to be permitted at any time during the delivery period, unless specifically excluded at the time of negotiation of Contract. Unless otherwise agreed such part deliveries to be in minimum lots of:—
   Antimony, Magnesium and Nickel—10,000 kg, Cadmium—5,000 kg, Bismuth—1,000 kg, Selenium—500 kg, Mercury—50 flasks.
   Part deliveries need not be in the same warehouse.
7. Warehouse telex releases and Warehouse warrants shall identify and describe the goods, state the number of packages and the declared weights.
8. In this contract the term "first half of the month" shall mean the first fifteen calendar days of the month.
9. Mercury must be supplied in iron/steel flasks of 34.5 kg net.
10. Documentation in respect of Antimony and Mercury of Chinese origin need not show gross weights.
11. Claims in respect of weight and/or quality shall be notified to sellers by the buyers as promptly as reasonably possible and if required, shall be supported by weighing and/or sampling and assay certificates of established and recognized independent superintendence companies, and/or samplers and assayers. Such certificates shall show that there is prima facie evidence of the identity of the goods and that the packing is intact, allowing for such unpacking as may have been necessary to examine the goods. Claims for difference in weight to be submitted within ninety days, and claims on grounds of quality to be submitted within twelve months of transfer of title.
12. Any dispute arising out of this contract which cannot be resolved by negotiation, is to be submitted to arbitration. The parties to the dispute may by mutual agreement nominate a single Arbitrator from the MMTA Panel of Arbitrators; otherwise they must each nominate an Arbitrator from the Panel. The two Arbitrators must nominate an Umpire also from the Panel, to whom the reference shall be submitted in the event of failure by the Arbitrators to agree an Award.
   The Arbitrator or Arbitrators, shall have discretion to direct the parties as to the submission of statements of case, defence and reply, and shall fix a convenient date for the hearing with adequate notice to the parties.
   The hearing shall take place in London, under the terms of the Arbitration Act 1950; but with the assent of the Arbitrator (or both Arbitrators if two are appointed) the hearing may be held elsewhere and subject to the rules of Arbitration procedure in the country of the place chosen for the hearing.
13. The "Exemptions" provisions of Article 74 of U.L.I.S. are expressly incorporated into this contract.
   To be read in conjunction with MMTA Directive dated 12th December 1978 which supersedes these terms where applicable.

**Figure 6.** (continued)

including storage and insurance (about ¼ percent per month), inspection (about $100), and analysis (about $150). Ask if the firm is marking up the metal, making a "spread," or if the commission is the only source of income.

Be sure that you inquire as to whether the commission covers both the purchase and sale, or whether you must pay a commission to buy and a separate commission to sell your metal. Ask if the commission and/or front load covers the sampling and assay charges and preparation of the warehouse receipt. If not, include them in your total cost figure.

### Scrutinize Your Confirmation of Purchase
The more specific the confirmation of purchase, the better. Check the amount, grade, origin, price, commission, front load, administrative charges, and delivery conditions. Delivery point is the seller's option, but you can negotiate.

### Arrange for Storage
Rotterdam is the traditional storage location for minor metals for several good reasons. For one thing, it is a free port. No taxes are levied on shipments that enter the warehouses, and no taxes are paid as they leave Rotterdam. Since warehousing is a time-honored, respected profession there, the personnel are very professional in their approach.

A number of Rotterdam warehouses are approved by the London Metal Exchange (LME). They are clean, orderly, well kept, and the structures are usually ideally suited for metals storage. These warehouses also perform services such as weighing, bundling, shrink wrapping, and filling bottles, sacks, cartons, and tins. Charges run about 3 percent per year, including insurance.

Pilferage appears to be related to the state of the market, as thieves seek to "home in on" metals that are in demand and fetching high prices. Some of the thieves simply read about these metals in the paper just like investors do, and often don't know what they look like. Sometimes they get confused, as in the case of the gang that stole what they thought was tungsten. It turned out to be tin ore.

Producers routinely ship their output to the free port of Rotterdam if not directly to a consumer, and much of the free-market tonnage is stored there. Therefore, freight charges for your purchase will be minimal or nonexistent. If you want the

## STATEMENT REGARDING FEES

As we have received numerous questions regarding the fees involved in trading strategic metals, it seems relevant to clarify the situation.

The account opening fee is allocated to:

1. marketing costs
2. accounting fees charged by the Chartered Accountant to: set up the individual client trust account and receive and verify the relevant documents of title
3. fiduciary fees charged by the bank

The transaction brokerage fee is allocated to:

1. telephone and communications expenses
2. shipping charges
3. weight and purity analysis certification
4. insurance of certified documents of title by both C. Steinweg and D. C. Griffiths

The storage insurance and administration fee is allocated to:

1. warehousing costs C. Steinweg
2. insurance costs from Lloyd's of London
3. quarterly statements issued by Barclays, and the Chartered Accountants

It was and is the objective of Strategic Metals Corporation to provide these services to the individual clients at the most reasonable fee possible.

Strategic Metals Corporation made a profit on the above services in the past calendar quarter of approximately $70 per $25,000 of client purchases.

That is less than $3/10$ of 1%.

We realize that such fees seem a bit high when compared to fees charged for stocks or shares. We can only emphasize that buying strategic metals is quite different from a paper/computer transaction in the stock or commodity market.

**Source:** Strategic Metals Corporation, London. Used by permission.

**Figure 7.** *Statement from One Investment Firm on How They Determine Their Fees.*

material moved to a special warehouse in another location, you will undoubtedly have to pay for it, except in the most unusual cases.

The warehouse used most often by investment firms is C. Steinweg Handelsveem B.V., the largest of the Rotterdam warehouses that store metals. By all accounts, Steinweg is excellent, but there are at least six other equally reputable LME-approved metals warehouses in Rotterdam.

### Scrutinize Your Warehouse Warrant

In the end, the warehouse warrant will prove to be the most important piece of paper in the entire minor-metals transaction. It is recognized as good delivery against a sales position. Once the warrant has been signed over to you, the seller has in effect met his or her obligation. You may then in turn sell that metal, and use your warrant to back up your sale. Title to the warrant changes when it is signed over to the new owner. In the case of "bearer" warrants, the title belongs to whoever possesses it. More about that later.

A warehouse warrant should include the following:

1. The name and address of the warehouse. Check with the London Metal Exchange to make certain that the warehouse is LME and/or MMTA approved.
2. The warrant number, identifying the actual warehouse document.
3. Reference number. Refer to it when querying the warehouse or broker about the lot being stored. It refers to the paperwork on the shipment.
4. The name of the dealer—that is, the name of the party, whether investment broker or merchant, who executed the transaction in your behalf. Having both names—that of the investment house and that of the dealer—is even better. In many cases, this will appear only on the contract.
5. The packing description. Is the metal in drums? Wooden cases? Plastic bottles? The warehouse warrant should specify.
6. All identifying marks and numbers. The identification marks and numbers that appear on the containers should be recorded on the warehouse warrant.
7. The contents. A description of what is in the containers, leaving no doubt about the name, grade, purity, and

form of the metal. Some of the descriptive information will vary from metal to metal. For example, a warehouse warrant for chromium might say "electrolytic chromium," while one for titanium might read "titanium sponge, T.G. 100 brand." If not on the warrant itself, this information should be on an accompanying document, such as the contract or assay report.

8. The weight. This should be listed in both net and gross figures, and the unit—pounds, kilos, short tons, long tons, or metric tons—should be specified.
9. The warehouse location. This could be a building name and/or location, and the actual storage site within the building. Some warehouses are very large, containing several buildings and/or enormous floors.
10. Identification number. A number assigned to the metal itself by the warehouse when it is accepted for storage.
11. The date of storage. The date the material arrived at the warehouse.
12. The charges. In some cases, the charges are not spelled out on the warehouse warrant, but are on an accompanying storage contract.

Delivery of the warehouse warrant generally takes thirty to sixty days.

### Watch Out for Falsified Warehouse Warrants

If you can't go to Rotterdam to have a look at your metal, the warehouse warrant will be the basic proof of purchase. But what is to prevent a swindler from taking an old warehouse warrant, some correcting fluid, and a good photocopier, and turning out phony warehouse warrants, which he will send you after you have sent him your money?

There are no simple suggestions for how to keep from getting swindled other than to check out the firm you are about to deal with, ask for a bank reference, and examine your warehouse warrant carefully. If you have the slightest doubt, do not send in any cash. Put the burden of proof on the firm. Ask to know more about the transaction: who the purchaser was, where the metal is coming from, whom you can call at the warehouse, and so on.

If you can go to Rotterdam to check the warrants against any physical goods, by all means do so, or send someone you trust in your place. A periodic inspection by an auditor should

# C. Steinweg
# Handelsveem B.V.

P.O. BOX 1068 3000 BB ROTTERDAM ● TELEX STEINWEG 22227/21275 ● TEL. (010) 14.77.11

NON NEGOTIABLE

## WAREHOUSERECEIPT 0001

Herewith we undertake to deliver against presentation of this original warehousereceipt, duly stamped/signed by:

Messrs.

unto Messrs/Mr/Mrs

| MARKS AND NUMBERS | PACKAGES | SAID TO CONTAIN | SAID TO WEIGH IN KOS | |
|---|---|---|---|---|
| | | | NETT | GROSS |
| | | | | |

Not insured by us

Stored in warehouse, in bond

Under rotation no.:

Date of storage:

Warehouserent as agreed payable each six months:

Physical delivery from warehouse can only be effected against payment of warehouserent and other accrued charges.

C. STEINWEG
HANDELSVEEM B.V.

voor condities z.o.z. - for condition p.t.o. - fur Bedingungen b.w. - pour conditions t.s.v.p.

Courtesy of C. Steinweg (Handelsveem B.V.), Rotterdam. Reprinted by permission.

**Figure 8.** *Sample Warehouse Warrant*

also be arranged. But remember, if you have been swindled, any discrepancy may well be discovered too late.

### Should the Warehouse Warrant Be in Your Name?
There is some disagreement among investment experts on the question of having the warehouse warrant in your name.

If it is put in your name, then no one else may sign over the metal to a buyer. If it were to be lost, it would be nonnegotiable by the finder. The warehouse could be notified of the loss and eventually you would be issued a copy of your warrant.

There is one drawback to this. When you wish to sell, you must sign over the warrant and forward it to the merchant or other appropriate party. This could take some time, during which the price and market conditions could change.

Some firms offer to hold your warehouse warrant for safekeeping. If the warrant is in your name, this is unwise, because the merchant will have to send the warrant to you, and you must sign it and return it to him before you can sell it. Thus, you lose even more time.

Your other option is to have the warehouse warrant read "Bearer." If you lose this receipt, you've got a problem, because the "Bearer," whoever that may be, can negotiate it. However, bearer warrants do assure ease of sale, since no signatures are required. If you decide to have the warrant read "Bearer," you should allow your dealer to keep it for you. Your main objective is a rapid sale, and your holding it would add another step. In addition, if you are particular about privacy, bearer warrants have that extra benefit.

Make sure that you feel comfortable with the firm that holds your bearer warrant, and ask where it will be kept. If you keep the original, leave a photocopy of the warrant with your broker. Some firms are reluctant to hold bearer warrants.

If your warehouse receipt is in the hands of a merchant or broker and it is a bearer receipt, there is nothing to prevent the firm from borrowing against the receipt, using the holdings as collateral. In some cases, a firm could borrow as much as 90 percent of the value of the metal in storage.

Not only is this a form of fraud, but it could lead to the loss of your holdings. If the firm were to run into financial difficulties and default on its loan, the bank would simply take possession of the metals. They would be first in line for collection of the bad debt.

Of course, no honorable bank would permit this to occur.

But it could easily be done without their knowledge, since the bearer receipt says nothing to indicate that a third party bought and paid for the metal in question.

Francis Vassallo of Chase Manhattan Bank in London says that this kind of possibility serves to underscore the importance of dealing with a top-notch company. Nevertheless, Mr. Vassallo is one of many who do prefer the bearer receipt approach because of the ease of sale.

Ideally, the bearer warrant or document of title, along with the other paperwork (assay, sampling certificates, and so on), should be kept in a bank vault, and this paperwork should be insured against loss by the bank. Insist on a photocopy of each item, as well as a confirmation of the transaction as carried out in your behalf by the dealer and the amount of money you paid out.

### Make Sure Your Purchase Is Properly Evaluated

When you buy gold or silver, the ingots have already been assayed and marked with the purity and weight. But minor metals are sold as industrial raw materials in just about every conceivable physical state, and it is usually not possible to determine much by simply looking at them. There is always a possibility of a misunderstanding between buyer and seller. It is therefore essential that you or your agent employ an independent inspection company to evaluate your consignment. It is wise to choose an assayer approved by the London Metal Exchange.

Years ago, when minor metals were traded by buyers and sellers who knew each other well, evaluation was necessary only on occasion. But the practice of assaying is becoming more widespread as a result of increasing investor participation. In addition, periods of tight supply in the free market have resulted in substandard metal being passed off as prime grade. Swindles are difficult to detect without the help of an independent assayer.

Investors are especially vulnerable for several reasons. A purchase of minor metals by an investor almost always involves more than two parties, and the risk of a "misunderstanding" increases with every middleman. Also, since the investor won't be using the metal, he or she will not be able to determine whether it is as good as the seller claims it is. Further, the investor does not know who the eventual user of the metal will be, much less the exact specifications that user will require.

In addition, a great deal of time may elapse between the date the investor buys the metal and the time of sale. Thus, if a problem is not discovered until the time of sale, it might be difficult to go back to the dealer—who sold it to the investor several years ago—to demand satisfaction.

*Do not rely on documentation provided by the seller!* Such documentation may not be regarded as sufficient by the party you try to sell to. Even worse, should the metal be accepted and turn out to be a lesser grade or quantity than the document indicates, you could lose a good deal of money. Again, your purchase should be evaluated by an independent assay firm, and be completed within a short time after the transaction has occurred. Usually, transactions are contingent on the results of the weighing, sampling, and analysis.

There are exceptions. In the trade, independent evaluation is often conducted only in the case of a dispute or the filing of a claim. It is common, for example, for the trade to purchase metals (antimony, bismuth, cadmium, and others) from the People's Republic of China, relying on the validity of the Chinese documents if the packing seals and containers are undisturbed. If you are purchasing from a reputable dealer, you may wish to forgo independent evaluation if the purchase is directly from the producer, or the dealer so advises.

How are metals evaluated?

**Sampling.** The sampler inspects the location of the metal in the warehouse, making sure there are no contaminants or atmospheric conditions that could adversely affect the metal. He or she then checks the documents, verifying that they relate to the metal itself, and makes certain that there are no discrepancies. In some cases, the sampler will have the metal emptied from its containers to make certain that it is consistent in appearance and quality from top to bottom.

The sampler will then inspect the metal for signs of substandard grade and casting defects and examine the shapes of the bars and ingots. He or she will then make certain there are no leaks, wet material, or other contaminants present, that the containers are suitable for the contents, that they are properly sealed, and that they are out of the way of harmful traffic. The sampler also weighs the metal, making sure the scales used are accurate. Then a specimen representative of the lot is taken.

# Daniel C. Griffith & Company Ltd.
**2 Perry Road, Witham, Essex, CM8 3TU**
Telephone: Witham (0376) 515081  Telex 995281  Telegrams Gryffydd Witham
Established 1850   International Commodity Samplers and Analytical Chemists

A.C. Israel Woodhouse Co. Ltd.,
21 Mincing Lane,
LONDON
EC3R 7DN.                                        7th October, 1980

<u>REPORT NO: A14/11630 A</u>

<u>CERTIFICATE OF INSPECTION, WEIGHING AND ASSAYING</u>

Material                : LOW CARBON FERRO CHROME
Located at              : C. Steinweg Handelsueem B.V. Rotterdam
Steinweg Ref.           : PB 778

------------------------------------------------------------------------

This is to certify that Daniel C. Griffith & Co. Ltd., have inspected,
sampled and assayed the above consignment and that our findings are as
follows:-

Date of Inspection      : 19th September, 1980

Description of            13 Green painted, 200 litre capacity, metal
Containers              : drums, with fitted lid, secured by bolted clamp
                          ring.   Second hand rusty condition.   Each drum
                          marked with its individual number, 1-6, 14-20.
                          Drums not sealed at time of inspection, but
                          sealed DCG No. NL 13 afterwards.

Description of            Bright silver coloured, hard, brittle, metallic
Material                : lumps of irregular shape, varying in size from
                          25 to 150 mm, and having a crystalline
                          structure at the fractured faces.   Material
                          was clean and free from contamination.

Gross Weight            : 9 356
Tare Weight             :   247
                          ------
Nett Weight             : 9 109 kilos
                          ------

Assay                   : 71.76% CHROMIUM


                        for and on behalf of
                   DANIEL C. GRIFFITH & CO LTD.,

                        J. Rendall


TR/sp

Directors:  Alastair R. Griffith (Executive Chairman). K. S. Axon MA, CEng, MIChemE, MBIM, (Managing).
        Brian F. Studd PhD, MRSC, MIMM,  F. E. Evans MSc. CChem, MRSC., R. Hampson CChem, MRSC
Registered Office: Perry Road, Witham, Essex CM8 3TU. Registration England 638315

Courtesy of Daniel C. Griffith & Company Ltd. Reprinted by permission.

**Figure 9.** *Sample Inspection Certificate and Assay Report*

# Daniel C. Griffith & Company Ltd.
## 2 Perry Road, Witham, Essex, CM8 3TU
Telephone: Witham (0376) 515081  Telex 995281  Telegrams Gryffydd Witham
Established 1850  International Commodity Samplers and Analytical Chemists


REPORT NO: A14/11630 A (Addendum 1)


ANALYSIS


Relating to material in its state as sampled:-


CHROMIUM          :              71.76%

CARBON            :              0.05%

SILICON           :              0.31%

PHOSPHORUS        :              0.041%

SULPHUR           : less than     0.01%


for and on behalf of
DANIEL C. GRIFFITH & CO LTD.,


TR/sp

Directors:  Alastair R. Griffith (Executive Chairman), K. S. Axon MA, CEng, MIChemE, MBIM, (Managing),
Brian F. Studd PhD, MRSC, MIMM,  F. E. Evans MSc, CChem, MRSC., R. Hampson CChem, MRSC
Registered Office: Perry Road, Witham, Essex CM8 3TU. Registration England 638315

**Figure 9.** (continued)

**Analysis.** An assayer, who should be LME-approved, analyzes the specimen provided by the sampler, using a method that is appropriate for the metal involved, ensuring a high degree of precision in determining the metal's exact chemical composition. Common techniques include colorimetry, emission spectrography, and atomic absorption spectrophotometry. Analyzing can cost $800 or more at current rates, another reason why small metals purchases are impractical. But the assayer's report can save you a lot of heartache.

The MMTA will arbitrate disputes arising within one year after you accept the metal. If you were to come back several years later claiming that you were sold the wrong grade, the seller would be most unwilling to accommodate you. After all, how does the seller know that the material has not been switched or altered? Therefore, resolve all disputes promptly.

Most traders claim that they rarely encounter problems—the assay usually matches the seller's description. Still, the assay is not a waste of money. Besides verifying your purchase and forming the basis for resolving any dispute, the assay report is evidence of what you have stored in the warehouse. When you go to sell it, should the assay report ordered by your buyer not be close to your own, you know the problem originated in the warehouse delivery to you.

**Insure Your Purchase**
You should be insured for the customary risks: physical loss or damage, including those resulting from fire and flood, as well as strikes, riots, and other civil disturbances. Lloyd's of London is quite familiar with this kind of policy for minor metals, but there are several other reputable insurance companies that will also write a policy of this kind. Generally, insurance companies will not insure quality or grade of a metal.

Very few insurance people know much about the metals they are insuring, so if you file a claim don't expect the same kind of service you would get if the tape deck from your car was stolen.

It usually pays to use an insurance company that works closely with the investment firm or merchant you are using. Such firms will be more familiar with the procedure and more responsive to your needs and problems.

In most cases, investment firms arrange insurance as part of a package that includes storage and inspections as well as

**Frank B. Hall & Co. of Massachusetts, Inc.**
89 Broad Street
Boston, Massachusetts 02110

#1258

## CERTIFICATE OF INSURANCE

This is to certify to........ Buyer

Address................10 Wilson Avenue, Boston, Massachusetts

that the following described policies are in force at this date.

Name of Insured:............Your Name

Policy No...................XYZ 90764 ....................**Expiring**....November 30, 1983

| INSURER AND<br>DESCRIPTION OF COVERAGE | LIMITS |
|---|---|
| XYZ Insurance Company | $3,500,000<br>(deductible $250 per<br>claim) |
| All risk of physical loss or damage<br>on stock of strategic metals while<br>stored in the ABC bonded warehouse in<br>Rotterdam, The Netherlands, including<br>but not limited to applicable exclusions<br>of transit, war and nuclear contamination. | All losses payable in<br>U.S. dollars. |

Frank B. Hall & Co. of Massachusetts, Inc.

Date Issued....December 15, 1982

**AUTHORIZED REPRESENTATIVE**

In the event of cancellation of the Policy the Company issuing said Policy will send notice of cancellation to the Certificate Holder at the address shown herein, by registered mail, not later than 10 days prior to such cancellation or change.

Telephone (617) 482-3100
Telex 940251 Cable HALLMASS

**Figure 10.** *Sample Certificate of Insurance*

insurance. The charges broken down will make it easier to compare prices. However, since such costs will ultimately prove minimal, you would not want to abandon a firm you like over a fraction of a percent. On the other hand, if the firm was clearly "gouging" you, it could be a sign of lack of integrity, which could spill over into other, more costly and critical services.

### Request an Annual Statement

The annual statement (you should request one) should be based on an annual audit, which includes a sight inspection. It should show the original cost, storage and insurance terms, costs to date, any advisory or administrative expenses, the current market value, and, if possible, the profit or loss on the open position, based on the current price.

The sight inspection not only reaffirms the accuracy of the warehouse receipt, but also ensures that storage is proper and that the consignment isn't deteriorating. For example, even under the best storage conditions, magnesium will oxidize in about six months. Improper storage can cause this to occur even more rapidly. Storage in excessively moist areas can be harmful to many metals, especially if they are bundled rather than packed in watertight containers. At the sight inspection, all seals should be examined and determined to be intact.

Some investment firms recommend semiannual or quarterly inspections as an added precaution, while others will provide a statement (without the sight inspection) every three or six months as an update for the client's convenience.

### SELLING

No dealer in this business can guarantee to buy back metal they sell unless they are willing to risk getting stuck with it if the market should soften. Frankly, dealers don't want to assume such a risk. London trader Bryan Webb tells investors, "We'll sell to you, but don't regard us as a terminal market, . . . because we might well want to structure the business so we are totally short [speculating that the price will go still lower]. We won't want someone else's discarded stuff."

Should you wish to sell during a weak market, you want to be able to exercise all your options in locating a buyer, phoning every dealer, broker, even corporate purchasing agent in an attempt to liquidate. Thus, when purchasing your metal, there is no advantage in signing an agreement to sell it back through the firm you bought it from unless that firm is willing to buy it back from you under any circumstances, at a fair market price (within an acceptable range of the published free-market prices).

If you have the financial resources to trade minor metals, you probably have several tax considerations. It is wise to consult your accountant, or one who is familiar with commodity transactions, before selling, so that you can derive maximum tax benefit from your profit or loss.

# INVESTMENT VEHICLES

## TEN

**A**S OF THIS writing, no investment vehicles specifically designed for minor metals have reached full maturity. But
here is a short history from conception to the present day.

First, several world watchers spotted what they termed an
investment "opportunity" in minor metals. This talk was bolstered by geopolitical warnings raised in Washington and other
Western capitals. Following that, a few aggressive risk takers
with the money to back up their gumption took the plunge,
raising eyebrows on Wall Street and catching the imagination
of those in the investing public who enjoy keeping track of
international politics, world affairs, and new investment
opportunities.

When the public takes a fancy to something, the question
the investment community loves to ask is, "How can we make
money off this new interest?" Regarding minor metals, the
question remains largely unanswered even today. But Wall
Street is changing and the major firms are not about to thumb
their noses at the "hard asset" type of investments/inflation
hedges. Doing so caused them to miss out on a large amount of
gold, silver, and other hard-money business in the seventies.

While the Street racks its collective brain to come up with
suitable packages and programs, many have been unwilling to

wait and have stepped into the minor-metals arena at a time when it is still the domain of industrial merchants. Those who feel queasy about buying metals that cannot be traded simply by calling one's friendly Merrill Lynch or Shearson broker would be wise to stand aside. But take heart in the news that your wait probably won't be very long.

Let's take a look at the investment vehicles and programs that are currently operational, in preparation, or taking shape in the planning offices of investment firms.

## PHYSICAL PURCHASES

The ownership of the actual metal, paid in full and stored in a warehouse, is the most popular investment method to date for two reasons: it is the easiest and simplest way to participate; and the trade deals primarily in physicals, so this is the best method of dovetailing with them, an important consideration since the trade does the bulk of the business.

### Advantages

Aside from the ease of investment, the most important advantage of purchasing physicals is that it is a "pure play." You are not forced to participate in another related business that could complicate and possibly reduce your profit potential. When you purchase pure germanium, that is precisely what you get. By contrast, when you invest in a mine through the purchase of shares, the price of the metal you are interested in is only one of the many factors affecting the profit potential.

### Disadvantages

One disadvantage of purchasing minor metals is that it is really a new form of investment. Although the basic trading mechanics and transactions are time-tested, they are relatively unfamiliar to the investment community and may have undiscovered pitfalls. Further, it is often difficult to get an accurate picture of supply and demand, and almost as difficult to monitor the price accurately.

Although the dollar value of the world output is quite substantial, the free market isn't always very liquid, and there are the added costs of warehousing, storage, insurance, and audits to consider. Obviously physical metals pay no dividends, so you might want to consider the loss of interest on the money tied up in metals as an additional cost. For example, suppose you have $50,000 in minor metals, and interest rates average 12 percent for the year you hold them—you've lost about $6,000 in interest.

### Managed Accounts

If you have a managed account, you give a sum of money to a professional manager, preferably one with some experience in the field of minor metals, who is given limited power of attorney to make decisions on your behalf. He or she may buy and sell metals without consulting you, but every time this is done you should receive written confirmation of the trade and the management charges.

The chief advantage of the managed account is indeed the manager. A good one has the knowledge, experience, and expertise to buy and sell when the time is right, often enough to make you some money. His or her power to make transactions even when unable to contact you is very important in fast markets, which do occasionally occur in minor metals.

Even though the manager is not required to consult you if you have granted power of attorney, the two of you should maintain a dialogue in order to gain insight into his or her thoughts on the markets. If you strongly disagree with these opinions or disapprove of your manager's actions, you can always close your account.

Since minor-metals investment is such a new field, there are very few experienced managers around. Many gold and silver experts are attempting to fill the void, but knowledge of precious metals does not necessarily qualify them as experts in minor metals. A word of caution is justified when selecting a manager.

If you are adopting a buy-and-hold approach, a managed account program is probably a waste of money. You could certainly use some expertise in selecting the metals, as well as advice on when to sell. But when there is so little trading involved, it seems rather unnecessary to share your profits with a manager. A good dealer should be able to give you the kind of advice you need. If not, get an "adviser," perhaps on a flat-fee basis.

**The Cost of Managed Accounts.** A managed-account program can be quite expensive. Most managers will charge a fee based upon a percentage of your account's assets, perhaps 0.25 to 0.50 percent per month. They are also likely to charge an additional incentive fee, which is based on new appreciation or profits. This incentive fee is supposed to encourage the manager to do the level best for your account, since he or she will make money if you do. However, it does not necessarily serve as a deterrent to the manager's taking outlandish risks; if you lose money the manager simply misses out on an incentive fee, but loses no cash of his or her own.

Incentive fees usually range from 10 to 20 percent of new appreciation, and are traditionally computed on a quarterly basis. (Because of the nature of the metals markets, however, several management programs have decided to take incentive fees on an annual basis to allow more time for price movement.) No fee is taken until the account balance rises above the level of the last profitable quarter. When a loss occurs in a quarter, no incentive fee is taken at all. In the following example, the incentive fee is 15 percent.

| | | |
|---|---|---|
| Original value of portfolio | $75,000 | |
| Value at the end of 1st quarter | 82,000 | Mgmt. fee = $1,050 (15% of $7,000 profit) |
| Value at the end of 2nd quarter | 70,000 | Mgmt. fee = 0 |
| Value, 3rd quarter | 80,000 | Mgmt. fee = 0 |
| Value, 4th quarter | 85,000 | Mgmt. fee = 450 (15% of $3,000 profit) |

Always be clear on how the account value is being assessed, that is, on what price quotes it is based.

Another problem is the actual payout of management-incentive fees. Using the previous example, let us suppose the manager spent the entire $75,000 in the portfolio purchasing metals in the first quarter. At the end of the first quarter, a profit is shown, but the manager hasn't sold any of the metals. Where does the $1,050 fee come from? If the manager doesn't see fit to turn some of your metal holdings into cash, you will have to reach into your pocket and come up with additional funds to pay. Otherwise, the manager may be forced to sell some of your metal just to produce the cash to pay the fee.

Some managed-account programs and funds charge an up-front fee, ostensibly for administrative costs involved in setting up the account or fund. Certainly, some of the fee goes toward such costs, but most of it winds up in the hands of the salespeople as commissions.

It pays to shop around to get an idea whether the "front

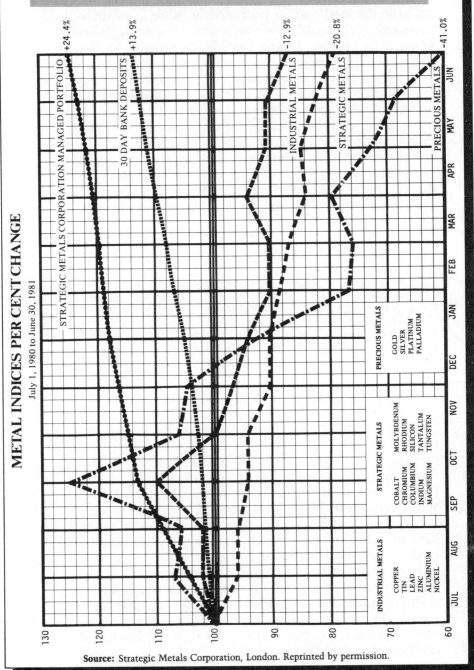

This chart indicates the relative changes in value of different types of investments during the same period. Note especially that while the value of strategic metals in general declined, the value of a managed portfolio of strategic metals increased.

METAL INDICES PER CENT CHANGE

July 1, 1980 to June 30, 1981

STRATEGIC METALS CORPORATION MANAGED PORTFOLIO    +24.4%

30 DAY BANK DEPOSITS    +13.9%

INDUSTRIAL METALS    -12.9%

STRATEGIC METALS    -20.8%

PRECIOUS METALS    -41.0%

| STRATEGIC METALS | |
|---|---|
| COBALT | MOLYBDENUM |
| CHROMIUM | RHODIUM |
| COLUMBIUM | SILICON |
| INDIUM | TANTALUM |
| MAGNESIUM | TUNGSTEN |

| PRECIOUS METALS |
|---|
| GOLD |
| SILVER |
| PLATINUM |
| PALLADIUM |

| INDUSTRIAL METALS |
|---|
| COPPER |
| TIN |
| LEAD |
| ZINC |
| ALUMINIUM |
| NICKEL |

JUL  AUG  SEP  OCT  NOV  DEC  JAN  FEB  MAR  APR  MAY  JUN

130  120  110  100  90  80  70  60

**Source:** Strategic Metals Corporation, London. Reprinted by permission.

**Figure 11.** *Metals Indices Percent Change*

# STRATEGIC METALS CORPORATION

```
                        STATEMENT OF ACCOUNT


                        MANAGED PORTFOLIO
                        PERFORMANCE RESULTS


                 July 1, 1980 thru June 30, 1981

            Account number: (Example of $100,000 Account)

                                      U.S. Dollars          Percent

Funds available for
purchase                          $   100,000.00            100.0%


Gross Appreciation                     33,458.31             33.5%

Less: Storage, Insurance and Administration
      (1/4% per month)                 (   3,000.00)        (3.0%)


         Appreciation net of Storage,
         Insurance and Administration  $   30,458.31         30.5%


Less: Research and Management Fee (20%) (   6,091.66)        (6.1%)


         Net Appreciation              $   24,366.65         24.4%


Value of Account at June 30, 1981      $  124,366.65
```

The above example is based on actual audited performance achieved.

As account opening fees and brokerage/transaction fees vary depending on
the amount of purchase, they are not included in the above example.
Please refer to the current schedule of fees.

500 CHESHAM HOUSE        150 REGENT STREET        LONDON W1R 5FA        ENGLAND
TEL: 01-439 6288                                                   TELEX 261 426

**Source:** Strategic Metals Corporation, London. Reprinted by permission.

**Figure 12.** *Sample Statement of a Managed Account*

load" you are being asked to pay is out of line with the rest of the pack. If it is, there had better be a very good reason.

### Advisory Accounts

An advisory account is just what the name implies. You pay a fee for advice given on a regular basis by a professional analyst or money manager. But you make all trading decisions—the adviser has no authority to make a trade without your approval. What you gain in control, you lose in timing, because a valuable opportunity may slip away.

### Funds

Since minor-metals trading lots are large, a large amount of money is needed to trade responsibly, and it should be money that can be tied up for months and years if necessary. Relatively large investors are in a position to do this. But funds offer a way for the small investor to participate. By buying several units of a fund for a small amount (usually around a $5,000 minimum investment), the investor can be part of a minor-metals partnership that, when fully subscribed, is often on the order of several million dollars and up.

The big question you must ask is, "What will the fund managers do with the money?" In some cases, the manager may buy and hold the metals portfolio over the long term. In others, the fund manager will actively trade the money, jumping in and out of the metals market.

One London-based mining expert has been working on a fund that would have essentially three components: the physical metals, substantial holdings in shares of metal fabricators, and the "ground," or the actual mining sites of economic deposits. Using his knowledge and experience, this expert proposes to "hunt" the ground, that is, search for areas that are rich in deposits of these metals. This approach is fascinating, but it obviously requires a wide range of knowledge and expertise on the part of the fund's managers.

At this juncture, neither Wall Street nor the metals traders know precisely how the possible proliferation of funds will affect the market, but certainly the presence of a dozen or so multi-million-dollar funds with the ability to buy and sell large amounts of minor metals will change things a bit.

The advantages of a fund are obvious: only a small amount of cash is required to participate, and the size of the fund allows it to diversify, that is, to buy a basket of metals rather than risk its fortune on one or two.

But funds allow you even less control over your money than managed accounts. There will be many investors in the fund, so it is unlikely you will ever get to speak directly to the person making the decisions, except perhaps at a large meeting. You should be kept abreast by the account executive who solicited your participation and by some sort of monthly or quarterly report. The manager is required to state his or her intentions and methods as clearly as possible in the fund prospectus, and he or she is bound to adhere to them.

Funds cost a great deal when you tally up all the accounting, legal, and administrative expenses. Then comes the manager's fee, which is usually an incentive fee based on profits, and sometimes a percentage of the assets as well. Trading commissions are often extra, but should be much less than an individual would pay because of the volume involved. On top of that, the general partners and/or manager get some equity participation in the fund in exchange for services rendered.

## INVESTING IN METALS SHARES

As discussed in Part I, the U.S. mining industry has performed poorly since World War II because of poor planning, increased competition from abroad, governmental intervention (environmental regulations and taxation policies), increased costs, recession-related lowering of demand, and other factors. The outlook for strategic or minor metals is bright, but can't be divorced from the mining industry as a whole.

### Trends

Almost every mining expert believes that the cost of mining will appreciate in excess of the inflation rate due to costly labor contracts, environmental regulations, and high interest rates. For these and other reasons, the United States is at a distinct disadvantage when in direct competition with foreign mining concerns. A U.S. miner needs a much greater return on investment to justify an attempt to exploit a particular deposit. In addition, much of the high-grade, easily recoverable U.S. ore has already been mined. The U.S. mining industry shows signs of a revival based upon the inflow of dollars from large oil concerns, possible relaxing of environmental restrictions, and popular pressure to become less dependent upon imports. However, it is unlikely that this activity will reverse the trend toward importing most of our metals and refined products from abroad.

In addition, the use of metallics will continue to decrease because of the reduction in the use of heavy machinery, the reduction in the amount of material required by each individual product as a result of miniaturization, and the increased use of man-made materials such as ceramics and composites. Service industries have been gaining over hard goods, with computer technology, electronics, and advanced communications playing a greater role in the world economic output.

### The Impact of By-products

In many cases, the difficulties of the U.S. mining industry were partly offset by the substantially increased impact of by-products, precious metals, and superalloys on earnings. Copper, for example, is associated with at least a dozen by-products, including gold, silver, nickel, cobalt, and molybdenum. Lead and zinc are each associated with eight or nine, such as antimony, bismuth, cadmium, cobalt, gallium, germanium, indium, thallium, gold, and silver. Tin is associated with columbium, tantalum, and silver.

During the last decade, the unit value of by-products increased about 718 percent, compared with a much more modest 88 percent increase for the base metals. One of the primary factors in this tremendous rise was precious metals, whose unit value climbed by 1,464 percent during that period.

The impact of by-products varied from situation to situation, depending on the ore grade involved, the by-product content of the ore mined, and the price variation during this period. In some cases, the earnings impact of by-products was so substantial—some copper companies earned so much more from silver that they could more correctly be referred to as silver companies—that the by-product eclipsed the base metal in importance. In other cases, some of the by-products became co-products—not more important than the base metals but certainly significant enough to sit side-by-side with them in terms of earnings. But in many cases, the impact of the by-products was rather minimal, adding very little to the earnings of the mining operation.

The supply/demand situation surrounding by-products is

much more difficult to assess than that of the more widely used base metals, because the appearance of new production capacity is often independent of demand. New production capacity in the by-products may be the direct result of an increase in output of the base metal. If demand for the base metal is strong, we may automatically get some increased capacity for the by-product, regardless of the demand for the by-product. This kind of situation (and its converse—by-product shortages resulting from slack demand in base metals) causes the by-product market to be volatile, often reacting to shortages and excesses.

A recent trend in the mining industry is to rely on by-product credits in the development of new projects: base-metal production costs are linked with by-product credits. This is an extremely tenuous situation. New accounting practices in the mining industry have created an additional profit center; we have one for the base metal and one for the by-products. Depending on how the numbers are juggled, the by-products can produce as much as half a company's earnings; all the expenses and costs are ascribed to the base metal.

**Independent Mining of Minor Metals.** Some deposits of metals can be mined independently of a base metal if the price is right. If a shortage were to produce a price rise that renders such deposits economic, we could see the opening of more minor-metals mines, in which they—not the base metals—are the primary product. Tantalum, for example, has long been mined in conjunction with tin. But the recent price surge has resulted in several plans to mine tantalum reserves independently.

**Pitfalls.** Chilean metal analyst Alexander Sutulov and other mining experts warn against extreme optimism about the economic future of by-products. In spite of their overall large dollar-value increase, not all minors went up in price from 1970 to 1980. Cadmium and bismuth actually declined. Vanadium, selenium, and several others increased, but at a slower rate than the base metals. And others such as cobalt, nickel, tantalum, rhenium, and molybdenum rose so rapidly that few analysts expect further significant upside movement for quite some time. Some by-products have even shown signs of price weakness now that the conditions that brought about the price rise have begun to change. Molybdenum began the seventies at $1.72 per pound and ran up to $31.50 on the spot markets in 1979, only to drop back to $6.00 in 1981. Cobalt was $2.20 per pound in 1970, got as high as $45.00 on the free market in 1979, and was trading at around $13.00 at the start of 1982.

New capacity, the economic cycle, and changes in the political climate could cause by-product prices to fall on a greater scale than the price of the base metals—a reversal of the trend of the seventies. This would almost certainly result in the abandonment of several important minor-metal development projects, and would probably assure a new era of tight supply and high prices sometime in the future. For this reason, many analysts view any substantial drop in the price of minor metals as a buying opportunity.

Note: The investor should not assume that all minor and strategic metals are by-products. Many, such as chromium, manganese, and the platinum group metals, are not. Others, like cobalt and vanadium are not always by-products.

### Why Metal Shares?

For most of this book, we have been discussing the purchase of the physical commodity itself. But there are many reasons why you might prefer to invest in stocks, or shares, of a mining firm rather than play the physical market or futures. One reason is risk—the risk of forward-contracts trading on a futures exchange may be greater because they are more highly leveraged. And physicals have the added problem of liquidity. Generally, stocks represent a lower risk and an investment medium that is more recognizable and familiar. They also allow you to enter with a much smaller amount of money, and are far more liquid. Further, stocks are easier to follow and analyze.

The major problem in investing in mining shares (specifically with strategic or minor metals in mind) is that the investment is limited domestically to perhaps a half-dozen stocks. There are very few companies of investment grade with a significant participation in minor metals.

Let's consider a few suggestions for selecting mining shares:

**Buy Quality.** Usually, it is wiser to choose a firm that is established in the mining business and growth-oriented—that is, embarking on significant expansion or plant modernization projects that will allow it to capitalize on the technology boom and the changing picture of the world raw-materials scene.

**Invest in Firms with Experienced Management.** Minor

metals have recently entered the limelight. Many natural resource people with experience in oil and gas and other related areas are forming firms and getting involved in the business. Others entering the field may come from strong international business backgrounds and have the connections abroad, but lack the expertise needed to pull off a major mining venture in this country. It is always better to get involved with a firm that has at least several experienced mining people in upper levels of management.

**Consider the Deposits.** It is very easy to be vague or unclear when describing the nature of the holdings of a mining firm. For one thing, remember that *ore* is an economic rather than a geological term. An ore is simply a mineral from which metal can be extracted at a profit. Ore bodies, therefore, expand and contract as the price of the metal changes. And whether or not a deposit is classified as ore is dependent not only upon the selling price but on factors that influence the cost of extraction, such as location. What is ore in one place may not be ore in another. For example, a copper deposit in the United States may be ore, but a very similar deposit in the Arctic may not be because of the cost of mining in a frigid climate. When reading a description of a mine's holding, make sure that it specifies the resources that are ore (or economic).

Sometimes mining companies will refer to the "gross value" of their deposit. In other words, they will compute the actual amount of recoverable metal in the ground and then multiply that by the current price of the metal to come up with an approximate value of the deposit. This kind of figure has almost no meaning, because it does not take into account an accurate calculation of costs. Consider the remoteness of the find. What about the scale of operation? How large will it be? How costly? How difficult is it to get machinery in and out of the area? Will roads need to be built? Will the company have to build shelters for the miners? How expensive will the recovery of the ore be? Is the metal easy or difficult to extract from the rock? Does it involve a basic, simple, surface kind of mining, or must extensive digging and strip mining take place? Must the mine pay royalties, or does the company own the land outright? Are there any smelting problems? Which refining processes are involved? Are they difficult or energy-intensive? What are the costs of milling and shipping? At the projected rate of production, how long are the reserves expected to last?

**The General Financial Health of the Firm.** Debt-to-equity ratio is often considered an important measure of the overall financial health of a firm. During the period from 1956 to 1978, the debt-to-equity ratio in the mining industries rose much faster than in all other manufacturing areas. The mining companies have generally been carrying long-term liabilities, which could hamper their ability to expand and prosper.

Recently, oil companies have capitalized on this trend by taking over many mining firms. Oil industry executives have reasoned that mining companies are wise acquisitions for several reasons. Oil and gas exploration is reasonably similar to mining metal, so that many of the oil industry experts feel that they can successfully apply their expertise. Antitrust problems exist when an oil company attempts to expand by acquiring other oil companies, but this problem is much less serious when it involves the acquisition of natural resource companies not directly involved in oil and gas. The oil companies, flush with cash, look at the mining firms—saddled with heavy debt, tight for cash, requiring an infusion in order to prosper and grow—and see an opportunity to buy low, turn these companies around, and then possibly sell high. Indeed, it may be wise to invest in a mining firm that seems ripe for acquisition and also stands a very good chance of having a bright earnings picture in the future.

When selecting a stock for investment, it is very important to have a clear idea of who owns the firm and to know whether the firm is held by other mining firms or other major conglomerates. It is also important to understand whether the mining firm you have targeted for investment has holdings or interests in other mines, refineries, fabricators, or other companies worldwide. There have been many situations in which the principal operation of a company has been less than spectacular, but earnings have been significant because one or several of the holdings it has outside of its primary operations have done spectacularly well.

**Supply and Demand in the Selection of Stocks.** In selecting a mining company on the basis of the future of some of its by-products, keep in mind that the price of the by-product will usually have a much more significant impact on the profits of the firm than the sheer amount of by-product that it sells. Suppose you examine a company's projections: it appears that the firm will be increasing its output of by-products by 20 or 30 percent per year, but predictions indicate that the price of those by-products will remain somewhat flat. You might conclude that investment in the firm is unwarranted, even though they will be selling more and more of a very good by-product. Ronald Shorr of Bear Stearns says, "It's rare for volume alone to make a major earnings impact. Certainly, in comparison with price, volume is a distinct second."

In the mining business, increased output doesn't necessarily mean increased profit margin. Once the basic fixed and variable costs are covered, there could actually be a situation in which increased output actually forces metal out of the ground at a lower profit margin (see "The Cost Structure of the Metals Producers," p. 187). When demand is strong, a smart company will take only the better contracts for the higher-grade, higher-margin ore, thereby upgrading the product line and producing a higher profit margin rather than a larger amount of overall metal production.

Even when considering shares, the information that we have given about the physical markets of the metals will prove invaluable, since supply and demand will ultimately have a very strong effect on the earnings of the company and the price of its shares. You should apply what you have learned about analyzing the supply and demand picture for minor metals before investing in a company intimately connected with them. To understand the importance of by-products, you must first do some homework on the base metals that the company is producing. The ebb and flow of the base metal markets have a significant impact on the supply, demand, and price of the minors.

**"Pure play"?** Because most miners and producers of by-products are also major producers of base metals, it is very difficult to buy shares in a "pure play" company, whose dominant activity is the production of one or several minor metals. For example, INCO produces many by-products, including cobalt, but it cannot be considered a "pure play" in the strategic or minor-metals area, because it is overwhelmingly affected by the price of nickel (which is considered industrial, not strategic). Therefore, no matter now high the cobalt price and how good the fortunes of other by-products of nickel, we could not expect much from INCO if the price of nickel itself were to be soft.

The absence of "pure plays" makes it very difficult to invest in these metals through securities or equity vehicles. Says Ronald Shorr, "From an investment point of view, there are so few vehicles one can play to participate, it almost makes it a useless practice to spend a lot of time on it. Usually, so-called pure plays involve tiny companies, not investment-grade, and certainly not institutional caliber. In most cases, the deposits involved are just in the 'think about' or possibly financing stages."

## Other Investment Opportunities

When looking for shares that might appreciate in a minor-metals boom, it would be very shortsighted indeed to look only at mining firms. The production, distribution, and use of minor metals is a very complex business, involving many interlocking and interrelated firms. Unfortunately, most refiners are owned by mining conglomerates, therefore making it difficult to invest in a company whose sole business is the refining of minor metals. In addition, the majority of refiners put most of their attention on refining base metals, taking out minor metals as a by-product.

Several refiners do specialize in buying by-products from base metal refiners and then working with them to produce an industrially usable minor metal. For example, some refiners specialize in buying up the flue dust or leftover by-products from the refinement of zinc. Taking that by-product, they are able to extract cadmium, germanium, and sometimes gallium. Regrettably, however, there are almost no refiners that are independent of other mining concerns and involved purely in this kind of operation. This is unfortunate, since such companies would represent much more of a pure play in minor metals.

If you are willing to venture further away from the mining and refining business, there are companies that offer investment opportunities and are in businesses related to the mining and utilization of minor metals.

**Fabricators.** Fabricators fashion basic parts and forms out of the raw metals. In the titanium industry, for example, fabricators are the first to benefit from a surge in demand; while the metal itself may be plentiful and available, a particular industry may be clamoring for specific parts, and the fabricators operate at full capacity long before the mines do. This is the case in the aerospace industry. In 1979 and 1980 there was no shortage of titanium ore, but production of sheets and other forms of titanium metal used in the construction of jet aircraft and military equipment was backed up for many weeks because the fabricators were unable to keep up with the strong demand. The lead time in the delivery of those titanium parts increased by as much as sixty-five weeks since 1975.

Fabricators are much more flexible than mines, and they are able to adapt their operations to the different phases of the business cycle a lot more easily. For instance, during a recession a fabricator can simply close down, or significantly reduce the amount of metal parts and forms it actually produces, adjusting to the demand and to the number of orders it has in-house. Mines, on the other hand, are more difficult to close during such a period. There is often an attempt made to reduce capacity, but it is not always possible. Another strategy, switching to a higher grade, is also possible only in certain circumstances. So, in general, a fabricator can cut losses a lot more easily than a mine.

There are a fair number of fabricators in the United States, as well as many in Japan, South Africa, and Europe, so investment opportunities exist. However, as with refiners, fabricators are often owned, wholly or in part, by larger conglomerates or multinational firms. For example, in titanium, Allegheny Ludlum, ARMCO, and Oregon Metallurgical (Ormet) are principal fabricators, but with the exception of Ormet, titanium fabrication is far from their principal business. Thus, the opportunity in titanium is very limited. Fansteel is a major fabricator of tantalum parts, but Fansteel is a subsidiary of the Cabot Corporation, a large firm involved in mining, oil, and gas as well as fabrication. Teledyne Wah Chang also does some fabrication, but it is a subsidiary of Teledyne, which is involved in many activities. In tungsten, the principal fabricators in the United States are Kennemetal and AMAX. In beryllium, Brush Wellman and Kawelki Berylco are the principal fabricators.

**Companies with Low Vulnerability** If one feels strongly that sooner or later the import dependence of the United States companies will come back to haunt them, it would make sense to look for firms that would be relatively self-sufficient and able to function effectively during a crisis. For example, a manufacturerer of metal parts or industrial equipment that had long-term contractual relationships with North American metal suppliers would obviously be in a position to increase its business significantly if its competitors were cut off from their supplies of metal from abroad. A jet-engine manufacturer that gets its cobalt from Canada would be in a much better situation than one that had to rely on Zaire. These supply situations are constantly changing, and in order to isolate and identify such companies one must rely on solid research from a major brokerage firm. You might want to carefully examine the annual reports of firms involved in the minor-metals industry.

Another kind of firm that could possibly benefit during times of a supply shortage or cutoff would be one that has strategic metals assets in the continental United States—for example, Noranda, a Canadian firm with major holdings in the United States' only cobalt mine, the Blackbird Mine in Idaho, which could become active if we were faced with a cutoff of cobalt from Africa. Scattered around the North American continent are many mining firms that produce primarily base metals but own some deposits of tantalum, cobalt, titanium, and other minor metals that could be mined at a profit if the price were high enough and the demand were in evidence. Again, one should be very vigorous in monitoring the activities of these firms, since these deposits change hands very rapidly. Make sure that the firm is in a position to exploit the deposits if the opportunity arises.

**High-Technology Firms.** Minor metals are becoming more important primarily because of the rapid development of new technologies in the electronics, energy, chemicals, and communications industries. Several firms are involved in the research and development of new alloys and new techniques for reducing the amount or cost of raw material in certain products, and in the development of subsitutes for rare or costly metals. Given the complexity of the minor-metals market and the difficulty of investing in physical metals, a high-technology firm involved in this area might be a very good bet. For one thing, these firms have flexibility. If tantalum were to become very expensive or be in short supply, a firm could capitalize by developing a substitute or a technology that reduces the amount of tantalum used. Therefore, the firm could increase its earnings without actually getting involved in the purchase of tantalum deposits or metal. Many of these firms are involved in exporting metallurgical technology to the developing nations of the Third World and even to the industrialized nations of Europe and Asia.

**Financial Institutions Specializing in the Mining Industry.** Because of the tremendous capital requirements for mining and mining expansion, the industry almost always has to seek outside sources to finance its operations. Certain firms specialize in financing mining ventures and stand to benefit from the forecasted boom in the production of minor metals worldwide, assuming that their management exercises good judgment regarding which companies to lend money to and which companies to buy into.

Whenever one speaks of minor-metals mining, one must consider the international scene; most of these financial institutions invest in companies outside of the United States— in South Africa, Latin America, and Southeast Asia. Thus, they are exposed to great losses if a company in which they had invested (or to whom they had lent money) is expropriated or nationalized by a new government. Nevertheless, most of the capital institutions involved in this area learned their lesson in the sixties and seventies, and are extremely cautious when participating in mining ventures outside the United States.

## How to Select an Investment

We have refrained from recommending specific investments because a book is completed many months before its publication, and selecting a stock involves many factors that are constantly changing. However, the discussion of the kinds of companies involved and what to look for should help you make an intelligent analysis of any investment opportunity that comes your way under the guise of a strategic metals play. If you have a trusted stockbroker, you might tell him or her that you are very interested in participating in a company involved in minor metals, giving an idea of the kinds of companies you are interested in. Perhaps he or she will come back to you with several options. Study those companies' annual reports, keeping in mind the criteria we have discussed. Talk it over with your broker, and if possible speak to the person or persons involved in researching the mining and metals industry.

Mining economics and accounting can get very complicated; if you become confused by the projection or balance sheet of a mining firm, do not hesitate to ask for assistance. The minor-metals or strategic metals issue has been appearing in the newspapers frequently, resulting in a mystique around any company that claims to be involved in the area. This mystique alone can be a major reason for the price of a stock to rise, although in the long run it would not be able to sustain the increase. Already there have been several firms whose shares have doubled or even tripled on the crest of a metals boom, only to fall back when it became clear that some of the minor-metals activities they announced were only in the planning or financing stages, and that the slack demand would probably slow up the development of mines.

Already there has been a huge price-earnings multiple runup in several mining shares. For this to sustain itself, there must be earnings to justify it very soon, or a real shortage in one or several of these metals—a scenario that will live up to the predictions. And at the current time, it does not seem likely that we will see such a serious shortage.

## FUTURE POSSIBILITIES FOR MINOR-METALS INVESTMENT

### Options

Options are contracts that grant you the right, though not the obligation, to buy from or sell to the grantor a fixed amount of a commodity at a specified price at any time prior to the expiration date of that option. To obtain this option contract you must pay a premium, which is paid in full at the time the option is purchased.

While an option may simply be bought, held to maturity, and either exercised or abandoned, some may be traded, meaning that the option contract itself may be bought and sold. In London, such contracts are called dealer options, and they are similar in certain respects to stock options traded on the Chicago Board Option Exchange (CBOE) and to commodity options traded on several commodity futures exchanges in the United States.

Unfortunately, none of the legalized options are in minor metals, although several London-based firms might well be writing options on behalf of well-heeled clients with large amounts of minor metals in storage. They are willing to write options against a portion of this metal to provide a means by which inventory can produce income.

In order to make money in options, the metal must have a price movement that allows you to register a profit in excess of the premium. But this has to happen in the time specified by the option contract. Minor metals go through periods of extreme volatility, but more often they move very slowly.

Naturally, if you are trading "on the news," and you think that a particular political event, such as the fall of South Africa, is likely to take place within a three-month period, you might consider a three-month chromium or vanadium option a worthwhile risk.

A sudden surge of investor cash into one or several minor-metals markets could have quite an effect on price, as we have seen. In such circumstances, options could become quite interesting.

Minor-metals dealer options differ from precious-metals options in one very important manner: since there are futures markets for precious metals, it is possible to "hedge" or lock in a profit, or minimize a loss during the option period using gold or silver futures. But since there is no futures market in minor metals, you have only your option to play with.

**Futures**

A futures contract is one that requires that a specified amount of a commodity be delivered at a specified date sometime in the future for a specified price. Such contracts are standardized, and as such are traded on exchanges. This means that a holder may liquidate his or her obligation to deliver or to take delivery before the contract comes due.

There are two principal futures exchanges for metals: the Comex in New York and the London Metal Exchange (LME). The LME deals in copper, lead, tin, zinc, silver, aluminum, and nickel, while the Comex actively handles copper, silver, and gold futures. Comex also has a zinc contract, but there is very little trading in it.

There is no futures trading in minor metals at the present time, but clearly some traders would like to see it happen. Lambert's Howard Masters says, "It is my opinion that future trading activity will be required to provide two basic functions: (1) to more accurately reflect the basic supply and demand positions; (2) to establish a more realistic price level for each metal traded. It is these two functions which . . . lead ultimately to the possibility of the establishment of a small terminal market, which could take several forms but would most likely be an LME-type ring once a week or so." An established futures market would also eliminate the discrepancies between published prices by setting a benchmark price for the free market. The obvious location for a futures exchange is London, where the bulk of minor-metals traders are already situated.

In spite of the enthusiasm for a minor metals futures

exchange, the prospects for one are rather dim, at least in the near future. There are some very specific conditions that must be met before such talk can be taken seriously.

**Standardization.** Currently, there are so many different grades, origins, types, and purities of each minor metal that you would never know what your contract meant. For a futures market to work, each contract must be for exactly the same amount of the same thing so they can be traded as identical, interchangeable units, like stock.

**Trade Hedgers.** History has shown that in order for a futures market to get off the ground, you can't count on the participation of the speculators alone. The trade must use the markets for some sort of price protection. At present, the trade doesn't appear to be terribly interested in such transactions, probably because they have some form of price protection from the producer contracts.

**Packaging Problems.** Because gold and silver are neatly stamped with weight, grade, and assayer's seal, it is easy to verify that deliveries meet contract specifications. But minor-metals deliveries are more complex. They come in all sorts of containers and in several grades. Futures exchanges would have to unpack each shipment and then repack it.

**A Fighting Chance for Speculators.** One needs a great deal of specialized knowledge and information to trade minor metals successfully. A futures market must be able to attract speculators, and very few would feel as comfortable about trading manganese as they are about trading copper, silver, gold, or aluminum.

**Liquidity.** The worldwide turnover of minor metals appears to be too small to justify a futures exchange.

In sum, a viable futures market must serve the best interests of both the trade and the speculators. Small and large purchasers must be able to get in and out easily and safely. Margin or leverage trading must be feasible. Taking and making delivery must be orderly and standardized.

If you wish to participate in the futures market, you may trade platinum and palladium on the New York Mercantile Exchange. Both of these metals have been gaining in importance. Considered precious metals, their prices have tended to run in tandem with gold and silver, which are also strategic to some extent but have been influenced more by factors such as inflation fears, world instability, and interest rates than by their uses in high technology. There are signs, however, that platinum will eventually break away from gold as it becomes more in demand as a critical advanced material rather than as "hard money."

As of this writing, minor-metals and base metal prices are depressed due to the economic slowdown. Those who suggest the purchase of minor metals point out that in these circumstances the profit potential might be just as great in zinc, aluminum, copper, or platinum, metals that are traded either on the Comex or the London Metal Exchange, or both.

### Greater Liquidity in Smaller Amounts

Responsible firms that are seeking to serve the investment public realize that the more or less traditional trading units can often be too large for clients. They are forced either to invest in a single metal, join a fund or a pool, or sit it out.

Eliot Smith of Bache believes that large unit size is an important built-in safeguard for customer suitability. Commercial-size lots prevent the customer from overdoing it, by putting money in minor metals when he or she can't really afford it.

But others disagree. Let's say an investor can afford to spend $15,000 on 5 metric tons of antimony. Wouldn't it be more advantageous to buy tradable lots of three or four different metals for around the same money, thus diversifying his or her portfolio? The main argument for smaller units is that larger ones prevent investors from buying a basket.

However, there are already signs that things might be changing. Some traders are beginning to deal in smaller lots, because they can make larger commissions and markups in relation to the size of the lot, and make them more often.

If we get an influx of investors in minor metals, the size of the lots traded could indeed get smaller: the investor holding, say, a single drum of electrolytic chromium (400 pounds) could conceivably find another investor eager to buy it, even though the trade won't touch less than a ton. If this were to continue on a large scale, even the trade would be obliged to accept smaller amounts, because a sizable portion of the above-ground supply of a metal could be traded that way. A user who is hungry for chromium might be forced to buy a 10-ton shipment from thirty different individuals. Such a transaction might be handled through one or two dealers who had a large investor-client roll representing a large number of private, small metal holdings.

As a rule, traders are flexible. If the profit incentive were there, and they would not be jeopardizing their existing business and client relationships, they would probably consent to sell smaller amounts.

### Other Possible Changes

The minor-metals pricing system is woefully inadequate for investment purposes. The quotes given by the trade publications are simply not reliable enough. It is hoped that some sort of standardized trading units will evolve, along with a pricing system similar to the Automated Quotation System of the National Association of Securities Dealers (NASDAQS), used for over-the-counter trading.

Many believe that eventually the trading houses will take on individual clients, or at least enter into arrangements with investment brokerage firms and commission houses. Such an approach is justified because it will bring the investment business out in the open, where the market can better assess the speculator interest and its overall effect on the price. Investor participation offers a genuine opportunity for traders to make a profit, and clear, well-structured arrangements should reduce their risks.

Metals firms will probably do less speculating as they turn their attention to providing financing, clearing, and other services that can ultimately prove more profitable, and certainly less risky.

Producers, their earnings dampened by depressed base metal markets, will probably seek to get a better return on their by-products. Thus, they will be cutting sharper deals with merchants, reducing the profit potential from basic trading.

# STRATEGIES AND TECHNIQUES

# ELEVEN

**T**HE MOST IMPORTANT minor-metals strategy of all is the simplest: *Be careful not to overinvest.* Invest only what you can afford to tie up for a relatively long time without the benefit of income. Assess your risk and the potential reward, and leave yourself plenty of room in case you have an unexpected financial setback.

We have seen the same problem occur time and time again with gold and silver buyers: people put more money into "hard assets" than they can readily afford. Then a slight financial setback forces them to liquidate because they need cash, and the liquidation frequently takes place at the least advantageous time. Strive for *control* over your investment. Buying minor metals requires the patience and finances to buy at the right time and the ability to choose the right time to get out. If your son or daughter is entering college next year, don't put the tuition money into minor metals in hope of making a killing in six months.

Gold and silver can be bought and sold in small amounts, as coins and small ingots. So if you buy 100 Krugerrands, and you need some ready cash, you can always sell off 25. But if you buy minor metals, you will not be able to sell part of your holdings, unless your holdings are so immense that even a portion of them would be considered a tradable lot.

Remember, strategic metals is not a form of "hard money."

## BUY-AND-HOLD

As the name implies, buy-and-hold is a strategy in which the investor accumulates one or several metals in the belief that over a long period of time the price will rise. Success with a buy-and-hold approach is more than a matter of selecting a metal or metals that will eventually go up in price. It raises several basic questions, such as: How much metal should you buy? How long should the metal be held before taking profits or considering it an investment that didn't pan out? If there is an unexpected run-up in price after only a few months, should you take profits rather than continuing to hold?

In order for a buy-and-hold investment to break even, the price of your portfolio must appreciate at a rate equivalent to the rate of inflation. If it increases at a greater rate—taking into account all costs such as warehousing, insurance, audits, and commissions—it is fair to say that the investment is profitable. But another factor is the prevailing interest rate over the buy-and-hold period. You must ask, "If I had taken the money and put it into government securities or CDs instead of buying metals, how much would I now have?" Remember that such investments are, for all intents and purposes, risk-free. Minor metals clearly are not. So, to justify an investment in minor metals it is only reasonable that your objective be profits in excess of the average interest rates over the holding period.

The buy-and-hold is, of course, more than a numbers game. Many investors adopt this stance for psychological reasons. Some have a desire to place some stored value outside the country, as a "hedge" against war or political turmoil. Others hold fully diversified portfolios with plenty of money in real estate, stocks, bonds, bills, and so on. They simply want to try something new. Such reasons are just as valid as the purely numerical ones, as long as you recognize exactly why you are buying and what your ultimate objectives are.

James Sinclair, one of the few metals specialists on Wall Street willing to take a stand on the relative importance of minor metals to private investors, recommended in 1981 that

15 percent of one's hard-assets investment portfolio be in minor metals, and another 10 percent in minor-metals shares (Sinclair uses the term *strategic*).

If you favor the buy-and-hold approach, make it clear to the broker or dealer you select. Let him or her know that you expect to remain in regular contact throughout the holding period so as to carefully monitor your investment, and that you expect to be notified of dramatic changes in the market and other important news.

Any reputable firm with foresight will be eager to stay in touch with you, advising you of additional buying opportunities and points at which to sell. The more transactions they execute for your account, the more income they generate for themselves. If they make an initial recommendation to buy a metal and hold it for three years, and that metal doubles in eight months, they will probably be most happy to urge you to take profits, since they want the good press and referrals generated by successful trading.

For example, several of the firms in the field opened their doors touting a basket of minor metals as a long-term investment. However, many of those baskets included germanium, and those who bought some in the last quarter of 1980, when most of these firms really got started, saw the price rise from $550 per kilo to more than $1,200 in only six months. Now most of these firms are boasting of the stellar performance of their strategic metals investment programs, although most prices didn't rise significantly during this period. The short-term success has been fueled by a single metal—germanium. But if you were wise or lucky enough to be holding germanium during this period, and you chose to take your profit, don't be too concerned about having violated the spirit of buy-and-hold.

## THE TRADING APPROACH

Active trading of minor metals has been the traditional domain of dealers, and it has proven difficult even for them. Says Howard Masters, "General economic cutbacks coupled with the low margins and speculative nature of minor metals . . . have led many companies to lose money. When they examined the situation and saw large amounts of money being turned over with small [profit] margins being obtained, and then considered general company overheads, many of the medium-sized companies dropped minor metals altogether." Those that have remained in the trading business hold smaller positions, not only because of the fear of losses, but because of the recession and high cost of money.

Nevertheless, money can be made trading minor metals. But unless you immerse yourself in the markets, your chances are slim. Since that is probably impractical for you, the only sensible approach is to affiliate with a knowledgeable, experienced trader who has good market connections.

The markets have become so complex that many minor-metals traders have subspecialized, dealing in less than half a dozen metals. The entire field of metals is thus covered by a group of traders, each with his or her own special area of expertise. In some cases, a firm may elect to trade only four or five metals, referring investors to another firm for those it does not deal in.

It is not surprising that most investment experts advise individuals against attempting to trade minor metals aggressively. In fact, most firms currently dealing with the public are not properly equipped to offer trading programs. They lack the contacts, the clout, and the daily trading volume necessary to assure clients that they can get them in and out cleanly and quickly. Even more important, they lack the knowledge and expertise, since most are relative newcomers to the field.

There are exceptions to this generalization. First, if you want to trade frequently and are willing to educate yourself and to spend some time keeping up with the more accessible events affecting the markets, a dealer might be willing to take you on as a trading client. The dealer will use his or her knowledge and skill to help you, provided you don't take up a great deal of time and the dollar amounts involved make it worthwhile.

Recently, several "old school" professional traders have entered the investment business, making their trading skills available to investors on a managed-account basis. Since these programs involve considerable incentive fees, it is in their best interest to use all their abilities to make a profit for such accounts. Putting your money in the hands of someone who has been trading for years may well be the best way to participate in an aggressive trading program.

## THE TRADE-AND-HOLD

This is our term for what many consider the soundest strategy of all. Quite simply, you buy an initial portfolio, accumulating a "core" position intended for a long-term buy-and-hold, and to that you add an extra, or "marginal" amount, intended for a more aggressive trading investment. In this manner, you have the flexibility to capitalize on short-term opportunities and a basic holding for the long term.

The core of your portfolio should be the most liquid grade, which you should be able to sell even in times of surplus. In a buyer's market, the best will sell first. This affords you a little extra protection.

The marginal portion of your portfolio should be a little more freewheeling. For example, if your merchant sees an opportunity to pick up some metal at "fire sale" prices, but you have to compromise a little in grade or origin, you might want to go ahead and buy it for your "marginal" portfolio. This decision would, of course, depend on market conditions and the perceived demand for the less-liquid grade. If the price of the stuff were to move up several weeks later, you could take your money and run, knowing that you had plenty of that metal in a higher grade on hand to sell should the price continue to rise.

You can use the trading portion of your holdings in some of the more sophisticated strategies outlined in this chapter.

## FORWARD CONTRACTS

A forward contract is an agreement to purchase a certain amount of metal for delivery at some point in the future. The price paid could be based on the price of the metal at the time of delivery, but in most cases, it will be based on the current price of the metal.

It makes sense to buy a forward contract at today's price for delivery in six months if you believe that the price of the metal will be significantly higher by then. Even if you have no use for the metal, you could sell it to another party at a higher price and pocket the difference.

On the other hand, if you think the price of the metal is going to be lower in six months, you might opt to "sell short"—selling a certain amount of the metal to another party at the current price, promising delivery in six months. If you are correct, and the price is lower six months down the road, you will purchase the metal at the lower price, and deliver it to the buyer, receiving the higher price agreed on six months ago. Then you pocket the difference between the price at which you purchased the metal, and the higher price you sold it for. Thus, you profit from a drop in the price.

The principal advantage of a forward contract is *leverage*. At the time you enter you need only put up a margin, or good faith payment, of about 25 percent. Thus you are able to invest in a lot of metal for only one-fourth of its value. And since your profit or loss on the contract is based on the value of the entire lot, that small margin can lead to a possible profit several times greater than the money you had to tie up. Technically, there is no limit to how much you can make because there is no limit to how high the price might rise.

Suppose, for example, you purchase a contract for 100 troy ounces of rhodium at $500 per ounce, to be delivered in six months. The value of that contract is $50,000, and your margin might be $12,500. If at the end of the six-month period rhodium is trading at $575, your contract is valued at $57,500 and you can realize a profit of $7,500. That is a sixty percent return on your investment in six months, exclusive of commissions or administrative charges.

Industrial users rely on forward contracts not as speculative tools, but rather to protect against wide price swings, using a technique known as *hedging*.

The price for a forward contract may be *based* on the current price, but is, in fact, slightly different. It usually reflects the spot price, that is, the price of the metal for immediate delivery, plus a "carrying charge"—the cost of holding the metal until you are ready for it when delivery comes due in three months, six months, or whenever. This carrying charge is referred to by London metals traders as the *contango*. Usually, the further away the delivery month the higher the contango.

In certain cases, demand for immediate delivery is so strong that buyers will actually be willing to pay more for metal that can be delivered now than they will for metals for forward delivery. In such cases, the price of the spot metal or the nearby forward contracts (those about to come due) will actually be higher than the far outs (those contracts with delivery a long way off). This is called *backwardation*, and is often a sign to traders that there is a serious short-term supply squeeze taking place. Even if you never trade forward contracts, discussing their price structure with a dealer can be very helpful.

The big disadvantage to dealing in forward contracts is the risk. Consider the damage to your equity if the rhodium contract mentioned earlier were to drop in price, with rhodium falling to, say, $450 after six months. You would be obliged to buy the rhodium at $500 and sell it at $450, for a loss of $50 per ounce, or $5,000. In six months you would have lost 40 percent of your original margin money ($12,500).

There is no limit to how low the price could go, and therefore no limit to how much you can lose. If the price were to drop to $300 for an ounce of rhodium, you would lose $20,000, which is far more than your original margin investment. You would be required to cover your loss with additional funds. An experienced minor-metals dealer will usually be able to prevent this by helping you get out of the forward contract before it comes due or loses much of its value.

Selling forward contracts is a tricky business for a speculator, and sometimes curls the hair of even the most experienced traders. For one thing, selling a forward contract is a commitment to deliver the goods. In a market still mostly comprised of industrial players, it is likely that the buyer of your forward contract will actually need the metal and will fully expect you to come up with it. Suppose there is a real squeeze and you are having a problem finding the metal to purchase to cover your contract. To meet your obligation, you may have to pay an absolutely outrageous price or "borrow" the metal from another party until the market loosens up. Both approaches are quite costly. In some cases, you might be able to get out of the contract by paying the other party the cash profit he would have made by buying from you at the contract price. But that is something that a speculator, who is in it purely for the money (or a trading firm that knows you might not be able to come up with the metal), is more likely to agree to.

In general, minor-metals forward contracts are written for as short a time as three months, or as long as a year. Obviously, the closer the delivery date the greater the risk, because you have less time to cover and there is little time remaining for the price to move in your favor. Currently, you may trade in minor-metals forward contracts only through London, as they are not yet legal in the United States.

You may recognize this kind of approach as being akin to commodity futures. It is, although not exactly the same. Forward contracts in minor metals are not exchange-traded. There are no industry-wide standardized delivery months and dates. Rather, forward contracts usually specify delivery three months from the agreement date. In most cases, you will make or take delivery and then enter the free market as necessary to convert your position to cash. In the futures market, you can usually get out of contracts with a single phone call, since they tend to have large volumes and are therefore liquid. This is not always the case with forwards. And commodity futures offer greater leverage, with margins consisting of as little as 5 percent to 10 percent of contract value in many cases.

## JOBBING THE MARKET

This is essentially the act of lending metals. Suppose there is a shortage of spot tungsten available for immediate delivery. A user puts out the word that he wants to buy a quantity of the metal for immediate delivery, but will guarantee the seller the opportunity to buy it back some months later at an agreed-upon price. The user is obviously concerned about meeting his immediate needs, but is confident that he will eventually be able to secure enough to pay back what he borrowed. Word of this proposition reaches a broker or merchant who knows you are holding a large amount of tungsten. He or she phones and asks if you would be willing to enter into such an arrangement. If you bought the tungsten for the purpose of holding it over a long term, what would be in it for you if you agree to sell now under this "jobbing" agreement?

This kind of deal is a numbers game. If you agree to lend the user the metal, you should be able to buy it back later at a price equal to or possibly less than its current selling price. But that is only part of it. You also get to hold the cash paid to you by the buyer, and you may draw interest on it during the lending period. A potential borrower who is really desperate for the metal might even be willing to pay a premium above its current price.

Jobbing is only feasible with large holdings. No user who is looking for metal is going to get very excited about a small lot, because it probably won't help much. Besides, the numbers involved begin to look attractive only on a large scale.

There are risks for both sides in a jobbing arrangement, and we suggest you discuss the proposition with a dealer before making an agreement. Suppose, for example, the borrower goes bankrupt. The contract would then be voided for all intents and purposes. True, you would still have the cash, but the borrower's obligation to sell you back the metal at the agreed-upon price would be meaningless.

If you are interested in jobbing, your dealer should, ideally, be in possession of your warehouse receipt and you should let him or her know you are open to such arrangements. Hearing of an opportunity, the dealer will advise you of the offer and give you an opinion as to whether you should take it. But do not sign or authorize the deal until you understand it fully.

## FINANCING

In most cases, purchasing minor-metals physicals means paying for them in full. As noted earlier, you must put some money down at the time of the order and pay the balance a short time later, usually on or before delivery.

Suppose a trading company wishes to contract for a given quantity of silicon, but does not have a buyer for it as yet. The company is of the opinion that taking possession of the silicon is wise, because it believes that it will be able to sell it very soon at a favorable price. Some banks will lend the trading company the funds necessary to make the purchase *if* they are convinced the transaction is sound. But banks are very particular about such financing, and the policy of most lenders is not to finance private speculators. In certain cases, a bank might decide to finance one or several of its good customers in a minor-metals venture, but the margins would be high. A speculator would be able to finance perhaps 50 percent, while a trading company, under the right circumstances, might be able to finance up to 90 percent.

In general, bank financing of minor-metals purchases is not an option for the investor. If the merchant or investment company has a good relationship with a bank, however, it is possible that the company itself could arrange financing and pass it on to a client. The trading company would then assume the risk of lending to an investor, the very risk the bank is unwilling to take. But the trading company may have confidence in the investor's integrity. Besides, the trading company might feel certain it could sell the metal should the investor default.

More common is the act of collateralizing a loan with a warehouse warrant. Again, it is worth about 50 percent of its value to the private investor seeking funds from a bank. If it is a bearer warrant, anyone in possession of it could probably walk into a bank and borrow against it. If you have your warehouse warrants made out to "Bearer," and let your broker hold them, make sure that nobody is using them as collateral. If they default, the bank gets the metal, and you are left holding the bag.

## SELLING SHORT AGAINST YOUR HOLDINGS

Suppose you are holding a particular metal. You think that the price is going lower over the next six months, but you don't want to sell your holdings because you could be wrong—which would force you to buy it back at a higher price—and because you believe the price will go higher over the long run. So you sell a six-month forward contract, backed by your marginal portfolio. If you are right, and the price goes lower, you simply buy the metal at the lower price in the free market and deliver on the contract for a profit.

On the other hand, if the price were to rise, you would have several options. You could buy the metal at a higher price and sell it to the contract holder at a loss. Or you could simply deliver some of the metal you are holding in your portfolio. There is a loss involved, because at the higher price your metal is worth more than it was six months ago. But you wouldn't have to pay out any additional cash.

Further, selling short when you are backed by the actual metal is less risky. If there is a shortage six months later, you *know* that you can make delivery because you have the metal in the warehouse.

## "THE BASKET"

It is difficult to get traders to agree on anything. But every trader, investment adviser, and analyst we spoke with believes that the most responsible and potentially profitable approach to minor-metals investment is the "basket" strategy. Basket is just a code word for a diversified portfolio. You buy several selected metals, spreading your money around rather than investing it all in one or two metals.

The reason for such an approach is obvious: if you guess wrong about one or two metals, you might still be right on the others. Depending on the relative changes in price, you should stand a better chance of making a profit, while at the same time taking steps to cut your losses.

The basket approach doesn't always work. Obviously, it is possible for all the metals in your portfolio to decline in price at the same time. Or one or two could sell off so severely that even a healthy rise in the price of the rest would not offset the loss. Probably the best thing you can do to avoid such a scenario is to select metals that are affected by different market factors. In other words, don't purchase a basket of metals consisting only of those that will rise if southern Africa has political problems, or only those that will rise if solar energy catches on. Rather, pick one or two linked to Africa, one or two linked to technology, one or two linked to economic recovery.

# PART III

## Minor-
## Metals
## Investment
## Profiles

# INTRODUCTION TO THE INDIVIDUAL PROFILES

## THE PITFALLS OF PROJECTIONS AND PREDICTIONS

Any follower of the economy is well aware of the inability of economists to make acurate predictions. The situation is not much different for minor metals. Projected demand, projected supply, estimated increase in production capability, surplus, and shortages are crude estimates, not to be relied upon too faithfully.

Recently, several leading think tanks have applied econometric and other models to the minor-metals markets. In consulting them, caution should be exercised, as many of these models rely too heavily on historical information, and forecasters are often too quick to change their predictions when a set of economic figures changes. In general, they have oversold their ability to forecast.

The supply/demand analyses computed by the Bureau of Mines are quite interesting and enlightening, but not completely objective. Rather, they are a meld of mathematical predictions and the input of several industry and government experts. In addition, they are often presented in wide ranges, and the disparity between the high and low ends of the ranges can make a big difference in whether or not an investment is advisable.

In reading through the metals profiles, keep in mind that this information is provided only to familiarize you with the metals and to give you a perspective on the fundamental factors and participants in the markets. Each outlook is a broad sweep, based on a careful look at the figures and the opinions of several metals experts, including merchants and academic and industry experts. Each is intended to provide background and overview rather than serve as a source for specific investment decisions.

## HOW THE METALS WERE SELECTED

As noted earlier, the term *strategic* has little relevance to investment feasibility, and even *minor metals* is often a misleading term. The choice of metals for review in this section is based on several factors. First, we felt obliged to include those most often discussed as potential investments. As such, we have included twelve metals cited in a recent *Metals Week* survey of eight firms selling minor metals: cobalt, chromium, tantalum, titanium, indium, germanium, manganese, columbium, silicon, tungsten, rhodium, and cadmium.

We also felt strongly that certain overlooked metals should be represented, as they may prove to be profitable in the long run. A third category is metals that are not feasible for investment at this time, but could prove interesting and profitable in the future.

## KEEP UP-TO-DATE

In the previous chapters we examined the variables affecting price, the shifting forces of supply and demand, and the mechanics of dealing in minor metals. As you apply this information to various metals, candidates for investment will begin to emerge. But the investment picture for metals changes rapidly, and what looks like a good buy one month may be quite a mistake several months later. Therefore, you should seek up-to-date information from other sources.

Read the principal trade publications. Many of them publish market outlooks for many of the metals and up-to-date appraisals by industry experts. In addition, the Bureau of Mines can supply you with monthly or quarterly *Mineral Industry Surveys* for most metals and with the monthly publication *Minerals and Materials*. These surveys can be quite valuable in tracing the markets, but remember that the figures are more relevant to the U.S. domestic mining industry. In some cases, foreign countries will make similar reports available to you through their mining bureaus, and in the case of a major producing nation such reports can be quite helpful. Most important, always get an appraisal from your investment adviser or a metals dealer before taking the plunge. They will often have information on the markets long before it reaches print.

Once you have narrowed down the choice, you must learn to be patient. Wise buying is largely a sense of timing. It is also a good idea to keep in mind that the right price is very important. Your analysis and your broker's recommendations may lead you to select five metals for *possible* purchase, but you will want to *buy* only the best values—the metals that have the best potential given the current price.

## SELECTION CRITERIA

To sum up our previous discussions, here are some of the things you should look for when investigating a particular metal.

### Supply Factors

**Import Reliance.** How dependent on foreign sources are we and other consuming nations? Are the consumers vulnerable to actions or disruptions in the producing nations? Are the producing nations stable politically? Are they part of the Third World? Are they at odds with us philosophically? Is there a recent history of aggression by or against other nations, strikes, coups, or terrorism? Do any of these factors jeopardize the mines themselves? Are there other potential sources? Would they be much more expensive to utilize? Do we have domestic reserves that we are not using now?

**Producer Control.** How much of a grip do the producers have on the market? Could a group of producers become aggressive and run the price up? Consider the relative strength and weakness of the producers who control a dominant share of the market. Most experts prefer markets with more players, but some believe that it often makes sense to ride the coattails of producers that are in a good position to dictate price.

**By-products.** Is the metal mined primarily as a by-product of another metal? If so, what is the supply/demand outlook for the base metal? How will it affect the supply of the by-product you are interested in?

**Recycling Potential.** Is recycling at maximum efficiency now? Is it possible or likely that additional supplies can be obtained from further recycling? How much additional supply can enter the market if the demand should require it? Is the metal consumed, or is much of it discarded as waste?

**Stocks.** How much above-ground supply exists in refined form? In raw form, as residues, or as other mining by-products? Where are the stocks and who owns them? How quickly is the stock being depleted or replenished? Do the owners desperately need cash that could be raised from selling stocks? Did they obtain their stockpile at low enough prices so that a sale at the current price would bring a handsome profit?

**Government Stockpile Status.** Is the government currently holding a stockpile? Does it have more than it needs? Are sales of stocks anticipated?

**New Mines and Refiners.** Where are they? How many? What is their capacity? How long is the projected lead time before they begin to produce?

**Regulation.** What has been the effect of environmental regulations on mining, processing, and refining? Will any new restrictions, current and future, result in the closing of any major operations? Will the exploitation of new reserves be prohibited? What about import controls by the United States or export controls by the producing nations?

**Elasticity of Supply.** How price-elastic is the supply of the metal? Are there any short- or long-term time factors that might change that? How about cross elasticity—is the supply of the metal likely to be affected by a change in the price of another metal?

### Demand Factors

**Relationship to Economic Cycles.** Does demand for the metal have a tendency to slack off as the world economy slumps? Does it pick up as the economy booms? Is demand for the metal in phase with the economic cycle, or slightly out of phase (that is, does the metal get strong well before or well after the economic upturn begins)? Past tendencies should not be mistaken for accurate predictions of future price and demand behavior. However, they will help you get a fix on how demand factors interact with the international economic scene as a whole.

**Current and Future Use Patterns and Projections.** Is the use of the metal growing? In what applications is its use decreasing? What industries are involved, and how does their future look? In assessing these patterns, always look at the tonnage involved and what percentage of overall output and consumption the tonnage represents.

**New Technologies.** Is the metal associated with any new technological processes or products? How soon will these come on stream, and are they expected to catch on? If they do, how much metal will be used?

**New Demand Sources.** Are there developing countries that previously had little use for this metal, but now require it for their industries? Nations like Brazil, South Korea, and Israel are developing high-technology industries that will require the use of several specialty metals.

**Substitutability.** Is substitution a possibility? In what applications? At what price? Will loss of performance result? Are there new research and development programs that might lead to substitutions? Once a substitution is effected, how easy would it be to revert back to the original metal if it was to become cheaper or turn out to be more efficient? Are consumers eager to strengthen their hand by becoming less dependent on the metal?

**Stockpile Status.** Are government purchase plans in the works? Any new tax programs that might encourage private stockpiling? Might the governments of producing nations buy up metals to keep prices high?

**Military Spending.** Are there any defense programs that require the metal? If so, how much will be needed over how many years? What about defense programs in other large nations?

**Government Intervention.** Is the government subsidizing any programs—for example, alternative energy research—that might lead to increased demand for the metal? Are there any government regulations restricting the use of the metal?

**Elasticity of demand.** How price-elastic is the demand for the metal? Are there any short- and long-term factors that might change that? Is substitution likely to have an effect on elasticity? What about cross elasticity of demand—will the demand of the metal be affected by a change in the price of another?

## Cost Factors

**Energy.** In general, what is the cost of energy in all forms, and how rapidly is it rising? What about the specific energy costs associated with the metal? What percentage of the overall production cost does energy account for?

**Capital Requirements.** Is new, expensive, specially designed machinery needed to extract and/or process the ore, or to meet environmental or conservation standards?

**Environmental.** Has the cost of production been increased by additional taxes, large finds, or money for land, air, or water cleanup?

**Labor.** Are the workers well organized, if not unionized? Do they have a recent history of demanding wage hikes in excess of the rate of inflation? Will new health and safety programs drive up costs substantially? Are labor costs unusually high because of the difficulty of getting skilled labor to work in remote areas?

**Reserves.** How much did the company pay to purchase or lease the land?

## Feasibility Factors

**Liquidity.** What is the tonnage and dollar volume of annual world-market consumption? How many buyers are involved? How many sellers? How much metal is in free-market hands? How balanced is the market between buyers and sellers? How is the market reacting to large sales and purchases?

**Size.** How much of a metal must you buy to be assured that you may sell it easily when you are ready? What is the minimum size of a lot commonly traded among industrial users?

**Storage Feasibility.** How long is the shelf life? Any special problems with storage? How bulky is the shipment? What form is it in?

**Volatility.** How volatile has the price been in the past? Does it appear to be heading for a volatile future? What does the market think about the metal's overall volatility?

**Optimum Holding.** How long a holding period is necessary

to maximize the chances of making a profit? Can you comfortably hold that long?

**Foreign Exchange.** What currency is the metal traded in? If not dollars, what is the outlook for that currency and is it wise to hedge?

**Grade.** How liquid is the grade? Is the price you have been quoted a proper one considering the grade being offered?

# Antimony

**Principal Uses and Demand.** Mainly used as an alloying constituent of lead and other metals, antimony is found in storage batteries; power, transmission, and communication equipment; solder; and ammunition, where it is used as an alloy to harden bullets, and in chemical form to emit light in tracer bullets. Its use in automobile batteries has declined as manufacturers have substituted tin, calcium, and cadmium. But its fire-resistant properties have led to the use of non-metallic antimony in fabrics and plastics. It is also used in ceramics and glass. End-use distribution for 1981: flame retardants, 55 percent; transportation (including batteries), 15 percent; ceramics and glass, 15 percent; chemicals, 5 percent; others 10 percent.

The Bureau of Mines predicts an annual increase in demand of 3.1 percent through 1990.

**Major sources.** U.S. producers supply less than 10 percent of the primary demand, a trend that is expected to continue. Domestic resources are in Idaho, Nevada, Alaska, and Montana, but nearly all production has been by two companies, one in Idaho, where antimony is obtained as a by-product of silver-lead ores, and one in Montana, where antimony ore is mined. Some is also recovered from the smelting of lead ore.

China, which has more than half the world's known reserves, supplied 39 percent of U.S. antimony metal imports between 1977 and 1980. Bolivia, Mexico, and South Africa are other major producers (South Africa supplies 46 percent of the antimony that comes in chemical form), and several other suppliers produce in small amounts.

**Import Reliance and Stockpile.** For 1981, net import reliance as a percentage of consumption: 51 percent. The U.S. stockpile goal is 36,000 tons; present inventory, 40,728 tons.

**Substitutes and Recycling.** There are various substitutes for antimony, mainly other strategic metals. Compounds of titanium, chromium, tin, and zirconium can replace antimony chemicals; alloys using calcium, strontium, tin, copper, selenium, and others can be used in hardening lead; aluminum oxide and various organic compounds are acceptable as flame retardants. However, cost and availability factors often favor the use of antimony.

Approximately 47 percent of 1981 domestic consumption was derived from scrap, mostly from battery plates.

**Trends.** Much research is under way on developing technology for recovering usable antimony in the secondary lead industry, since current recycling is inefficient. The Bureau of Mines also is researching better recycling methods. There is concern over the depletion of high-grade ores in Mexico, Bolivia, and South Africa, and there is concern also about our dependence on China.

**Outlook.** The big question with respect to antimony's future appears to be, Will industry find new uses for it?

The role of antimony as an industrial metal appears to be in decline, but it is still an important component of many batteries. While its use in chemicals and flame retardants is dropping, its use in the production of plastics, ceramics, and glass is growing somewhat.

Currently, there appears to be more than enough antimony to meet demand. Eventually, it is expected that battery improvements will reduce if not eliminate the amount of antimony currently used.

Additional capacity from ASARCO, Bolivia's plan to double production, and an expected GSA stockpile sale could contribute further to an oversupply in 1982–1983.

These factors and the high rate of recycling make the outlook for antimony rather dismal. No significant price moves are expected in the near future, even as the economy picks up.

What antimony needs is a new application that the market can get excited about.

**Grades.** The most commonly traded grades of antimony metal are 99.5 and 99.65 percent, with an arsenic content below 0.2 percent. The Chinese grade is usually 99.65 percent minimum and 0.15 percent arsenic. The metal usually comes in ingots weighing 20 to 50 pounds, traded in metric ton units, usually 5 tons or more.

# Beryllium

**Principal Uses and Demand.** Strong and exceptionally light, beryllium is used in nuclear reactors and in the aerospace industry (40 percent of 1981 consumption); as an alloy in electrical equipment (35 percent); in miniaturized spring elements and contacts in electronics (15 percent); and others (10 percent). It is, however, a very toxic substance whose emissions are regulated by the Environmental Protection Agency. One of its main functions is as a copper alloy; used in small amounts, it produces a metal hard and strong enough to be used in aircraft engines. It is also crucial in certain defense-related applications—for example, in optical systems in missiles. Demand varies with defense spending and general economic conditions.

The Bureau of Mines predicts an annual increase in demand of 1.3 percent through 1990.

**Major Sources.** The United States has very little of the raw materials needed to produce beryllium. We rely mainly on imported ores, which are processed in Utah, Ohio, and Pennsylvania; production increased significantly in 1980, although the industry says strict environmental standards threaten closings.

The world reserve base is not well delineated. The main producers are communist nations and Brazil. Between 1977 and 1980, Brazil supplied almost half the U.S. imports, China 25 percent, India 12 percent and Argentina 8 percent. Exact figures on U.S. production are withheld by the Bureau of Mines.

**Import Reliance and Stockpile.** Beryl ore, beryllium-copper alloy, and beryllium metal are all stocked. The first two are almost up to established inventory goals, but beryllium metal is about 43 percent of its goal. The percentage of imports is not available.

**Substitutes and Recycling.** Steel, titanium, and graphite composites can substitute for beryllium metal, and phosphor bronze for beryllium-copper alloys, but the loss of performance quality is significant. Where its light weight, high strength, and conductivity are needed, beryllium use is expected to continue.

Old scrap is too costly and too difficult to reuse; new scrap is often recycled by companies that generate it.

**Trends.** Regulations by the Occupational Safety and Health Administration that lower the maximum exposure to beryllium by workers are still under consideration and, if adopted, will add significantly to production costs.

Recovery of by-product uranium from bertrandite ore (from which beryllium hydroxide is made) may encourage production.

The industry expects increased use in microprocessors and electronic controls for automobiles and appliances.

**Outlook.** From 1971 through 1976, there was a decline in beryllium consumption; this was primarily due to the reduction in defense and aerospace programs following the Vietnam War. Since then, consumption has increased annually. Many experts expect beryllium consumption to increase if we undergo a major defense buildup. Construction of the MX missile system will also increase demand.

In the United States only one company, Brush Wellman, Inc., mines beryllium ore. In fact, it is the only free-world producer of beryllium metal. Considering the lack of production facilities in the free world, our dependence on imported ore, and beryllium's role in the defense industry, the metal could prove interesting in the future. However, trading beryllium presents practical difficulties because there is almost no merchant activity in this metal. The reasons for this are manifold. The lack of producers makes the appearance of any marginal tonnage unlikely. And because there is virtually no recycling of beryllium, no alternative source of tradable free-market metal exists.

With advanced technology in recycling, we could see the appearance of a scrap beryllium market, and if demand were to get stronger we could also see beryllium metal arriving from other nations.

**Grades.** Because of its toxicity, pure beryllium metal is rarely, if ever, traded. The most common form of beryllium is a master alloy of beryllium and copper, which has a content of up to 5 percent beryllium.

# Cadmium

**Principal Uses and Demand.** This soft, malleable metal is a by-product of zinc processing, and is used most in plated hardware (34 percent of 1981 consumption). Batteries are its second most important application (22 percent), followed by transportation (17 percent), pigments (13 percent), and plastics (11 percent), and others (3 percent). Because it is so ductile and so easily soldered, it is widely used when plated parts have to be stamped or formed. It also has excellent resistance to alkali and salt spray and therefore is used in sea environments.

The Bureau of Mines predicts a 1.8 percent annual increase in demand through 1990.

**Major Sources.** Canada and the United States have the best reserve bases of cadmium, the production of which is dependent on zinc ore supplies, The closing of a large zinc mining operation in 1980 led to the loss of some 3 million pounds of cadmium, an example of how the zinc industry affects cadmium supplies.

In addition to the United States and Canada, major producers include Japan, Belgium, Australia, and the U.S.S.R. The United States gets 25 percent of its imports from Canada, and the rest from Mexico, Australia, Belgium, West Germany, Peru, and others in small quantitites.

**Import Reliance and Stockpile.** Import reliance in 1981 was 76 percent of apparent consumption. The stockpile goal is 5,307 metric tons; inventory contains 2,871.

**Substitutes and Recycling.** There are substitutes for most major uses. Coatings of zinc or certain types of aluminum can replace cadmium in some plating applications, but with a loss of durability. Zinc and iron can replace cadmium pigments, but performance is often diminished.

Very little recycling is done; it is practical now only with nickel-cadmium batteries and some alloys.

**Trends.** The Bureau of Mines is researching cadmium pollution-control techniques, methods of recovering cadmium from primary and secondary materials, and substitutes for plating applications.

There are large potential resources in the zinc-bearing coals of the United States. If it becomes economic to do so, these resources could be tapped even before the coal itself is used. Experts believe there are anywhere from 5 to 50 million tons of undiscovered cadmium resources in the world.

There are major potential applications in solar energy cells and as window coating for passive solar heating systems in buildings.

**Outlook.** Cadmium is primarily an industrial metal, and therefore its consumption tends to run in tandem with the business cycle. However, it has recently been discovered to be highly toxic and efforts are being made worldwide to reduce cadmium in pigments and stabilizers, as well as in certain forms of cadmium plating.

As a result of the recession, zinc consumption has dropped considerably, and production along with it. Closely linked to zinc, cadmium production has declined as well. Even though production has decreased, stocks seem to be increasing, largely because of a decline in consumption and an increase in imports. In such situations, consumers tend not to hold stocks because they know they can get the metal anytime they need it from the producers, so the producers are forced to stockpile.

Soft markets and growing inventories among cadmium producers should keep the market dull for some time. An economic rebound would, of course, increase consumption and demand for cadmium, but it would take a bit of time before this brought higher prices, due to the high stock levels on hand.

Some experts believe that there are some promising new markets for cadmium in the battery, solar cell, and pigment areas. Indeed, demand for cadmium in the nickel-cadmium battery market has continued to be strong throughout this lackluster period.

While market watchers find it difficult to get excited about cadmium given the current recession, high stock levels, and its toxicity, there is a lot of cadmium around and it is very freely traded. But if you are astute and watch the market carefully, it does present certain profit opportunities provided you adopt an aggressive trading strategy.

**Grades.** There are several forms in which cadmium is traded, depending entirely on the end use. Purity is usually 99.95 percent minimum, but some chemical purposes require 99.99 percent purity. Cadmium comes in balls for use in plating, sticks for use in chemicals, and ingots for use in alloys.

# CHROMIUM

**Principal Uses and Demand.** The chrome trim on cars and refrigerators actually accounts for about 6 percent of the chromium used in the United States. It is one of the most important ferroalloys, and a key ingredient in stainless steel, 14 to 20 percent of which is composed of chromium. And stainless steel is found just about everywhere in an industrial society. In 1981, 19 percent of domestic chromium was used in the construction industry; 17 percent in machinery and equipment; 12 percent in transportation; 12 percent in refractories; and 40 percent elsewhere. Its use in defense production—there is no substitute for it in aircraft engines—is so important that early in World War II the makers of Lucky Strike cigarettes switched from green packages to white, announcing with great fanfare, "Lucky Strike Green Goes to War." Chromium is used in pigments and dyes, and green cigarette packages were deemed less vital than military uses. In all, 18 percent of chromium is used in the refractory industry, 25 percent in the chemical industry, and 57 percent in metallurgy. Due to its ability to enhance strength, hardness, and resistance to corrosion, oxidation, heat, and wear, chromium is indispensable.

In 1981, consumption dropped by more than 30 percent from the previous year's level, reflecting reduced demand in chromium-consuming industries, especially steel. But growing demand in developing countries and stepped-up defense spending here portend increased demand.

The Bureau of Mines predicts an annual increase of 3.2 percent through 1990.

**Major Sources.** Chromite—containing chrome, iron, and oxygen—is the principal ore, and it is found in varying grades. Whatever deposits the United States has are inferior grades found in California and Montana. The best grades and the largest reserves are in South Africa, Zimbabwe, and the Soviet Union; 99 percent of world resources are in southern Africa. Once, the United States manufactured ferrochrome, an alloy of chrome and iron, from imported ores, but now it is increasingly dependent on imported ferrochrome. This is largely due to Japan's emergence as a major ferrochrome producer (it has no ores of its own), and South Africa's decision to sell less raw material and more ferrochrome, which adds considerable value to its exports. Cheap labor, cheap energy, and the absence of environmental restrictions are important advantages in ferrochrome production.

Known resources are sufficient to meet every conceivable demand for centuries. But distribution of reserves is uneven, and certain political factors influence supply. The combined 1980 mine production of South Africa and the Soviet Bloc was seven times greater than that of all market economies. The Soviet Union, faced with production problems and enormous demand, cut back its exports dramatically. Of our imports of chromite from 1977 to 1980, 44 percent came from South Africa, 16 percent from the Philippines, 15 percent from the Soviet Union, and 9 percent from Turkey. Of imported ferro-chrome, South Africa supplied 71 percent, Yugoslavia 11 percent, Zimbabwe 7 percent, and Sweden 4 percent.

**Import Reliance and Stockpile.** The Bureau of Mines lists our 1981 import reliance as 90 percent. The remaining 10 percent was recycled. The stockpile goal for metallurgical-grade chromite is 3,200,000 tons; current inventory is 1,957,000.

**Substitutes and Recycling.** There is no known substitute for its use in stainless steel. For other applications, various elements or materials may replace chromium, but cost, performance, and other factors restrict their use. Nickel, zinc, or cadmium can replace chromium for corrosion protection; aluminum and plastic can replace it in decorative trim; molybdenum, nickel, cobalt, and vanadium can replace it as an alloy; titanium can be used in chemical-processing equipment; cadmium can be used as a replacement pigment in some cases.

Recycling of stainless steel scrap provides 9 percent of chromium demand; more can be recycled, depending on the price of the metal and environmental restrictions.

**Trends.** Bureau of Mines research focuses on recovering chromium from low-grade ores and laterite deposits; improved recycling methods; conservation procedures; and substitutions. No domestic mining is likely at current prices.

**Outlook.** People who deal in strategic metals love to talk about chromium. They tout it as a terrific investment because there are no known substitutes for many of its critical uses, and because the major supplies emanate from southern Africa, certainly one of the world's tinderboxes. The program to stockpile chromium is one of the most ambitious and important in the entire government stockpile program.

How does this situation affect chromium's investment feasibility? Let's look at chromium demand. The most important use for chromium is in the manufacture of stainless steel, which is related to the overall worldwide economic situation. It is an industrial metal, and although its growth is expected to be high and steady over the long term, chromium is very susceptible to any economic downturn or recession. In fact, 1980 world demand for chromium was the lowest recorded since 1975; U.S. consumption was down 14 percent from 1979.

Significant developments in the process of manufacturing chromium have allowed end-users to utilize lower grades. In the past, when the producers received ferrochrome, they had to remove the carbon before making steel. But recent technological advances have made it possible to remove most of the carbon in the actual steel-making process. Therefore, users have been able to make do with higher-carbon ferrochrome, a lower-grade of chromium commonly called charge chrome. It is not impossible that mining firms in the United States, armed with advanced technology, will find a way to utilize much of our domestic, low-grade chromium reserves. That, of course, would reduce our dependence on overseas suppliers.

Investors should approach the chromium market with a bit of caution. It is expected that as we come out of the recession, the demand for the metal will rise. The increased costs of freight, fuel, electric power, labor, and coke needed for its production will also have an effect. Thus, the case for higher prices seems reasonable.

Although the bulk of the chrome business is done between producers and large consumers, namely the major steel-making conglomerates and mills, there is a very healthy and respectable merchant business as well.

**Grades.** Most of the chrome produced is in the form of: (a) its ore, chromite, or (b) ferrochrome, which is an alloy of chrome and iron. It is produced in several grades, which are related to the amount of chromium metal in the ore and the amount of carbon present. Charge chrome, for example, contains about 55.0 percent chrome. High-carbon ferrochrome contains about 5.0 percent to 8.0 percent carbon, and low-carbon ferrochrome contains less than 0.1 percent carbon. Some chrome is sold in the form of ferrosilicon chrome, containing some silicon metal.

There is some disagreement among investment advisers and metal specialists as to the grades that would be most acceptable for long-term investment. Some traders feel that because most of the chromium in the world is sold in the form of ferrochrome, that form is best. Others maintain that the purchase and storage of ferrochrome is not feasible because of the extra bulk involved. In most cases, you must store as much iron as you store chrome, along with some carbon content as well. They contend that storing pure chromium metal is a better bet for investors. While chromium metal is much less frequently traded, it is felt that during a chromium shortage there will always be users willing to take the pure chrome metal and work with it. Therefore, from a buy-and-hold standpoint, it makes sense to purchase pure chrome metal. In a trade-and-hold situation, it might be a good idea to hold some pure chrome for a long-term investment, and trade in and out of the market with the ferrochrome. Since you don't intend to be holding it for very long, the storage costs won't be very significant.

# Cobalt

**Principal Uses and Demands.** Once used mainly in ceramics and pigments—the blue in Ming dynasty porcelain, for example—cobalt has found other, more critical uses. Thanks to its heat resistance, strength, and superior magnetic properties, it is a vital alloying ingredient in aerospace and electrical products. Jet engines can't be built without cobalt for their turbine blades, and cobalt is also used in landing gear, engine mounts, structural components, and other parts of airplanes. The military uses it in missiles, tanks, armor-piercing shells, propulsion systems, and communications gear. Cobalt is used in much of the country's machinery—tool steels, high-speed steels, dies, valves, sleeves, springs, mills, presses, cutting tools, and drill bits. Cobalt is also used as a catalyst in oil refineries, in the chemical industry, in synthetic fuel gasification, and in other areas—even as a nutritive agent for livestock.

In 1981, demand for cobalt declined, probably because users had overreacted to earlier price shocks. Still, the United States consumed an estimated $250 million worth. Forty percent of it was used in superalloys; 15 percent went to the electronics industry for use in magnets; 12 percent was used in drying agents for paint; 12 percent in catalysts; metal cutting and mining tool bits accounted for another 10 percent of consumption; and other uses 11 percent.

The Bureau of Mines predicts an annual increase of 2.5 percent through 1990.

**Major Sources.** U.S. production ceased at the end of 1971. Reportedly, the Blackbird Mine in Idaho and the Fredericktown Mines in Missouri are good potential sources, capable of supplying 20 to 30 percent of U.S. needs. Environmental restrictions and economics will determine if they are to be exploited in the next few years. Noranda's Blackbird Mine is adjacent to an area of 50,000 acres felt to have a high potential for cobalt, and that region was excluded from Wilderness Area protection. With cobalt prices dropping, however, the domestic deposits may be uneconomic. Production may also hinge on the world copper market, since most producers of cobalt extract it as a by-product of copper mining. Blackbird, however, is not a by-product mine.

Forty percent of world reserves are in Zaire; Zambia is next, with reserves about a third as large as Zaire's. On the basis of production, Zaire is even more solidly in first place; it was responsible for more than half the world's production in 1981. The Soviets were a distant second, but new facilities may enable them to increase production to 10,000 tons by 1985. Canada and South Africa also announced plans to expand production, and a new plant is being built in New Caledonia, an important producer.

The United States obtained 42 percent of its cobalt from Zaire between 1977 and 1980; 15 percent came from Belgium-Luxembourg, 14 percent from Zambia, 7 percent from Finland, and 22 percent from elsewhere.

**Import Reliance and Stockpile.** The Bureau of Mines lists the United States as 91 percent import-reliant; the rest comes from recycled scrap. Stockpile goal is 42,700 short tons; 20,996 are in inventory. The recent agreement to purchase 5.2 million pounds raised the inventory to 53 percent of its goal.

**Substitutes and Recycling.** In some applications, nickel may be substituted for cobalt, but not without some loss of strength and durability. Other potential substitutes include: platinum, barium or strontium ferrite, and iron for use in magnets; tungsten, ceramics, molybdenum carbide, and nickel in machinery; nickel and ceramics in jet engines; nickel in catalysts; and copper, chromium, and manganese in paints.

Recycling accounted for 10 percent of consumption in 1981.

**Trends.** The Bureau of Mines and private industry are searching for substitutes, better ways to recover scrap, and new methods of extraction. The political situation in southern Africa, progress on the Blackbird Mine, and Law of Sea negotiations (cobalt is found in the nodules on the ocean floor) will all affect the future market.

**Outlook.** As with chromium, much ado has been made about cobalt by investors who are bullish on strategic metals.

The reasons are obvious: we rely on outside sources for our cobalt, and much of it comes from southern Africa; and for many years, cobalt was thought of as having few suitable substitutes for many of its applications.

But very high prices and fears of shortages resulting from the Shaba incident have taught us a few things. Substantial substitution by other metals has occurred, particularly in the magnet and hard-facing industries. While demand continues to be strong in aerospace and jet engine technology, recent advances in the development of new alloys have reduced the use of cobalt in that area as well. In the meantime, Zaire and Zambia, countries that rely heavily on their mining industries for foreign exchange, are expected to continue to produce cobalt and possibly expand production. While Zaire remained the major producer in 1981, its strict adherence to its producer price weakened its position in the market. Although producing more than half of the world's cobalt, it captured perhaps only 15 percent of the market, apart from the stockpile sale to the United States.

The recent recession has brought about a reduction in demand. At the same time the plans for increased cobalt production in Zambia have so far not materialized due to technical and labor problems. Producers' stocks of cobalt appear to be high, while consumer stocks are relatively low. Hopes that demand for cobalt might increase because of stockpiling suffered a setback when many countries shelved their plans. In the United States, the General Services Administration acquired 5 million pounds of cobalt for $75 million, immediately causing the free-market price to drop. Apparently, the market is sufficiently soft to be able to take occasional stockpile purchases without running up the price.

Supply should remain ample over the short run, and the price will probably remain soft. Over the long term, it is expected that the demand for cobalt will increase in the chemical industry for use in carbides, and that the substitution that has taken place in the manufacture of magnets will level off. A slight decrease is expected in cobalt use in superalloys.

Many experts feel that investing in cobalt at this time can be justified by two factors: (1) buying for the recovery—it is possible that cobalt prices will get firmer as we recover from our economic slump and industrial demand increases, especially since cobalt inventories are at all-time lows; (2) the possibility of some kind of political crisis in Zaire, Zambia, or

Zimbabwe, although a supply disruption would have to be quite severe to produce the kind of price movement that we experienced in 1978.

Some analysts fear that cobalt is very susceptible to cartel formation. However, there has been no evidence that a cartel of cobalt producers could hold together and exert any meaningful price influence at this particular time. Supply/demand equilibrium is not expected to return to the market for quite some time.

**Grades.** Cobalt metal usually carries a minimum purity of 99.6 percent and often trades in higher grades. The most common trading form is broken cathodes. The large, flat cathodes of cobalt metal are crushed and broken up, and the pieces are then packed in drums, which usually weigh about one-quarter ton each.

Since the Shaba incident, there has been a very active free market in cobalt.

# Columbium
Also Known as Niobium

**Primary Uses and Demand.** Columbium is used in a number of specialty steels, for beams and girders in buildings, for offshore drilling towers, special industrial machinery, railroad equipment, ship plating, automobiles, and increasingly in gas and oil pipelines. It is also important in superalloys for jet engines, missiles, and other military applications. Its use in the nuclear and electronics industries is growing. End-use distribution for 1981: transportation, 32 percent; construction, 31 percent; oil and gas industries, 16 percent; machinery, 11 percent; and others, 10 percent.

The Bureau of Mines predicts an annual increase of about 6 percent through 1990.

**Major Sources.** Produced from columbite, pyrochlore, euxenite, and columbium-tantalite, the metal is primarily used in the form of ferrocolumbium. Since 1959, there has been no domestic mining of columbium; eight companies produce the metal ferrocolumbium and other alloys from raw materials imported chiefly from Canada, Nigeria, and Brazil, which contains about 80 percent of the world's known reserves. Other sources include Thailand, the Soviet Union, Zaire and Uganda. In previous years Brazil was the largest exporter, but in 1981 its CBMM, the world's largest producer, stopped exporting columbium concentrates in favor of more refined products. The exact amount of Soviet reserves is unknown but is thought to be about the same as Canada's, which ranks a distant second to Brazil.

**Import Reliance and Stockpile.** The United States is 100 percent import-dependent. The stockpile goal for columbium concentrates is 5,600,000 pounds; the inventory is 911,000. The stockpile currently contains almost 598,000 pounds of ferrocolumbium.

**Substitutes and Recycling.** In high-strength steels and superalloys, vanadium and molybdenum can be used; and in high-temperature applications, molybdenum, tungsten, tantalum, and ceramics can take the place of columbium.

Recycling is insignificant.

**Trends.** Columbium has potential for increased use in superconductors of electricity at extremely low temperatures, a growing area. Producers expect increased use in pipelines and defense. There are some 800 million pounds of columbium in identified deposits in the United States; they were uneconomic at 1980 prices, but could be tapped in the future.

**Outlook.** In recent years, columbium has found quite a large number of uses in the specialty-steel area. There has been strong demand for ferrocolumbium pipeline steels, and there has been increased worldwide use of superalloys containing ferrocolumbium. Even automobile manufacturers are interested in utilizing more columbium in the manufacture of lightweight steels that can provide better gas mileage.

Some high-purity grades of ferrocolumbium are used primarily in the growing aerospace industry. In addition, since the amount of columbium being used in the manufacture of oil pipelines is about to increase, should oil exploration continue unabated there could be an increase in demand.

In recent years, prices have gone very high, due to a shortage in 1979. However, by 1980, supplies were plentiful and they have remained so. Producers have increased capacity, and even though there is some growth in demand predicted, it is likely that there will be supplies available for some time to come. For that reason, the subsitition programs that were stimulated by high prices in 1979 have slowed down considerably. In fact, many producers are trying to promote columbium as a substitute for tantalum in machine tools and for cobalt in aircraft superalloys. No major movement of price is anticipated in the short term. In 1981, prices for high-purity ferrocolumbium dropped by 14 percent, but the standard grades held steady.

Weak demand related to oversupply and the recession not only has discouraged substitution, but has also encouraged the search for new uses.

The use of columbium in superconductors may add to columbium demand. However, this is a long-term prospect based on advances in the electronics industry. Potential uses of superconductors are in magnetic coils, fusion reactors, and switching circuits for computers.

**Grades.** Columbium is most commonly traded in alloy form as ferrocolumbium, usually made of up to 60 or 70 percent columbium (the balance is iron and small amounts of impurities). It comes in lump form, packed in drums.

Pure columbium metal is rarely traded.

# Gallium

**Principal Uses and Demand.** More than 90 percent of the gallium consumed in 1981 was in electronics, where it is an important component of semiconductors. Gallium compounds are used to produce light-emitting diodes for visual display panels in calculators, radios, televisions, clocks, and instruments.

The Bureau of Mines predicts an annual increase of about 6 percent through 1990.

**Major Sources.** Most of the world's gallium is recovered as a by-product of the extraction of aluminum from bauxite; the second major source is by-product recovery from smelting zinc ore. Only a small part of the gallium in these ores is recovered, due to cost factors and low demand levels. While the Bureau of Mines is unable to estimate current world reserves, bauxite is plentiful. But if aluminum production is slow, less gallium can be produced. Zinc reserves are also quite large.

The United States produces gallium, but consumption exceeds domestic capability at current prices. Of the amount imported, 68 percent comes from Switzerland, 12 percent from West Germany, 12 percent from Canada, and the rest from a few others.

**Import Reliance and Stockpile.** In 1981, the United States imported 40 percent of its gallium. It is not held in the stockpile.

**Substitutes and Recycling.** Silicon and germanium can replace gallium in many semiconductor applications. Liquid crystals made from organic compounds are used in visual display panels, but gallium provides superior performance and is used despite its higher cost.

About 25 percent of the gallium used in fabricating compounds for solid-state semiconductors is reprocessed.

**Trends.** If current research on the direct conversion of sunlight to electricity is commercially successful, demand for gallium, which is used in photovoltaic cells, should increase considerably. Some experts believe gallium will replace silicon chips in many semiconductors during this decade. It is also being used in fiber optics. On the supply side, higher prices could generate better ways to recover gallium from zinc and bauxite operations, where much of it is now discarded with waste.

**Outlook.** The demand for gallium is expected to increase significantly due to its use in electronics. With the advent of bubble memory technology in computers, gallium demand could become very significant in the next decade.

While gallium is quite plentiful—more abundant than antimony, silver, molybdenum, and tungsten, and almost as abundant as lead—its supply is closely tied to that of zinc and aluminum. Since zinc and aluminum are industrial metals, we can expect the supply of above-ground gallium to run with the business cycle.

Demand on the other hand may not be as cyclical and may tend to grow steadily. So it is possible that we could see a short-term supply squeeze if zinc demand and bauxite demand were to remain depressed and gallium demand were to grow. It should be noted, however, that there are many zinc and bauxite processing circuits that do not recover gallium at present. If they were equipped to do so the supply of gallium would be increased tremendously, even if zinc and bauxite production were to drop overall. Nevertheless, it is fair to say that gallium does represent the kind of high-technology metal that is worthy of investment, if one can keep a very close eye on the supply/demand situation.

**Grades.** Since gallium is used primarily in high-technology applications, very high purities are usually required. Gallium usually trades in ingot form, with purities ranging from 99.9 to 99.9999 percent.

Except for some gallium supplied by the Eastern Bloc, and during periods of severe shortages, there is little free-market activity.

# Germanium

**Principal Uses and Demand.** In 1981, 66 percent of all domestic consumption was for instruments and optical equipment; another 29 percent was used in electronics, mainly in semiconductors for calculators and watches; 5 percent was used in other applications. Germanium has also been used in the fabrication of fuel elements in atomic reactors and, importantly, as a key ingredient in infrared and laser guidance systems. This military use is one reason for growing interest in the metal.

The Bureau of Mines predicts an annual increase of 5.8 percent through 1990.

**Major Sources.** A by-product of zinc and other base metals, germanium is produced in the United States from domestic and imported raw materials. It is believed that most of the germanium consumed in the United States is produced domestically. However, there was a sharp increase in imports in 1981 (almost six times more than in 1980). Major import sources are Belgium-Luxembourg, 33 percent; Switzerland, 26 percent; the U.S.S.R., 11 percent; and West Germany, 10 percent.

**Import Reliance and Stockpile.** Exact figures on import reliance are not available. The United States has no germanium stockpile.

**Substitutes and Recycling.** Silicon, which is plentiful and inexpensive, has been used increasingly as a replacement for germanium in certain electronic applications. Some tellurium, selenium, indium, and gallium bimetals are also used, but germanium is considered more reliable for high-frequency and high-power requirements and is more economical for use in light-emitting diodes. In infrared guidance systems, zinc selenide or germanium glass can substitute for germanium metal, but performance quality is sacrificed.

While more than half the metal used during the manufacture of electronic and optical devices is recycled as scrap, very little germanium is returned because it is so dispersed. Eventually, high-purity optical devices may become a good source of recyclable material.

**Trends.** Since germanium supplies hinge on zinc and other base metal production, current worldwide operations are more than adequate to meet projected demand. Research has been directed toward finding new uses and perfecting existing applications. Recent high prices have forced consumers to use germanium more efficiently, which has in turn held prices and demand down a bit.

It may become possible to recover germanium from ash and flue dusts resulting from burning certain coals. According to the Bureau of Mines, if this were done, worldwide germanium resources would grow to several billion kilograms; worldwide production in 1981 was 125,000 kilograms.

**Outlook.** Germanium has attracted a great deal of attention primarily because of the rapid rise in the demand pattern. The demand is expected to increase substantially in the early years of this decade, mainly because of the development of infrared optics systems. Germanium's use in the electronics industry, particularly in transistors, has declined quite markedly. However, the demand in infrared has more than compensated for that drop. In addition, germanium continues to be used in the manufacture of light-emitting diodes. The use of germanium dioxide as a polyester fiber catalyst also continues to be strong, and germanium's use in a gamma ray detector is expected to bear on its future growth.

New applications include fiber optics, which use germanium tetrachloride. Fiber optics are expected to play a very important role in communications, especially in telephone, computer, and cable television applications in the coming decades. If fiber optics technology is adopted on a wide scale and germanium continues to be used in their manufacture, we could see a very substantial increase in demand over and above what has already taken place. Research continues to be conducted on the use of germanium in solar cells, medicine, and superconductors. However, as of this date no major breakthroughs have been announced.

The outlook for germanium certainly appears promising. But let's take a close look at the supply side. Germanium, as pointed out earlier, is a by-product of zinc and copper. Although there has been a substantial increase in demand over the past several years, the germanium industry has failed to establish new production sources. Prices rose about 50 percent during 1980, but no new production was announced. This is largely due to the difficulty of transporting germanium-rich zinc residues to U.S. smelters from the African countries, notably Zaire, that mine zinc and copper. However, all parties involved are aware of the potential for a buildup of a short-term dislocation situation, and it is expected that there will be an adequate supply of germanium in the near future. Of course, many analysts failed to anticipate the current market conditions, so we have to watch the situation very closely. If the producers continue to be slow in making germanium-rich zinc residues available, we could expect still higher prices as the demand continues to grow. Germanium supply is only partially dependent on an increase in zinc output because so little of the available germanium is actually recovered from zinc residues. Even if the zinc output were to remain flat, germanium output could be increased substantially if a concerted attempt was made to recover more and more germanium from the existing residues.

In 1981, Jersey Miniere Co. (JMZ) began producing germanium from residues of its Tennessee zinc smelter.

Substitution is possible for some applications, and it is expected that zinc prices will rebound, stimulating production and making more germanium residue available.

Currently, the markets are quite tight, and the supply and demand situation is highly restricted. But the price has stabilized as germanium producers scramble to make more available. In fact, the free-market price premium, which was once 25 to 35 percent above the producer price, fell as low as 5 percent by the end of 1981. Investor buying of germanium, a popular "strategic" play, has subsided.

Germanium has been recognized as a potentially critical material by the U.S. government. But it is felt that industry stocks can be kept high enough and substitution utilized, making a national stockpile goal for germanium unwarranted. However, industry stocks are at their lowest levels in quite some time. If there was some disruption in the supply of zinc residues from abroad, a problem could develop, especially in the wake of the military buildup. Prices could rise once again.

Germanium can be recovered from copper also, and the United States continues to mine a great deal of that metal. Copper and zinc are distributed around the world, and there are about a dozen different companies involved in some phase of germanium production. These companies are not only in

Zaire, but also in France, Italy, Belgium, Austria, Canada, the United States, and Libya, with the refiners in Japan, Germany, the United States, and Belgium.

Germanium's price pattern actually places it in a class with precious metals, but the market is very small. Total annual world production is around 100 metric tons, and world capacity appears to be about 200 metric tons, including the central-economy nations. With the current supply squeezes and the rapid run-up in price, there has been an increase in free-market activity. But since germanium is used in highly technical applications where the actual amount of raw material needed is very small, the main concern of manufacturers is not to get the best possible price, but to have a steady supply. Germanium users have a distinct preference for dealing with producers. The manufacturers of infrared night-sights, electronic instruments, and gamma ray detectors need the assurance that they will be able to get that small bit of germanium required for each unit they manufacture. This relative price inelasticity can be good for the investor, but it does make the free market slightly illiquid.

There has been some concern about the potential for someone to corner the market because of the small annual world output. Certainly, based on dollar value, it is possible for somebody to get a big piece of the market, but germanium producers usually sell directly to consumers rather than to the free market, so it is unlikely that speculators, unless they were very sophisticated and well organized, could get their hands on enough metal to corner the market or cause a speculative run-up. As previously noted, available germanium supplies can and probably will be increased, and that could serve to offset any attempt to corner the market.

**Grades.** Because germanium is widely used in a number of electronic applications, electrical resistance is an important consideration in determining the grade. Fifty ohms is a common high grade, although germanium commonly trades in grades down to 30-ohm resistivity. Purity rarely goes below 99.99 percent minimum.

It is usually sold in ingot or crystal form, as pure metal or germanium dioxide. The dioxide is less expensive—beware of a broker who quotes you the free-market price of the metal and offers you a "great deal" at a cheaper price. It may turn out to be dioxide.

# Hafnium

**Principal Uses and Demand.** Because it has the ability to absorb neutrons, this gray sister-metal of zirconium is principally used in the reactor control rods that slow down nuclear chain reactions. Use in control rods accounted for about half of the total hafnium consumption in 1981. It is also used as an alloying agent in high-temperature refractory metals and in ceramics. Its use in cutting-tool alloys is expected to increase, as hafnium-columbium carbide replaces the more costly tantalum carbide.

The Bureau of Mines predicts an annual increase of 5 percent through 1990.

**Major Sources.** Hafnium comes almost exclusively from the mineral zircon, which usually contains about one percent hafnium. It is recovered as a by-product in the production of nuclear-grade zirconium. World resources are thought to exceed 500,000 tons, giving the United States about 28 percent of the world's supply. South Africa and Australia are the main producers.

Between 1977 and 1980, our main import source was Mexico, which accounted for 71 percent of imported hafnium.

**Import Reliance and Stockpile.** Figures on U.S. import dependence and worldwide production are not published. Hafnium is not stockpiled, but it is estimated that the United States has 140,000 tons of hafnium resources available in its 14 million tons of domestic zircon.

**Substitutes and Recycling.** In naval nuclear-reactor control rods, and in refractory metal alloys, there are no known substitutes. In some refractories and in ceramics, zirconium oxide and zirconium metal can be used. There is no significant recycling.

**Trends.** Hafnium is expected to be available at reasonable cost as long as demand continues for reactor-grade zirconium. Increased use in the nuclear industry is projected.

**Outlook.** Stringent government requirements on nuclear reactor specifications make it easy to predict what the hafnium demand in nuclear power plants will be at least through the middle of this decade. Based upon nuclear power plant construction or planned construction around the world, it appears that there is more than enough hafnium to meet demand in that particular application. The reasons: the recent protests and criticism of nuclear power plant construction, and the long lead time needed for their registration and deployment.

However, there are several factors that may prove interesting to potential hafnium investors. At least for the near future, hafnium production is entirely dependent upon the production of reactor-grade zirconium. Suppose some significant new uses for hafnium were to be found. With the nuclear power market depressed, if zirconium demand decreased while hafnium demand increased, it is possible that we could find ourselves with some sort of supply squeeze. At the present time this does not appear likely. But for those who are sanguine on the future of nuclear power, the time to buy hafnium and its sister-metal zirconium may be now, just when nuclear power seems to be under siege. We may not see much movement in the price of this metal for a while because of the long lead time required to develop new power plants, but if there were to be an acceleration of nuclear power, we could find that by the end of the decade the demand for hafnium and zirconium could outstrip production capacity, which could cause a run-up in price.

No zircon ore is mined in the United States. A major portion of it comes from Australia and the Soviet Union, as well as from China and India. Thus, the United States is more or less import-dependent. A countervailing force is the fact that as much as 75 percent of the hafnium used in U.S. foundries could be recovered if necessary.

**Grades.** Hafnium metal is produced as sponge or ingot; there are also hafnium dioxide forms and a crystal-bar hafnium iodine form. World production is estimated at around 100 short tons per year with domestic consumption in the United States about 45 short tons.

# Indium

**Principal Uses and Demand.** This soft, malleable metal with a low melting point has a variety of uses, chiefly in electrical and electronic components, which accounted for 40 percent of its 1981 consumption. Solders, alloys, and coatings accounted for another 40 percent. Research and other uses accounted for the remaining 20 percent. Established uses include plating on electronic components; alloys for bearings, glass lens grinding and polishing, fire sprinklers, and dental products; coating on electrical contacts and nuclear-reactor control rods; infrared detectors; as a catalyst in purification systems used in manufacturing man-made fibers.

The Bureau of Mines predicts an annual increase of about 3 percent through 1990.

**Major Sources.** Indium is a by-product of ores mined for other metals, mainly zinc. Identified resources occur primarily in zinc sulfide ores, although the indium content varies. Major producers are Canada, Japan, Peru, and the U.S.S.R. Of the 50,000 troy ounces of indium thought to constitute worldwide reserves, over a quarter are in the United States and Canada; Eastern Bloc nations contain about 10 percent of the world's supply. Major import sources are Peru (31 percent), Belgium-Luxembourg (29 percent), Canada (15 percent), and the United Kingdom (11 percent).

**Import Reliance and Stockpile.** Import reliance and exact production figures are not published by the Bureau of Mines, but U.S. dependence is felt to amount to about half of its consumption. The United States has no stockpile program for indium.

**Substitutes and recycling.** For most of indium's uses, alternatives are available. Silicon has replaced germanium-indium in transistors. In dental alloys, gallium can be used, but at a higher price. Hafnium and boron carbide can replace indium in nuclear-reactor control rods.

A small amount of indium is recycled, mainly from alloy scrap.

**Trends.** New uses for indium include: as a transparent, electrically conductive coating on glass, such as that used for wristwatch and calculator displays; in infrared detectors and nuclear-reactor control rods; in solar cells; as a coating on aluminum wire, which is expected to be used more widely for electrical circuits.

**Outlook.** Like germanium, indium is recovered primarily as a by-product of zinc, and therefore its supply is intimately connected with the economics of the zinc industry. Improvements in recovery methods and the increase in demand for indium can increase the amount recovered from zinc residues. However, since zinc is a base metal, it is subject to changes in the business cycle and a depressed zinc industry could result in a shortage of indium. This could create a short-term tight supply situation and a run-up in price. As long as indium prices remain sufficiently high, it can be expected that zinc producers will continue to recover it.

The best way to approach investing in the indium market is to monitor carefully the economics of the zinc industry and the impact of the business cycle on it, as well as the general demand and new uses for indium in high-technology applications.

The indium market is dominated by Canada, the largest producer, along with several other major producers in the United States. Most of the larger consumers receive their supply through contracts directly with the producers, but there is an active free market conducted by several merchants who specialize in indium and other rare metals. These merchants get their supply from the Soviet Union and from Japanese and South American producers.

**Grades.** Usually indium is traded in ingot form and the purity runs from 99.97 percent to 99.99 percent. The 99.99 percent is the more commonly traded. The slightly lower grade is usually priced at a discount off the quoted price.


# Lithium

**Principal Uses and Demand.** The lightest metal known to man, lithium is highly reactive and malleable. It is used mainly in compound form. Lithium carbonate is used primarily in aluminum smelting; it is also used in the production of ceramics and enamels, in certain lightweight alloys, and in the manufacture of steel. Lithium hydroxide is used in the production of multipurpose greases (about 60 percent of all greases produced in the United States are lithium-based). In addition, lithium compounds are used in making bleaches, disinfectants, synthetic rubber, and glass. Small quantities are used in batteries.

The Bureau of Mines predicts an annual increase of 5.7 percent through 1990.

**Major Sources.** Although Chile contains 59 percent of the world's known reserves, it produces very little lithium. The United States, with 17 percent of the world's reserves, is the leading producer and also the leading consumer. Following, each with reserves about a third the size of the U.S. reserves, are the U.S.S.R., Zaire, and Canada. China is also believed to have significant deposits and has been increasing its exports.

In the United States, the principal producers of lithium products are Foote Mineral Company and Lithium Corporation of America.

**Import Reliance and Stockpile.** The United States is a net exporter of lithium. The metal is not included in the strategic stockpile, but some is maintained for the Department of Energy.

**Substitutes and Recycling.** Calcium and aluminum can be used in greases; zinc, magnesium, calcium, and mercury can be used as anode materials in batteries; sodium and potassium can be used in ceramic and glass manufacture.

No lithium is recycled.

**Trends.** Ongoing research will determine if lithium batteries can be used to power passenger vehicles. An increase in automation could also mandate more lithium-battery use in industry. Other new uses—for example, as an alloy with aluminum for high-strength, low-weight applications—are being researched. The two major U.S. producers have committed major funds for expansion, and will open plants in Chile and the United Kingdom. There are pollution and contamination problems associated with lithium production, and considerable capital expenditures are required to comply with environmental regulations.

The Bureau of Mines is researching ways to recover lithium from clays, and the U.S. Geological Survey continues to search for lithium-bearing deposits. The Department of Energy is researching the use of lithium in energy storage, and in fuel cells to generate electricity, steam, and hot water. And if fusion power becomes a reality, it will require lithium.

The use of lithium in glass-making is also expected to increase.

**Outlook.** A major drawback to lithium use is that it reacts violently with water and must be stored in strictly dry conditions, something to keep in mind if you are planning to buy any lithium for storage in a warehouse. To some degree, demand is dependent upon the aluminum industry, since lithium is used primarily (in carbonate form) in aluminum smelting.

There is great cause for optimism based on the potential use of lithium in batteries since they appear to outperform regular batteries. However, safety problems result when lithium batteries are severely bruised. Other industries that can affect lithium demand include ceramics, lubricating grease, and rubber.

Currently, there is more supply than there is demand, and it is unlikely that domestic consumers will be vulnerable to any supply squeeze since so much lithium can be produced here. However, the world market for lithium is much more vulnerable, as it is being supplied primarily by the Soviet Union and to some degree by South America, Western Europe, Japan, and recently China. The Soviet Union has been showing signs of using more of its own lithium and selling less on the open market. Therefore, a squeeze could develop later on if the Soviets were to stop exporting lithium to any great extent. In addition, if someday it were to become economically advantageous for lithium producers in the United States to use imported ores, a shortage of lithium ore for other producing nations could result.

The price of lithium chemicals increased by about 10 percent in 1981, but this was largely the result of higher energy costs. In the future, price increases will probably be tied to the U.S. inflation rate.

Because of the U.S. domination of this market, price competition has been small, and therefore merchant activity is also very small. Lithium can be purchased, however, because the Soviet Union has a tendency to use merchants to dispose of their export stocks, in their usual sporadic manner. While lithium bears watching, it should not be considered a primary metal for investment purposes at this time.

**Grades.** Pure lithium is rarely traded, partly because it reacts strongly with water and must be kept very dry. It is also a difficult metal to work with. Most of the applications are for compounds such as lithium carbonate, lithium hydroxide, lithium chloride, and lithium fluoride.

# MAGNESIUM

**Principal Uses and Demand.** The lightest of the structural metals, magnesium is an essential ingredient in aluminum production—57 percent of total consumption in 1981 was used in manufacturing aluminum-based alloys. As an alloy, it is found in a wide range of consumer goods—easy-open cans; luggage, sports equipment, tools, lawn mowers, and automobiles, where it is expected to be used increasingly as manufacturers try to cut down on weight. Magnesium is also used in aircraft engine parts, lightweight military equipment, and structural parts for missiles. As a powder, it is important in flashbulbs and explosives.

After aluminum alloys, the largest uses of magnesium are for castings and wrought products (18 percent of the 1981 total), reducing agents (8 percent), cathode protection (7 percent), the manufacture of nodular cast iron (4 percent), and others (6 percent).

The Bureau of Mines predicts an annual increase of 5 percent through 1990.

**Major Sources.** Forming about 2.5 percent of the earth's crust, and recoverable from seawater, brines, and dolomite ore, magnesium is abundant. The reserve base is virtually unlimited; indeed, natural brines are considered a renewable resource. In 1981, the United States produced 165,000 tons of magnesium, just under half the world's production. The U.S.S.R. (83,000 tons) and Norway (44,000) are the next largest producers. We import some from Norway, the Netherlands, Canada, and Italy.

**Import Reliance and Stockpile.** The United States is a net exporter. Magnesium is not stockpiled.

**Substitutes and Recycling.** In castings and wrought products, aluminum and zinc can be used in place of magnesium. In 1981, about 20 percent of the total metal consumed (20,000 tons) was from old scrap.

**Trends.** Because of the emphasis on fuel-efficiency and lighter-weight vehicles, automobile manufacturers are experimenting with magnesium, and significant increases in use are expected as long as the energy cost of producing it does not exceed the rewards. By mid-decade, at least one U.S. manufacturer is expected to use a die-cast magnesium transmission case. Many small structural parts currently using fabricated steel or cast aluminum are expected to be replaced by magnesium in the future. The Volkswagen Beetle has been a major user of magnesium for years, and Brazil—where Beetles are still made—has been one of the major importers. Projections by the auto industry for the use of magnesium by 1985 range from an average of 4 pounds per car to 30.

Producers continue to make strides in reducing the energy required to process magnesium. Amax Specialty Metals and Dow Chemical recently announced breakthroughs in this area.

The Bureau of Mines is researching superplastic magnesium alloys and technology to improve magnesium corrosion resistance.

**Outlook.** Magnesium is generally not considered a strategic metal or even a minor metal. But it should not be overlooked, because it is definitely a growth metal. In the first place, magnesium's increasing use in the automobile industry is expected to contribute to an increase in demand. Secondly, magnesium is considered a primary substitute for aluminum in many applications, and the price ratio between aluminum and magnesium has been getting closer to equal. As recently as 1980 it has ranged from 1.3 to 1 to 1.7 to 1, which is attractive enough to make many users consider choosing magnesium over aluminum in many applications. Furthermore, magnesium is used as a fuel in the production of titanium. So, as titanium demand increases, which it has as a result of the aerospace boom and the defense buildup, we can expect that more magnesium will be used.

However, magnesium is a plentiful metal, and production capacity has been expanding all over the world. Although economic recovery is some years away, virtually unlimited amounts of magnesium are available from seawater. Producers have managed to keep a pretty tight hold on the price, and once again it is the Soviet Union that provides the real stimulation to free-market merchant activity.

Because of its many industrial applications, magnesium is very sensitive to business cycles, and might even be considered to behave more like a base metal than a minor metal. As of this writing, both minor and base metals are still generally depressed as a result of the slow rate of industrial growth, and magnesium could be considered a sensible investment. However, one must monitor the situation carefully. While nobody expects anything spectacular over the next year, many experts are predicting a boom in the magnesium market by the mid to late 1980s.

**Grades.** Magnesium is traded in ingot form, the purity running between 99.8 percent and 99.9 percent. The ingots usually weigh between 5 and 20 kilograms each.

# Manganese

**Principal Uses and Demand.** About 95 percent of all manganese is consumed in the steel-making industry, where it is used both to extract oxygen and sulfur and as an alloying agent. High-quality steel can't be made without it. Lesser amounts are used in pharmaceuticals, dry-cell batteries, fertilizer, aluminum alloys, and the chemical industry. Its ultimate end uses in 1981 were: construction, 23 percent, transportation, 20 percent; machinery, 16 percent, other, 41 percent.

Demand is linked directly to steel production, which in turn rises and falls with worldwide economic activity. The Bureau of Mines predicts an annual rate of increase of 1.6 percent through 1990, but demand outside the United States could grow faster.

**Major Sources.** In 1981, there was no domestic production of ores containing 35 percent or more manganese. World reserves are overwhelmingly concentrated in the U.S.S.R. and South Africa, which together contain more than 80 percent of the total. Australia, Brazil, and Gabon also have major deposits, but their combined total amounts to less than a quarter of South Africa's.

The United States gets 40 percent of its imports from Gabon, site of the world's single most productive mine (owned in part by U.S. Steel); 19 percent comes from Brazil, 15 percent from Australia; 14 percent from South Africa; 12 percent from elsewhere. Those figures are for manganese ore. Ferromanganese imports are divided this way: South Africa, 39 percent; France, 25 percent; other, 36 percent. Ferromanganese is produced from manganese ore, and is the most commonly used form of the metal. France gets most of its ore from South Africa. So do Japan, Germany, and other European nations.

The United States contains some deposits of low-grade manganese ore, considered uneconomic at current prices. Large amounts of manganese are contained in nodules on the ocean floor.

**Import Reliance and Stockpile.** in 1980, 98 percent of the manganese used by the United States was imported; the rest was taken from stockpiles. The stockpile goal for metallurgical ore is 2.7 million tons; inventory holds 2.4, plus adequate amounts of ferromanganese and lower-grade ores.

**Substitutes and Recycling.** In its major applications, there are no satisfactory substitutes for manganese. Recycling is not significant.

**Trends.** A stagnant world economy, plus the trend to smaller, fuel-efficient automobiles, has hurt the demand for steel, and therefore manganese. The industry predicts a pickup in 1983–1984, and any increase in economic activity will require more manganese for steel production. The worldwide political situation, relations with South Africa, and Law of Sea negotiations will all affect the future for manganese.

**Outlook.** The manganese market is very large. The most common form, ferromanganese, is very bulky and is traded in large amounts. Because of this, manganese presents little profit opportunity to the trader, since the cost of storing and shipping ferromanganese and turning it over to a third party often erases the possible profit margins. From time to time, some major producers will sell to merchants at a discount, thus bringing in a minimal profit and allowing them to trade the metal around. For the most part, however, manganese and ferromanganese are sold through contracts with large consumers.

Manganese is considered a strategic metal for two reasons: most of it is produced by the Soviet Union and South Africa; and most of the steel in this country could not be made without it. However, there are other producers of manganese, such as Australia, Gabon, India, China, Brazil, and Mexico. Combined, they account for about 40 percent of the world manganese production. Thus it is unlikely that the United States supply would ever be cut off entirely. The export of manganese ore is an important source of foreign exchange for the Soviet Union and unlikely to cease very suddenly. And while seabed mining is potentially a tremendous source of manganese, it is considered to be at least a decade away. But if there was an emergency, the predicted date for the start of seabed mining could be moved up.

Barring any major supply dislocation resulting from political instability or hostility, the future of the manganese price is intimately linked to steel production, and to steel production forecasts. So far, the slack in steel demand has taken its toll on prices. The only cause for optimism is that an economy recovery will bring with it increased steel demand and therefore increased demand for manganese, which should produce a modest but significant rise in price. Unless you feel very strongly about the possibility of political disruption involving the Soviet Union and/or South Africa, we do not suggest investment in manganese at this time.

**Grades.** Pure manganese metal usually comes in an electrolytic form, sold in lumps with the purity between 98.8 percent and 99.9 percent minimum. The most commonly traded forms of manganese are ferromanganese, which contains up to 80 percent manganese, and silico manganese, which contains up to 20 percent silicon. The prices for ferromanganese and silico manganese vary with the manganese content and the amount of impurities.

# Molybdenum

**Principal Uses and Demand.** By far, the most important use of "moly" is as an alloying agent. It increases strength, hardness, durability, and corrosion resistance, and for those reasons is important in the military, where it is found in submarines, combat vehicles, and aircraft carriers. Automobiles, mining equipment, machine parts, and other applications of strong steel require molybdenum. It is considered indispensable in oil and gas pipelines, particularly in severe environments.

In all, iron and steel producers accounted for 75 percent of the molybdenum used in the United States in 1981. End-use distribution was: machinery, 34 percent; oil and gas industry, 20 percent; transportation, 17 percent; chemicals, 13 percent; electrical, 8 percent; other, 8 percent.

Despite a decrease in demand in 1981, the Bureau of Mines predicts an annual increase of 4.2 percent through 1990 and a slightly higher rate in other countries.

**Major Sources.** The United States is the largest producer of molybdenum by a long shot; its 1981 output was five times greater than either of the two closest competitors, Canada and Chile. Our reserve base is equally impressive—more than double Chile's quantity, and six times higher than the combined total of the communist nations. The biggest U.S. producer by far is the Climax Mine in Colorado, a division of AMAX. There, molybdenum is not a by-product of copper production, as it is about 30 percent of the time.

**Import Reliance and Stockpile.** The United States is a net exporter of molybdenum. The metal is not included in the strategic stockpile program.

**Substitutes and Recycling.** For the major applications of molybdenum—as an alloying element in steels, cast irons, and nonferrous metals—there is little substitution. In fact, it is most often thought of as a potential substitute for less abundant metals, and industry has been researching ways to use it in that capacity. Yet there are possible substitutes for molybdenum: chromium, vanadium, columbium, and boron in alloy steels; tungsten in tool steels; graphite, tungsten, and tantalum for refractory materials.

Some molybdenum is recovered, but the amount is small.

**Trends.** Between now and 1985, significant new additions to production are expected, mainly in the United States and Canada but also in Mexico, Peru, and elsewhere. Large deposits in Alaska, Colorado, and Washington are being evaluated for potential development. The Soviet Union, which purchased substantial amounts of molybdenum in the late 1970s, has taken steps to bolster its production and to acquire new supplies from Mongolia. This is expected to reduce Soviet dependence on Western markets.

On the demand side, major increases are expected, primarily as a result of the worldwide drive to discover and develop new energy sources. Molybdenum also has important uses in pollution control. New developments in military aircraft, railway, and automobile technology are expected to require significant amounts of molybdenum.

**Outlook.** Like manganese, molybdenum is consumed mainly by the steel industry. But since molybdenum steels have very special applications, prices and demand are not greatly affected by fluctuations in the steel industry as a whole. In fact, molybdenum is one of the few major industrial metals with increasing applications in highly technical industries.

Molybdenum steel provides high strength and resistance to the corrosive attack of oil and gas on drilling and piping equipment. It is necessary, in the case of many wells, to employ stainless steel or nickel-base materials alloyed with molybdenum to resist the highly corrosive environment. Molybdenum high-strength/low-alloy steel (often referred to as HSLA) provides the highest quality pipe for the high-pressure gas lines in Arctic conditions. This steel has superior weldability and excellent toughness, making it an outstanding choice for severe environmental conditions, including deep underwater applications. It is expected that in the future the construction of synfuel plants will require large amounts of molybdenum, and that coal liquefaction technology will use molybdenum catalysts, also stimulating demand. The metal is used in the manufacture of a special kind of stainless steel used in solar collectors, and if this particular application were to grow it could have a significant effect on overall demand. Molybdenum also plays a role in pollution control devices, especially in the construction of scrubbers. Front-wheel-drive cars require higher molybdenum carbonizing steels, and molybdenum is also used in high-temperature applications in turbochargers and diesel engines.

The long-term outlook for molybdenum appears to be quite favorable. However, molybdenum production has been increasing and there is currently a surplus in the wake of new capacity and very slack demand. Molybdenum provides investment opportunity because in recent years we have seen both severe short-term shortages and surpluses. The supply/demand situation is quite active.

As with other domestically produced metals, producers favor long-term supply contracts with major consumers. The free market, however, does offer opportunities, especially in times of shortage or surplus, when trading increases. However, as supply and demand approach equilibrium, free-market trading can become quite soft and provide little or no opportunity.

Fortunately, because the metal is produced in the United States, you can invest in molybdenum by buying shares in one or several producing companies.

**Grades.** Most of the metal is traded in oxide form or as ferromolybdenum, an alloy of molybdenum and iron, when it is between 60 percent and 80 percent molybdenum. There is a very small market for metallic molybdenum, which is usually sold in the form of ingots, sheet, and wire of high purity.

## PLATINUM GROUP METALS
Platinum, Palladium, Iridium, Osmium, Rhodium, Ruthenium

**Primary Uses and Demand.** Chemically inert refractory metals with excellent catalytic qualities, the platinum group metals are used in a variety of industries, with this distribution in 1981: automotive, 30 percent; electrical, 26 percent; chemical, 14 percent; dental, 12 percent; other, 18 percent. As catalysts they are important in the chemical, petroleum refining, and automotive industries. They are used to upgrade the octane values of gasoline, to substitute for poisonous lead, and, in catalytic converters, to curb air pollution. Because of their corrosion resistance, they are important in chemistry, electronics, glassmaking, medicine, and dentistry. Platinum is also used in fuel cells that convert hydrogen-rich fuels to electricity.

Rhodium, the most expensive of the group, has a very high resistance to corrosion. Used to coat steel and brass for protection against sea water, rhodium is also being used increasingly in the jewelry industry, and in automobile emission systems, when alloyed with platinum. Because it reflects so well and does not tarnish, rhodium is also used in optical equipment.

In Japan, platinum has always been more highly valued than gold for jewelry.

The Bureau of Mines predicts an annual increase of 1.5 percent through 1990.

**Major Sources.** The six metals occur together in nature, platinum and palladium being the most common. Whatever domestic production there is comes as a by-product of copper mining. Essentially, however, all U.S. requirements other than that which is recycled from scrap are imported: 55 percent from South Africa, 18 percent from the Soviet Union, 11 percent from the United Kingdom (which processes concentrates from South Africa and Canada) and 16 percent from elsewhere. Throughout the seventies, the U.S.S.R. accounted for about half the world's production, and South Africa for 40 percent. The gap between the two has evened out in the last few years, however, as the Soviet Union cut back shipments to the West and South Africa expanded production. There are differences between the two main sources: platinum group mining in the Soviet Union is nearly all a by-product of copper-nickel sulfide ores, while South African mining is done with ores almost exclusively of the platinum group; Soviet production yields three times more palladium than platinum (palladium is less expensive), while South African production is predominantly platinum.

In 1981, the two nations accounted for more than 95 percent of the world's production. In terms of reserves, South Africa is unsurpassed, with nearly five times greater reserves than the Soviet Union, and one hundred times more than the next largest competitor, Canada. World reserves are about twenty times greater than the predicted demand through this century; the problem, of course, is unequal distribution. The United States is thought to have reserves of about one-ninth that of Canada. But a potentially huge deposit—the largest in this hemisphere—is being evaluated at the Stillwater Complex in Montana. The land is under national forest, which could, along with economic factors, slow down development.

**Import Reliance and Stockpile.** In 1981, the United States imported 85 percent of its consumption, but just about every-thing not imported was recycled scrap. The strategic stockpile contains three members of the group. The platinum goal is 1.3 million ounces, and the inventory is 453,000; the palladium goal is 3 million ounces, with inventory at 1.2; the iridium goal is 98,000 ounces, and the inventory is 17,000.

**Substitutes and Recycling.** In electrical/electronic uses (the prime application of palladium), gold, silver, and tungsten can be substituted. In catalytic uses, nickel, vanadium, titanium, and the rare-earth metals can be used.

In 1981, about 350,000 ounces of platinum group metals were refined from scrap, an amount equivalent to 18 percent of sales to industry.

**Trends.** New or improved engines and fuels could reduce the use of the platinum group in emission control catalysts in automobiles. Consumption in that area has already declined due to the sagging auto industry and recycling of old catalytic converters. The future, according to industry sources, depends largely on the U.S. automobile industry and the Japanese jewelry industry. Synfuels is a potential growth area, as is the electronics industry.

Each member of the platinum group should be considered separately when assessing the investment outlook and the grade.

## Platinum

**Outlook.** Platinum itself is traded on an exchange, and therefore is much easier to invest in, and better regulated than other platinum group metals. Although often grouped with gold as a precious metal, it has many strategic uses. Indeed, 80 percent of it is used in industry, compared with 17 percent of gold. As a catalyst, platinum is very important in achieving chemical reactions in the petroleum industry as well as in the pharmaceutical and chemical industries. The fastest growing uses of platinum appear to be in electronics and computers.

Many people consider the high price of platinum to be a lot more solidly grounded than gold since it is more useful, has greater applications in industry, and is much harder to find. Many experts feel that even if gold prices were to continue soft as a result of continued deflationary trends, the price of platinum could rise, due to the strong demand and limited supply that could result from an upturn.

But platinum is still used as a precious metal, not only in the minting of coins, a practice favored by the Russians, but also in the manufacture of jewelry. In fact, Japanese consumption of platinum for jewelry has become an increasingly significant factor in the market.

When investing in platinum keep in mind that it has not separated itself completely from the price movements of gold, and for that reason it must be considered to act as a precious metal in terms of price. Therefore, inflation is a price factor, as it is with gold. Many experts feel that in the long run, platinum will divorce itself from gold as gold fluctuates with other economic factors. Even if gold prices drop, platinum could continue to go up as its demand as a strategic metal steadily increases.

Over time, the demand in the oil and petroleum industry will have a significant impact on the price of platinum. Also, if there is a significant reduction in the use of platinum in catalytic converters or if some new energy technology requires less use of platinum catalysts, the price of platinum could soften.

In general, platinum is a reasonably sound investment based on its long-term use picture, the feasibility of investment through exchange trading, and the existence of several almost "pure plays" in mining shares (that is, investments in companies that mine primarily platinum), especially in South Africa. If one desires to invest in the platinum group for the shorter term, it might be wise to consider some of the lesser-known members, which are less intimately linked with gold and are known as industrial metals.

Platinum futures are traded on the New York Mercantile Exchange, where the minimum purity for delivery is 99.5 percent.

**Grades.** Generally, the minimum purity of platinum on the free market is 99.9 percent, and in fact most producers will sell material that is at least 99.95 percent. The absolute minimum standard is on the order of 99.89 percent, which is considered to be low-grade material. Most of the platinum is sold in ingots weighing about five kilos in plates of about 50 troy ounces. There are other forms such as sponge, sheet, wire, and powder.

## Palladium

**Outlook.** This metal is similar in use and supply factors to platinum, but is considered almost completely free of the monetary forces affecting precious metals; the market is controlled almost entirely by industrial supply and demand. Palladium is mined as a by-product of platinum, which in turn may be mined as a by-product of several other metals such as nickel and gold. Thus, the suppliers of palladium are the same as the suppliers of platinum; primarily South Africa and the Soviet Union.

Much of the palladium is used in the form of an alloy with platinum and other metals to make jewelry, catalytic converters, and other antipollution devices. Palladium is also used to manufacture electrical contacts in the electronics industry, especially in telephones, and to make thermocouples. It has widespread uses in the chemical industry as well.

The outlook for palladium very closely parallels the outlook for platinum. It is expected that its use in automobile emission controls will be phased out in the years ahead, and that its use in jewelry will decline as well. However, palladium demand in the telephone industry is expected to remain strong, and the trend is toward increasing use in the dental and medical industries, as it continues to replace gold in prosthetic dentistry.

Palladium is traded in the futures market at the New York Mercantile Exchange, where the minimum trading unit is 100 troy ounces, and the minimum purity is 99.8 percent. The market there, however, is not considered very liquid.

**Grades.** The minimum purity on the merchant market is usually 99.9 percent. Once again, the producers usually supply 99.95 percent or an even higher 99.99 percent purity. Commonly, palladium is traded in ingot or sponge form and is sometimes made available as powder, rod, wire, even tubing. Ingots may weigh from 2.8 to 7.5 kilos.

## Rhodium

**Outlook.** Another member of the platinum group, rhodium is also a by-product of platinum production. But it is different from platinum in several ways. It has an extremely high resistance to erosion from seawater and other highly corrosive elements. It has very high reflectivity, which is particularly important since rhodium is also completely untarnishable. Thus, its use in the optical equipment industry is becoming more widespread—when used as a coating on optical surfaces, it provides high reflectivity with no loss of reflected value due to oxidation or corrosion. The Japanese like to use rhodium as an alloy in jewelry, and are sometimes very big buyers on the free market. Rhodium is also used as a catalyst, and is now being considered for the manufacture of a three-way catalytic converter.

Some experts feel that the future demand might exceed the amount of rhodium recovered from platinum. In other words, unless platinum production were to increase from its current levels, we could eventually fall behind in our ability to recover enough rhodium to meet demand. It is also possible, however, that the percentage of rhodium recovered from the ore could be increased. The amount of rhodium recovered from platinum ore may vary from year to year.

Rhodium is the most expensive of all the platinum group metals, including platinum itself, because of its rarity and the strong industrial demand for it. While the demand pattern for rhodium looks quite good, it is unfortunately a very difficult metal to invest in for several reasons: it is traded by a small group of specialists; the Soviet Union's supply policy is erratic; and the players and variables involved in trading are complex. Because rhodium is not traded on any major metals exchange, it cannot be bought as a futures contract. And it can be quite expensive to invest in. We do not recommend investing in rhodium on your own. However, it could turn out to be quite promising in the hands of someone who understands how to trade the metal.

**Grades.** Rhodium is traded like most other platinum group metals, in units of troy ounces with a minimum purity of 99.9 percent, but usually higher, 99.95 percent, and in the form of bars, ingots, sponge, or powder.

## Iridium

**Outlook.** Most traders don't like iridium as much as platinum, palladium, or rhodium. Iridium is a difficult metal to work with because it is hard and brittle. Therefore, it is usually used in the form of an alloy with platinum, making up only a small portion of the alloy. This platinum-iridium alloy is used in jewelry (because it is cheaper than platinum and rhodium), for setting diamonds, and also in the manufacture of electric contacts. Iridium is used with ruthenium and with osmium as an alloy for fountain pen nibs.

Iridium is extremely expensive and is traded by only a few precious-metal specialists. Once again, the suppliers are the Soviet Union, South Africa, and Canada. The market is very thin and the price is not greatly affected by price movements in the other platinum group metals. However, there are some new uses for iridium, such as in special electrical contacts, aircraft engines, and certain chemical applications, which could produce a surge in demand.

This market must be watched very carefully. We do not recommend investing in iridium at this time. However, it could take its place alongside the other platinum group metals with strategic importance, and its pricing could move closer in line with the other near-precious platinum group members.

**Grades.** Iridium is sold in ingots with a minimum purity of 99.9 percent. But unlike other platinum group members, it is usually sold in the form of powder.

## Osmium

**Outlook.** Osmium is not in widespread use at the present time. In fact, in 1974 it was estimated that 64,000 ounces of osmium were mined, but only a few thousand ounces were actually refined. The reason: lack of demand. In processing, osmium is often considered a waste product and is therefore discarded.

But there are some highly sophisticated applications for osmium. This may point toward increased use in the future, resulting in tight supplies. One reason for the possible tight supply picture is that osmium constitutes only a small portion of the platinum group metals found in the common ore.

Osmium is rarely traded, and most is obtained from South Africa. It is not recommended as a good trading or investment metal.

**Grades.** Osmium is available in sponge form, purity ranging from 99.5 percent minimum to 99.9 minimum. It is priced and traded in troy ounces.

## Ruthenium

**Outlook.** Ruthenium is curious in that it happens to be one of the rarest metals and yet also the cheapest of all platinum group metals. The reason is that so far there are very few uses for ruthenium that cannot be better served by other metals. Like osmium, it is rarely traded and rarely used. A 300-ounce order of ruthenium would be considered a healthy one, although a mere pittance in most other metal markets.

Ruthenium's principal use is as an alloy with platinum in jewelry. But like the other platinum group metals, it is expected to play a greater role in the electronic and chemical industries in the future. The use of ruthenium as a catalyst is also expected to increase, especially since it offers price advantages and, at least for the time being, supply advantages over some of the other platinum group metals.

Although ruthenium bears watching, at this time it should not be considered a good metal for investment.

In summary then, investors seeking to participate in the platinum group should restrict their activity to platinum and palladium, which are traded on the futures exchange, and to the free market in rhodium, which is one of the more popular and widely used of the platinum group metals.

# RARE-EARTH METALS
Lanthanum, Cerium, Praseodymium, Neodymium, Promethium, Samarium, Europium, Gadolinium, Terbium, Dysprosium, Holmium, Erbium, Thulium, Ytterbium, Lutetium

**Principal Uses and Demand.** In 1981, the industrial consumption of this group of fifteen metals was estimated by the Bureau of Mines as follows: petroleum catalysts, 40 percent; metallurgy, 37 percent; ceramic and glass, 20 percent; other (electrical, arc carbons, nuclear, superalloys, magnetic, and research), 3 percent. Small quantities of expensive, high-purity europium, terbium, and gadolinium compounds were used in electronics, in color TV tubes, and in X-ray screens.

The Bureau of Mines expects demand to increase at about 6 percent a year through 1990.

**Major Sources.** The United States was the world's principal producer and consumer of rare earths in 1980, and was a major exporter of rare-earth concentrate, compounds, and metals. As a group, the rare earths are in abundant supply domestically and around the world. A large amount of gastnaesite, a rare-earth-bearing mineral, is mined in California. The United States imports monazite from Australia (79 percent), Malaysia (17 percent), and Thailand (4 percent). Monazite, a principal source mineral, is a by-product in titanium and zircon mining.

**Import Reliance and Stockpile.** The Bureau of Mines does not publish import reliance figures. The stockpile currently contains 488 short tons of rare-earth oxide, all of which is authorized for disposal.

**Substitutes and Recyling.** In major use categories, there are no satisfactory substitutes. For other applications, alternatives are available, but are generally less effective.

Only samarium and europium are recycled, and those in small amounts.

**Outlook.** Eight of the rare earths are considered commercially valuable. Important uses are: in the production of catalysts for petroleum refining and other chemical processes; for camera and instrument lenses, and other optical equipment; and in metallurgy, such as the manufacture of crucibles for the melting of titanium and other reactive metals, and in the production of certain steel alloys. In spite of the recession, demand for most rare earths has remained stable or increased slightly.

When we speak of rare earths, since we are discussing fifteen metals, it is hard to generalize about their relative abundance. Some are quite plentiful while others are considered rare. The three most common ones, neodymium, cerium, and lanthanum, are collectively more abundant than nickel or copper.

Increasingly, users and producers are referring to rare earths by a more scientific name, *lanthanides*.

The future for rare earths appears bright, as the major applications in electronics and other advanced technologies—such as lasers, bubble memories, optics, microwaves, and phosphors—are expected to increase. Also, their use in steel alloys and in chemical processes is expected to continue to be strong, with steady growth in glass polishing, decolorizing, and ceramics. Of the top hundred important new technological developments of 1981 noted by *Industrial Research and Development* magazine, four involved the use of rare earths.

One of the major problems in investing in rare earths is that there are so many of them. While they tend to be lumped together, one rare-earth element may become highly desirable while another may fall out of favor.

Investing in the rare earths really involves following minerals that contain a mixture of rare-earth oxides (REO). The principal rare-earth minerals are monazite, a rare-earth phosphate containing about 55 to 70 percent REO, and bastnaesite, a fluorocarbonate mineral containing about 75 percent REO. Because of their extremely specialized uses, rare earths are usually sold by producers and processors directly to the consumer. Thus, there is very little merchant activity in rare earths.

Investing in rare earths may be promising, but it should be undertaken only if you can become a student of this group, or at least retain somebody who is.

The most recent edition of *Metal Statistics* lists only one dealer offering monazite, and no dealers for any other rare earths. *Metals Week* does not publish rare-earth prices in their weekly quotations. The Bureau of Mines keeps track of monazite and bastnaesite prices.

# Rhenium

**Principal Uses and Demand.** By far the main use of rhenium, accounting for 92 percent of its 1981 consumption, is in catalysts for producing low-lead and lead-free high octane gasoline. The other 8 percent was used in thermocouples, heating elements, X-ray tubes and targets, flashbulbs, vacuum tubes, electrical contacts, and metallic coatings.

The Bureau of Mines predicts stable demand through 1990 because of lowered use in petroleum refining; other sources predict an increase in rhenium use because it will replace platinum to a large degree as a catalyst.

**Major Sources.** The metal is recovered as a by-product of molybdenite concentrate found in porphyry copper deposits and is produced here; the U.S. reserve base is estimated at 2.6 million pounds, about the same as that of Chile, and accounting for more than a third of the world's known reserves. Of the amount imported, about half comes from West Germany and the other half from Chile. In 1977, the last year for which figures are available, the United States imported all its rhenium; the year before that, only 47 percent.

**Import Reliance and Stockpile.** Import figures for rhenium are not published by the Bureau of Mines. The United States does not stock rhenium.

**Substitutes and Recyling.** Alternative catalysts are being evaluated continually. In one application, iridium has achieved commercial success as a catalyst. Other metals being looked at include gallium, germanium, indium, selenium, silicon, tin, tungsten, and vanadium. Cobalt and tungsten can replace rhenium in X-ray targets; rhodium and rhodium-iridium can be used for thermocouples; tungsten and platinum-ruthenium on electrical contacts; tungsten and tantalum for electron emitters.

Recovery of rhenium from scrap is small.

**Trends.** Since rhenium is used almost entirely as a catalyst, technology can alter the market at any time. Another factor that could be significant is the environmental cost in the copper and molybdenum industries.

**Outlook.** A by-product of molybdenum and copper production, rhenium has physical and chemical properties, as well as applications, that are similar to those of the platinum group metals. A lot more rhenium is mined than is actually extracted each year, either because many producers of molybdenum don't have the facilities to extract it or because the low prices of rhenium have tended to make extraction unprofitable. But recently the price of rhenium has surged. During 1979 it tripled, primarily because rhenium can be used as a substitute catalyst for lead in petroleum production and for platinum.

It is difficult to determine the outlook for rhenium at this time. On the plus side, demand continues to be high, and unlike platinum it is primarily produced in the United States—we are not dependent upon the Soviets or South Africans for a steady supply. On the minus side, molybdenum is very plentiful, and there would be many additional rhenium sources if producers were willing to acquire the equipment necessary to extract it from the ore. Since rhenium is used primarily as a catalyst, it can be recovered and reused (the very definition of catalyst suggests that the material itself does not take part in the chemical reaction but only facilitates it).

Still, many experts feel that the applications of rhenium are only beginning to be tapped, and that there is significant cause for optimism with respect to its price. It is unlikely, however, that the price of rhenium will ever again equal the gains it made from 1979 to 1980. Indeed, it was in 1979 that merchant activity in rhenium began, and since then the market has been quite active. Metal specialists dealing in rhenium have obtained most of their supplies from the Soviet Union and some of the smaller molybdenum refineries, which have only small amounts of rhenium to buy and sell.

**Grades.** The most common grades for rhenium trading are a metallic powder with a purity of 99.9 percent and an ammonia-rhenium compound containing about 70 percent rhenium.

# Selenium

**Principal Uses and Demand.** The major users of selenium now, and probably in the future, are the photocopying and electronics industries. In 1981 they accounted for 35 percent of all consumption. Close behind is glass manufacturing, where selenium is used as a decolorizer for beverage and food containers. Glass manufacturing used 30 percent of the selenium in 1981. Another 25 percent was used in chemicals and pigments. The rest was divided among a number of other users, such as the pharmaceutical, rubber, steel, and explosives industries. The best market continues to be the photocopying industry, where selenium and its alloys are used as coatings on photocopier drums.

The Bureau of Mines predicts an annual increase of 2.8 percent through 1990.

**Major Sources.** As a by-product of copper ores, selenium production is pegged to copper demand. The percentage of selenium per unit of copper, however, is quite low. Further, with current methods, much of the selenium content is lost during smelting and refining.

U.S. selenium production decreased by 15 percent in 1980, largely due to a copper strike. Production was about half that of Canada and Japan, the leading suppliers, although America's raw material reserve base is a close second to that of Chile. Zambia, Peru, and Canada also contain significant reserves. Of the selenium imported by the United States in 1981, 40 percent came from Canada, 19 percent from Japan, 10 percent from Yugoslavia, and the remaining 31 percent from a variety of other sources.

Photocopier selenium scrap is a major source, competing with "virgin" selenium.

**Import Reliance and Stockpile.** In 1981, the United States imported 49 percent of its selenium needs. The material is not held in the strategic stockpile.

**Substitutes and Recycling.** In rectifier and semiconductor applications, selenium can be replaced by silicon, germanium, and cadmium. Tellurium is a good substitute in electronics, pigments, and rubber compounding. Cerium oxide can be used in glass manufacturing.

About 210,000 pounds of selenium were recycled in 1981—one-fourth of total consumption. Obtained from used electronic and photocopier components, the recycled selenium was processed mainly in Canada.

**Trends.** As worldwide interest in information processing grows, so should the demand for selenium. In addition, new applications are cropping up in photovoltaics, catalysts, biochemistry, and nutrition. The animal feed industry considers selenium an essential nutrient, and its value in disease prevention in humans is being researched. The use of selenium-based solar cells could boom if the metal's ability to reduce glare and transfer heat is applied. Another area where demand could increase is in maintenance-free batteries, where selenium is used as an alloying agent. Currently, the photocopier market continues as the major source of growth in demand.

On the supply side, the Bureau of Mines reports that in addition to the large reserves contained in identified copper deposits, three times more is believed to exist in undeveloped, undiscovered, or uneconomic deposits. Selenium might one day be recovered from coal as well.

**Outlook.** Selenium is a very interesting metal from an investment point of view even though most experts do not consider it a strategic metal. Since almost all the selenium produced is as a by-product of copper production, there are reserves on each continent. The principal world refiners are in Belgium, Canada, Chile, Finland, Japan, Mexico, Peru, Sweden, the United Kingdom, the United States, the Soviet Union, Yugoslavia, and Zambia. Therefore, we could not consider selenium to be strategic from the point of view of possible supply cutoffs resulting from a single political event. Its uses are very important to industry, but in most cases not critical for defense. However, its uses are growing very rapidly.

The wide range of applications for selenium makes many experts believe that demand for it will continue to grow steadily in the next decade. At the current time supply appears to exceed demand, but that can easily change, especially in light of reduced copper production that will, in turn, curtail selenium supplies. Indeed, the Bureau of Mines estimates that although the current supply of selenium is sufficient to meet domestic needs, the forecasted supply will not be sufficient to meet the forecasted demand. This would obviously lead to a shortage, and while the Bureau predicts that such a shortage will cause a decrease in demand as users turn to substitutes such as cadmium, zinc, and germanium, there is no doubt that any kind of shortage in the selenium industry would first produce a period of high prices. Consumers would need some time in order to reduce their dependence on selenium, and during that time speculator profits could be taken.

If demand for selenium was to remain strong, and the demand for copper was to remain depressed as a result of the generally slow industrial growth, we could see a supply/demand dislocation somewhat similar to that which occurred in the zinc/germanium relationship. The free market in selenium is very volatile, for some basic reasons: small production, inelastic demand, and the fact that it is a by-product (which means there is very little control over the available supply). These factors also contribute to the possibility that the market can be manipulated from time to time. Consumers need selenium, and rarely shy away from it because of price appreciation. On the other hand, there are many producers of selenium scattered around the world, and no single producer is strong enough to dominate or completely control the price. In the past decade, there has been very little interest by nontrade buyers in the selenium market.

We are of the opinion that selenium could prove a very interesting investment vehicle in the future. While North American producers continue to sell by contract and to adhere to a producer price, more and more producers, particularly the Japanese, have turned to the free market.

**Grades.** Selenium is usually traded in granule or powder form, and the purity is either 99.8 or 99.5 percent minimum.

# SILICON

**Principal Uses and Demand.** Most of the silicon used in the United States is in the form of ferrosilicon, which is used as an alloying agent in the iron and steel industries. Silicon metal is used mainly in the aluminum industry. Other uses for the metal are in the electronics industry, particularly in computers, calculators, and communications equipment. The end-use distribution of silicon in 1981 was: transportation, 33 percent; machinery, 20 percent; construction, 14 percent; chemicals, 12 percent; other, 21 percent. Demand is pegged to activity in the steel, iron, and aluminum industries, and those directly reflect worldwide economic conditions.

The Bureau of Mines predicts an annual increase of about 3 percent through 1990.

**Major Sources.** Resources in most producing countries are more than adequate to meet world requirements for a long time, since the principal raw materials are sands and pebbles. Silicon is the second most abundant element in the earth's crust (behind oxygen). Supply problems, therefore, are not related to raw materials, but to the cost of production. Making ferrosilicon or silicon metal from cheap raw materials requires a great deal of costly electrical energy, pollution control (responsible for 20 percent of capital costs and 10 percent of operating costs), and transportation, as the raw materials are not always found near market areas.

The United States and the Soviet Union are the two principal producers, and Norway is the chief exporter to the world. Of the silicon the United States imported in 1981, 28 percent came from Canada, 27 percent from Norway, and the rest from other countries such as Yugoslavia and South Africa.

**Import Reliance and Stockpile.** In 1981, the United States imported 20 percent of its consumption, up from 8 percent in 1980, although we also exported 23,000 tons of silicon metal. Silicon is stockpiled in the form of silicon carbide, an abrasive compound, and the inventory is more than double the requirement.

**Substitutes and Recycling.** In some of its applications, ferrosilicon can be replaced by a number of metals and alloys—aluminum for one—but at higher cost. In semiconductor and infrared applications, germanium is the principal substitute. Silicon is more often thought of as a substitute for other, less abundant metals. Small quantities of silicon carbide are recycled.

**Trends.** Because of its abundance, silicon is being considered as a replacement for cobalt, nickel, and chromium in alloys. Ceramics containing silicon have substitution potential and are being researched. The use of silicon in photovoltaic cells is also being researched, and considerable progress has been made in reducing the cost of manufacture. Pollution control, energy costs, and the growth of the computer industry should all influence the market.

**Outlook.** Silicon is traded mostly by contract between producers and consumers. But there is a large and active free market, and most of the silicon that is traded by merchants comes from outside the United States, primarily from Europe. The production of silicon is energy-intensive; the cost of the electrical energy needed to drive the arc furnace used to refine silicon from ore is much greater than the actual cost of the ore itself. So to some extent the future price of silicon will depend upon energy prices. However, one should note that in the past the price of refined silicon has not increased nearly as much as the price of energy. This is due in part to the great competition that exists between producers. Rapidly increasing energy prices and slowly increasing silicon prices obviously do not present a very pleasant picture for the producers in terms of profits. Therefore, there is little incentive for them to expand in capacity.

From the demand side, however, the use of silicon in the aluminum industry and in the chemical industry in the manufacturing of silicones has increased very rapidly. The possibility that silicon photovoltaic cells may eventually become economically competitive is another factor that may cause a tremendous increase in demand in the near future. The demand for silicon will to a large degree be dependent on the success of current research on new applications.

In spite of its abundance, the lack of adequate production capabilities and high energy prices could translate into a shortage in the future, possibly in the next few years. Like selenium, silicon is not considered a strategic metal. However, since there is an active free market in the metal and demand appears to be growing, it could turn out to be a very interesting investment vehicle in the next decade.

**Grades.** Silicon is usually sold in lump form with a minimum purity of about 98.5 percent. Much of the accepted silicon in lump form does have some calcium and iron content, usually less than 0.5 percent. However, sometimes higher silicon purities are required, especially in the chemical industry. Most silicon is consumed in the form of ferrosilicon, and the most widely used grade contains about 75 percent silicon.

# Tantalum

**Principal Uses and Demand.** Largely replaced in the steel industry by lighter, more abundant columbium, tantalum is now used primarily in electronic components. The electronics industry consumes 73 percent of the tantalum produced. Another 19 percent is used in machinery and tools, while small amounts are used in transportation, the chemical industry, and surgical applications.

The Bureau of Mines predicts an annual increase of about 4 percent through 1990.

**Major Sources.** The world's largest consumer of tantalum, the United States mines no raw materials for producing the metal. Most of the world's reserves are in Thailand, Australia, Nigeria, Zaire, and Canada. However, the largest known producers are Brazil and Canada, followed by Australia and Thailand. In the past few years there has been a steady increase of tantalum produced from tin slags, chiefly from Thailand and Malaysia. Of the tantalum imported by the United States in 1981, 36 percent originated in Thailand, 11 percent in Canada, 11 percent in Malaysia, and 5 percent in Brazil. Official estimates of Soviet production and reserves are not available, but some sources claim that production was five times that of Canada.

**Import Reliance and Stockpile.** In 1981, the United States was 91 percent import-dependent. The stockpile goal is 8.4 million pounds; inventory contains 1.4 million pounds of stockpile-grade minerals, and 1.1 million in lower grades.

**Substitutes and Recycling.** Possible substitutes include columbium in high-strength steel, superalloys, and carbides; aluminum and ceramics in electronic capacitors; silicon, germanium and selenium in electrical rectifiers; tungsten, rhenium, columbium, molybdenum, iridium, and hafnium in high-temperature applications. In most substitutions, performance is compromised or cost is increased. However, demand has been hurt by the substitution of aluminum capacitors used in automobiles and electronic entertainment equipment.

Recycling of scrap accounted for about 5 percent of the total raw materials consumed in 1981.

**Trends.** Mine expansions are underway in Canada and Australia. Some countries, notably Thailand and Australia, are tending toward upgrading their raw materials before exporting.

The aircraft industry is a small but growing user of tantalum in high-performance alloys in jet engines. Larger, more expensive capacitors used in defense, telecommunications, and computers should not lose ground to substitution, the industry feels.

**Outlook.** The outlook for tantalum is somewhat complicated because of many factors related to the current supply/demand situation. Tantalum has become increasingly popular in applications in the electronic industry, particularly for its use in capacitors. Its popularity in this area coincided with increased demand at a time when supplies were not really adequate to meet that demand, and the result was a marked increase in price. Between 1979 and 1980, the price tripled. Since then, it has dropped significantly, partially as a result of the classical reactions to a tight supply–high demand situation: an increase in supply due to increased output and production capacity, and to additional discoveries of tantalum source materials, primarily in Australia and Canada; a slackening in demand as users, dismayed over the tremendous escalation in price, began to look for less expensive substitutes. Add to that the deep recession.

However, many experts feel that this will lead to at least a short-term price rebound in the near future, as lower tantalum prices discourage the continued expansion of production and supply. With demand slack, the high-grade tantalum is moving out while the lower grades are expected to remain in stockpiles until the price goes up again. One should keep in mind that along with germanium, silicon, and several others, tantalum is very important to the electronics industry. And electronics has repeatedly shown itself to be less affected by recession or slow economic periods than the heavy industries. Therefore, demand is expected to remain strong, regardless of the state of the world economy in years to come. Whether that steady demand will lead to higher prices or only to greater production remains to be seen. Thus, it is very difficult to predict whether the supply/demand situation will dislocate sufficiently to cause another tremendous price run-up. Note that even though the electronics industry is less affected by recession, it is not immune to it. Indeed, many of the metals used in the electronics industry have come down in price during the recent period of slow growth.

Tantalum and other metals that have appreciated greatly in the wake of important applications are vulnerable to substitution. As the years go by, tantalum's role in the electronics industry may lessen. It is expected that any new applications will be in highly specialized areas, and at this time it does not appear that they will have much impact on overall tantalum demand.

The Bureau of Mines does not expect the United States to produce its own tantalum much before the year 2000. However, our principal suppliers—Brazil, Canada, Thailand, and Australia—are all considered allies, or are at least in our sphere of influence. With the possible exception of Thailand, our suppliers are reasonably stable. The producers maintain a fairly strong grip on the price, and much of their business is done by contract. Usually tantalum ore is traded on the free market, but there is some activity in scrap or recycled tantalum metal.

**Grades.** Tantalum is most commonly traded in its ore form, tantalite, which comes in two basic grades, one about 60 percent tantalum pentoxide, the other a lower grade containing approximately 30 percent tantalum pentoxide. The metal is traded in minimum purity of 99.9 percent, and the forms available are powder, sheet, and bar.

# TELLURIUM

**Principal Uses and Demand.** Tellurium is used mainly as an additive to steel and copper, and as a chilling agent for malleable cast iron. Iron and steel products accounted for 65 percent of its end uses in 1981; nonferrous metals used 20 percent; chemicals, 10 percent; and other applications, 5 percent. Tellurium is used as a curing agent and accelerator in rubber compounding; in the production of semiconductors in devices such as thermoelectric junctions, infrared detectors, and photoelectric cells; and in chemical catalysts, and the production of synthetic fibers and petrochemical products.

Demand for tellurium has decreased in the iron, steel, and automobile industries.

The Bureau of Mines predicts an annual increase of one percent through 1990.

**Major Sources.** Tellurium is recovered as a by-product of the electrolytic refining of copper, and to a lesser degree from zinc, lead, and gold telluride ores. Production is closely linked to copper output. Statistics on U.S. production are not published, but the U.S. reserve base is the largest in the world, containing almost 20 percent of the total. Peru and Canada, both large producers, contain substantial reserves. Not counting the United States, Japan is the world's leading producer, although some estimate that production in the Soviet Bloc might be as great.

Between 1977 and 1980, the United States imported tellurium from Canada (43 percent), Peru (11 percent), Fiji (17 percent), Hong Kong (9 percent), and other nations (20 percent).

**Import Reliance and Stockpile.** Import figures are not published; there is no tellurium stockpile.

**Substitutes and Recycling.** The chief substitute materials are selenium, bismuth, and lead in metallurgical applications; selenium and sulfur in rubber compounding; selenium and germanium in electronics. There is no significant recycling.

**Trends.** The Bureau of Mines reports that catalytic applications of tellurium show promise of increasing. The Department of Energy has been supporting research on the use of cadmium telluride for use in making photovoltaic solar cells.

As with other copper by-products, potential resources far outnumber the known reserve base.

**Outlook.** Tellurium is somewhat of a neglected child in the metals industry. It has been kicked around by the fortunes of other metals such as copper and, curiously, gold and silver. While all tellurium is recovered as a by-product of copper, according to the Bureau of Mines recovery is economical only because the process of extraction is done in order to recover gold and silver. Thus, if the copper ore does not contain sufficient quantities of gold and/or silver to make extraction worthwhile, the mining industry does not feel justified in refining the ore just to remove the tellurium. With such an unpredictable supply situation, and the fact that there is virtually no use for tellurium that cannot be handled by a substitute, it is not surprising that the market is very small at the current time and that industry uses tellurium only if and when the price is right.

During 1980 and 1981 there was a permanent shutdown of a chemical process that uses tellurium as a catalyst, a serious blow to tellurium consumption. The general economic slowdown also hurt tellurium in two ways: by restricting the supply as a result of reduced copper production and by decreasing industrial demand. In fact, the recession has hurt tellurium demand so much that inventories have been growing in spite of declining production.

However, tellurium bears watching as a possible investment. New uses of the metal are being researched, including applications in photoelectric chemical solar cells and other thin-film forms of solar cells. New technologies promise an increase in tellurium production, not only in recovery from copper but also from gold ores, coal, and manganese nodules. Even though use of tellurium as a catalyst has declined recently, many experts are very optimistic that new uses for tellurium catalysts will be found in the next few years. Tellurium may in fact be where tantalum and germanium were just a few years ago, before anybody thought that they would be of any great significance. But for now, there is a very small free market in tellurium and most of the marketing is handled directly by producers or their representatives. The only significant free-market sources have been the state-controlled copper-producing economies of Eastern Europe, and merchants who have been acting as intermediaries for those countries. The United States will probably be producing less tellurium in the future because more and more copper ore is being shipped out of the country for refinement and extraction elsewhere, and with it will go the tellurium contained in that ore.

**Grades.** Tellurium is sold as ingots, slabs, or powder. The purity ranges between 99.7 and 99.9 percent minimum.

# TITANIUM

**Principal Uses and Demands.** Lighter than steel but just as strong, titanium is strategic because of its defense applications and its ability to resist corrosion. In 1981, about 60 percent of titanium consumption was in jet engines, airframes, and space and missile applications. Of the remainder, about half was used in chemical processing, power generation, and marine ordnance; the other half was used in steel and other alloys. The average aircraft now uses twice as much titanium as it did in 1968.

Titanium dioxide, the nonmetallic form of titanium, is widely used for making pigment. End uses for 1981: paints, varnishes, and lacquers (47 percent), paper (26 percent), plastics (11 percent), ceramics (2 percent), and other products (14 percent).

The Bureau of Mines predicts an annual increase of 6 percent through 1990 for titanium metal, and 2 percent for titanium dioxide.

**Major Sources.** The mineral sources of titanium products are rutile and ilmenite. Rutile, less common, is used to produce titanium sponge, as the metal is called. Both rutile and the more abundant ilmenite are used for pigment production. Ilmenite can be used to produce the metal, but it is not considered economic, and the United States has not developed the capacity. The Soviet Union uses ilmenite, and is the world's largest producer by far. U.S. production figures are withheld.

The major sources of U.S. imports between 1977 and 1980 were, for sponge metal: Japan, (74 percent), U.S.S.R. (14 percent), China (9 percent), United Kingdom (3 percent); for titanium dioxide, Germany (34 percent), Canada (15 percent), United Kingdom (15 percent), France (8 percent), other (28 percent). Between 1975 and 1978, we imported 88 percent of our rutile from Australia, with Japan and India supplying most of the remainder. Our ilmenite also came mostly from Australia (55 percent), with Canada supplying another 42 percent.

**Import Reliance and Stockpile.** For titanium metal, statistics concerning net import reliance as a percentage of consumption are withheld by the Bureau of Mines. U.S. import dependence for titanium dioxide was 9 percent in 1980. The stockpile goal for titanium sponge is 195,000 tons. Inventory stands at 21,465. Titanium is considered vitally important by Congress, which may well take action that will make it easier to build the stockpile.

**Substitutes and Recycling.** In the aerospace industry, there are essentially no substitutes for titanium metal. In general industrial uses, high-nickel steels and superalloy metals can be used to a limited extent. So far, no cost-effective replacement for titanium dioxide pigment has been found.

A considerable amount of scrap metal is recycled; no known recycling of titanium dioxide occurs.

**Trends.** Once, the U.S.S.R. was a chief exporter to the West. This stopped during the seventies, presumably because the Soviet military buildup required large amounts of titanium. Its new submarine, the world's largest and deepest-diving, has a titanium hull, and there are reports of a nuclear-powered submarine that would require more than 20 million pounds of titanium. Such military applications portend a huge demand. As the United States also steps up defense spending, there have been calls for the application of the Defense Production Act to generate greater capacity to produce titanium metal. Since the United States has ample ilmenite, we might gear up to produce titanium from that raw material. With larger amounts being used in airplanes (a Boeing 747 uses 4 tons of titanium) and increases in defense spending approved, demand surged into mid-1981, until the recession and the decline in commercial aircraft orders began to take their toll. The unexpected reductions left both producers and consumers with large inventories.

New sponge-producing plants are planned or under construction in Australia, Canada, India, Brazil, South Africa, and the United States.

**Outlook.** Strategic and profitable are not synonymous terms. Everybody loves titanium because it is of such critical importance to industry and defense. But it might not be as vital to an investment portfolio.

Titanium's light weight, strength, and corrosion resistance makes it an ideal metal for aerospace applications. In the sixties and seventies the major aircraft companies built many planes and used a great deal of titanium. With rising energy costs, even more attention is being paid to producing aircraft that can withstand the strain of flight but are light enough to reduce fuel consumption. There are indications that the automotive industry is interested in titanium for the same reasons. Thus, titanium's importance is likely to increase. However, a shortage or tight supply situation is unlikely in the near future.

While the trend is clearly toward lighter aircraft, and the demand for such is likely to increase in the future, we are currently experiencing a slowdown in orders for commercial aircraft because of the slow economy. There has been a great deal of talk about increased defense spending, which would consume a large amount of titanium and increase demand somewhat. It appears, however, that the lead time for deliveries of titanium parts has been increasing, but not the price.

Titanium production has been expanding rapidly over the past few years, partly because of the Soviet Union's decision to stop exporting titanium sponge (they have resumed those exports recently, but on a much smaller scale). There is a great deal of titanium ore in the world, and now that its importance has been recognized, mining geologists are looking for it and indeed have been finding it. Apart from any serious supply disruption based upon political or environmental problems, it is quite likely that there will be more than enough titanium to meet demand at least until the end of the century.

Titanium can be conserved. One of the simplest ways of doing this is to divert some of the titanium that is being used in the steel industry to areas where titanium's special properties can be better utilized. This is already being done to some extent. In addition, a great deal of progress has been made in alloy technology, not only with ceramics and other man-made materials but also with special titanium-aluminum alloys that in certain applications perform just as well if not better than titanium metal itself. This reduces the amount of titanium required to do the job. Also, recycling methods can be improved to conserve the metal.

It is possible, though, that some of the titanium mining operations could harm the environment; thus expansion could be impaired unless new ways are developed to reduce pollution.

Both the price of titanium and the method of trading it are controlled by producers. Much of the trading is done by contract, and the real source of free-market titanium appears to be companies abroad rather than domestic supplies. Quantities are occasionally made available by the Soviet Union, China, and Japan. The market for scrap titanium is far more active; merchants and dealers are buying up scrap from aerospace companies around the world and then reselling it to steel mills and other fabricators.

**Grades.** Titanium is most often traded with specific end uses in mind, and is therefore sold in fabricated forms, such as sheets, bars, and slabs. However, it is also traded in the form of sponge, usually with 99.6 percent minimum purity.

# Tungsten

**Principal Uses and Demand.** Its hardness and high melting point make tungsten valuable in a variety of applications. Basically, its uses fall into four main categories: tungsten carbide for cutting tools, drill bits, welding, and hard-facing rods; as an alloy in tool and die steels; in light-bulb filaments; in chemicals and chemical compounds. End uses in 1981 were distributed as follows: metalworking and constructing machinery, 78 percent; transportation, 9 percent; lamps and lighting, 6 percent; electrical, 4 percent; other, 3 percent.

Much of our tungsten finds its way into military equipment: tanks, armored cars, shells, aircraft parts, armor-piercing ordnance, and high-speed tools used to make munitions. There, its toughness and heat resistance are crucial.

The Bureau of Mines predicts an annual increase of 5 percent through 1990.

**Major Sources.** A major consumer of tungsten, the United States produces less than 7 percent of the world's total. The leading producer in 1981 was China, with more than one-quarter of the total. The Soviet Union was second, followed at a distance by Australia, Bolivia, South Korea, Canada, and the United States.

The China connection may be important in the future. Once our leading supplier, China possesses an estimated 55 percent of the world's tungsten resources, five or six times the amount found in either Canada or the Soviet Bloc. Other areas with significant potential include North and South Korea, Burma, Malaysia, Thailand, Australia, and parts of South America. In 1981, U.S. imports came from: Canada (30 percent), Bolivia (24 percent), China (11 percent), Thailand (10 percent), and other countries (25 percent).

U.S. resources are largely low grade, and production is further hampered by environmental considerations, investment costs, and other economic factors. The Bureau of Mines states: "Unless economic methods of recovering tungsten from these low-grade sources are developed, greater imports will be required."

**Import Reliance and Stockpile.** In 1981, the United States imported 52 percent of its apparent consumption. The stockpile goal for tungsten ore and concentrate is 55,450,000 pounds; the inventory exceeds that, with 56,657,000, plus about 30 million pounds of lower-grade ores. Tungsten is one of the materials the General Services Administration has been selling; 3.4 million pounds are authorized for disposal.

**Substitutes and Recycling.** In some wear-resisting applications, titanium carbide, tantalum carbide, and columbium carbide can replace tungsten. Molybdenum tool steels and tungsten tool steels are virtually interchangeable. Depending on a variety of factors, some ceramics and coatings can substitute for tungsten economically. During 1981, 15 percent of consumption was from scrap. The use of reclaimed tungsten carbide has been growing.

**Trends.** In addition to relations with China and the ability of domestic producers to use low-grade ores, several significant new production sources will influence supply. General Electric's Springer Mine in Nevada is due on stream any day; it has the potential to increase U.S. production by 25 percent. Plans are under way for production in the Yukon, New Brunswick, Iowa, Texas, and elsewhere, and important deposits in Australia, England, Thailand, and other locations are being evaluated.

Oil and gas production, military spending, and the general state of industry in the West are all important demand factors.

**Outlook.** The tungsten market is one of the most free-wheeling of all the minor metals and one of the most exciting to trade. During certain periods the free-market price actually can change several times daily. But as far as the investment outlook is concerned, there appears to be no sign of an imbalance between supply and demand in the near future. Production of tungsten has been slowly but steadily increasing, and the Chinese, already the world's largest producer, have become more aggressive in their export policy.

We are now coming out of a recent large-scale expansion of tungsten production, which occurred between 1975 and 1980. During that period, production increased about 34 percent in the West; adding China's exports, the total free-world supply increased by about 40 percent.

Since it is a major component of carbide drilling bits, tungsten is an obvious beneficiary of the boom in oil and gas exploration. However, with the current surplus in petrochemicals we could see a decrease or tapering off of that boom. Another major user of tungsten is the cutting tools industry, which is subject to changes in industrial cycles. There appears to be steady growth also in the chemical applications of tungsten.

While the short-term investment outlook is uncertain, the long-term picture for tungsten is a great deal more encouraging. World resources are certainly not overly abundant, and demand is expected to increase at a steady rate. While there are good substitutes for tungsten in many of its applications, the Bureau of Mines believes that 40 to 50 percent of its present uses are essential and nonsubstitutable at the current level of technological development. In addition to the use of tungsten in cutting tools and drill bits, we can expect increased use in various kinds of machinery. It is still possible that the automotive industry may turn to turbine engines in the future, and this would greatly increase demand for tungsten.

The tungsten market is almost entirely a free-market situation. China acts as a price leader, with other producers in Thailand, Southeast Asia, and South America following its lead. Merchants are supplied by the Chinese, the Eastern Europeans, and the Soviet Union. The Chinese are similar to the Soviets in that their marketing and sales policies are somewhat inconsistent and erratic. Rather than supplying the market steadily they will often hold back when the price seems too low, and then sell vigorously when the price is favorable. The North American producers follow their favorite pattern of selling by contract directly to consumers, but they are clearly in the minority. The market is extremely volatile and speculative, and it is very difficult to get an accurate handle on the price of tungsten at any given time. The International Price Index for tungsten was started in 1978, using data derived from both consumers and producers in the Western world in an attempt to arrive at an accurate price.

**Grades.** Tungsten is traded in the form of concentrates, and there are many types, such as wolframite and scheelite, ferrotungsten, and ammonium paratungstate (APT). The concentrates are sold in short ton, long ton, and metric ton units (MTUs) containing 20 pounds, 22.4 pounds, and 22.046 pounds per unit of tungsten trioxide ($WO_3$) respectively. The commonly traded commercial grades contain about 65 to 70 percent MTUs per metric ton, or 65 to 70 percent tungsten trioxide per metric ton. Most of these concentrates have various impurities such as tin, phosphorus, sulfur, and copper, and these can affect the price. Some pure tungsten metal is traded in the form of powder, but this is a very small portion of the market.

# Vanadium

**Principal Uses and Demand.** Vanadium is used mainly as an alloying ingredient to increase strength in iron and steel. High-strength, low-alloy vanadium steel is found in oil and gas pipelines; in lightweight, energy-efficient vehicles; and in structural applications that need a high ratio of strength to weight. In addition, vanadium is used in titanium-based alloys for jet engines and aircraft frames. As a catalyst, it is used in the production of sulfuric acid and in oil refining, but in small quantities.

Demand for vanadium rose slightly in 1981, principally because of increased use in steel. In 1980, end-use distribution was: transportation, 35 percent; construction, 27 percent, machinery, 25 percent; chemicals, 4 percent; other, 9 percent.

The Bureau of Mines predicts an annual increase of about 4 percent through 1990 in the United States.

**Major Sources.** Domestic resources are sufficient to supply the current level of demand, but a substantial portion of U.S. consumption is import-based because of price advantages. We imported mainly from the following sources between 1977 and 1980: South Africa, 8 percent; Chile, 16 percent; Canada, 7 percent; others, including the U.S.S.R., 19 percent. South Africa and the U.S.S.R. were main producers in 1981, with about 62 percent of the world's production between them. China is another important producer, and is expected to become a larger exporter soon. We do not know the extent of China's reserves, but the rest is overwhelmingly in South Africa and the Soviet Union: of the estimated 40.8 billion pounds of vanadium reserves in the world, 17.2 billion are in South Africa, and 16 billion in the Soviet Union. Australia, Chile, and the United States are far behind, but contain significant reserves.

**Import Reliance and Stockpile.** In 1981, the United States imported 42 percent of its consumption. The stockpile calls for 17.4 million pounds of vanadium pentoxide and 2 million pounds of ferrovanadium; inventory contains 1,082,000 pounds of the former and none of the latter. Excess capacity could be utilized to build the stockpile.

**Substitutes and Recycling.** Various combinations of other alloying metals can replace vanadium in steels. Columbium, molybdenum, manganese, titanium, and tungsten can also to some degree be used as substitutes, but their use hinges on cost factors. Platinum can substitute for vanadium compounds in chemical processes.

Vanadium is recycled from tool steel scraps, and as a minor component of scrap iron and steel alloys. Waste from chemical operations often contains large amounts of vanadium, but it is not economic to recover it.

**Trends.** Increased use in pipelines and aircraft is expected, and so, to a smaller extent, is the use of vanadium in concrete reinforcing bars, in automotive equipment, and as a replacement for nickel, molybdenum, and other more expensive alloying elements. Stockpiling in the United States and Europe is expected to occur shortly. On the supply side, Australia began mining in 1980, and China has entered the world market for the first time.

**Outlook.** Vanadium is considered a strategic metal primarily because half of the world's supply comes from South Africa and the Soviets also supply a significant amount. However, the United States has considerable resources of vanadium, and if necessary much of it could be exploited to reduce our dependence on foreign sources.

Currently the only operable mine in the United States is a Union Carbide mine in Arkansas. Recently, vanadium has been recovered from uranium ores, and Energy Fuel Nuclear Inc. is producing some vanadium at its White Mesa Mill in Utah. China has recently been offering some for sale to the United States, and as previously noted, Australia is now an exporter. Thus, the number of suppliers has been increasing around the world. The content of vanadium in the earth's crust has been estimated at 140 parts per million, which makes it even more abundant than copper, lead, and zinc. However, it is more widely distributed and not as easy to recover as the base metals.

Since vanadium is used in the manufacture of steel alloys, its demand is very closely linked to the steel industry. Vanadium is also an important ingredient in the manufacture of oil pipelines, and the specialty steel used for that purpose could benefit from a continued boom in oil and gas exploration.

Other metals such as molybdenum and tungsten can be substituted for vanadium, and these potential substitutes keep producers from raising the price unrealistically. On the other hand, vanadium could well wind up being a substitute for nickel or molybdenum in the manufacture of certain alloy steels. This, of course, is a function of price in many cases. It also should be noted that vanadium has been part of the U.S. strategic stockpile, and even though the goal has been reduced from 25.3 million to 17.4 million pounds, the government has only about 1.08 million pounds currently stockpiled. Even if the United States buys slowly and carefully, its pursuit of the stockpile goal should be a significant factor in keeping demand steady and strong.

Vanadium is currently almost completely controlled by producers, with merchant activity relatively small, except in times of shortage. The Soviets are a source of free-market material, and it is expected that the Chinese will also supply some vanadium to the merchant market in the future. The price is still firmly controlled, however, by the producers operating on a contract basis. Serious political trouble in South Africa would probably mean higher vanadium prices, but barring that vanadium does not appear to be the most efficient way to invest in minor metals. If one were very interested in vanadium, one might consider several South African mining firms. A significant price rise in vanadium could be expected to increase the price of the mining shares themselves. The drawback to investing in South African shares is that if there was a revolution in South Africa and the price of vanadium went up, the price of the shares would probably go down or be worthless, since the mine might no longer be functioning smoothly, if at all.

**Grades.** The most common form of vanadium is ferrovanadium, containing about 50 percent or 80 percent vanadium, the rest being iron.

# Y TTRIUM

**Principal Uses and Demands.** Ninety percent of yttrium consumption in 1981 was in color televisions, where it is used in phosphors (a substance that can be stimulated to emit light); another 5 percent was used in electronics; the remaining 5 percent was used in alloys, refractories, ceramics, crystals, lasers, jewelry, nuclear equipment, and research.

The Bureau of Mines predicts an annual increase of about 6 percent through 1990.

**Major Sources.** Because of limited demand, yttrium is produced with relatively small-scale equipment; thus costs are high. Large-scale methods can be adopted to produce the metal if demand increases sufficiently. Most yttrium produced in the United States is derived from imported xenotime ore, a by-product of tin mining.

Production and import figures are not published by the Bureau of Mines, which anticipates "no problems in supply or production capacity." Australia is the leading world producer, with more than double the output of its closest competitor, Malaysia. However, India contains more than half the world's known reserves. Some U.S. supplies come from Canada in the form of uranium residues.

**Import Reliance and Stockpile.** Percentage of consumption figures for imports are not available. The U.S. stockpile contains 237 pounds of yttrium oxide, all of which is "authorized for disposal."

**Substitutes and Recycling.** In most uses, especially phosphors and jewelry, there are no practical alternatives, but in some minor applications cost factors often permit substitution. No yttrium is recycled.

**Trends.** New applications are anticipated if ways to lower production costs are found. Large resources of yttrium are thought to be available worldwide in sands.

**Outlook.** The outlook for yttrium most closely parallels that of the rare earths, and indeed the Bureau of Mines includes yttrium in its discussion of rare-earth metals. The use of yttrium with nickel, cobalt, and chromium for the manufacture of superalloys and high-intensity magnets is expected to grow very rapidly through the beginning of the next century. Research into and development of new applications bear watching, but so do the sources of supply, which are expected to grow sufficiently to keep pace with demand. As we have seen, however, rarely do supply and demand grow in a state of equilibrium. There is usually some short-term surplus or tightness in a growing market, and that produces profit opportunities. Unfortunately, there is virtually no merchant market for yttrium and there are only two domestic producers of high-purity yttrium oxide in the pentoxide form. However, this situation could change.

# ZIRCONIUM

**Principal Uses and Demand.** Zirconium metal is used in nuclear reactors, and therefore its use has decreased substantially in the last two years in the United States. Nonnuclear applications are principally in corrosion-resistant alloys and chemical processing. The metal is used to construct valves and thermocouple pockets. Much of current consumption is for reloading present nuclear plants.

Zircon mineral is used mainly in foundries and refractories, and to a lesser degree in ceramics, abrasives, and a number of minor applications.

The Bureau of Mines predicts an annual increase of 4 percent through 1990, although developments in the nuclear industry can alter any forecast significantly.

**Major Sources.** Australia is by far the world's largest producer of zircon, with almost 80 percent of the total. South Africa's output is about 20 percent of Australia's. India, Brazil, and Malaysia produce much smaller quantities. U.S. production figures are withheld. We do have significant reserves—8 million of an estimated 50 million tons worldwide. Australia has 14 million and South Africa 12. Ninety percent of our imports come from Australia.

**Import Reliance and Stockpile.** Figures on import-dependency are withheld. There is no present goal or inventory in the stockpile.

**Substitutes and Recycling.** Chromite and some aluminum silicate minerals can replace zircon in certain foundry applications. In the steel industry, ferrotitanium can be used as a substitute.

No significant recycling is done.

**Trends.** Present metal production capacity is sufficient for the short term, since any new nuclear plants will take years to license and construct. The major growth areas for mineral zircon should be in refractories, abrasives, and chemicals; for zirconium metal, in corrosion-resistant alloys and nuclear reactor construction. New production facilities in South Africa, Japan, and Utah have just been completed.

**Outlook.** The demand for zirconium is closely tied to the proliferation of nuclear power plants, and at present the licensing and construction of these plants has been slowed considerably, especially in the United States. In other parts of the world, such as France and Japan, almost twice as much time is required to license and construct a plant as in the United States. So even if expansion continues at full tilt it would take some time for zirconium demand to pick up.

Zirconium does have other uses outside the nuclear field—in fabricated metal products and in the manufacture of superconducting and electromagnetic magnets. If something serious was to happen to the titanium supply, it is possible that zirconium could be looked to as a possible substitute because of its high corrosion resistance. In addition, there are several other uses for zircon ore.

The outlook for zirconium investment is not very good. The raw material is plentiful, and demand is not expected to grow significantly in relation to supply. Nuclear power may gain wider acceptance if tighter safety measures are adapted. But the financial burden is very large—utilities can't afford to build nuclear plants without help. It is very likely that in the future, the recycling technology for recovering zirconium will be improved. The refinement and production of zirconium metal, however, is quite expensive because it requires magnesium, and it is possible that we could see a significant rise in price based not on slow supply or slack demand but on high production costs.

**Grades.** Zirconium metal for use in the nuclear industry is commonly marketed as zircaloy. Zirconium alloys include tin, chrome, nickel, iron with tin, and in some cases columbium. The ore form zircon is usually between 65 and 66 percent zirconium dioxide. The metal is usually sold as ingot or sponge. In this rather dull merchant market, most dealers and merchants confine their activity to scrap or the ore form.

# APPENDIX

**Members of the Minor Metals Traders' Association**

ACLI International
Acli Metal & Ore Division
110 Wall Street
New York, New York 10005
Tel. 212-943-8700
Telex 232261

Ametalco Trading Ltd.
29 Gresham Street
London EC2V 7DA
Tel. 01 6068800
Telex 885541

Ayrton & Partners Ltd.
Friendly House
21–24 Chiswell Street
London EC1Y 4SN
Tel. 01 6385588
Telex 887648

Basmont Metal Co. Ltd.
Victoria House
Vernon Place
Southampton Row
London WC1B 4DN
Tel. 01 4055065
Telex 27312

Bocmin Metals Ltd.
Broadway Chambers
Hammersmith Broadway
London W6
Tel. 01 7410661
Telex 934849

Brandeis Goldschmidt & Co.
4 Fore Street
London EC2P 2NU
Tel. 01 6385877
Telex 84401

Brookside Metal BV
Vredenberg L24
3511 BB Utrecht
Holland
Tel. 30 313851
Telex 40555

Cambridge Metals Ltd.
7 All Saints Passage
Cambridge CB2 3LS, England
Tel. 0223 312111
Telex 817570

Chloride Metals Ltd.
Manor Metal Works
Harrow Manorway
Abbey Wood
London SE2 9RW
Tel. 01 3104444
Telex 896948

Cominco (UK) Ltd.
50 Finsbury Square
London EC2A 1BD
Tel. 01 6384000
Telex 886563

Commodity Analysis Ltd.
37–39 St. Andrews Hill
London EC4V 5DD
Tel. 01 2489571
Telex 883356

Continental Metals
Corporation
820 Second Avenue
New York, New York 10011
Tel. 212-421-9811
Telex 425589

Copalco International Ltd.
200 Park Avenue, Suite 354
New York, New York 10017
Tel. 212-697-7260
Telex 127758

R L Cusick Metals Ltd.
Cusick House
Church Street
Ware
Herts, England
Tel. 0920 61181
Telex 817395

Entores Ltd.
79–83 Chiswell Street
London EC1Y 4TB
Tel. 01 6066050
Telex 261932

Erlanger & Co.
(Commodities) Ltd.
Moor House
London Wall
London EC2Y 5ET
Tel. 01 6386691
Telex 8813155

Exsud Ltd.
237–247 Tottenham Court
Road
London W1P OBU
Tel. 01 6314959
Telex 264751

FLT & Metals Ltd.
1–5 Long Lane
London EC1A 9HA
Tel. 01 6061272
Telex 8811917

Gerald Metals Ltd.
Europe House
World Trade Centre
St. Katherine-by-the-Tower
London E1 9AA
Tel. 01 4810681
Telex 884377

Gill & Duffus Ltd.
201 Borough High Street
London SE1 1HW
Tel. 01 4077050
Telex 887588

Greendown Trading BV
Bozembocht 23
Rotterdam
Holland
Tel. 10 13207
Telex 23508

Grondmet
Rochussenstraat 125
Rotterdam
Holland
Tel. 10 361933
Telex 21689, 25218

Intsel Ltd.
83–87 Gracechurch Street
London EC3V OAA
Tel. 01 6233691
Telex 8811981

AC Israel Woodhouse Co. Ltd.
21 Mincing Lane
London EC3R 7DN
Tel. 01 6233131
Telex 883136, 883139

Lambert Metals Ltd.
506–508 Kingsbury Road
London NW9 9HE
Tel. 01 2049422
Telex 23844

Leopold Lazarus Ltd.
Gotch House
20–34 St. Bride Street
London EC4A 4DL
Tel. 01 5838060
Telex 265544

Leigh & Sillivan Ltd.
Knights Pools
Windmill Street
Macclesfield
Cheshire SK11 7HR, England
Tel. 0625 31331
Telex 668363

Lonconex Ltd.
29 Mincing Lane
London EC3R 7EU
Tel. 01 6264383
Telex 885016

Maclaine Watson & Co. Ltd.
2–4 Idol Lane
London EC3R 5DL
Tel. 01 2838611
Telex 883854

Arthur Matyas & Co. Ltd.
Pearl House
746 Finchley Road
London NW11 7TH
Tel. 01 4588911
Telex 8812123

Metaleg Metall GmbH
Graf Adolph Strasse 22
4000 Dusseldorf 1
West Germany
Tel. 211 631011
Telex 8582610

Metallbodio Ltd.
PO Box 296
CH-4010 Basel
Switzerland
Tel. 61 238953
Telex 62270

Metramet Ltd.
Kingswell 58–62 Heath Street
London NW3 1EN
Tel. 01 7941131
Telex 25479

Minor Metals Inc.
1 Gulf & Western Plaza,
Room 918
New York, New York 10023
Tel. 212-541-8880
Telex 426965

Minwood Metals Ltd.
Paterson Road
Finedon Industrial Estate
Wellinborough
Northants, England
Tel. 0933 225766
Telex 311394

Nemco Metal International
Ltd.
9 Harrowden Road
Brackmills
Northampton NN4 OEB,
England
Tel. 0604 66181
Telex 826433

A J Oster Co.
50 Sims Avenue
Providence, Rhode Island
Tel. 401-421-3840
Telex WUD 927747

Powell Metals & Chemicals
(UK) Inc.
62 Hills Road
Cambridge CB2 1LA, England
Tel. 0223 51775
Telex 817669 Powcang

Primetal Italia
20124 Milano
Via Cappelini 16
Italy
Tel. 2 667124
Telex 33439

Derek Raphael & Co. Ltd.
DRC House
2 Cornwall Terrace
Regents Park
London NW1 4QP
Tel. 01 4869931
Telex 261916

Redlac Metals Ltd.
148 Buckingham Palace Road
London SW1W 9TR
Tel. 01 7032276
Telex 888885

Rhonda Metals Co. Ltd.
Rhonda Works
Perth
Mid-Glamorgan
Wales CF39 9BA
Tel. 044 3612881
Telex 49562

Rothmetal Trading Ltd.
PO Box 1549
Argus Insurance Building
Wesley Street
Hamilton, Bermuda
Tel. 80929 27980
Telex 3368 BA

William Rowland Ltd.
Powke Lane
Cradley Heath
Warley
West Midlands B64 5PX,
England
Tel. 021 5593031
Telex 331376

Sassoon & Co. Ltd.
203 Avenue Louise
PO Box 4
1050 Brussels
Belgium
Tel. 2 6406783
Telex 63605

Jack Sharkey & Co. Ltd.
Middlemore Road
Smerthwick
Warley
West Midlands B66 2DP,
England
Tel. 021 5587444

Skandinaviska Malm-Och
Metallaktiebolaget
Kungsgatan 6
Box 7547
S-103 93 Stockholm
Sweden
Tel. 8 233520
Telex 19552

Sogement
161 Avenue Charles
deGaulle
92202 Neuilly sur Seine
France
Tel. 1 6375760
Telex 820242

Spencer Metals & Minerals
Ltd.
25 London Road
Newbury
Berks, United Kingdom

Steetley Chemicals Ltd.
Berk House
PO Box 56
Basing View
Basingstoke
Hants RG21 2EG, England
Tel. 0256 292292
Telex 858371

Sterling Enterprises Metals
Ltd.
Sterling House
328 Holloway Road
London N7 7HJ
Tel. 01 6077381
Telex 27325

Tennant Trading Ltd.
9 Harp Lane
Lower Thames Street
London EC3R 6DR
Tel. 01 4805701
Telex 884724

Trans-World Metals Ltd.
Walsingham House
35 Seething Lane
London EC3N 4EL
Tel. 01 4805701
Telex 8951322

Unimet GmbH
Stahl, Rohre und Metalle
Cecilienallee 21
4000 Dusseldorf 30
West Germany
Tel. 211 450914
Telex 08582622

H A Watson & Co. Ltd.
119–120 High Street
Stourbridge
West Midlands DY 8 IDT,
England
Tel. 03843 77801
Telex 337034

Rene Weil SA
77 Rue de Monceau
75008 Paris
France
Tel. 1 5630488
Telex 280445

Wheatstock Ltd.
4 Fore Street
London EC2Y 5EH
Tel. 01 5887081
Telex 8814900

Wogen Resources Ltd.
17 Devonshire Street
London W1
Tel. 01 5805762
Telex 28820

**Several Minor Metals Firms Dealing with the General Public**
Bache Halsey Stuart Metal Co., Inc.
  100 Gold Street
  New York, New York 10038

Millenium Metals Ltd.
  45 Belden Place
  San Francisco, California 94104

Strategic Metals Corporation
  500 Chesham House
  150 Regent Street
  London W1R 5FA

Strategic Metals & Critical Materials, Inc.
  90 Broad Street
  New York, New York 10004

**Information on Minor Metals**
Commodities Research Unit
  26 Red Lion Square
  London WC 1 4RL

General Services Administration
  General Services Building
  18th & F Street NW
  Washington, DC 20405

Minor Metals Traders Association
  69 Cannon Street
  London EC 4N 5AB

National Association of Recycling Industries
  330 Madison Avenue
  New York, New York 10017

Roskill Information Services Ltd.
  2 Clapham Road
  London SW9 OJA

World Bureau of Metal Statistics
  41 Doughty Street
  London WC 1N 2LF

**Pertinent Financial Publications**
*American Metal Market*
  7 East 12th Street
  New York, New York 10003

*Metal Bulletin Ltd.*
  45-46 Lower Marsh
  London SE 1 7RG

*Metals Week*
  McGraw-Hill Inc.
  1221 Avenue of the Americans
  New York, New York 10020

*Engineering & Mining Journal*
  McGraw-Hill Inc.
  1221 Avenue of the Americas
  New York, New York 10020

## U.S. GOVERNMENT PUBLICATIONS

### U.S. Bureau of Mines
Mineral Commodity Summaries. An up-to-date summary of eighty-nine nonfuel mineral commodities. Published annually.

Minerals Yearbook. An annual publication that reviews the mineral industry of the United States and foreign countries.

Contains statistical data on metals and minerals, and their products, and includes information on economic and technical trends and developments. The yearbook is published in three volumes: Volume I, Metals and Minerals; Volume II, Area Reports, Domestic; and Volume III, Area Reports, International.

Mineral Industry Surveys. Periodic statistical and economic reports designed to provide timely statistical data on production, distribution, stocks, and consumption of significant mineral commodities. The surveys are issued monthly, quarterly, or at other regular intervals, depending on the need for current data.

Perspectives. Reports which present timely data on mineral developments in foreign geographic areas.

Bulletins. Reports that describe major Bureau of Mines investigations or studies that are considered to have permanent value.

Information Circulars. Reports that primarily compile, review, abstract, and discuss various activities and developments in the mineral industries.

Reports of Investigations. Reports that describe the principal features and results of minor investigations or phases of major investigations, to keep the mineral industries and the public informed on progress in original Bureau of Mines research.

These and other Bureau reports are described in the monthly release "New Publications—Bureau of Mines," which is available free upon request from the Branch of Production and Distribution, Bureau of Mines, 4800 Forbes Avenue, Pittsburgh, PA 15213.

**Geological Survey**
Professional Papers. Comprehensive reports on the results of resource studies and of topographic, hydrologic, paleontologic, and geologic investigations, including longer contributions to the literature on scientific and engineering subjects.

Bulletins. Either final or progress reports on the results of resource studies and of topographic and geologic investigations; shorter contributions to economic and general geology;

and descriptions of Geological Survey instruments and techniques.

Circulars. Timely, scientifically sound, and accurate reports for which a simpler and less permanent format is deemed adequate. In general, the treatment of the subject is less comprehensive and final, or the report is of relative local or restricted interest or of relatively temporary usefulness.

Maps and Charts. Numerous maps and charts pertaining to mineral resource investigations are published. These include: mineral investigations field-studies maps; and mineral investigations resource maps.

These Geological Survey publications are described in the monthly release "New Publications of the Geological Survey," which is available free upon request from the Branch of Distribution, Geological Survey, 1200 South Eads Street, Arlington, VA 22202.

# INDEX

Accuracy of statistics, 162–63
Administered price, 168–69
Advisory accounts, 242
*Affluence in Jeopardy* (Park), 87
Afghanistan, 53, 71, 85
Africa, 61
  Soviet inroads in, 54–60
    rail lines and, 56–58
    sea lanes and, 58–60
    worst-case scenario and, 55–56
  *see also individual countries and* Third World
African National Congress (ANC), 108, 109
Alaska Lands Bill, 127
Albania, 48
Albier, Robert, 80
Allegheny Ludlum, 253
Allende, Salvador, 73, 74
Allied Chemical, 147
Alloys, 12–13, 146
  new, 146–48
Aluminum, 14, 18, 25, 79, 141, 166, 186, 257

substitution and, 142, 143, 144, 145, 147, 148, 193
AMAX, Inc., 121, 130, 253
American Mining Congress, 15, 124, 125
  stockpiling and, 134, 135–36, 139
Anaconda, 129, 133
Analysis of the purchase, 234
Andrews, E. F., 17, 83–84, 104, 105
Angola, 3, 4, 10, 111
  government of, 84–85, 89
  Soviet Union and, 49, 54, 58, 59
  transportation of ore in, 57
Annual statements, 235
Antimony, 7, 15, 25, 26, 38, 101, 246
  profile of, 281–82
ARMCO, 253
Armed Services Subcommittee on Military Construction and Stockpiles, 124
Arsenic, 199

ASARCO, 183, 200
Asbestos, 98, 101
Assay report, 232–34
Australia, 57, 79, 81, 82, 102
Austria, 67

Bache Metals, 203, 259
Backwardation, 267
Barium, 43, 145
Barnett, Richard, 65
Barometric price leaders, 170
Base metals, 165–66
    supply of minor metals and,
        183, 196–98
"Basket" strategy, 270–71
Battleground, 73–122
    cartels and, *see* Cartels
    future in the Third World, 84–
        90
    legacy of colonialism, 74–75
    new economic order, 75–77
    Republic of South Africa and,
        100–112
    Zaire and, 90–96
    Zambia and, 94–96
    Zimbabwe and, 96–100
Bauxite, 43, 67, 68, 79–80, 138,
    142
Bear Stearns, 251
Belgium, 66, 68, 90
Beryllium, 7, 20, 22, 25, 26, 144,
    149, 253
    profile of, 283–84
    Soviet Union and, 45
    substitution and, 192
Bismuth, 246, 247
Blackbird Mine, 128, 254
Black market, 177–78
Boron, 147
Botha, P. W., 105
Botswana, 111
Boyd, James, 118
Brazil, 48, 59, 81, 82, 101, 170
Brennan, Justice William J., 132–
    33
Brezhnev, Leonid, 61
Bronze, 12–13
Brush Wellman, 253
Bureau of Land Management
    (BLM), 123

Bureau of the Mines, U.S., 20, 23,
    113, 114, 137, 139, 145,
    148, 150, 152, 158, 181,
    190, 198
    publications of, 275, 276
Burford, Robert, 123–24
Burns, John F., 97
Bush, George, 123
Business cycles, 161–62
*Business Week*, 115, 119, 191
Buy-and-hold strategy, 262–63
Buying minor metals, 208–37
    annual statement and, 236
    choosing a firm, 215–18
        high-pressure sales and, 217–
            18
        knowledgeable staff and,
            216–17
        prices and, 216
        reputation and, 215–16
    commissions and, 221, 224
        statement regarding, 225
    confirmation and purchase
        and, 224
    contracts for, 220, 222–23
    dealers and, 212–14
    evaluation of purchase, 230–34
        analysis and, 234
        sample inspection certificate
            and report, 232–33
        sampling and, 231
    feasibility of, 208–12
    insuring your purchase, 234–36
        sample certificate, 235
    investment firms and, 214–15
    payment and, 223
    quotes and, 219–21
    selling and, 236–37
    service provided by brokers,
        218–19
    small amounts and, 221
    storage and, 224, 226
    warehouse warrants and, 226–
        27
        falsified, 227, 229
        sample, 228
        should it be in your name?,
            229–30
    *see also* Investing in minor
        metals; Investment vehicles

By-products, 183
impact of, on metals shares, 246–48
independent mining and, 247
pitfalls of, 247–48
stocks of, 196–98

Cabot Corporation, 253
Cadmium, 15, 38, 246, 247, 252
price of, 149
profile of, 284–86
speculation in, 199
Calingaert, Michael, 9, 95
Canada, 66, 79, 116, 134
U.S. and, 81, 102, 172
Cape of Good Hope, 58, 59, 102
Capitalism, 61
Carbon, 147
Carrying charge, 266
Cartels, 77–84, 100, 106
feasibility of, 80–81
introduction, 77–78
new forms of, 82–83
Soviet Union and, 55–56
strength of, 78
substitute sources and, 82
unlikelihood of metals, 79–80
worst-case, 83–84
Zaire-Zambia cobalt, 95–96
Carter, Jimmy, 4, 71, 110, 122
Castro, Fidel, 4, 70
Center for Strategic and International Studies, 49, 82
Ceramics, 147
Cerium, profile of, 320–22
Chad, 54
"Charter of Economic Rights and Duties of States, The," 75–76
Chile, 70, 73, 79
China, 114, 174
"Choke points," 58
Chrome, 17, 26, 145, 148, 150, 152
resource wars and, 66, 67, 68, 69
Soviet Union and, 43
in Zimbabwe, 98–99
Chromite, 48–49, 54, 66, 71, 128
Chromium, 4, 9, 15, 17, 20, 25,

38, 40, 92, 101, 102, 118, 151, 211, 248, 259
domestic deposits of, 115–16, 128, 146
profile of, 286–90
Soviet Union and, 43, 44, 47, 48–49, 55, 59
substitution for, 147, 148, 149, 150
Zimbabwe and, 98, 99, 100
Church, Frank, 124
CIA, 70, 73, 84
CIPEC (International Council of Copper Exporting Countries), 80
Clark Amendment, 111
Clean Air Act, 133–34
Coal, 57, 67, 83, 98
Coar, Richard J., 191
Cobalt, 14, 15, 19, 20, 25, 38, 40, 118, 125, 128, 146, 152, 246, 247, 251
GSA's purchase of, 206–7, 219
market structure and, 171, 174, 175–76, 177, 188, 189
price of, 10, 25, 63, 191, 201, 220, 247–48
profile of, 290–93
Soviet Union and, 54, 55
stockpiling of, 135, 138, 140, 141
substitution for, 145, 147, 148, 149, 150, 191
under the sea, 153, 155
vulnerability and, 253, 254
Zaire and, 4–5, 8–9, 11, 26, 57, 68, 90–96, 253
Zambia and, 94–96
Coke, 57
Cold War, 22–27
resource war and, 62–63, 64, 70
Collender, Dr. Frederick, 192, 193
Colonialism, legacy of, 74–75
Columbium, 4, 15, 20, 22, 25, 38, 59, 93, 138, 141, 167, 170, 246
demand for, 113–14
profile of, 293–95

Comex exchange, 257, 259
Commerce Department, U.S., 119, 139, 155
Commissions, 221, 224
  Advisory accounts and, 244
  funds and, 245
  managed accounts and, 240–41, 244
  statement regarding, 225
Commodity Futures Trading Commission (CFTC), 163–64
Complements, 189
Confirmation of purchase, 224
Congo, the, 54, 57, 59
Conservation, 200–201
Consumption and demand, 197–98
Contango, 266
Contracts, 171–72
  "cost plus," 171
  fixed-price, 171
  flexible, 171–72
  forward, see Forward contracts
  free market and, 172
  options, 256–57
  samples of, 222–23
Copper, 4, 11, 12, 14, 18, 19, 32, 73, 79, 94, 98, 128, 202, 257
  by-products and, 246
  substitution and, 142, 143–44, 148, 192, 194
  under the sea, 153, 155
  U.S. production of, 118, 119, 129, 141
  in Zaire, 91, 92, 93, 177
Corrosion, 146, 147
"Cost plus" contract, 171
Cost structure, 187–88
Council for Mutual Economic Aid (CMEA), 50
Council for Mutual Economic Assistance (COMECON), 44, 45, 48, 55
  free market and, 173
Council on Economics and National Security (CENS), 55–56
Critical metals, see Strategic metals

Crocker, Chester A., 108, 110, 111, 112
Cronkite, Walter, 110
Cross elasticity of demand, 189–90
Cruft, Dr. Edgar, 118, 150
Cuba, 4, 10, 53, 85, 89
  resource wars and, 69, 70, 71
  Soviet Union and, 54, 55, 58, 59
Czechoslovakia, 67

Dealers, 178–79
  buying and selling through, 212–14
  choosing, 215–18
Defense Department, U.S., 113, 139, 140, 148–49
Defense Industrial Base Panel, 23–24
Defense Production Act of 1950, 24–25, 141
De Klerk, F. W., 106
Demand and consumption, 197–98
Demand for metals, 183–84, 278–80
  consumer preferences and, 184
  level of related metals and, 183
  liquidity and, 209
  need for finished products and, 183–84
  number and size of customers and, 183
  price and, 188–90
Dempsey, H. Stanley, 130
Diamonds, 101
Dominant firms, 170
Dykstra, Franz, 47–48, 69, 126–27, 150
Dysprosium, profile of, 320–22

Eagle Picher, 197
East Germany, 10, 53, 54, 55
  see also Germany
Eckes, Alfred E., 64–65, 67, 68
Ecology, 119, 123, 129–34, 183
"Economic cannibalism," 61
Electronics industry, 19–20
Elliott, Dr. John F., 46, 47, 80
Energy costs, 201–2

Energy sources, new, 20, 22
Environmental Protection Agency (EPA), 119, 123, 133
Erbium, profile of, 320–22
Etheredge, Dennis, 106
Ethiopia, 49, 53, 54, 55, 58
European Economic Community (EEC) imports of strategic metals, 40, 41
Europium, profile of, 320–22
Evaluation of purchase, 230–34
Export-Import Bank, 88
Extraction line, 199–200

Fabricators, 252–53
Fansteel, 253
Federal Emergency Management Agency (FEMA), 138, 140, 141–42
Federal Surface Mining Act, 124
Fees, see Commissions
Ferroalloys, 19, 25, 66, 121, 142
Ferrochrome, 99, 101, 102, 211
Ferromanganese, 101
Financial conditions, personal, 166
Financial institutions specializing in the mining industry, 254–55
Financing purchases, 269–70
Fine, Daniel I., 45, 46–47, 48–49, 50
Fischer, Fritz, 65
Fixed-price contracts, 171
Flexible contracts, 171–72
Flue dust, 152, 252
Fluoride, 43
Fluorspar, 15, 38, 101, 137
Foreign Affairs, 108
Foreign exchange, 212
Fortune, 44, 45, 60, 147, 149
Forward contracts, 265–68
    Commodity Futures Trading Commission and, 164
    delivery of the metal and, 267
    described, 265–66
    hedging and, 266
    leverage and, 266
    risk and, 267
    spot price and, 266–67
    time frame of, 267–68

France, 3, 65–66
Free market, 172–75
    buyers, 173–75
    contracts and, 171, 172
    defined, 163, 172–73
    "excess" tonnage and, 173
    international crises and, 174
Free-market price, 169, 174–75
    two-price marketplace and, 175–77
Frei, Eduardo, 73
Frost & Sullivan Inc., 89
Funds, 242–43
Futures, 257–59

Gabon, 48, 82, 101
    transportation of ore in, 57
Gadolinium, profile of, 320–22
Gallium, 20, 22, 25, 144, 246, 252
    profile of, 295–97
Gardiner, David, 133
General Accounting Office (GAO), 122, 125
General Services Administration (GSA), 139–40
    cobalt purchases by, 206–7
Geological Survey, U.S., 88, 127
Germanium, 20, 25, 26, 246, 252
    "cornering the market" for, 204–5
    investing in, 263
    profile of, 297–300
    zinc and, 190, 196–97, 199–200
Germany, 65, 134, 142
    resource wars and, 65–69
    see also East Germany; West Germany
"Get rich quick," 165
Giscard d'Estaing, Valéry, 85
Glagolev, Igor, 61–62
Gold, 6–7, 12, 98, 99, 101, 246, 257, 258–59
    investing in, 261
Gorsuch, Anne, 123
Gourlay, James, 206
Government intervention, 206–7
Grades of metals, 211
Great Britain, 65–66
Guatemala, 70
Guayule, 142
Gulf Oil, 84–85, 89

Hafnium, 22
  profile of, 301–2
Haig, Alexander, 5, 59–60, 86, 87
  South Africa and, 110, 111–12
Hanks, Robert J., 58, 59
"Hard assets," 261–62
Harriman, Averell, 71
Harris, James R., 124
Hedging, 266
High-pressure sales tactics, 217–18
High technology, 162
High-technology firms, 254
Hillyard, Leonard, 178
Hitler, Adolf, 67, 69
Holding period, optimum, 212
Holmium, profile of, 320–22
House Armed Services Committee, 23–24
House Foreign Affairs Committee, 111
Hudson Institute, 23, 26
Hungary, 67

Ilmenite, 116, 145
Imports of strategic metals, 37–43
INCO, 251
India, 48, 50, 66, 82
Indium, 20, 22, 25, 246
  profile of, 302–4
Indonesia, 67
Industry output, 181–82
  changes in capability of, 186–87
Inflationary hedge, 161
Information:
  accuracy of, 162–63
  dealers and, 179
  investing and, 170
  overload of, 163
  substitution, 190
  trader's provision of, 218
  up-to-date, 276–77
Inspection certificate, 231–33
Institute for Policy Studies, 65
Insurance, 234–36
  sample certificate of, 235
Interest rates, 262
Interior Department, U.S., 125–26, 157

International Bauxite Association, 79–80, 83
International Economic Studies Institute, 17, 35, 40, 80
Investing in minor metals, 161–66
  accuracy in statistics and, 162–63
  business cycles and, 161–62
  feasibility of, 208–12
    foreign exchange and, 212
    grade and, 211
    liquidity and, 208–9
    optimum holding period and, 212
    size of trading quantities and, 210–11
    storage feasibility and, 211
    tax advantages and, 212
    volatility and, 209–10
  financial suitability and, 166
  getting rich quick and, 165
  high-sounding terms and, 165–66
  high technology and, 162
  inflation hedge and, 161
  information overload and, 163
  jurisdictional confusion and, 163–64
  political unrest and, 162
  politics, morals, and, 164–65
  selection criteria, 277–81
    cost factors, 280
    demand factors, 278–80
    feasibility factors, 280–81
    supply factors, 277–78
  two market system and, 163
  variables and, 162
  see also Buying minor metals; Strategies and techniques of investing
Investment firms, 214–15
  choosing, 215–18
Investment vehicles, 238–60
  future possibilities, 256–60
  futures, 257–59
  options, 256–57
  other possible changes, 260
  small quantities, 259–60
  metals indices percent change, 242

Investment vehicles *(cont'd)*
 metals shares, 245–56
  by-products and, 246–48
  fabricators and, 252–53
  financial health of firms and, 249–50
  firms with experienced management and, 248–49
  firms with low vulnerability and, 253–54
  high-technology firms and, 254
  how to select an investment and, 255–56
  ore deposits and, 249
  other investment opportunities, 252–55
  "pure play" and, 251–52
  quality and, 248
  specialized financial institutions and, 254–55
  supply and demand and, 250–51
  trends, 245–46
 physical purchases, 239–41, 243
  advantages of, 239
  advisory accounts, 244
  disadvantages of, 239–40
  funds, 244–45
  managed accounts, 240–41, 243, 244
Ion implantation, 148
Iran, 48, 53, 70, 81, 86, 108
Iraq, 53
Iridium, 4
 profile of, 318–19
Iron, 13, 14, 15, 19, 120, 147, 148
 resource wars and, 66, 67, 68
Iron Ore Exporting Countries, 80
Irregularities in markets, 219
Italy, 66, 67, 134

James Sinclair and Company, 206
Japan, 63, 134, 151, 158
 imports of strategic metals, 40, 42
 processing of ores, 42, 114, 119, 120, 129
 resource wars and, 66–68

Jet engines, 25, 113, 150, 152, 171, 253
Jobbing the market, 268–69
Jurisdiction over minor-metals trading, 163–64

Katrak, Dr. Firoze, 200
Kaunda, Kenneth, 95
Kennecott, 121
Kennemetal, 253
Kenya, 111
Kewelki Berylco, 253
Kilmarx, Dr. Robert, 49, 82–83
Kissinger, Henry, 5, 60
Korean War, 113, 114, 115, 134, 141, 158
Kroll, Bud, 210
Krueger, Paul, 138–39, 140, 141

Labels, 165
Lambert Metals Ltd., 204, 214, 257
Landsberg, Hans H., 19
Lanthanum, profile of, 320–22
Laterite, 145–46
Law of the Sea Treaty, 83, 153–56
 objections to, 154
Lead, 15, 19, 32, 246, 257
 Soviet Union and, 45
*Lean Years, The* (Barnett), 65
Leith, Dr. C. K., 32
Lenin, Nikolai, 87
Leontief, Wassily, 18
L'Esperance, Robert, 48
Leveraged contracts, 165, 266
Libya, 54, 89
Liquidity, 208–9, 265
 small amounts and, 259–60
Lithium, 98
 profile of, 304–6
 Soviet Union and, 45
Lloyd's of London, 234
London Metal Exchange (LME), 224, 226, 230, 234, 259
 futures and, 257
Long run, 186, 265
Lutetium, profile of, 320–22

McClure, James, 124
McGovern, George, 104–8, 124
Machel, Samora Moïsés, 85

McPherson, M. Peter, 97–98
Magnesium, 15, 118, 144
  profile of, 306–8
Malenbaum, Wilfred, 18
Malone, James L., 154
Managed accounts, 240–42
  cost of, 240–42
  sample statement of, 245
Managed price, 168–69
Manganese, 4, 9, 15, 17, 19, 25,
    26, 38, 40, 92, 101, 135,
    146, 149, 150, 248
  cartels and, 80, 82
  profile of, 308–11
  resource wars and, 66, 67, 68,
    69, 71
  Soviet Union and, 43, 44, 47–
    48, 54, 87
  transportation of, 57
  under the sea, 153, 155
Market behavior, 180–207
  conservation and, 200–201
  demand and, 183–84
  energy and, 201–2
  extraction line and, 199–200
  government intervention and,
    206–7
  prices and, see Prices for
    metals
  speculation and, 202–6
  stocks of by-product metals
    and, 196–98
  substitution and, see Substi-
    tution
  supply and, 180–83
  supply overhang and, 198–99
Market structure, 167–79
  black market and, 177–78
  dealers and, 178–79
  free market and, see Free
    market
  producer market and, see Pro-
    ducer market
  two-price marketplace and,
    175–77
Massachusetts Institute of Tech-
    nology (MIT), 45, 46–47
Masters, Howard, 204, 214, 257,
    263–64
Melting points of metals, 20, 21

Metal Bulletin, 179
Metals, 12–13
  alloys, 12
  bronze, 12–13
  search for, 13–14
  strategic, see Strategic metals
  utility and value of, 12
Metals shares, see Investment
    vehicles, metals shares
Metals Statistics, 213
Metals Week, 179, 276
Metglas, 147
Mexico, 81
Meyer, Herbert E., 44, 60
MHO, 197
Microcrystalline, 147
Military-industrial complex, 24
Mineral Industry Surveys, 276–
    77
Minerals and Materials, 276–
    77
Mining, see United States
Minor metals, 7, 165–66
  see also specific metals
Minor Metals Traders Associa-
    tion (MMTA), 166, 178,
    213–14, 216, 226, 234
  contracts of, 220, 222–23
Mitterand, François, 85
Mobutu Sese Seko, 3, 91, 92, 93,
    94
Models of minor-metals markets,
    275
Molybdenum, 15, 19, 20, 22, 25,
    67, 147, 151, 172, 181, 246,
    247
  profile of, 311–13
  Soviet Union and, 47
Moody's Investor Service, 121
Moral convictions and investing,
    164–65
Morgan, Dr. John D., 20, 23, 114,
    116, 158
  stockpiling and, 136, 140–41
Morocco, 48
Mott, William C., 55, 61
Mountain States Legal Founda-
    tion, 123
Mozambique, 49, 54, 58, 111
  government of, 85

Mugabe, Robert, 96–100
Munroe, George B., 119, 143

Names, 165
Namibia, 54, 58, 61, 85, 105, 111
National Association of Securities Dealers, Automated Quotation System of, 260
National Commission of Supplies and Shortages, 135
National defense, 22–27
  increased spending for, 24–25
  metals and arms buildup, 25–27
National Defense Stockpile, 134
National Materials Advisory Board, 9, 194
National Mineral Security Act, 124, 157–58
National Research Council, 149
National Security Council, 62, 70
Neodymium, profile of, 320–22
Netherlands, the, 67, 68
*New Leader, The*, 11–12
*New Republic*, 61–62
*Newsweek*, 61
New York Mercantile Exchange, 258
*New York Times, The*, 37, 89, 97, 98, 99, 163, 220
Nickel, 4, 15, 20, 25, 38, 92, 98, 128, 138, 141, 145, 146, 148, 151, 152, 246, 247, 251, 257
  resource wars and, 66, 67, 68–69
  Soviet Union and, 45, 47, 54
  under the sea, 153, 155
Nigeria, 111
Niobium, *see* Columbium
Nixon, Richard, 61
Noranda Mines, 128, 141, 254
Nord Resources, 118, 150
Norway, 67
Nuclear reactors, 22
Nuclear war, 71

Occupational Safety and Health Administration, 133

Office of Surface Mining (OSM), 124
Oil, 7, 15, 37, 58, 78, 79, 81
  corporate takeovers and, 250
  Persian Gulf and, 53–54
  resource wars and, 66, 67, 69
  substitutions for, 20, 22, 142, 144, 148, 191–92
Oligopolies, 167–68
OPEC, 37, 77, 78, 80, 81, 83, 105, 191–92
Options, 256–57
Ore, 249
Oregon Metallurgical (Ormet), 253
Organization of Petroleum Exporting Countries, *see* OPEC
Orionova, Galina, 61
Osmium, profile of, 319
Outer space, mining of, 156
Overseas Private Investment Corporation, 88
Overton, J. Allen, 15, 124, 125
Oxygen, 143

Palladium, 4, 128, 148, 150, 258
  profile of, 317
Papp, Daniel S., 87
Papua New Guinea, 118
Park, Charles F., 87, 126
Persian Gulf, 53–54, 61
"Persian Gulf of Minerals," 90–112
  Republic of South Africa, 100–112
  Zaire, 90–96
  Zambia, 94–96
  Zimbabwe, 96–100
  *see also individual countries*
Phelps Dodge, 118, 119, 143
Photovoltaic cells, 22
Physical purchases, *see* Investment vehicles, physical purchases
Plastic, 143, 144, 146–47
Platinum, 4, 15, 20, 25, 38, 40, 67, 71, 101–2, 128, 135, 136, 137, 248, 258–59

Platinum *(cont'd)*
  profile of, 315–16
  Soviet Union and, 43, 44, 48, 49, 101, 102
  substitutes for, 148, 149
Platinum group metals, profile of, 313–20
Political beliefs and investing, 164–65
Political unrest, hedge against, 162
Polymers, 146–47
Popular Movement for the Liberation of Angola (MPLA), 84
Powder metallurgy, 152
Power of attorney, 218
  managed accounts and, 240
Prasadam, S. P., 178, 209
Praseodymium, profile of, 320–22
Pratt & Whitney, 171, 191
President's Council of Economic Advisers, 123
Price elasticity of demand, 188–90
  cross elasticity and, 189–90
Price elasticity of supply, 185–88
Price leaders, 170
Prices for metals:
  "average," 176
  black market and, 177–78
  choosing a firm and, 216
  dealers and, 178–79
  demand and, 188–90
    overall budget and, 188–89
    prices of other metals and, 189–90
    substitutes and, 188
    time frame and, 188
  excessive markups of, 220
  free market, 169, 174–75
  forward contracts and, 265–68
  inadequacy of system of, 260
  industry capacity and, 181–82
  producer, *see* Producer price
  quotes on, 219–20, 223
  "spread" and, 219–20
  stocks of by-product metals and, 197–98
    supply overhang and, 198–99

substitution and, 188, 190–92, 193
supply and, 185–88
  cost structure of producers and, 187–88
  cross elasticity and, 189–90
  industry output capability and, 186–87
  time frame and, 186
  two-tier marketplace and, 175–77
  volatility in, 209–10
Primary Tungsten Association, 80
Producer market, 167–72
  defined, 163, 167
  financing and, 167
  low margins and, 167–68
  mergers and takeovers and, 168
  as oligopoly, 167–68
  prices and, *see* Producer price
  scarce raw materials and, 167
Producer price, 168–69
  contracts and, 171–72
  fixing of, 169–70
  free-market price and, 169–70
  investors and, 170
  role of price leaders and, 170
  two-price marketplace and, 175–77
Production and reserves of strategic metals, 51
Promethium, profile of, 320–22
"Pure play," 251–52
  physical purchases as, 239

Quotes, price, 219–21

Rare-earth metals, profile of, 320–22
Reagan, Ronald, 24, 64, 72, 89, 97, 116, 158
  Law of the Sea and, 153–55
  mining policy of, 122–34
  South Africa and, 110–12
  stockpiling and, 138, 142
Recycling metals, 151–52
  cost and, 151
  future of, 152
  market behavior and, 200–201
  obstacles to, 151–52

Refiners, 252
Republic of South Africa, 43, 44, 54, 55, 57, 61, 85, 114, 116
  are supplies threatened?, 102–3
  cartels and, 79, 82, 83, 84
  diplomatic tightrope of U.S. and, 109–12
  disruption scenarios, 104–8
  mineral abundance of, 101–2, 103, 149
  as "Saudi Arabia of minerals," 100–112
  sea lanes and, 58, 59
  stability of, 108–9
  Zimbabwe and, 96, 97, 98, 100
Reserves of strategic metals, 32–35
  classification of, 34
  expansion of, 181
Resources for the Future, 19
Resource war, 5–6, 53–72
  Cold War bombast or, 62–63
  competition or, 60–63
  history of, 64–69
  introduction, 53–54
  need for objectivity and, 63–64
  post–World War II era and, 69–71
  present-day, 71–72
  Soviet grand design and, 60–62
  Soviet inroads in Africa and, 54–60
    rail lines and, 56–58
    sea lanes and, 58–60
    worst-case scenario and, 55–56
Rhenium, 247
  profile of, 322–24
Rhodesia, 48, 56, 66, 96
  see also Zimbabwe
Rhodium, 4, 266, 267
  profile of, 317–18
Richardson, Elliot, 153–54
Risk/reward ratio, 210
Rubber, 142
Ruthenium, profile of, 319–20
Rutile, 68, 116

"Sagebrush Rebellion," 123
St. Joe Minerals, 121
Salpeter, Eliahu, 11

Samarium, profile of, 320–22
Sampling of the purchase, 231
Santini, James, 5, 9, 22–23, 44, 57, 60, 61, 64, 80, 82, 93, 94, 98, 99, 102, 107, 126, 130, 135, 138, 149
  National Mineral Security Act and, 124, 157–58
Sassi, John, 85
Schneider, Dr. William, 23, 26
Science, 19, 118, 151
Sea, mining of, 153–56, 181
  reserves and, 181
Selenium, 20, 22, 247
  profile of, 324–26
Selling, 236–37
Selling short, 265–66
  against your holdings, 270
Senate Appropriations Subcommittee on Foreign Operations, 111–12
Senate Energy and Natural Resources Committee, 124
Senate Environment Committee, 133
Senate Foreign Relations Committee, 104–8, 111
Shaba province, 3–12, 26, 57, 63, 91, 92, 93, 94, 95, 107, 128, 145
  market structure and, 174, 177
  see also Zaire
Shakespeare, Frank, 60
Shorr, Ronald, 251–52
Short run, 186, 265
Siad Barre, Mohamed, 61
Sieberling, John F., 123
Sierra Club, 123, 127, 133
Silicon, 14, 22, 25, 142, 143, 147, 194
  market behavior and, 172, 201–2, 206
  profile of, 326–28
Silk, Leonard, 37
Silver, 148, 246, 257, 258
  investing in, 261
Sinclair, James E., 6, 46, 106, 262–63
Slay, Gen. Alton D., 23
Smith, Eliot, 203, 259

Smith, Ian, 56
South Africa, *see* Republic of South Africa
South African Foreign Affairs Association, 106
South-West Africa People's Organization (SWAPO), 111
South Yemen, 53, 58
Soviet Union, 24, 26, 67, 69, 76, 95, 116
  in Africa, 54–60, 108, 112
  cartels and, 82, 83, 84
  defectors from, 61–62
  free market and, 173
  future of the Third World and, 84, 85, 86, 87, 100, 106
  naval strength of, 58–59
  resource war and, *see* Resource war
  Shaba province invasion and, 4, 9, 10–12
  strategic metals endowment of, 43–52
    change from exporter to importer, 44–45
    problems of, 46–49
    sinister implications of, 49–52
    South Africa and, 101, 102, 103, 104
    speculating on motivation, 45–46
SOZICOM, 207
Spain, 69
Speculation, 202–6
  "buffer stock" and, 206
  "cornering the market," 199, 204–5
  effects of, 204
  private, 203–4
  "shorting" and, 203
  staying power and, 205–6
  supply overhang and, 199
  taking positions and, 202–3, 204
Speer, Albert, 69
Spot price, 266
Stainless steel, 17, 26, 149–50
  recycling of, 151–52
Standard and Poor's, 121

Stalin, Joseph, 61, 87
State Department, U.S., 11, 62, 88, 92, 94, 99, 139
Steel, 13, 14, 17, 19, 47, 69, 80, 146, 158
  costs of production, 118, 120–21, 144
  strategic metals and, 22
  substitution for, 147, 148, 150
Stillwater Complex, 128
Stockpiling, 134–42
  alternatives to, 140–41
  Defense Production Act and, 141–42
  deficient, 138
  economic, 135–37
  future of, 140
  goals, and present inventories, 136–37
    determination of, 138–39
    manipulation of, 134–35
  National Mineral Security Act and, 157
  new purchases, 138
  revised stockpile act, 135–36
  transactions, 139–40
Stocks of by-product metals, 196–98
Stoner, Bruce, 163–64
Storage, 224, 226
  feasibility of, 211
  warehouse warrant and, 226–27
    falsified, 227, 229
    sample, 228
    should it be in your name?, 229–30
Strait of Hormuz, 53, 58, 59
Strategic and Critical Materials Stock Piling Act, 134
Strategic and Critical Materials Stock Piling Revision Act, 135, 140
Strategic metals, 14–15
  battleground over, *see* Battleground
  defined, 165
  demand for, 15–17
    changing pattern of, 18–22
    increase in, 17–18
    U.S., 27–31

Strategic metals, demand for (cont'd)
  world, 28–31
electronics and, 19–20
on engines, 25
as gold of the eighties, 6–7
implications of Shaba invasion on, 8–10
import-dependency in, 37–43
  EEC and, 40, 41
  implications of, 40–43
  Japan and, 40, 42
melting points of, 20, 21
national defense and, 22–27
  increased spending for, 24–25
  metals and arms buildup, 25–27
production of, 51
reasons to be bearish about, 7–8
reasons to invest in, 7
reserves of, 32–35
  classification of, 34
  production of, 51
resource war and, *see* Resource war
solving problems with, 20, 22
Soviet Union and, 10–12, 43–72
  *see also* Soviet Union
steel industry and, 22
stockpiling of, *see* Stockpiling
substitution for, *see* Substitution
in telephones, 16
transportation of, 56–60
  by rail, 56–58
  by sea, 58–60
Strategic Metals & Critical Materials, Inc., 223, 224
Strategic Metals Corporation, 178, 189, 209
  commission of, 223–24
Strategic Minerals Task Force, 123
*Strategics Review*, 46, 106
Strategies and techniques of investing, 261–71
  "the basket," 270–71
buy-and-hold, 262–63
control over investment, 261
financing and, 269–70
forward contracts, 265–68
"hard assets" and, 261–62
jobbing the market, 268–69
most important, 261
selling short, 270
trade-and-hold, 265
trading approach, 263–64
Strauss, Simon, 183, 200
Strontium, 20, 145
Substitution, 9, 20, 27, 47, 146–50, 190–95
cobalt and other metals, 148–49
functional, 148
high prices and, 190–91
innovation and, 192
looking for new alloys, 146–47
material, 148
platinum, 148
price elasticity of demand and, 188
projected use pattern and, 194
relative price and, 192, 193
subjective variables and, 194–95
substitution ladder and, 195
suitability and, 192–94
technology and, 142–45
time and, 191
time/price combination and, 191–92
uncertainty and, 149–50
Sudan, 49
Sudden changes in markets, 218–19
Sulfur, 168
Supply of metals, 180–83, 277–78
base metal production and, 183
cost of production and, 182
ecology and, 183
expansion of economic reserves and, 181
industry output and, 181–82
liquidity and, 209
price and, 185–88
  cross elasticity and, 189–90
technology and, 182
Supply overhang, 198–99

Supreme Court, U.S., 132–33
Sutulov, Alexander, 247
Sweden, 67, 136
Syria, 48, 53

Tantalum, 4, 20, 25, 38, 93, 138,
    141, 193, 246, 247, 254
  profile of, 329–31
  Soviet Union and, 45, 49, 59
Tanzania, 54, 57, 58, 111
Tax advantages, 212
Tax laws, 157, 158
Technology:
  demand for minor metals and,
    143–44
  investing and, 162
  substitution and, 192
  supply of minor metals and,
    142–43, 182
Teledyne, 253
Telephones, 16, 143, 148
Tellurium, 22
  profile of, 331–33
Terbium, profile of, 320–22
Thallium, 246
Thermoplastics, 147
Third World, 6, 8, 10, 12, 54, 254
  cartels and, *see* Cartels
  as food importers, 37
  future in, 84–90
    adapting to the new eco-
      nomic order and, 87–89
    ambiguous signals from
      Washington and, 89–90
    pragmatism over ideology
      and, 85–86
    time of transition and, 86–
      87
  Law of the Sea and, 153–54
  legacy of colonialism, 74–75
  new economic order and, 75–
    77, 87–89
  resource wars and, 70, 71, 72
  risks and, 49–50
  *see also specific countries*
Thulium, profile of, 320–22
Thurmond, Strom, 124
*Time*, 89, 121
Timing of trades, 218
Tin, 12, 13, 14, 246, 247, 257

Titanium, 20, 22, 24, 25, 101,
    138, 141, 145, 148, 150,
    177, 186, 202, 254
  conservation and, 200–201
  domestic deposits of, 116
  fabricators and, 252–53
  profile of, 333–36
  Soviet Union and, 45, 49
  in submarines, 26
Trade-and-hold strategy, 265
Trading approach, 263–64
Trading quantities, 210–11
  small size, 223
"Traffic" in metals, efficient han-
    dling of, 219
Transportation of ore, 56–60
  by rail, 56–58, 92
  by sea, 58–60
Tshombe, Moise, 3
Tungsten, 4, 15, 19, 25, 114, 141,
    144, 147, 253
  free market and, 174
  profile of, 336–39
  resource wars and, 68, 69
Turkey, 48
  resource wars and, 66, 67, 69
Two-price    marketplace,    163,
    175–77
  consumer loyalty and, 176–77
  lower producer prices and, 177

Ukraine, the, 66, 67
Union of Soviet Socialist Repub-
    lics (USSR), *see* Soviet
    Union
United Kingdom, 65–66
United Nations, 75, 83, 88, 105,
    109, 111
United States, 36–43, 113–58
  changes in government mining
    policy, 122–24
  clean air versus minerals, 129–
    34
    Clean Air Act and, 133–34
    public and, 132–33
    regulation and, 130–32
  decline of domestic mining,
    114–17
    government    policies    and,
    115

United States, decline of domestic mining *(cont'd)*
  price and, 115–17
  demand for strategic metals, 27–31
  extraction methods and, 145–46
  future of the Third World and, 84–90, 97
  as import-dependent in metals, 37–43
    EEC and, 40, 41
    implications of, 40–43
    Japan and, 40, 42
  invention and innovation, 142–45
    demand and technology, 143–44
    supplies and technology, 142–43
  national minerals policy, 156–58
  National Mineral Security Act, 157–58
  outer space and, 156
  public lands and, 124–29
    conservation argument, 127–28
    exploration without destruction, 126–27
    how much is off limits?, 125–26
    if public land is opened up, 128–29
  recycling and, 151–52
  sea and, 153–56
    Law of the Sea and, 153–54
    mining the sea and, 155–56
  as self-sufficient in metals, 36–37
  South Africa and, 109–12
  state of the mining industry, 117–22
    crunch on capital and, 120–21
    expense and, 117–18
    government and, 121–22
    reasons for increased costs, 118–20
  stockpiling by, *see* Stockpiling

  substitution and, *see* Substitution
*United States and the Global Struggle for Minerals, The* (Eckes), 64–65
*U.S. News and World Report*, 3
University of Pennsylvania, 18
Uranium, 114

Vanadium, 4, 19, 22, 25, 101, 138, 142, 149, 247, 248
  profile of, 339–42
  Soviet Union and, 43, 45, 49
Vassallo, Francis, 230
Vietnam, 54, 59
Volatility, 209–10

*Wall Street Journal*, 80, 85
Warehouse warrant, 226–27, 269, 270
  falsified, 227, 229
  sample, 228
  should it be in your name?, 229–30
*Washington Post*, 61, 151
Watt, James, 64, 123, 124
Webb, Bryan, 166, 178, 218, 235
Wharton School of Finance and Commerce, 18
Weidenbaum, Murray, 123
West Germany, 114, 119, 134, 151, 158
  *see also* Germany
Wilderness Act, 124, 127
Wilderness Society, 133
World Affairs Council of Pittsburgh, 60
World Bank, 88
World War I, 65–66
World War II, 37, 59, 84, 134, 150
  resource prelude to, 66–68
  as resource war, 68–69

Ytterbium, profile of, 320–22
Yttrium, 7, 20
  profile of, 342–43
Yugoslavia, 67

Zaire, 3–12, 54, 55, 68, 79, 83, 86, 88

Zaire *(cont'd)*
  cobalt and, 90–96, 140, 175–76, 207
  mineral wealth in, 4–5
  Shaba province and, *see* Shaba province
  Soviet Union and, 4, 9, 10–12
  transportation of ore in, 57–58
  Wall Street and, 6–8
Zambia, 5, 50, 54, 55, 79, 83, 88, 111
  cobalt and, 94–96, 175–76
  transportation of ore in, 57
Zimbabwe, 43, 54, 55, 83, 95, 96–100, 111, 116
  caution in, 99
  government of, 96–98
  minerals in, 98–99
  prognosis for, 98
  transportation of ore in, 57
  West and, 100
Zinc, 15, 18, 19, 32, 246, 252, 257
  germanium and, 190, 196–97, 199–200
  production of, 120
Zirconium, 7, 15, 22, 101, 223
  profile of, 343–45